WAR, DIPLOMACY, AND HISTORY: PAPERS AND REVIEWS

Raymond G. O'Connor

Copyright © 1979 by

Raymond G. O'Connor

All rights reserved
Printed in the United States of America
ISBN: 0-8191-0790-5

Library of Congress Catalog Card Number: 79-88951

For Susan, Verna, Virginia, and Carol

ABOUT THE AUTHOR

RAYMOND G. O'CONNOR was born in St. Louis, Missouri, in 1915, and served in the United States Navy from 1935 to 1955. He received his Master of Arts degree from The American University in 1948 and his Doctor of Philosophy degree from Stanford University in 1957. He has taught at the University of California, Stanford University, the University of Kansas, Temple University, and, since 1969, at the University of Miami. As a visiting professor he has taught at the University of Costa Rica, Stanford University, the University of California, Santa Barbara, Brown University, and Arizona State University. He held the Ernest J. King Chair at the Naval War College 1967-1968, and lectured at the American Studies Research Center, Osmenia University, Hyderabad, India, Summer 1978. His books include <u>Perilous Equilibrium</u> (1962, 1968); <u>Readings in the History of American Military Policy</u> (ed., 1962); <u>Readings in Twentieth Century American History</u> (co-ed., 1963); <u>American Defense Policy in Perspective</u> (ed. and co-author, 1965); <u>Presidential Powers in Foreign Affairs</u> (co-author, 1966); <u>A History of American Military Affairs</u> (co-author, 1968); <u>The Japanese Navy in World War II</u> (ed., 1969); <u>Diplomacy for Victory: FDR and Unconditional Surrender</u> (1971); <u>Force and Diplomacy: Essays Military and Diplomatic</u> (1972); and <u>War, Diplomacy and History</u> (1979).

ACKNOWLEDGEMENTS

1. This paper was delivered as a lecture on the occasion of the author being appointed a Presidential Scholar at the University of Miami, February 1976.

2. "War, Diplomacy and the Historian" was published in _Proceedings of the Conference on War and Diplomacy, 1977_ (The Citadel, Charleston, S.C., 1979), and is reprinted by permission.

3. "The Navy and American Foreign Relations" was published in _The Society for Historians of American Foreign Relations Newsletter_, VII, No. 4 (December 1976) and is reprinted by permission.

4. "The Imperialism of Sea Power" was published in _Reviews in American History_, IV, No. 3 (September 1976) and is reprinted by permission.

5. "Maritime Dimensions of the American Revolution: Commentary," was published in _Maritime Dimensions of the American Revolution_ (Washington, Government Printing Office, 1977), and is reprinted by permission. The papers commented on were "Naval Policy of the Continental Congress," by Frank C. Mevers, and "Defeat at Sea: The Impact of American Naval Operations upon the British, 1775-1778," by David Syrett. The papers and commentary were read in a session at the annual meeting of the Organization of American Historians, April 1976.

6. "The Navy on the Frontier" was published in _The American Military on the Frontier: Proceedings of the Seventh Military History Symposium, 30 September - 1 October 1976_, ed. James P. Tate (Washington, Government Printing Office, 1978), and is reprinted by permission.

7. "Origins of the Navy 'General Staff'," was published (without the footnotes) in _American Defense Policy in Perspective: From Colonial Times to the Present_, ed. Raymond G. O'Connor (New York, John Wiley & Sons, 1965), and is reprinted by permission.

8. "The Great Aberration of the 1890's," was published in the _American Studies_, IV (Spring 1963), and is reprinted by permission.

9. "Peace Making After the First World War: Commentary," was read in a session at the annual meeting of the Pacific Historical Association, May 1963. The Papers commented on were "General Tasker Bliss and the Versailles Peace Conference," by David Trask, and "The Washington Conference, 1921," by Thomas H. Buckley.

10. "The 'Yardstick' and Naval Disarmament in the 1920's" was published in The Mississippi Valley Historical Review, XLV (December 1958), and is reprinted by permission.

11. "The Influence of Disarmament Upon Technology: Commentary," was read in a session at the annual meeting of the American Historical Association, December 1965. The papers commented on were "The Effects of Disarmament on the Design of Cruisers, 1930-1940," by Robert S. Woodbury; "Disarmament and Technology in the Weimar Republic," by Thomas P. Hughes; and "The Influence of Disarmament Upon Aircraft Design," by Lee Scamehorn.

12. "Naval Policy Between World Wars: A Review Article," was published in The United States Naval Institute Proceedings, 95 (January 1969), and is reprinted by permission.

13. "U.S. Amphibious Doctrine and Naval Policy in the 20th Century," was published under the title "The U.S. Marines in the Twentieth Century: Amphibious Warfare and Doctrinal Debates," in Military Affairs, XXXVIII (October 1974), and is reprinted by permission. Originally it was delivered as an address at the First Marine Corps Conference on Military and Naval History, Quantico, Virginia, April 1972.

14. "Did FDR Want War in 1941?" was published in American Defense Policy in Perspective: From Colonial Times to the Present, ed. Raymond G. O'Connor (New York, John Wiley & Sons, 1965), and is reprinted by permission. This article is based on a paper read at the annual meeting of the Pacific Coast Branch of the American Historical Association, December 1958.

15. "Naval Strategy in World War II" was presented as a lecture at the Naval War College in 1968.

16. "Strategy for Victory in the Pacific: Commentary," was read in a session at the annual meeting of the American Historical Association, December 1975. The papers commented on were "Admiral Ernest J. King," by Clark Reynolds; "General George C. Marshall," by Forrest C. Pogue; "Admiral Chester W. Nimitz and the Central Pacific Offensive, 1943-45," by E. B. Potter; and "General Douglas MacArthur and the War in the Southeast Pacific," by D. Clayton James.

17. "The European Second Front in World War II: Commentary," was read in a session at the annual meeting of the Pacific Coast Branch of the American HIstorical Association, August 1971. The papers commented on were "American Public Opinion and the European Second

Front," by Richard W. Steele; and "The Second Front in Europe: The Soviet View," by Foster Anderson.

18. "Reflections on the Characteristics of a Commander" was published in the <u>Naval War College Review</u>, XXI (October 1968), and is reprinted by permission. It is a modified version of a commentary on papers presented in a session at the Military History Symposium, Air Force Academy, 1968. The papers commented on were "Jellicoe and Beatty as Commanders-in-Chief, Grand Fleet," by Arthur Marder; and "The Command Personality: Some American Naval Officers of World War II," by E. B. Potter. These papers and the commentary are published in <u>Command and Commanders in Modern Warfare</u>, ed. William Geffen (2nd ed., Washington, Government Printing Office, 1969).

19. "The Foreign Relations Papers, 1940-1943," was published in the <u>Pacific Historical Review</u>, XXXIV (August 1965), and is reprinted by permission.

20. "The Politics of Strategy and Peace in World War II" was presented as a lecture at the Naval War College in 1974.

21. "The Historical Dimensions of War Guilt," was read in a session on The Historical Dimensions of War Guilt at the annual meeting of the Pacific Coast Branch of the American Historical Association, August 1972.

22. "Sea Power in a Multi-Polar World" was read at the Regional National Security Seminar, University of Connecticut, November 1973. Portions of this paper reflect material in "The Soviet Navy in the Mediterranean and Indian Ocean," <u>The Virginia Quarterly</u>, 49 (Autumn 1973), by Raymond G. O'Connor and Vladimir P. Prokofieff.

23. "The Maya Culture and America: A Comparison," consists of two papers under the theme "The Rythm of History--Upbeat or Down?." The papers are titled "Ingredients that Stimulated the Rise of the Maya Culture, and a Comparative Analysis of the Ascendancy of the United States," and "Causes of the Decline of the Maya Culture, and Analysis of Present Day Parallels." These papers were read at a Symposium on The Rise and Fall of the Maya Culture, and Its Present Day Parallels, held at the Museum of Science, Miami, Florida, under the sponsorship of The Institute of Maya Studies, January-February, 1974.

24. Book Reviews (acknowledgment follows each review).

FOREWORD

This volume consists of miscellaneous papers and reviews written by the author during the past twenty years, and it represents his conviction that they merit circulation in book form. Most of the papers and the reviews have been published in journals or conference proceedings, and their source is indicated in the foregoing acknowledgments. Some effort has been made at organization along topical and chronological lines, although the diversity of subject matter renders impossible an ideal coherence. Each piece does, however, seem to fit within the categories of war, diplomacy, and history without straining the accepted definition of these terms. Because many of the topics are closely related the reader will find occasional instances of repetition, an unavoidable occurrence in bringing together writings of this nature. Historians, we are told, often repeat each other, and repeating oneself may constitute a milder form of plagiarism.

The shorter book reviews in the last chapter have been arranged in approximate chronological order and divided into two categories: military and diplomatic.

Some of these papers were written for publication, others for oral delivery, and none have been revised or rewritten. Nor has any effort been made to standardize editorial peculiarities or citation form. All items are reproduced as originally presented to readers or listeners, with the hope that a wider audience will benefit from their accessibility.

Deserving of a special note of appreciation is Rosemary McEwen, whose expertise in preparing the manuscript on a word processing machine was equaled by her meticulous care in striving to save the author from errors. Credit for whatever faults exist is claimed by the undersigned.

> Raymond G. O'Connor
> Coral Gables, Florida
> March 1979

WAR, DIPLOMACY, AND HISTORY
Papers and Reviews

CONTENTS:

	Page
Acknowledgments	i
Foreword	iv
1. War and the American Dream	1
2. War, Diplomacy, and the Historian	15
3. The Navy and American Foreign Relations	35
4. The Imperialism of Sea Power	47
5. Maritime Dimensions of the American Revolution: Commentary	53
6. The Navy on the Frontier	63
7. Origins of the Navy "General Staff"	77
8. The Great Aberration of the 1890's	89
9. Peace Making After the First World War: Commentary	95
10. The "Yardstick" and Naval Disarmament in the 1920's	103
11. The Influence of Disarmament Upon Technology: Commentary	127
12. Naval Policy Between World Wars: A Review Article	133
13. U.S. Amphibious Doctrine and Naval Policy in the 20th Century	143
14. Did FDR Want War in 1941?	161
15. Naval Strategy in World War II	171
16. Strategy for Victory in the Pacific: Commentary	181

Contents (cont.)   Page

17. The European Second Front in World War II:
    Commentary   185

18. Reflection on the Characteristics of a
    Commander   191

19. The Foreign Relations Papers, 1940-1943:
    A Review Article   201

20. The Politics of Strategy and Peace in
    World War II   211

21. Historical Dimensions of War Guilt   224

22. Sea Power in a Multi-Polar World   231

23. The Maya Culture and America: A Comparison   243

24. Book Reviews   253

    A. Military

        1. Sea of Glory: The Continental Navy
           Fights for Independence, 1775-1783,
           by Nathan Miller   253

        2. "Old Bruin:" Commodore Matthew C.
           Perry, 1794-1858, by Samuel Eliot
           Morison   254

        3. The United States Navy in the Pacific,
           1909-1922, by William Reynolds
           Braisted   256

        4. Race to Pearl Harbor: The Failure of
           the Second London Naval Conference
           and the Onset of World War II, by
           Stephen E. Pelz   258

        5. Bargaining for Supremacy: Anglo-
           American Naval Collaboration,
           1937-1941, by James R. Leutze   259

        6. The Navy League of the United
           States, by Armin Rappaport   260

        7. Strategy and Command: The First
           Two Years, by Louis Morton   261

        8. D-Day: The Normandy Invasion in
           Retrospect, no editor   263

Contents (cont.)   Page

    9. Silent Victory: The U.S. Submarine
       War Against Japan, by Clay Blair, Jr.   264

  10. The Quiet Warrior: A Biography of
      Admiral Raymond A. Spruance, by
      Thomas B. Buell   266

  11. Nuclear Navy, 1946-1962, by Richard
      G. Hewlett and Francis Duncan; and
      Mobility, Support, Endurance: A
      Story of Naval Operational Logistics
      in the Vietnam War, 1963-1968, by
      Edwin Bickford Hooper   268

  12. The Soviet Naval Offensive: An
      Examination of the Strategic Role
      of Soviet Naval Forces in the East-
      West Conflict, by Edward Wegener   269

  13. Gunboat Diplomacy: Political
      Applications of Limited Naval Force,
      by James Cable   270

  14. The Question of National Defense:
      A Critique of Our Military
      Preparations and Policies,
      by Oskar Morgenstern   271

B. Diplomatic

    1. Prologue to War: England and the
       United States, 1805-1812, by
       Bradford Perkins   273

    2. The United States and Huerta,
       by Kenneth J. Grieb   274

    3. Gunboat Diplomacy in the Wilson
       Era: The U.S. Navy in Haiti,
       1915-1916, by David Healy   276

    4. The United States and the Far
       Eastern Crisis of 1933-1938,
       by Dorothy Borg   277

    5. General Stilwell in China, 1942-1944:
       The Full Story, by Chin-Tung Liang   278

    6. E. R. Stettinius, Jr., and James F.
       Byrnes, by Richard L. Walker and
       George Curry   280

Contents (cont.)   Page

7. *Imperialism at Bay: The United
    States and the Decolonization of the
    British Empire, 1941-1945*, by
    William Roger Louis   281

8. *Foreign Relations of the United
    States, 1946, The Far East*,
    Department of State   284

9. *Foreign Relations of the United
    States, 1946, The Far East: China*,
    Department of State. *Foreign Rela-
    tions of the United States, 1947,
    The Far East*, Department of State   286

10. *Foreign Relations of the United
    States, 1947, The Far East: China*,
    Department of State. *Foreign Rela-
    tions of the United States, 1948,
    The Far East: China*, Department of
    State   287

11. *Containment and Revolution*, edited
    by David Horowitz   288

12. *Intervention and Negotiation, The
    United States and the Dominican
    Republic*, by Jerome Slater   291

13. *From Colony to Empire: Essays in the
    History of American Foreign Relations*,
    ed. William Appleman Williams   293

14. *Competitive Interference and
    Twentieth Century Diplomacy*, by
    Richard W. Cottam   294

WAR AND THE
AMERICAN DREAM
Chapter 1

The American people, we have been told, are peace-loving, unlike others, especially Europeans, whose past is replete with fighting indiscriminately among themselves and with foreigners. Yet in 1922 the Secretary of War published a list of "official" American wars that totaled 104, and since that date at least three major involvements have added to the record. Violence may not be as American as cherry pie, as has been claimed. But the United States has not been remiss in participating in what used to be called "the sport of kings." Our history demonstrates that a representative government can indulge in the organized, legalized destruction of life and property as often if not as effectively as any dictatorial or totalitarian regime. War has played a vital and at times determinant role in the development of the nation. The question is whether the employment of this ultimate arbiter in disputes between persons and nations is compatible with the American Dream as expounded by spokesmen or shared by the people during the 200 years of our existence.

The essence of the American Dream, it seems to me, was brought to the colonies by many Englishmen in the 17th and 18th centuries. Frustrated by political and religious persecution, deprived of social mobility and economic opportunity, these discontented migrants saw this new land as a place to pursue a life bereft of the evils and ills that plagued Europe. Unwittingly endorsing Voltaire's dictum "happy is the nation that has no history," these colonists rejected the unpalatable institutions and practices of England and the continent. Separated by three thousand miles of ocean and by ethical and moral convictions different from many of the prevailing mores in their homeland, these utopian pioneers exulted in a feeling of psychological and material superiority.

One English heritage brought to the colonies and enthusiastically embraced by most colonists was an aversion to militarism. Too often liberties had been subverted by a leader supported by a professional army, so the typical form of defense in the colonies became the local militia. Composed of farmers, artisans, and community leaders, these organizations of part-time warriors drilled periodically and were called up to combat Indians and participate in the international wars that shook the Western world during the

17th and 18th centuries. The Indians, resenting the occupation of their lands, waged war in their own fashion with their own form of terrorism. The mother country was involved in rivalry with continental powers for overseas empire, and the New World became the stakes as well as the battleground. When the colonists became sufficiently incensed over actions of the British government to rebel, they had the training and experience to make it difficult for the then major super-power to prevail. War at that time, as before and since, was a struggle to impose the will of one group on another, and as the conflict escalated from the objective of a redress of wrongs to a war for national liberation, it spread to become a world conflagration. By declaring independence the nation was able to attract allies, and the coalition, whose war aims were not always identical, was able to wrest from Britain its most valuable possession.

Emerging from the crucible of war, the new nation, impoverished and underdeveloped, sought to survive in a hostile world that resented the example of a liberated colony and a republican form of government. The principles embodied in the Declaration of Independence promulgated a dream embracing a government that governed with the consent of the governed and a dedication to "life, liberty, and the pursuit of happiness." The development of a sense of national identity, where loyalty to the mother country had been superceded by a primary allegiance to the United States, was a composite of grievances and aspirations that threatened the existence of the new republic. Dissolution was feared as some states rights adherents, having won their freedom from the tyranny of King and Parliament, now opposed the tyranny of a national government. This issue, like independence, eventually was to be resolved on the battlefield. But this division of opinion further imperiled the existence of the new nation, for it created an altercation over defense policy. The dispute reflected different versions of the American Dream, for the problem of federalism was intensified by sectional differences and disagreement over agrarian or maritime priorities. An army was needed to fight the Indians; a navy was needed to protect commerce from pirates and Barbary corsairs in the Mediterranean. President George Washington's messages to Congress and those of his successors are filled with recommendations on these matters, and the Annals of Congress are replete with arguments pro and con as protagonists debated their respective versions of American fulfillment.

On occasion, indignation over a violation of American rights, often put in the context of national honor, aroused the people and the Congress to the point where a consensus for action was reached. The first such occasion arose from French assaults on American shipping. Engaged in another conflict with Great Britain, France, endeavoring to hurt her insular adversary, directed privateers and warships to capture neutral merchant vessels. The United States, through Congressional resolutions in 1776 and 1784, had promulgated rules stipulating rights that neutral nations should enjoy during time of war. These rules, which had been incorporated in the 1778 treaty with France, were being flaunted. The material losses were significant, but the French disregard for American rights revealed a lack of respect for the government and the nation, and was a blatant insult to the young republic. So the reaction was a combination of economic distress, emotional fervor, and political reality. Hitherto diverse interests united to authorize the construction of warships, the establishment of a Navy Department, and the waging of a limited naval war against French armed vessels. President John Adams could boast of tangible financial benefits and a vindication of the national honor.

The allegedly pacifist Thomas Jefferson, on assuming the presidency in 1801, found himself faced with a renewal of Barbary depredations in the Mediterranean, where treaties involving tribute had been made with these four North Arican countries - Morocco, Tunis, Algiers, and Tripoli. American ships and cargoes were being captured, while passengers and crews were being held for ransom or sold into slavery. Jefferson, unsure of his Constitutional authority, dispatched a squadron to the Mediterranean with orders to "sink, burn, or otherwise destroy their ships and vessels, wherever you find them." Although not so enthusiastic as his predecessor about overseas commerce, Jefferson was acutely aware of the image projected by the nation. If American rights could be defied with impunity by any country, then others would follow suit, and eventually the republic would be subject to conquest or disintegration. Resistance to violations of American neutral rights reached a crescendo with the resumption of war between Great Britain and France, while the issue was aggravated by the British practice of forcing American seamen to serve in the Royal Navy. The government responded by moving from diplomatic protests to the imposition of an embargo on goods and shipping in an effort to coerce the belligerents into observing American neutral rights. Finally President James Madison asked Congress to authorize war against England on the grounds that the former mother country was abetting Indian hostilities on the frontier and ignoring the precepts of international law. As in the case of the Quasi-War with France, a multitude of motives was represented in the Congressional vote for war, among them a desire for the conquest of Canada or the Spanish Floridas. Jefferson, writing from retirement in his Monticello home, condoned the step as necessary to uphold the national honor and prevent further insulting, degrading treatment. Yet widespread support for the war was lacking, and none of the declared objectives of the war was achieved in the final peace signed on Christmas

Eve in 1814. Positive results accrued from a resurgent patriotism inflamed by a few victories, a stimulation of domestic industries, and a further demonstration that the young country would fight to defend its interests.

As the nation emerged and encountered the international anarchy of the time, the diversity that had characterized the colonial period conflicted with the realities of survival. An early doctrinal affiliation with the French Revolution had been overcome by an affront to American interests. But the issue resurfaced when independence movements shook the western world during and after the Napoleonic era.

Spain, torn by war, saw her Latin American colonies begin to revolt, and the halls of Congress reverberated to debate over the extent of aid, moral or material, that should be extended by the modern precursor of colonial independence. In 1821, Secretary of State John Quincy Adams, that staunch defender of American principles, faced the dilemma by announcing the policy that was to be followed, with notable exceptions, by subsequent administrations. The United States, he declared, "goes not abroad in search of monsters to destroy. She is the well-wisher in the freedom and independence of all. She is the champion and vindicator only of her own." But in 1823 President James Monroe declared that the Western Hemisphere was no longer available for colonization; warned that European nations should not attempt to extend their system to the newly independent states; and, as a quid pro quo, disavowed American intervention in Europe's internal affairs. The uprising in Greece in the 1820's, that in Hungary in 1848, and accompanying liberal movements, found the nation divided over the course to be taken when other were striving to achieve what some regarded as American ideals.

These American ideals, in the minds of many who espoused them, were founded in natural law, spurred by the 18th century French Enlightenment and Christian humanitarianism. Immutable and eternal as the physical laws of the universe discovered by Isaac Newton, they were destined to prevail. These natural laws that regulated the conduct of humankind had been subverted through ignorance and perversity. Now, having been applied in the United States, they were ordained to prevail everywhere, and in the great scheme of things this nation was decreed to be the vehicle for the adoption of these "self-evident truths." This sense of mission was shared by many Americans to a greater or lesser degree at different times, and it provided a justification or rationalization for aggressive ventures employing armed force with or without hostilities.

This sense of mission, the product of conviction and experience, was less often the source of debate than was the extent of commitment and the means by which it should be implemented. The vision that the United States would one day occupy the entire North American continent, a vision expressed in the term "manifest destiny," derived in part from a kind of geographical determinism that fit into a concept of the natural order of things. But whether this should be accomplished by diplomacy or force was what often agitated the government, the press, and the people. In explaining the acquisition of Indian lands, some troubled leaders contended that it was part of a civilizing process. In Rousseau's words, forcing the redman to be free by driving him into the white man's society. When, in the 1830's and 1840's it became evident that this acculturation was not working, another and this time avowedly supernatural justification was invoked, namely, territorial utilization and regeneration of the soil. The Indian simply was not fully exploiting the land, and Biblical injunctions compelled a more efficient cultivation of the wilderness. Meanwhile, in the 1850's, a group of political hopefuls emerged in the Young America movement, dedicated to the spread of republican institutions throughout the world. Adding to the earlier compulsions of duty and destiny was a conviction that the American system, based on the consent of the governed, could not long endure in the midst of nations dedicated to monarchy, elitism, and special privilege.

These various manifestations of the American Dream were displayed in the enthusiasm and crusading zeal that accompanied the Texas Revolution, Texan independence, its annexation, and the subsequent war with Mexico. As usual, opinion was divided over the justice or propriety of the war, and the so-called "spot resolution" introduced by the young Congressman Abraham Lincoln denounced the President for his deceitful behavior in bringing on hostilities and subverting the Constitution. As Commodore Matthew C. Perry was coercing Japan by threat and intimidation to accommodate itself to intercourse with the western world, opposing domestic philosophies of government in the American Dream accelerated to a more acute stage, and the compromise that had saved the Union on earlier occasions was not forthcoming. Convictions had hardened, the issues had become too volatile, and with the election of the Republican Lincoln certain southern states acted on that principle embodied in the Declaration of Independence, that of "the Right of the People to alter or to abolish [a government], and to institute new Government."

The shots fired on Fort Sumter may not, as at Lexington and Concord, have been heard 'round the world. But they served as a catalyst to ignite sentiment in the North, and the long, bitter, bloody Civil War was underway. To Lincoln, the issue was the preservation of the Union, and every step he took was designed to achieve this end. For the Confederacy, the issue was that of self-determination. Each stand was based on a principle, an ideal encompassed by the American Dream, of that last best hope of man on earth. Lincoln, in his effort to enforce the laws and suppress a domestic insurrection, at times exercised dictatorial powers. Jefferson Davis, equally determined to pursue his ideal, was driven to similar excesses of authority. The war for the Southern dream of independence had failed. The war of Yankee agression had succeeded. The fulfillment of one dream denied. The preservation of another dream accomplished. The ideal of national unity had prevailed over that of local autonomy, each an objective of different men of 1776.

The American Dream of transcontinental domination became a reality as the nineteenth century neared its end with the final elimination of armed resistance by the indigenous population. But the dream of expansion abroad had never died, and circumstances combined to, as one historian has put it, thrust great world power status on the United States. A war waged against Spain ostensibly to liberate Cuba became a war of conquest with the acquisition of the Philippines, Guam, and Puerto Rico, while Hawaii and a part of Samoa were annexed in the process. Whether the impetus for what Secretary of State John Hay called a "splendid little war" was engendered by "crusading morality," a domestic "psychic crisis," commercial ambitions, or security considerations, the sudden creation of an overseas empire could be summed up under the compulsions of "Duty, Dollars, Destiny, and Defense." And this part of the American Dream as envisioned by jingoists was brought to fruition largely by the Modern American Navy. The peaceful military occupation of Cuba was not repeated in the Philippines, where pacification followed three years of vicious jungle warfare that left over 4,000 Americans and some 250,000 Filipinos dead. Opposition at home to this brutal operation was widespread. But the administration was not deterred from its efforts to civilize these "little brown brothers" and, incidentally, protect them from other predatory powers.

Soon after the end of the Philippine insurrection, President Theodore Roosevelt announced what came to be known as the Roosevelt Corollary to the Monroe Doctrine. To prevent European intervention in Latin American countries, the President in 1904 declared that if a nation defaulted on its foreign debts the United States would intervene to restore its finances. Intended to preserve the sovereignty of these nations and protect American commercial and defense interests, Roosevelt, Taft, Wilson, and Coolidge under this or other pretexts were responsible for military occupations of a number of Caribbean and Central American countries, occupations that often included hostilities. Woodrow Wilson's interventions in Mexico are especially notable for what has been called "missionary diplomacy," of wanting to provide that nation with a constitutional government rather than a dictatorship.

WAR AND THE DREAM

This highly principled, allegedly pacifist chief executive was responsible for launching more military ventures than any of his predecessors or successors. Wilson was not the first or the last president to clothe his action in abstract moralistic terms, although there seems little doubt that he meant what he said. His predilection for crusading morality reached its zenith when, after much agonizing, he asked Congress to recognize a state of war between the United States and Germany. Earlier Wilson had proclaimed that American foreign policy should be based on morality not expediency, and that we sought "the development of constitutional liberty in the world." His plea to Congress for war against Germany enumerated violations of American neutral rights through unrestricted submarine attacks on merchant vessels, and the exhortation to "make the world safe for democracy." War aims proliferated as the President announced his Fourteen Points for a durable peace, and America's first crusade in Europe became not just a defense of traditional concepts of international law, but a venture in reforming the international community. Wilson, the professional historian, southern born and bred, was aware of how the American Dream of federalism had triumphed over the minority dream of confederation. His League of Nations concept may have derived from the bitter experience of his beloved South, or it could have been from his reading of history and his own inability to keep the United States from being engulfed in the European conflict. The dangers inherent in a continuation of world anarchy were, to him, obvious.

Whatever Wilson's motives for expanding a war for American neutral rights into a crusade for international reform, the aftermath of World War I found the nation swept with a sense of disillusionment. The warnings of Washington and Jefferson were revived, warnings against permanent "entangling alliances" or any alliances at all. The experience of waging war and trying to make peace in concert with other nations had revealed the impracticability of attempting to reconcile the American Dream with the age-old ingrained habits of others. Not that relationships or associations were completely discouraged. Trade continued as before, and the United States cooperated on international problems such as disarmament and the suppression of traffic in white slavery and drugs. But the suspicion of corruption by political affiliation persisted, and was exacerbated by the onset of the depression and the emergence of authoritarian governments.

The Wilsonian dream of an extension of the American system to the rest of the world, a system that he and likeminded citizens believed would diminish if not eliminate the tensions that caused war, reflected a belief long shared by many Americans. Democracy meant not only constitutional government but an entire way of life. Yet the onset of the economic depression that began to exert its dire impact in 1930 cast doubts on the validity of that portion of the American Dream which virtually guaranteed the material necessities and the prospect of improvement. The dictatorships that rose from the chaos of economic distress seemed to offer an escape from the uncertainties and instability characteristic of pluralistic America and other nations that had been following a similar path. These dictatorships promoted a fanatic nationalism, one of whose manifestations was an aggressive drive, not wholly unlike earlier imperialistic surges. The United States, committed to the maintenance of the status quo, opposed these efforts to alter the existing situation because they threatened peace and American interests. On other and no less practical grounds, these movements jeopardized American principles and practices. As Germany, Italy and Japan extended their control through intimidation and belligerence, the United States joined other status quo powers in rearming and seeking ways to halt the alarming successes of the aggressors.

One aspect of the American Dream, not explicitly understood by much of the populace, related to the nation's dependence on the power structure in other parts of the world. Thomas Jefferson privately articulated the need for the maintenance of a balance of power in Europe to prevent any nation from becoming so dominant that it could ignore continental neighbors and thrust itself into the Western Hemisphere. Theodore Roosevelt perceived the dangers to American interests posed by a disturbance of the balance of power in Europe and in the Far East as well. Franklin Roosevelt, too, was aware of what an extreme alteration of the equilibrium in either area could mean to the United States. The doctrine of the two hemispheres, namely, the separation of Europe from the Western Hemisphere geographically, politically, and ideologically, had been proclaimed in the Monroe Doctrine. But Latin America was a constant temptation for European exploitation, and supremacy on the continent could enable an ambitious government to risk American displeasure. In the Far East, the United States had adopted the principle of the Open Door in China, or equal commercial opportunity which depended on the preservation of the territorial and administrative integrity of this vast country. Since a military commitment either in Europe or Asia was anathma in the American tradition, a balance of rivalries and capabilities was considered to be in the best American interests and foreign policy was conducted accordingly.

Therefore, when the equilibrium was being upset during the 1930's, President Roosevelt sought to lend assistance in resisting this change. He first tried diplomacy, next economic sanctions, then material aid to those opposing the aggressors, and finally pursued a policy that led the nation into formal war.

WAR AND THE DREAM

The appeals made by the President to secure support of the people, Congress, and the communication media were couched in the language of the American Dream. Addressing Congress on 6 January 1941, he stressed four universal human freedoms: freedom of speech, freedom of worship, freedom from want, and freedom from fear -- all consistent with cherished American objectives. Meeting with Prime Minister Winston Churchill off Newfoundland in August 1941, Roosevelt joined in issuing what was known as the Atlantic Charter, which promised, "after the final destruction of the Nazi tyranny," measures for peace and equal economic opportunity. The attack on Pearl Harbor brought a unity of effort and dedication that had been lacking in previous American wars. In simple terms, the enemy was bent on destroying the American way of life. Allied appeals for resistance to the Axis went out to all oppressed peoples, including those in a colonial status, holding forth the prospect of independence, republican institutions, and individual liberty -- essentially what had been won by the thirteen English colonies in America.

The incompatability of Roosevelt's professed ideals with the war aims of the Allies became more apparent as the defeat of the Axis powers neared. Britain and France were not inclined to dissolve their empires, and the Soviet Union embraced an ideology and a practice that clashed with those of America. Militarily, the United States and Russia emerged supreme. Any vestige of a balance of power in Europe and Asia was destroyed, and each of the victors sought to fill the vacuum. The high expectations raised and unattained in the colonies in Asia, Africa, and the Middle East exacerbated the situation, while positions hardened and lines of opposition were drawn. The United Nations Charter and the subsequent Universal Declaration of Human Rights had incorporated many of the principles inherent in the American Dream, originally and as it evolved. But interpretation and conflicting aspirations made universal application impossible and revealed that the new international organization was no panacea. Nor was it solely an instrument for implementing American policies.

The Cold War became official when President Truman, on 12 March 1947, declared that "One of the primary objectives of the foreign policy of the United States is the creation of conditions in which we and other nations will be able to work out a way of life free from coercion." This objective could not be realized, the President went on, "unless we are willing to help free peoples to maintain their free institutions and their national integrity against aggressive movements that seek to impose upon them totalitarian regimes." Therefore, he concluded, "It must be the policy of the United States to support free peoples who are resisting attempted subjugation by armed minorities or by outside pressure." This "Truman Doctrine" was thoroughly consistent with those portions of the American Dream that saw republican government and self-determination embedded in natural law, the obligation which devolved upon the nation to extend its system to others, and the implied belief that a hostile world environment endangered the Dream. Objections to what seemed an open ended commitment came from many quarters, including those who felt like John Quincy Adams that we should not go out to combat monsters, and that the attainment of the American Dream lay at home rather than abroad.

As the great debate continued so did the Cold War, and the polarization of the free world and the Communist block increased. The United States, in opposing Communism, supported totalitarian regimes, while economic, military and technological aid escalated into armed intervention in Korea. Justification shifted perceptibly from an ostensibly altruistic desire to maintain the area of freedom to a more frightening concern for collective security and resistance to aggression. American ideals were cited both to urge and oppose military intervention in the Chinese civil war, and to condone or condemn General MacArthur's contention that war's object was victory, not prolonged stalemate. Nuclear weapons and improved delivery systems brought about a further delineation of viewpoints, as did the stifling of liberation movements in East Berlin, Czechoslovakia, and Hungary.

Emphasis on the doctrinal incompatability of Communism and the American free world concepts reached its peak during the administrations of Dwight D. Eisenhower and John F. Kennedy. President Eisenhower's secretary of state, John Foster Dulles, branded the Truman containment policy "negative, futile, and immoral," while advocating a political and psychological offensive. The Eisenhower "New Look" in defense posture relied on "massive retaliation" at times and places of our own choosing as a deterrent to agression -- a policy that seemed to offer only the options of nuclear holocaust or retreat. Mutual security treaties proliferated until 43 nations were formally included in the American defense perimeter, and the brief flurry of "coexistence" with Communism was succeeded by even more dramatic confrontations.

Cold War oratory reached a new high in the inaugural address of John F. Kennedy. "Let every nation know," declared the President, "whether it wishes us well or ill, that we shall pay any price, bear any burden, meet any hardship, support any friend, oppose any foe, to assure the survival and success of liberty." By articulating what he conceived to be the feelings of most Americans, as spokesman for the people and the nation, and most likely what were his own sentiments, Kennedy became a prisoner of his own rhetoric. Relying on those perennially emerging aspects of the American Dream, his absolutes and superlatives raised expectations impossible of realization and led to disillusionment at home and abroad. The abortive Bay of Pigs venture tarnished the American image--and that of the new President-- more than had the failure of the Eisenhower administration to implement its "roll back of Communism" assertions. Kennedy once described himself as a "practical idealist." In the presidential campaign of 1960 he had taken a more vigorous stance in foreign policy than had his opponent, who was associated with an administration that also had promised a more forthright projection of American principles. In keeping with his claims, and to retrieve his and the nation's prestige after the abysmal Cuban invasion, Kennedy expanded the defense posture to provide for paramilitary operations, placed 10,000 troops in Thailand to stabilize Laos, became involved in the Congo civil war, declared himself a Berliner, and committed thousands more troops to Vietnam. His stand against missiles in Cuba was consistent with a cherished American ambition of not allowing a European government to pose an extreme threat to the safety and security of the Western Hemisphere, and especially to the United States. The Monroe Doctrine warning the European governments against extending their system to free nations in this hemisphere was not involved, for presumably the Soviet Union had not established the Castro regime.

That portion of the American Dream which visualized the immutability of republican institutions and the associated impermeable values received its greatest challenge in the context of the Vietnam War. The story of this involvement goes back to the revolt of the thirteen colonies against England and the rationale for rebellion, and the persistent if fluctuating missionary spirit that inspired expressions of sympathy and extension of aid, covert or overt, in support of liberation movements. Vietnam also presented the more realistic specter of a breach in the defense perimeter, which had come to circle the globe. Both ideals and self-interest were at stake, and credibility in meeting commitments was an issue. These and other factors were responsible for the escalation of intervention that followed President Truman's initial decision to send an advisory group in May 1950. Without attempting to analyze the complexities of the Vietnam War, it is apparent that various aspects of the American Dream were to some extent responsible for American participation in this Southeast Asian quagmire. In fact, in my opinion, if decisions had been based solely on defense considerations, it is unlikely that this painful excursion would have occurred.

Among the results of the Vietnam experience at least two can be singled out. First, it demonstrated that the United States was neither omniscient nor omnipotent, that it could not impose its will indiscriminately. Of course this shortcoming had been revealed previously, but the illusion of infallability persisted since failure was attributed to faulty decision makers. In keeping with this awareness of the inability of the Dream to prevail everywhere, the government has adopted an ostensible, but not yet clear, lower profile for America's role in world affairs. In Secretary of State Henry Kissinger's words following the Mayaguez incident, "the United States is not looking for opportunities to demonstrate its manhood."

Another result of the Vietnam experience was that it stimulated a closer scrutiny of the American Dream, of what this country stood for. Attention was focused on the grandiose phrases, the noble superlatives, and, more specifically, on the gap between accomplishing at home what we were trying to achieve abroad. Along with this introspection came an awareness that conditions in other countries might be different from those that had prevailed in the United States. Solutions to their problems could lie outside the American framework. The innocence and naivite with which many American approached world affairs had been shattered, and the repercussions are going to be felt in the domestic and foreign policies of this nation for the unforeseeable future.

The American Dream was based on universals shared by the colonists, proclaimed by the Founding Fathers, and elaborated by successive generations. Deemed implicit in the natural order, these truths were destined to prevail. Committed to the Aristotelian dictum that two contrary statements cannot both be true, many Americans could not accept views different from their own. Believing in the constancy of what was euphemistically called "human nature," namely, that all people behave the same way under the same or similar circumstances, they postulated and adhered to precepts that are being questioned today. The very foundations on which the Western world was built have been shaken, and the first crumbling of the edifice was revealed by the American Revolution. The rejection of elitism in government, of class distinction by birth, of the suppression of ideas, of the denial of mobility--the unacceptability of these anachronisms--was part of the original American Dream. Those aspects of the Dream have been weakened by its very diversity and the imprecision of its precepts. It has been a composite of similar, different, and even contradictory expressions of aspirations and ambitions that have been reflected in the dichotomous approach to war and peace, to isolationism and interventionism, to tolerance or truth, to principle or expediency, and to the acceptance or rejection of responsibility for one's actions. This pluralistic nature of the American Dream has been both its strength and its weakness. The paradoxes of the American Dream have made it possible for people to live together in an atmosphere of almost "countervailing power," of preserving the rights of at least certain minorities against the tyranny of the majority.

WAR AND THE DREAM

The venerable John Adams, writing in 1807, said "The principles of the American Revolution may be said to have been as various as the thirteen states that went through it, and in some sense as diversified as the individuals who acted in it:" This heterogeneity of the American Dream derived in part from the heritage that immigrants brought to the colonies. The French farmer, Hector St. John de Crevecoeur writing in 1782, asked "What, then, is the American, this new man?" He found the answer in unsettled land, the mixture of nationalities, their multitude of religions, and their chance to improve themselves. The variability of the American Dream has been exemplified by the philosophy of pragmatism which rejected absolute truths and substituted a variable but vague criterion for determining actions and values. To some extent extolling the virtues of doing one's own thing, it prompted the saying that "everything is relative," although unlike Einstein, it was not clear what it was relative to. In sum, the approach was one of absolute relativism. If tolerance is a virtue, then it is immoral to insist that other adhere to any standard.

Conversely, the Rockefeller Report on "Prospects for America," issued in 1961, concluded that in a world of considerable change, "What do remain fixed are American ideals and values," and that "It is the grand objective of foreign policy that the world order shall be of a kind in which the United States can be at home--spiritually, economically, and politically." The assumption that "our way" is "the way," that the world is to be viewed and judged through our own rose colored glasses, and that we should expect others to accept our dictates is a form of moral absolutism that seems out of place in recent and current times.

But back to the flexibility and vagaries of the American Dream, which, it seems, at one time or another has accommodated almost everything. The American Dream may have been an illusion, but at least the illusion was real. War has not been an illusion, and it has made the Dream possible. Crises have demanded dedication, a dedication stemming from convictions that certain things are worth fighting and dying for. The cliches and platitudes expounded in versions of the American Dream are no less real because they lack exactitude in definition or application.

Some of the harshest critics of the American Dream, in theory and practice, have been Americans. Some of the most perceptive critics have been foreigners. The United States has been the most criticized and most envied nation in modern history. The Americanization of much of the world has not been through military conquest but by demonstrating a way of life that offers advantages in human fulfillment not enjoyed by the majority of peoples who have inhabited the earth. The complexity of the American Dream offers others the opportunity to select or reject those elements of the Dream most compatible with their aspirations. As a contemporary folk song puts it, "we must have been doing something right these past 200 years."

WAR, DIPLOMACY, AND
THE HISTORIAN

Chapter 2

The sibling relationship of war and diplomacy has been one of the more stable constants in history. Perhaps this perennial popularity can be explained by the commonality of their activities. Both constitute risk, danger, and uncertainty, which add zest to the venture. They involve an adversary relationship, and an assessment of intentions and capabilities. Both include the Latin "machismo," or what Henry Kissinger called demonstrating our manhood. One finds the encounter, the foreplay in negotiation, the confrontation in the contact of forces, and the climacteric of disputation or battle. Each employs strategic and tactical maneuvering, with domination, or imposing one's will, as the objective, and conquest and submission signaling the outcome. This ultimate experience, whether real or vicarious, has its fascination. Each deals with the contact between peoples and their efforts to get along with each other and resolve their differences, and each displays both the consistencies and the inconsistencies of human behavior.

The words "war" and "diplomacy" have become so enmeshed with various categories of human relationships that they have been deprived of specific meaning. Mao Tse-tung's dictum that "politics is war without bloodshed, and war is politics with bloodshed," was followed by Dean Acheson's paraphrase of Mao and Clausewitz to the effect that "negotiation today means war carried on by other means."[1] My own inclination is to define war as "an act of organized violence conducted by a government to impose its will on others." Thus both the act and the purpose of the action are included. In regard to "diplomacy," technically the term pertains to negotiation, although it has been used so loosely that it has come to embrace the conduct of international relations, embodying both the formulation of policy and its execution by whatever means. So the historians of war and diplomacy enjoy a symbiotic relationship, for their fields invariably overlap. "History," of course, is easy to define: it is the record of human experience, the study of life in action.

So where does this leave the historian investigating war and diplomacy? We, too, can profit from the past, for there are many illustrious predecessors from whom we can learn, including the Bible, Homer, Herodotus and Thucydides, Machiavelli, Sir Walter Raleigh, Carl von Clausewitz,

Antoine Henri Jomini, and Alfred Thayer Mahan, as well as many distinguished contemporaries. We have been exposed to writers in the non-western world, especially Sun Tzu and Mao, who along with Machiavelli and Clausewitz concentrated more on the purpose of war than its conduct. This conference appears to be less concerned with the strategic and tactical aspects of military operations than with the way the armed forces can be used as an instrument to protect and promote national policies, as these policies were perceived by the decision makers at any particular time in space. Also, the historian should be aware that the conduct of military and diplomatic operations is almost as difficult as writing about them.

Not many years ago some historians were complaining that military history concentrated excessively on battle accounts, illustrating the nine principles of war in the American version, seven in the British, and from three to twenty-four depending on the predilections of the analyst.[2] This "drum and trumpet" treatment was attractive as entertainment and it provided "lessons" for the practitioners. Yet some believed that this version of military activity was not only a distortion of the true function of the armed forces but was a disservice to the military profession.[3] For the average student or reader, of what relevance was a knowledge of Hannibal's double envelopment at Cannae as compared with an understanding of the factors that led to the conflict between Carthage and Rome, why the latter was victorious, and the results of the outcome. Arnold Toynbee has graphically revealed how Carthage, in defeat, had a considerable impact on the life and institutions of the victor.[4] It is the role that war has played in the fate of peoples, nations, and civilizations that is most significant within the context of the human past. Not that the study of strategy and tactics should be denigrated, for the way a war is fought usually influences the peace. But it depends on the purpose of the study and the audience the historian wishes to reach.

Perhaps I am flaying a dead horse. Michael Howard has written, "Today the history of war is generally seen as an intrinsic part of the history of society,"[5] Maurice Matloff has contended that "military history lies on the frontier between general history and military art and science,"[6] and Allan Millett has acclaimed the "demilitarization of military history."[7] On the other hand, is it possible that the pendulum has swung too far, that the "new" military history tends to ignore the demoralizing, inhumane manifestations of human armed conflict. La Rochfoucauld has reminded us that "history never embraces more than a small part of reality," Marc Bloch has pointed out the abstractions that constitute the historian's version of events, and Arnold Toynbee is among those who have reiterated the shortcomings of any attempt to recreate the past. The trend in recent and contemporary studies of war has been toward viewing the armed forces in the totality of their role within the entire social context--as an institution and its effect on every dimension of human activity. The complexities of modern warfare and the appalling consequences of a general conflagration have prompted military affairs to move from the province of generals to politicians and finally to the realm of scholars. Thus the study of military history has become academically respectable.

Diplomatic history, too, has become legitimized within the framework of higher learning. "History," Burckhardt wrote, "is the record of what one age finds worthy of note in another."[8] Usually, the most valid history is that which is contemporary at all times, focusing on the basic and fundamental issues that have plagued humankind on this earth. Diplomacy has been called the world's second oldest profession, second only to prostitution. The reason for the close relationship being that they are the only two professions in which experience does not count. But diplomacy underwent a transformation in the last few hundred years from an episodic, part-time activity to a profession with its own rules and expertise. Scholarly concentration on this phenomenon was slow in coming, for in 1893 James B. Angell chose as the subject of his address to the American Historical Association, "The Inadequate Recognition of Diplomatists by Historians."[9] Even so, the recognition that he sought was along the lines uttered by Demosthenes, that "Ambassadors have no warships at their disposal, or heavy infantry, or fortresses. Their weapons are words and opportunities."[10] Persuasion and manipulation, guile and subterfuge were the weapons wielded by the diplomat, while overlooked was the Melian Dialogue, as reported by Thucydides, where the Athenian envoys told the Melians, "Into the discussion of human affairs the question of justice only enters where the pressure of necessity is equal, and the powerful exact what they can, and the weak grant what they must."[11] Theodore Roosevelt, in an address at the Naval War College in 1897, said, "The diplomat is the servant, not the master of the soldier." Roosevelt did not mean that the envoy was carrying out policy enunciated by the military hierarchy, but that the diplomat was able to perform his task adequately only if he had armed force to support his claims.

For the historian, the relationship between the civilian and military authorities is fundamental in understanding the correlation of ends and means. "A continuum of relationships," wrote Claude Welch, "exists between the power of the military and the power of civilian institutions relative to the enunciation, development, and implementation of policy."[12] In recent years writers have tended to emphasize the adversary, negative aspects of civil-military relations rather than the cooperative and positive functions. Alfred Vagts extolled the separation of roles in regard to World

War II, when, he said, "It contributed vastly to Allied victory that on their side the professional view prevailed, and on Hitler's side basically political ones."[13]

While many of us will disagree with this assessment, literature on the role of the military in society abounds with terms such as militarism, the warfare state, the garrison state, the war system, the military mind, and the like. The "politicization" of the military and the "militarization" of the civilians is described and deplored with varying degrees of intensity and alarm.[14] The military, while being urged to understand the political purpose for their existence, are told not to interfere in matters outside their area of professional competence. Civilian leaders are faulted, as Russell Weigley does John F. Kennedy, for perceiving "toughness" as "an index of merit," with a "willingness to employ military forces almost routinely as an instrument of policy" being "the gauge of toughness."[15] Apparently the opposite position is taken by Paul Schratz, for, he maintains, "American statesmen and strategists . . . insist upon the isolation of war from politics."[16] Perhaps the contrast derives from their respective civilian and military backgrounds and further illustrates what some consider a dividing line between exclusively differentiated groups that appear to have conflicting perceptions of disparate roles in pursuing the same ends.

The main purpose of a government is to provide for the safety and security of the people. In furthering this objective governments employ various methods, with armed force as the last resort in protection from enemies at home and abroad. Yet, as Clausewitz observed, "every means must influence even the ultimate purpose."[17] So the problem is to correlate force and diplomacy and subordinate both to the objective for which they are the means. In order to achieve this cooperative effort it seems imperative that the military become politicized and civilians become militarized so they can fulfill their distinct but coordinate functions in pursuing what should be common goals. As Mahan put it, "Diplomatic conditions affect military action, and military considerations affect diplomatic measures. They are inseparable parts of a whole." Further, "for a military establishment the distinction between a state of war and a state of peace is one of words, not of fact."[18] This simultaneity of occupation applies equally to the statesman, and the degree of influence that each has on the other is the crux of the matter. But as each adopts some of the characteristics of the other, what some consider a major distinction may be reduced, and the issue relegated to the <u>petit difference</u> that distinguishes men from women with each maintaining separate identities and complementary roles.

This brief excursion into the arena of prescription is not intended to divert attention from the study of the past, but to illustrate ways in looking at problems that are of concern to historians, especially those of war and diplomacy, where often the distinction between the two is marked only by the outbreak of hostilities. Clausewitz has been cited to contradict his oft-quoted maxim that war is merely a continuation of state policy by other means, and other authorities have been mentioned to support the emphasis given to war in dimensions other than battle accounts. Some of the more widesweeping statements regarding the impact of war on human society have been made by historians who have tried to encompass the totality of human experience. "War is the creator of all great things," Oswald Spengler asserted, for "All that is meaningful in the stream of life has emerged through victory and defeat."[19] Arnold Toynbee contended that "On the evidence of history, war has been the immediate cause of most of the breakdowns and disintegrations of civilizations of which we have a record."[20] "Most often in history," wrote William McNeill, "what makes most powerfully for social change is the application of force," and he concluded that war "has played a distinguished role in human history since at least 2000 B.C."[21] One authority, then, is praising the effect of war, another deploring it, and a third noting that its impact has been both constructive and destructive. A superficial reaction to these statements would lead one to belive that war, presumably unlike other human institutions, has both advantages and shortcomings as a device for the improvement of the human condition. A more careful analysis might provoke the historian of war and diplomacy to a greater appreciation of the enormity of his task and the challenge that awaits him in dealing with his subject matter.

The "new" military and diplomatic history, therefore, must encompass all phases of human activity. The narrow confines of tactics and negotiation are no longer tenable, and to practice our craft we must utilize the interdisciplinary approach which emerged from the multification of history as it originally was conceived.[22] This academic dismemberment of knowledge and the proliferation of disciplines, each embracing a methodology to justify its own existence, has proved puzzling and frustrating to many orthodox or traditional investigators of the past. The historian finds within his province all of the social, physical, and biological sciences, the humanities, and their offshoots. All is grist for his mill, and the historian's mill, like that of the gods, often grinds slow and exceeding fine.

Of the many expanding vistas opening up to the historian is that of "psychohistory," for if the historian is to explain as well as describe events he is drawn into an analysis of the objectives and the motivation of the participants. As the venerable John Bassett Moore put it, in "the study of the past. . . the element of real value is the motives, the thoughts and purposes by which events are inspired."[23] A familiar example of the way that some historians have dealt with this problem is the controversy over whether President William McKinley wanted war with Spain and the acquisition of overseas territory because he thought it would be popular, or whether it was part of a carefully devised plan to achieve what he believed was best for the nation and/or the peoples concerned.

This illustration is on the periphery of psychohistory, a technique that many historians have been practicing wittingly or unwittingly with varying degrees of competence or success. Perennially, the historian has been endeavoring to discover sources of performance in the personal qualities and characteristics of political and military leaders. Why did they behave the way they did, make the decisions they made, follow a specific course of action rather than another. One method for explaining choices is to determine the criterion used by the individual in selecting among various options. The debate over the national interest rather than abstract moral principles as a standard is an example. Theodore Roosevelt is heralded as a practitioner of the former with a reasonably successful foreign policy and Woodrow Wilson is condemned for following the latter with unfortunate results. A judicious application of both has been suggested, with the unenviable prospect of failing to apply either in the proper context or being in the predicament of a person who cannot make up his mind. Wilson, it seems, vacillated between his concept of the national interest, not clearly defined, and moralistic inflexibility. The tragic figure, perhaps, who was destroyed by a defect of character. Further, as Freud noted, "the discrepancy between men's opinions and their behavior is so wide and their desires so many-sided that things are probably not so simple."[24]

One trouble with the national interest as a criterion is that there is so little agreement on what it constitutes. During the Vietnam involvement those who supported the war and those who opposed it both used the national interests and moral considerations to support their position. Without attempting to resolve the issue, and if there were an answer it would no longer be a problem, often it is possible for the historian to determine the standard employed by the decision-maker in particular situations and provide a more substantive explanation of the reasons why an action was taken.

The foregoing may have little relationship to psychohistory, which some profess to be a delving into the wellsprings of human nature.[25] No doubt psychohistory was dealt a severe blow by the reception accorded Freud and Bullitt's _Thomas Woodrow Wilson: A Psychological Study_,[26] which even the Viennese master might have disavowed if he had seen the final product. Psychoanalysis may be more effective if the patient is not subjected to an inquisition on the couch, and William Langer, who did the study of The Mind of Adolph Hitler, is quoted as saying that psychiatric profiles are "90% guesswork."[27] Probably most if not all historians have lurking in their hearts, if not in their inkwell, a theory of the roots of human behavior. For psychology does help us to understand if not to explain, as do the psychohistorians, the rational and irrational behavior of our subjects when empirical evidence is lacking. Whether the rational faculty is able to comprehend the irrational, or the human mind is capable of understanding what the human mind is capable of, are matters of dispute. The role of fate, chance, and providence fall within the historian's bailiwick, and perhaps eventually he will be able to grasp those factors beyond human control that affect events and resolve the issue of free will or determinism, of acting rather than being acted upon.[28]

The historian's perception of the past that he is attempting to present is, as most of us probably would acknowledge, colored by his own vision of reality, which is a composite of inherited and acquired characteristics. The extent to which we are affected by current interests, passing fads, or whatever, is a factor that should be recognized and not necessarily rejected. What we should be aware of, regardless of our motives, is that a modified application of the Heisenberg Principle of uncertainty or indeterminancy is going to prevail; namely, that the behavior of the object observed is going to be influenced by the predilections of the observer. The actual conduct of the historical figure is not going to be altered, but the version of his conduct will be determined to some extent by the vision which the historian brings to bear on the evidence. This historical state of mind monitors the behavior of the subjects in absentia. So if the Croce belief that all history is contemporary history means that it is written from the viewpoint of the present, then we should be alert to the fact that not all historians see the present in the same way, and are reflecting the heterogeneity of a pluralistic society that is even further afield from the Virgin and dynamo contrast proposed by Henry Adams.

Perspective, of course, has many dimensions, and the historian of war and diplomacy is compelled to adopt more of a world or universal outlook than that circumscribed by the conventional national approach. His view may be myopic, distorted by his origins, but the phenomena he relates to are more associated with what Spengler called a Copernican rather than a Ptolemaic version of the past. In effect, he must emancipate himself from the customary orbit. Nations as well as people are acting and being acted upon, and this association between societies and cultures has constituted much of the story of humankind. Initial contacts involve negotiation or hostilities, with each group containing similarities and differences and each eventually absorbing or modifying some of the characteristics of the other. In describing and interpreting the nature of these relationships and their outcome, it is incumbent on the historian to expose himself to the myriad aspects of his field before he can describe much less explain. We console ourselve with the thought that there are degrees of ignorance, that secondary studies written by specialists will suffice for areas in which we have neither the time, the inclination, nor the ability to investigate in greater depth. We label peoples, policies, and historical periods by those traits which seem most distinctive, especially when they contrast sharply with those of others. We make order out of chaos in an effort to make it comprehensible, and follow the Aristotelian ideal of writing as though there were a beginning, a middle, and an end. After all, the historian usually has the advantage of knowing how things turned out.

So the historian of war and diplomacy is engaged in a search that leads him to all corners of the earth and to every type of record to obtain the evidence, evidence scattered and reposing in different places and in different forms of communication and degrees of reliability. For the historian usually is not an observer of the activities he is recounting, so much of his evidence consists of reports by others. The factual accounts that the historian uses to reconstruct the past are themselves past facts, not accessible to direct inspection. The epistemological question arises: if you have not observed the phenomenon how do you know that it occurred. This reliance on a "middleperson," an intermediary between the events themselves and the historian, imposes severe limitations on the quest for truth and unavoidably contributes to a betrayal of the past.

No less an authority than Polybius had said that documents provide only one third of a story and the rest must be supplied by a participant.[29] Perhaps the most telling answer to the "participant's version" thesis was made by James Fenimore Cooper in response to criticism of his account of certain events in his History of the Navy. "In most of these incidents," he replied, "those who have testified, either for or against, have had but one portion of the subject before them, while the author, viewing both sides of the question, has been better able to judge between the parties."[30] That the historian is more competent to present a complete and accurate version of an event than anyone who was there is pretty well accepted by members of our profession. Distorted perspective and self interest are among the ingredients that cast doubt on the efforts of a participant to produce a wholly reliable account. "It is my duty," wrote Herodotus, "to report what people say, but I am not required to believe it," and Thucydides complained that "eye-witnesses of the same occurrences gave different accounts of them, as they remembered or were interested in the actions of one side or the other."[31] The historian, by training and dedication to his profession, acts as judge and jury to produce the source of most of our ideas about the past; in effect, when we say "history tells us," we are saying it tells us what the historian says it tells us. In this sense there is more than a kernel of truth in Karl Popper's contention that there is no "meaning" in history other than that given it by the historian.[32] The atmosphere of chronic obscurity that envelopes the battlefield applies equally to much of the past available to the researcher.

Nonetheless, the historian of war does have at his command certain data often denied to his diplomatic colleagues, namely, what Lewis Richardson called Statistics of Deadly Quarrels.[33] In his study Richardson saw a direct correlation between the number of casualties suffered by each antagonist in relation to the total population, and the outcome of the conflict. Using more sophisticated statistical methods, others have endeavored to solve the enigma of "victory," or what subsequently was called "conflict termination."[34] Statistics can be useful in the study of diplomacy, for whether it is troops in uniform, warships at sea, or multiple individually targeted reentry vehicles at the ready, the figures constitute a significant factor in the outcome of negotiations as well as combat.

Parenthetically, our profession has suffered from the lack of a jargon, an esoteric nomenclature and an intricate methodology that separates the scientists who "know" from the non-scientists who do not know. Intelligibility breeds contempt, and the absence of models, cliometrics, original data, theoretical constructs, parametric tests, and the like eliminate the mystery of the historian's craft. Few have claimed, however, that quantification by simple statistics, data processing, or sophisticated computer programming constitutes a substitute for judgment on the part of the historian or the decision-maker. The term "systems analysis" that upset military leaders when Robert McNamara served as secretary of defense merely represented a more efficient method for considering all of the factors involved in making a decision. Yet as long ago as 1887, at the joint meeting of the American Historical and American Economic Associations, the Commissioner of the United States Bureau of Labor said, "The statistician writes history. He writes it in the most concrete form in which history can be written."[35]

Some social scientists have hailed the computer as the philosopher's stone that would end the quest for predictability. Others use statistics in an effort to demonstrate that a discipline is a science for the observation of phenomena, their classification, and their arrangement in such a way that general laws will be revealed. A learned group of historians once concluded that "Generalization from a single instance is dangerous,"[36] although my experience in studying history inclines me to the belief that trying to generalize from more than one "instance" is even more dangerous.

The historian of war and diplomacy has at least two basic problems in using quantitative methods in order to gain substantive insights into his subject matter. First, he has too few _identical_ occurrences to work with, and these occurrences _ordinarily_ are affected by factors largely unknown. Second, there are too many variables involved in the outcome of battles, campaigns, and wars, much less diplomatic relations. The bits and pieces of unquantifiable information about how and why decisions have been made and events have transpired are seldom capable of being fed into a computer and programmed to produce an analysis much less a conclusion.[37]

While the historian should use quantification methodology as a tool it should be his servant and not his master. The brain is the most effective instrument he possesses, and the choices that the historian makes in the selection, utilization, and interpretation of his material are the sum total of experience, education, contemplation, and acquired or inherited ability. His, as it were, "instinctual" or "intuitive" treatment of the material is a manifestation of his judgment being exercised at every step in his methodology, and is an ultimate expression of the creativity that he displays in his craft. For the historian is an artist operating in a medium different from that of the painter, sculptor, or composer, producing his version of the truth as he sees it. "Art," said Picasso, "is what nature is not," and if he meant that art is a more perceptive depiction of reality than the surface impression, then the historian is performing the same function.

Still, the restrictions imposed by the discipline deny the historian the license accorded many of those who reach a wider audience. The historian, in portraying the totality of his subject with a devotion to accuracy, finds his abstractions curtailed and his superlative laden generalizations suspect when trying to measure up to the canons of his profession. Within the context of the limitations imposed on the historian is that of speculation about things that might have happened _if_ the military commander or statesman had chosen to zig rather than zag in a particular situation, or certain circumstances had or had not been present at a specific time. "The primary duty of the historian," says Thomas Bailey, "is to tell what demonstrably happened, not what he guesses may have happened or should have happened,"[38] and _Time_ magazine has caustically referred to "a formula beloved by armchair historians and sore losers: what would have happened if?"[39] Others have felt that such reflection is worthwhile, and recently Daniel Boorstin urged historians to be aware of what he called "the otherwise," or what could have taken place as opposed to what did.[40]

Aside from the fact that part of life is made up of lost opportunities and that their contemplation can be fun, it seems that if the historian is going to attempt an explanation of how and why events took place he will be considering factors that were responsible. In doing so, it is difficult to avoid what Peter McClelland calls "counterfactual speculation." Obviously, says McClelland, "One cannot judge a cause to be indispensable without some thoughts about what the world [would] have been like if the indispensable had been dispensed with."[41] Many of us have indulged in this "want of a nail" approach in an effort to clarify and understand the factors responsible for an event and put them in some kind of order of importance without striving for a quantifiable multiple. The purchase of the Louisiana Territory is one example of something that might not have occurred when it did, if ever. Historical accounts emphasize Napoleon's failure to pacify Santo Domingo, but a number of other circumstances prevailed "without which" the transaction probably would not have been consumated. The Spanish-American War is another event that almost did not happen, and while one can stress the existence of the Modern American Navy that permitted an offensive war against Spain, there were many other "causes" where the absence of one or several might have prevented hostilities. In the study of war, Clausewitz wrote, we "have to consider the full extent of everything that has happened or might have happened," for "a great many assumptions have to be made about things that did not actually happen but seemed possible, and that, therefore, cannot be left out of account." How else can one analyse the multiplicity of the means much less the complexities of the ends?[42]

At this conference last year Charles B. MacDonald, in his paper on "The Five Big Decisions of the War in Vietnam," mentioned occasions on which the United States and the North Vietnamese could have terminated the war and avoided the bloodshed and suffering of the subsequent fighting, with results for both sides comparable to what eventually took place. Of course the United States did not take advantage of these opportunities because its objectives <u>at the time</u> would not have been realized. Why the North Vietnamese <u>did</u> not elect this choice is another matter, for, as MacDonald points out, they did achieve the objective they consistently sought. The "might have beens" do have their place in historical study.[43]

Perhaps the most challenging task for the historian of war and diplomacy, or at least the culmination of his efforts, is judging both the ends and the means involved in the events he is depicting. In assessing the merits of these inseparable parts of the whole he is going beyond the judgment exercised in the selection, arrangement, presentation, analysis, synthesis, and interpretation of the material; essentially, he is transcending the creative dimension of his craft. The hazards involved are evident, and the historian must be as conscious of the criterion or standard he applies as he is of that employed by the actors in his narrative. In similar fashion, when determining success or failure, he can use the values of the participants, his own, or whatever he chooses so long as it is clearly specified. He might find Theodore Roosevelt's concept of the national interest dominating his actions and resulting in compromise and concession when it was neither practicable nor in America's interest to strive for certain objectives. Woodrow Wilson could be viewed as a statesman torn between the concern for moral absolutes and a vacillating concept of the national interest with criteria, goals, and methods proving incompatable. The historian may find Roosevelt successful in his own and the president's terms; he may find Wilson successful in his own and not the president's terms, or the reverse in both cases. The historian may perceive the issues in short term or long term developments. But human beings are judging and being judged all the days of their lives, and the sharpening of judgment through vicarious experience is a value of history that the historian, of all people, cannot escape. Having neither responsibility nor authority for the events he is portraying, the historian should have no hesitation in pontificating on the mistakes of the past. Just as taking no action is taking action, so making no judgment is making a judgment. Besides, any topic worth writing about must be controversial.

In assessing performance the historian is compelled to be as familiar with the instruments at the disposal of his subjects as the subjects were themselves, to be coach as well as grandstand and Monday morning quarterback. Technology has revolutionized the military and diplomatic spheres, and the effort to comprehend the sophisticated weapons in the arsenals of "soldiers" and statesmen threatens to provoke a degree of humility that is anathma to the historian. Yet weapon effectiveness is at the core of much negotiation and warfare that has gone on and is going on in international relations.

Historians must consider both the means available to the decision-maker and the skill--or lack of skill--with which they were employed, whether as "bargaining chips" or to encompass the entire spectrum of his obligations in peace and war. Theodore Roosevelt is extolled for practicing the African proverb of speaking softly and carrying a big stick, although on occasion he spoke loudly and brandished the Navy. Harry Truman is praised and blamed for dropping the bombs on Hiroshima and Nagasaki and for practicing or not practicing atomic diplomacy. The historian must understand the limitations placed on military action and diplomatic negotiations by the inadequacy of the instruments available to the military and civilian leaders, limitations imposed by technological and logistic factors which may bear no relationship to other considerations that provoke or hinder decisions. The good old days of sail and smooth bore cannon evoke nostalgia and envy, while the controversies over the relative merits of eight-inch gun and six-inch gun cruisers, or battleships versus aircraft carriers, appear almost academic in light of the weapons systems that have emerged in the past thirty years. On a positive note, the historian can view the situation as one that enables him to bring into play a greater variety of talents and further exploit the potential of which he is capable.

In speaking on the vast subject of War, Diplomacy, and the Historian, there is a temptation, to which I shall yield, to comment on American foreign policy. Combining the discipline of a naval career and the objectivity of a historian, it seems appropriate for me to present a version that will probably invalidate some of the points that I have been trying to make in this talk.

The nation was conceived in the womb of mercantilist-imperialism and born in the crucible of war. The Founding Fathers were motivated by many considerations, but some were inspired by what has been called The American Dream, a theme selected by President Carter for his inaugural address. The American Dream has been defined as a desire to die with money in the bank, and many critics have characterized the United States as a nation dominated by materialism, a standard of living concept that denigrates basic human values. Yet the impetus that drew many colonists and immigrants to this country embraced more than economic advantages, and the phrases embodied in the Declaration of Independence and the Constitution have not been lost on the rest of the world, where they constantly surface in perorations from Fidel Castro to Idi Amin. The new nation formed by the thirteen colonies early faced the problem of ideals or reality in rejecting an overture from the Executive Council of Revolutionary France to enter into an agreement "to defend the empire of liberty wherever it may be embraced," and "to guarantee the sovereignty of the people."[44] In 1821 Secretary of State John Quincy Adams reaffirmed a nationalist policy when he declared that the United States "goes not abroad in search of monsters to destroy. She is the well-wisher in the freedom and independence of all. She is the champion and vindicator only of her own." As America matured and practices became policy and policies became principles, an imperialism of righteousness and opulence combined with other motives to project the United States to a position of material, political, and ideological preemenence that promised the Pax Americana envisioned by Charles Evans Hughes as a successor to the Pax Romana, Pax Catholica, and Pax Britannica. The rhetoric of Woodrow Wilson seemed to become a reality in World War II, which conceived of a world in the American image as we sought to impose on erstwhile enemies and allies alike the values and practices we proclaimed and often honored in the breech. The atmosphere of the Cold War heightened the divisiveness implicit in the pluralism of varying aspirations as goals and means envisioned by others appeared inimical to American interests if not to the natural order of things. The numerous alliances arranged during the 1940's and 1950's gave rise to the suspicion that in the event of a general war the United States would be fighting on both if not more sides. Under Truman, Eisenhower, Kennedy, and Johnson we sought to reform the world. Under Nixon and Ford we sought to stabilize the world. Under Carter, if Brezinski's article "America in a Hostile World" is any indication, we are obliged to adjust to the values and expectations of others to avoid a "slide into a siege mentality."[45]

Perhaps the United States is aging, as C. Vann Woodward argued at the American Historical Association convention in December 1976, by losing its innocence and sense of invincibility.[46] But aging can bring maturity, and one of the signs of maturity is not expecting everybody to behave the way we want them to. Has the Nixon-Ford-Kissinger combination ushered in a new era in foreign policy? Are we maintaining a lower profile, retreating from empire, an empire of military, economic, political, and ideological domination, or at least an <u>attempt</u> to dominate in these spheres? We have opened up a dialogue with Communist China, terminated a military involvement and commitment in Southeast Asia, reiterated what a host of presidents had said, namely, that manpower for a nation's defense should be supplied from its own population, and signed the Helsinki agreement which formalized a situation that had prevailed for decades. In the meantime we have become involved to a greater extent than ever before in sub-Sahara Africa, endeavored to destabilize the Allende government in Chile and possibly elsewhere, denounced the Arab oil embargo at the time of the October 1973 war in the Middle East as "blackmail" when the United States had used economic sanctions more often than anybody, interfered in the domestic affairs of the Soviet Union to promote emigration and defend the rights of dissenters, and actively supported or withdrew support from totalitarian regimes that imprisoned, tortured and murdered those of the opposition. The dilemma of ideals versus reality was vividly demonstrated last month by the Carter administration decision to curtail aid to Argentina, Uruguay, and Ethiopia because of their violation of human rights, while continuing aid to South Korea on grounds of national security in spite of similar governmental behavior.

"The United Nations," said Daniel Patrick Moynihan, "is a mirror of the world." The United States, in most respects a nation of immigrants and their descendants with its ethnic clusters, may be serving as a mirror of the world in microcosm. President Ford spoke of "the unhyphenated American promise," although we have not achieved the Crevecouer image of a country where "individuals of all nations are melted into a new race of men." Affluence is contributing to an already volatile situation, for, as F. Scott Fitzgerald wrote, "nobody feels sorry for a girl on a yacht."

The historian, viewing the past from the context of the present, should be endowed with greater breadth as well as depth of perception, find a less parochial, heliocentric not geocentric, macrocosmic rather than microcosmic, approach more compatible with the hitherto unfathomable human past. Most likely he will find his vision altered by future developments yet unknown, and fads in history become fashionable in many ways. The excursion in Vietnam found the communication media emphasizing the less pleasant aspects of war, which presumably reduced its fascination and led to pressures for its discontinuance. At least so Dean Rusk contended at the American Historical Association meeting in 1975, and the historian may be inclined to stress the "blood and guts" facet of war in an effort to discourage this vicious practice. But it is questionable whether this method of providing a "lesson" would have the effect desired. To paraphrase Robert E. Lee, it could be that people are fond of war because it is so horrible. Montaigne wrote that there is no idea so absurd but what men will die for it, and Arnold Toynbee has concluded that wars waged for ideals such as religion, democracy, and nationalism have been the most atrocious.

War is the ultimate form of competition and it demands the maximum in human performance. International rivalries that culminate in hostilities are the extreme manifestation of individual and group contentions for whatever aspirations happen to prevail. Peace is easy; all you have to do is let the other fellow have his way. Whether the urge to violence is inherited or acquired, conflict has been characteristic of human existence as has been the dichotomous presence of cooperation. The justification for military preparedness and war as an instrument or continuation of state policy seems to derive from a desire to maintain or alter an existing situation. The options a nation wishes to exercise and its perception of dangers or risks will determine its behavior on the international scene. For power is used to exert influence and impose control, and the fallibility of human beings is revealed by our awareness that statesmen and military leaders, like physicians, bury their mistakes. But the pages of history books are filled with the corpses of nations that failed to correlate their perceptions with their aspirations and their objectives with their resources.

Each field of history and each generation of historians has to earn its place in the profession, to become worthy of its heritage and contribute to that sum of knowledge and understanding that has enabled mankind to achieve a better life and provide greater opportunities for individual fulfillment. War and diplomacy have contributed immeasurably to the attainment of this condition, and the magnitude of the task in presenting the story in all of its ramifications places overwhelming demands on the historian. But, as Lord Nelson wrote, "If I had been censured every time I have run my ship or fleets under my command into great danger, I should long ago have been out of the service and never in the house of peers."[47]

FOOTNOTES

1. Dean Acheson, Doherty Lecture, University of Virginia, 7 May 1966.

2. "Principles of War: An Analysis," Army Quarterly and Defense Journal, July 1960, condensed and reprinted in Marine Corps Gazette, October 1960. This article reduces all "principles" to three: (1) Selection and maintenance of aim; (2) Concentration of force over weakness; (3) Offensive action.

3. See Dana Carleton Munro, "War and History," The American Historical Review, XXXII (January 1927), 225; Louis Morton, "The Historian and the Study of War," Mississippi Valley Historical Review, XLVIII (March 1962), 599, 612; Wilbur R. Jacobs, "Wider Frontiers--Questions of War and Conflict in American History: The Strange Solution by Frederick Jackson Turner," California Historical Society Quarterly, XLVII (September 1968), 220, 225.

4. Arnold J. Toynbee, Hannibal's Legacy: The Hannibalic War's Effects on Roman Life (2 vols, New York, 1966). Several authorities writing in 1918 concluded, "When this war comes to be reviewed in proper perspective its social and economic aspects will be found at least as remarkable as the military events, and perhaps more instructive." J. Maurice Clark, et al., eds., Readings in the Economics of War (Chicago, 1918), Foreword, ix.

5. Michael Howard, Studies in War and Peace (New York, 1972), 185.

6. Maurice Matloff, ed., American Military History (Washington, 1969), 2.

7. Allan R. Millett, "American Military History: Over the Top," in Herbert J. Bass, ed., The State of American History (Chicago, 1970), 159.

8. Jakob Burckhardt, *Judgments on History and Historians* (Boston, 1958), 158.

9. James B. Angell, "The Inadequate Recognition of Diplomatists by Historians," *Annual Report of the American Historical Association, 1893* (Washington, 1893), 15-23.

10. "The gift of persuasive speech has continued to be a primary quality for the diplomatist." D. P. Heatley, *Diplomacy and the Study of International Relations* (Oxford, 1919), 21.

11. "But there is a limit to what diplomacy can achieve. It cannot substitute for an existing relationship of forces." Henry Kissinger, Press Conference, 19 August, 1974.

12. Claude E. Welch, Jr., "Civilian Control of the Military: Myth and Reality," in Claude E. Welch, Jr., ed., *Civilian Control of the Military: Theory and Cases From Developing Countries* (Albany, N. Y., 1976), 3.

13. Alfred Vagts, *A History of Militarism: Civilian and Military* (Rev. ed., New York, 1959), 475.

14. Samuel P. Huntington saw "the nub of the problem of civil-military relations" in the possible incompatibility of the military function and the values of a society. *The Soldier and the State: The Theory and Politics of Civil-Military Relations* (Cambridge, Mass., 1959), 2. Convenient recent summaries are Larry H. Addington, "On Militarism: A study of Historical Interpretation Since the Mid-Nineteenth Century," in David H. White, ed., *Proceedings of the Conference on War and Diplomacy* (The Citadel, 1976), 20-28; and Russell V. Weigley, "Military Strategy and Civilian Leadership," in Klaus Knorr, ed., *Historical Dimensions of National Security Problems* (Lawrence, Kans., 1976), 38-77.

15. *Ibid.*, 67. Henry Stimson wrote of "the peculiar psychology of the Navy Department, which frequently seemed to retire from the realm of logic into a dim religious world in which Neptune was God, Mahan his prophet, and the United States Navy the only true Church." Henry L. Stimson and McGeorge Bundy, *On Active Service in Peace and War* (New York, 1947, 1948), 506.

16. Paul R. Schratz, "Militarism or the Military Virtues: The Changing Role of Military Force in National Policy," in John P. Lovell and Philip S. Kronenberg, eds., *New Civil-Military Relations: The Agonies of Adjustment to Post-Vietnam Realities* (New Brunswick, N. J., 1974), 273.

17. Carl von Clausewitz, On War, edited and translated by Michael Howard and Peter Paret (Princeton, 1976), 158.

18. Alfred Thayer Mahan to Theodore Roosevelt, 25 August 1911, in Robert Seager II and Doris D. Maguire, eds., Letters and Papers of Alfred Thayer Mahan (3 vols., Annapolis, Md., 1975), III, 276.

19. Oswald Spengler, The Decline of the West (2 vols. in 1, New York, 1939), II, 363.

20. Arnold J. Toynbee, A Study of History (12 vols., London, 1961), XII, 610.

21. William H. McNeill, Past and Future (Chicago, 1954), 9, 178. See also Quincy Wright, A Study of War (2 vols., Chicago, 1942), I, 254.

22. "History was the first of the social sciences to become an organized body of knowledge." Arthur M. Schlesinger, "History: Mistress and Handmaid," in Essays on Research in the Social Sciences (Washington, 1931), 139.

23. John Bassett Moore, The Principles of American Diplomacy (New York, 1905, 1918), ix.

24. Sigmund Freud, Civilization and Its Discontents (London, 1951), translated from the German by Joan Riviere, 7.

25. "Freud's fundamental discoveries--of the significance of man's individual and collective past--provide the basis for psychohistory." Robert J. Lifton, "On Psychohistory," in Robert Jay Lifton and Eric Olson, eds., Explorations in Psychohistory: The Wellfleet Papers (New York, 1974), 27.

26. Sigmund Freud and William C. Bullitt, Thomas Woodrow Wilson: A Psychological Study (Boston, 1967).

27. Time, 12 August 1974, 41.

28. Isaiah Berlin contended that "everything is in principle explicable, for everything has a purpose, although our minds may be too feeble or too distraught to discover in any given case what this purpose is." Isaiah Berlin, "Historical Inevitability," in Patrick Gardiner, ed., The Philosophy of History (London, 1974), 162. A contrary view is expressed by Pieter Geyl, who concluded that "in the sequence of cause and effect, of which the human mind will never have complete command, the category of the imponderabilia, passion and emotion, conviction, prejudice, misunder-

standing, have their organic function." Pieter Geyl, "The American Civil War and the Problem of Inevitability," The New England Quarterly, XXIV (June 1951), 168. "We can set no limits to the future expansion of the 'empire of the mind,'" conjectured James Conant. "A continued reduction in the degree of empiricism in our undertakings is both possible and of deep significance --this, in a few words, is the message that modern science brings to modern man." James B. Conant, Modern Science and Modern Man (New York, 1952), 111.

29. "They fail to catch the versimilitude of historical events, because nothing but personal experience can enable the historian to achieve that. . . The moral is that a preoccupation with documentary materials is only one-third part of an historian's task--and this the third in order of importance." Polybius, quoted in Arnold J. Toynbee, A Study of History, X, 166.

30. J. Fenimore Cooper, History of the Navy of the United States of America (2nd ed., 2 vols., Philadelphia, 1840), I, viii.

31. Thycydides "is the only great historian I can think of who concentrates rigidly and exclusively on the dynamics, the methods, the causes, and results of war between sovereign states." Bernard M. W. Knox, "Thucydides and the Peloponnesian War: Politics and Power," Naval War College Review, XXV (Jan-Feb 1973), 6.

32. Karl R. Popper, The Open Society and Its Enemies (4th ed., 2 vols, Princeton, 1963), II; and his The Poverty of Historicism (Boston, 1957).

33. Lewis F. Richardson, Statistics of Deadly Quarrels, edited by Quincy Wright and C. C. Lienam (Pittsburgh, 1960).

34. See Raymond G. O'Connor, "Victory in Modern War," Journal of Peace Research, VI (December 1969), 367-384.

35. Carroll D. Wright, quoted in Herbert B. Adams, The Study of History in American Colleges and Universities (Washington, D.C., 1887), 2. "Il est plus d'hommes qui savent calculer que raisonner." Moheau, Recherche et considerations sur la population de la France (1778), quoted by G. Ohlin, "No Safety in Numbers: Some Pitfalls of Historical Statistics," in Roderick Floud, ed., Essays in Quantitative Economic History (Oxford, 1974), 59.

36. The Social Sciences in Historical Study: A Report of the Committee on Historiography, Social Science Research Council Bulletin 64 (New York, 1954), 151.

37. "As a rule of thumb, historians who have fewer than two hundred cases, and who have for each case only a few pieces of information, will prefer to work by hand." Edward Shorter, The Historian and the Computer: A Practicable Guide (New York, 1971, 1975), 7. This work deals with quantification, statistics, and computer techniques.

38. Thomas A. Bailey, "Confessions of a Diplomatic Historian," Society for Historians of American Foreign Relations Newsletter, VI (June 1975), 10.

39. Time, 3 January 1977, 81.

40. Daniel Boorstin, Phi Beta Kappa address, as reported in the Miami Herald, 8 December 1976.

41. Peter D. McClelland, Causal Explanation and Model Building in History, Economics, and the New Economic History (Ithaca, N. Y., 1975), 160.

42. Clausewitz, On War, 159.

43. Charles B. MacDonald, "The Five Big Decisions of the War in Vietnam," in David H. White, ed., Proceedings of the Conference on War and Diplomacy 1976 (The Citadel, 1976), 12-19.

44. Edmund Randolph to James Monroe, 1 June 1795, American State Papers: Foreign Relations, I (Washington, 1832), 708.

45. Zbigniew Brezinski, "America in a Hostile World," Foreign Policy, No. 23 (Summer 1976), 65-96. The quote is on page 80.

46. Editorial, Washington Post, 31 December 1976.

47. Lord Horatio Nelson to Henry Dundas, Viscount Melville, First Lord of the Admiralty. Victory at Sea, 10 March 1805. Letter in possession of Raymond G. O'Connor.

THE NAVY AND AMERICAN FOREIGN RELATIONS

Chapter 3

The navy has been a microcosm of American life and a product of the nation's values, a reflection of the times and a response to the policies that administration and Congressional decision-makers adopted in an effort to protect and promote what they conceived to be paramount national interests. As an institution the navy has had a determining effect on the development of the nation, and its role in the anarchy of international competition has been its most notable contribution. An investigation of the navy's function in American history reveals the following: (1) the composition and distribution of the navy have reflected government priorities in foreign policy; (2) the navy has provided a flexible response to challenges to American interests at virtually every step in the escalation ladder, and has enabled the President to employ the appropriate amount of force commensurate with the "requirement, cost, and gain" formula; (3) the navy has served as an indispensable agent for stability and peace, and as a catalyst for adventuresome pursuits and imperialist ambitions. The evidence to support these conclusions is found in the record of the past.

The American colonies were spawned in an era of unbridled European struggle for overseas possessions that the contending nations perceived as the major factor in the balance of power, in both the New World and in Europe itself. The thirteen colonies, spread along the Atlantic coast, developed in the womb of England's mercantilist system and survived and thrived on the umbilical cord of maritime preeminence in trade and the sea lanes guarded by the Royal Navy. The Founding Fathers, nurtured in the environment of rivalry for empire, were acutely aware of the role that sea power had played in the destiny of nations. Most recently they had witnessed the outcome of the Seven Years' War, where the stakes had been the future of North America, a war that might well have ended differently had Britain not controlled and maintained the lines of communication with the Western Hemisphere.

Soon after the rebellion began in April, 1775, the Second Continental Congress responded to the increased military demands by authorizing a navy to interdict British supplies and support land operations, then expanded its activities and included privateering to harass enemy shipping. The escalation of the American Revolution from a civil conflict for a "redress of wrongs" to a war of national liberation was determined to a considerable extent by the course of hostilities and an awareness that French military support was necessary to ensure success. General George Washington's conviction that sea power was essential for victory on land was vindicated when Admiral de Grasse's fleet made possible the British surrender at Yorktown.

This further object lesson seems to have had little impact on the infant Confederation government which was heavily in debt and striking out on its own. Deprived of imperial preference and British protection, with a miniscule army and a disbanded navy, many leaders perceived that the future of this experiment in republicanism depended on a restoration of previous channels of trade. Such a resumption, in turn, could be achieved only through obsequious negotiations, for the American diplomats had no "force in being" to sustain their efforts. The disparity between objectives and capabilities was glaringly revealed by the Barbary states in the Mediterranean that captured and confiscated American ships and enslaved or held for ransom American citizens. John Adams as minister to England, and Thomas Jefferson, serving in the same capacity in France, differed as to how this costly and humiliating situation should be remedied. Jefferson, rankled by British depredations on American commerce while he was governor of Virginia, advocated building a navy to compel the corsairs to accede to the government's demands. Adams, convinced that Congress would not appropriate the funds to establish a navy, cited the European experience in urging negotiation and tribute. Finally, after some ten years of enduring the Barbary atrocities, a more affluent federal Congress, under President Washington's prodding, enacted legislation providing for the construction of six vessels. Perhaps influenced by this evidence of American intent, Algiers, the most persistent of the Mediterranean predators, agreed to a treaty incorporating acceptable tribute. President Washington, under the Congressional mandate to cancel ship construction in the event of an agreement, requested and received permission to continue building three frigates and thereby launch the first peacetime American navy. In this as in many subsequent cases, it was not a matter of trade following the flag but the reverse, since the protection and preservation of existing seaborne commerce had spurred the legislation for warships.

Moving backward to the period of the Confederation, the attitude of certain leaders toward the merits of a navy was clearly revealed. Washington, in his "Sentiments on a Peace Establishment," written in 1783, advocated "building and equipping a Navy, without which, in case of War we could neither protect our Commerce, nor yield that Assistance to each other which, on such an extent of Sea-Coast, our mutual safety would require." Prophetically, in light of the events of the War of 1812, he emphasized the importance of controlling the Great Lakes. Jefferson thought that a small navy would be effective against whatever portion of a European fleet could be sent across the Atlantic, and he, with James Madison, believed that a navy, unlike a standing army, would not pose a threat to the liberties of the people, a belief endorsed by the constitutional limitation on two year appropriations for the army. Writing in the Federalist Papers, Alexander Hamilton and John Jay joined Madison in extolling the advantages of a navy. To Hamilton, a navy would act as a makeweight between contesting powers and as leverage in bargaining for commercial privileges. Jay envisioned the role of a navy in the overall maritime development of the nation, and as an essential element in the equation of power and greatness. The Constitution, as did the Articles of Confederation, provided for a navy, but it appears that sectional differences on the subject emerged in the deliberation at the Constitutional Convention, and they surfaced repeatedly in subsequent Congressional debates on naval policy.

The new United States, impoverished, weak, underdeveloped, and anxious to survive and prosper, was not looked on kindly by many of the European monarchies, who wished to quarantine the "Republican Disease." The Congress, anticipating future European wars, incorporated the provisions of the "Plan of 1776" in its "Treaty Plan of 1784," which prescribed the rules for the rights of neutrals, including a definition of contraband and a refutation of "paper" blockades. Secretary for Foreign Affairs John Jay, warning the Congress that the United States would lose trade to other neutrals unless it became a "maritime power," found the members unable to resolve the question because of financial distress and sectional disputes. The controversy between those who foresaw national development in the exploitation of the sea and those who were continentally-oriented continued as factionalism developed following the formation of a new and stronger government. The Barbary depredations overcame some opposition to a permanent navy, but the outbreak of war between England and France in 1793 provided the circumstances which led to a resolution of the issue.

John Adams, who prided himself on his role in creating the Continental Navy, was president when French violations of America's concept of the rights of neutrals became most acute. Believing that "the trident of Neptune is the sceptre of the world," and projecting his Massachusetts attitude of maritime preeminence to the nation, he exploited a delicate situation to produce a crisis. Releasing the XYZ papers and taking advantage of the uproar that followed, he secured Congressional authority to establish a Navy Department, expand the fleet, commission privateers, and wage war first against French armed vessels in American coastal waters and finally anywhere in the world. Then he almost lost control of the crisis, and in his efforts to retain control he lost the presidency. Whether he would have secured a better settlement from France if he had continued fighting or expanded the war, as some politicians believed, is conjectural. But Adams conducted the new nation's first war with a major power and successfully resisted all attempts to escalate a limited naval conflict. Objectives were correlated with the commitment of resources, and while neither hostilities nor diplomacy were orchestrated to everyone's satisfaction, the compromise Convention of 1800 with France subsequently was approved by the Senate.

So, in the first decade of the fledgling government the prospect of a navy had influenced negotiations with Algiers, and the existence and employment of a navy in retaliation to French activities had induced the Directorate to make substantial concessions. Adams could report to the House of Representatives on 27 November 1800 that ". . . a navy, well organized, must constitute the natural and efficient defense of this country against all foreign hostility . . . . The great increase of revenue," he added, "is a proof that the measures of maritime defense were founded in wisdom. This policy has raised us in the esteem of foreign nations." The side effects of this response to French incursions were, in Adams' opinion, far-reaching.

The United States, it should be noted, has gone to war with European nations on three occasions ostensibly because of a violation of the American concept of neutral rights. The provisions incorporated in the Congressional "plans" of 1776 and 1784 persisted through the quasi-war with France, the War of 1812 with England, and the first war against Germany. Paradoxically, some political leaders who had been eager to adopt these neutral principles were opposed to fighting for them in 1812.

The preparations for hostilities with Algiers and the resort to war against France demonstrated to all nations that this pre-adolescent country was willing and ready to resort to that ultimate arbiter, armed force, to defend its interests. A perceptive, or perhaps more docile Congress, accepted an administration recommendation to reduce but preserve the navy, which was to consist of thirteen frigates, six active and seven in reserve. Adams signed the bill the day before he left office, and it remained for Jefferson to implement the act and deal with the problem of renewed Barbary raids.

Jefferson has been portrayed as a man of strong moral convictions who, upon becoming chief executive, rose above principle to practice his concept of what was best for the country. Also, depicted as a foe of the navy, his maritime enthusiasm seemed at times as inconsistent as his principles. John Adams, writing in later years to his former adversary, said that he "always believed the navy to be Jefferson's child." Parentage aside, presiding over naval reduction and faced with the earlier dilemma of what to do about the Barbary corsairs, Jefferson was now in a position to act. After wrestling with his conscience, his interpretation of the Constitution and two Supreme Court decisions arising from the quasi-war with France, and advice from his cabinet, Jefferson ordered the Navy to take the offensive in the Mediterranean. Apparently the first president to exercise this sort of discretionary power as Commander in Chief, subsequently he sought and obtained congressional authorization for the deployment of the navy against Barbary "piratical" behavior. Other presidents have followed this example of committing armed forces to combat without the permission of Congress, although it is not clear whether Jefferson's precedent was cited as justification. The instructions to Commodore Matthew C. Perry for the Japan expedition bade him "bear in mind that . . . the President has no power to declare war," but allowed "self-defense" to protect the ships and crews under his command. President James Buchanan, a rigid constructionist, contended that he could not permit the navy to defend merchant vessels from attacks by Latin American nations without the consent of Congress, whereas Franklin Roosevelt directed the navy to go from the defensive to the offensive against German submarines.

The latitude granted the president as commander in chief has often been debated but was never legislatively circumscribed until the War Powers Act of 1973. Perhaps some presidents were aware that a proposal advanced at the Constitutional Convention designated the president as "Admiral of the Navy." Evidently John Adams took this position, for it is said that during his presidency he lay awake nights devising strategy and tactics, and overruled Secretary of the Navy Benjamin Stoddert on a number of occasions.

As the services grew and the administrative hierarchy proliferated the role of the secretary often appeared ambiguous. President Madison found it necessary, on 12 June 1815, to clarify the relationship between himself, the Secretary of the Navy, and the newly-created Board of Navy Commissioners, with the latter subordinate to the secretary who was "the regular organ of the President for the business belonging to the Department." Some presidents later, Franklin D. Roosevelt, writing to Secretary of War Henry L. Stimson about a proposed reorganization of the War and Navy Departments, cautioned against any structure that would interfere with the direct link between the president and the chief of staff or the chief of naval operations. Military or naval planning and execution were evidently too important to be left to the secretaries. The well-known altercation between the Secretary of Defense and the Chief of Naval Operations during the Cuban missile crisis was more an indication of the political delicacy of the operation than the case of a civilian attempting to exercise tactical control.

The way that a president uses the navy as a means to secure objectives abroad is most clearly revealed by its employment in peacetime where the strategic and tactical professional intricacies of naval engagements are less likely to be involved. During much of the American experience the chief executive has utilized the navy to apply "force without violence" in order to influence the behavior of other nations. As a sanction or coercive device it has provided the greatest degree of flexibility in support of responses to anticipated or prevailing threats to American interests. The mere existence of a navy that had proved itself in combat may have been enough to induce Britain to refrain from taking a more aggressive stance in the Maine and Oregon border disputes, the "visit and search" rights in suppression of the slave trade, the Honduran, Nicaraguan, and Venezuelan controversies, the forays into Canada, the recognition of the Confederacy, and the abrogation of the Clayton-Bulwer treaty. It was not necessary for the United States to possess a navy comparable to that of Great Britain in order to affect the policies of that government. The British, in weighing the cost of pursuing a policy unpalatable to the United States, considered liabilities other than Canada as a hostage or the interruption of a lucrative trade. Spain's reaction to America's gradual acquisition of the Floridas was tempered by an awareness of the hazards in conducting military operations dependent on maritime support against a navy that had displayed its prowess against France, the Barbary states, and the Royal Navy; while after Appomattox Louis Napoleon saw the expanded, steam-powered, battle-tried Union fleet as a formidable obstacle to his dreams of empire in the Western Hemisphere.

Alfred Thayer Mahan's contention that "The surest way to maintain peace is to occupy a position of menace" may not be universally valid, for it can contribute to insecurity and increase tensions to provoke preventive or preemptive strikes. But during most of the nineteenth century the American Navy did not "menace" the European nations; it simply provided a counterweight in tipping the scales toward a peaceful solution of outstanding issues, issues that otherwise could have led to hostilities or the defeat of American policy. Statesmen customarily considered all of the factors involved in coping with problems long before the term "systems analysis" was coined, although a mathematical solution probably eluded them. To use a computer analogy, many statesmen were programmed different ways and attached more importance to certain factors than to others. Sea power, however, was never absent from the deliberations that preceded judgment, and the value assigned to this variable often contributed to the final decision.

NAVY AND FOREIGN RELATIONS

The navy has not always been able to meet American commitments abroad, but its composition and assignments have reflected the prevailing interests of the government if not the nation. Following the War of 1812 America experienced a surge of intense nationalism and devoted itself to domestic and internal development. Yet the Naval Act of 1816 was designed to provide for a "balanced" navy, and the decades that followed witnessed the assignment of warships to implement policies abroad to an extent never approximated for more than a century. The United States, moving from the status of a have-not, developing nation, sought to alter its role in world affairs and share in the exploitation of the available natural and human resources. The task assigned the navy was the projection of American influence and the protection and promotion of American interests throughout the globe. Priorities in foreign affairs were revealed not merely by voyages to distant lands but by the stationing of naval vessels in what were designated key areas. The establishment of the Mediterranean squadron in 1815 indicated a primary concern with the Barbary threat, although these units helped conclude a treaty with Turkey and coerce the Kingdom of the Two Sicilies into paying an agreed-upon debt. The founding of the West India squadron coincided with the acquisition of the Floridas in 1821 and the acceleration of piratical activity in the Caribbean. The Pacific squadron, authorized in 1818, was also a response to former privateers commissioned by revolting Spanish colonies, and to the war between Peru and Chile. It and the Brazil squadron, formed in 1826, were also to protect whalers operating in these waters and serve as a possible warning against attempts to restore Spanish rule in South America. The East India squadron was ordered to station in 1835 to protect merchantmen and impress Asian countries. The Home squadron, formed in 1841 during altercations with Great Britain, was to defend Atlantic coast ports; while the African squadron was assigned in 1843 to carry out the provisions of the Webster-Ashburton treaty in suppressing the slave trade and to reveal a continued regard for the fate of Liberia.

These dispersals of American naval power occurred at a time when the steam propulsion system was being introduced and the need for bases and coaling stations assumed an added significance. Secretary of the Navy Abel Upshur, in a report of 7 December 1842, "respectfully suggest [ed] that too little attention has heretofore been paid to the important interests of our country in the Pacific ocean," but the need for support facilities was not appreciated by other Washington authorities. After expressing deep gratitude for Commodore Matthew C. Perry's success in opening Japan through "coercive suasion," the administration disavowed his arrangements for rights and holdings on various Pacific islands.

The alleged decline in the post-Civil War expansionist urge has been coupled with the rapid deterioration of the navy, and the period of the 1870's and 1880's has been interpreted as an interlude or a gestation stage in preparation for a determined outward thrust. Continued interest in non-contiguous territories, the modernization of European navies, and burgeoning industry and agriculture, found ever-increasing demands for a navy that would enable the United States to compete in the New Imperialism era's contest for land and markets. President Chester Arthur, considered one of the fathers of the Modern American Navy, in his annual message of 1881 urging approval of a naval construction bill, declared, "We must be prepared to enforce any policy we think wise to adopt," without specifying what those policies might be. When Haiti offered Mole St. Nicholas for a naval base, Secretary of State Frederick T. Frelinghuysen opposed acceptance on the grounds that the navy was not prepared to defend it, while Secretary of the Navy William E. Chandler was proposing the acquisition of some fifteen bases and coaling stations ranging over much of the world. Bases constitute both assets and liabilities, providing support and having to be defended. President Arthur, stung by criticism of his "big-navy" program, defended himself in his third annual message by claiming that he did not want a navy able "to cope with that of the other great powers of the world." During the 1880's a number of Congressmen and publicists were clamoring for a modern navy and expounding on the uses to which it could be put. But at the executive level there seemed to be a hiatus, an unwillingness or inability to articulate a rationale for a navy to achieve first rank status in the world. So the new American navy began to grow like Topsy, but it grew exceedingly fast, and soon was able to perform some of the functions envisioned by those who sought an enhanced role for the United States in world affairs.

The controversy over American expansion abroad was to some extent endemic in the debate over naval strategy, namely, the respective merits of commerce raiding versus fleet action. Mahan, in his virtual obsession with the "command of the sea" concept, denigrated the "gunboat diplomacy" function of the navy in projecting American influence abroad. Yet Mahan was writing when the nation was in the process of deciding which direction it should take on the international scene, and this state of flux was reflected in the debates over naval policy. The adoption of a fleet action, control of the sea strategy, eventually determined the composition of the navy and was a manifestation of the expansionist sentiment that came to prevail in the government. Both the naval strategy and the foreign policy seemed to be vindicated when together they, in the words of William Graham Sumner, "knocked to pieces a poor, decrepit, bankrupt old state like Spain." Under Theodore Roosevelt the navy rose to rank second only to that of Great Britain, and he

NAVY AND FOREIGN RELATIONS

brandished this big stick in the Caribbean, at Gibraltar during the Algeciras Conference, and around the world to alert other nations to the new status of America as a "great" world power. The newly-elected William Howard Taft, basking in the light of this accomplishment, declared in his inaugural address that a strong navy was "the best conservator of our peace with other nations, and the best means of securing respect for the assertion of our rights, the defense of our interests, and the exercise of our influence in international matters." In his first annual message, Taft could boast of "the beneficial and far-reaching effect of our personal and diplomatic relations in the countries which the [Great White] fleet visited." Taft's abortive efforts to penetrate Manchuria and Persia witnessed no invocation of the naval force that permitted intervention in Nicaragua to ensure a stable government, and President Woodrow Wilson followed the Nicaraguan precedent to implement the Roosevelt Corollary to the Monroe Doctrine in Haiti and the Dominican Republic. Just how much influence these incursions had on other Latin American governments in promoting stability and fiscal responsibility is problematical.

Woodrow Wilson, often portrayed as the "pacifist" president, utilized overt armed force more often than any of his predecessors. His tardy conversion to the preparedness movement helped spur the concept of a "navy second to none," and the construction program of 1916 was designed to match Great Britain or whichever nation emerged victorious from World War I. Why Wilson, faced with German unrestricted submarine warfare, did not first resort to an embargo or a limited naval conflict is beyond the scope of this paper. But his naval policy was not predicated on the assumption that combatting undersea craft would be the navy's mission in any possible forthcoming war. His postwar naval plans reveal his concern that Britain not become the enforcer for League of Nations sanctions, especially in Latin America, which would have constituted a violation of American interests. Theodore Roosevelt had indignantly rejected the contention that Britain had protected the Monroe Doctrine, and Wilson did not intend to see it ignored under the guise of collective security.

The naval limitation conferences during the 1920's and 1930's were, to a great extent, a reaction against the competitive building after the First World War which stemmed from uncertainty about the ambitions of the victorious powers. The political and naval agreements reached at Washington in 1922 were based on an understanding to maintain the status quo, an understanding which the major naval powers confirmed at London in 1930 by extending controls to all categories of warships. Prospects for future attempts to alter the status quo were initially revealed by the reception of the London treaty in Japan and the refusal of France and Italy to adhere to the pact. As aggression erupted and spread in the 1930's, accelerated building programs reflected the policies of those who wanted to change the existing situation and those who wanted to resist such change. The invocation of the "escalator clause" by the United States and Great Britain was a response not just to Japanese construction but to the increasing international turmoil and the position that each nation was taking to promote or resist change through the use of force. Franklin D. Roosevelt could write in 1928 that additional cruisers were not needed, but later the joint compulsions of economic recovery and aggression led him to realize that the assumed equilibrium of naval power which these conferences sought to establish had failed to maintain the peace.

Of course the navy has not always served as an instrument for peace. At times its existence has led the decision makers to embark on courses of action which resulted in war. Would President Madison, in 1812, have made his appeal to Congress if one of his assets had not been a navy tempered by service against France and the Barbary states? Would President William McKinley have asked Congress for a free hand in resolving the Cuban insurrection if the modern steel, steam, and rifled-gun navy had not been at his disposal, a navy that made practicable an invasion of Cuba and Puerto Rico, the destruction of the Spanish fleet at Manila Bay, and the support of land operations in the Philippines? Not that war with Spain was spurred by a desire to demonstrate the effectiveness of a navy that had cost a good deal of money, but its control of the sea enabled the army to prevail on Spanish soil and provide victories for the acquisition of an overseas empire. Wilson may have been deterred from fighting Germany if the preparedness program had not been underway, and, conversely, the German high command, gambling on the time factor, might have refrained from launching its submarine offensive if the American maritime posture had been more formidable.

The naval balance in the Pacific during the 1930's contributed to Japan's decision to wage war against China and to America's muted response, for both Tokyo and Washington realized that the United States fleet was incapable of waging a successful campaign in the western Pacific. Did President Roosevelt take a more adamant stance toward Japan beginning in 1939 because he wanted to fill the vacuum in the Far East left by Britain's concentration on Hitler, or because he had more confidence in the effect that a reconstituted navy would have on the Japanese? Annual fleet maneuvers had continued to be held in the central Pacific in spite of protests from Tokyo, but the ultimate form of intimidation was the retention of the fleet at Pearl Harbor in 1940. This projection of the only force available to the President, intended as a deterrent to restrain Japan, has been criticized for placing the fleet in a position of less readiness and greater vulnerability. Roosevelt, who complained that he simply did not have enough ships to go around, was trying to use the navy most effectively in support of American policy without placing it in a hazardous and untenable position or subjecting it to accusations of provocation. The decision involved that perennial dilemma of political and military leaders, namely, in assessing the adversary's possible or probable reaction to initiatives, should the assessment be based on an estimate of intentions or capabilities? Granting that both factors must be considered, which should predominate? In retrospect it seems that the American planners relied primarily on their prediction of intentions, whether from strategic convictions or a misreading of the Japanese. Surprisingly, what appears to have had little impact on the thinking of American leaders was the effect of the transfer of substantial units to the Atlantic in May 1941. This reduction lessened the value of the Pacific fleet as a deterrent and made it a more feasible target for attack. Perhaps without this diversion of strength to assist Britain the visionary proposal of Admiral Isoroku Yamamoto would have been rejected, in which case the American fleet probably would have been sunk in the southwest Pacific in deep water with no prospect of recovery.

Japan may have been provoked to attack by the prospect of imminent, overwhelming, American naval superiority, as has been suggested by Stephen Pelz in his Race to Pearl Harbor. In which case the "two-ocean navy" program of 1940 contributed to the outbreak of war and frustrated whatever may have been Roosevelt's attempt to employ navel force as an instrument for peace. Ensuing events demonstrated the validity of Field Marshall Viscount Montgomery's contention that "The lesson is this: in all history the nation which has had control of the seas has, in the end, prevailed." Naval strategy during the conflict was designed to subdue the enemy and allow the diplomats a free hand in determining the peace. Campaigns were not based on or synchronized with detailed foreign policy objectives, and the navy carried out its assigned task of providing the goverment with options abroad.

When World War II ended, the American Navy dominated the oceans, and maritime supremacy coupled with possession of the atomic bomb promised a virtual Pax Americana. The battleship Missouri and other units sent to stabilize a situation in the Middle East were followed by the establishment of the Sixth Fleet to project American power into the Eastern Mediterranean and counter anticipated Soviet pressure. The naval presence in various portions of the globe influenced governments and provided that control of the sea which permitted military intervention in Korea, Lebanon, and Vietnam. President Dwight D. Eisenhower could speculate on what he might have done during the 1956 Hungarian uprising if access had been possible from the sea, for the logistics of warmaking and peacekeeping in distant places has demanded control of the ocean highways. This ability to appear on short notice anywhere in the world with credible force has proved a major factor in the preservation of American interests, and, as previously indicated, has enabled the United States to indulge in highly controversial ventures. The massive Soviet maritime offensive with each segment carefully synchronized had led some to prophesy a <u>Pax Sovietica</u> and highlights the struggle for the remaining most exploitable area of the globe.

The justifications for a navy articulated by early American statesmen have prevailed throughout the nation's history, but the naval mission has expanded in keeping with technological change and broadened aspirations and commitments. Basically, the magnitude of naval implementation of foreign policy has been increased phenomenally in recent decades by the ability to bring destruction to any point on the earth's surface. Gerald Graham has written that "In the eighteenth and nineteenth centuries sea power was probably most influential when it was least conspicuous." The entire American experience leads to the opposite conclusion, for the presence of "proximate" power, as manifested by warships, often has proved decisive in achieving American objectives. The navy consistently has covered, in almost every dimension, the entire spectrum of risk incurred by the nation. From the frigate protecting commerce, the gunboat intimidating a small country, the fleet defending American rights, to the impending <u>Trident</u> missile-launching submarines correcting the strategic balance, the navy has been an indispensable adjunct to diplomacy. The navy has been an agent of imperialism-political, economic, and ideological imperialism. It has stifled revolutionary upheavals as in Panama and Nicaragua, and has enabled liberation movements to succeed as in Cuba and Panama. It has provided that ingredient "without which" both desirable and undesirable steps in external affairs would not have been taken. The presence of American naval vessels abroad has reassured some and alarmed others, a clear indication of naval effectiveness. The navy has given statesmen the option of applying force as gently, moderately, or excessively, with or without violence, as the occasion warranted. The navy has been a symbol of America from the first sighting of the flag in a foreign port, and there is every reason to believe that it will continue to function as the all-purpose right arm of American foreign relations.

THE IMPERIALISM OF SEA POWER

Chapter 4

Alfred Thayer Mahan. Letters and Papers of Alfred Thayer Mahan. Edited by Robert Seager II and Doris D. Maguire. Vol. 1, 1847-1889. xix + 718 pp. Vol. 2, 1890-1901. xv + 745 pp. Vol 3, 1902-1914. xv + 873 pp. Illustrations, notes, bibliography, and index. Annapolis, Md.: Naval Institute Press, 1975. $95.00.

Historians have tended to devote more attention to the influence of Alfred Thayer Mahan on history than they have to the merits or short-comings of his version of the past. Charles Beard saw Mahan as one of a triumvirate, along with Theodore Roosevelt and Henry Cabot Lodge, that spurred American expansion abroad. In The New Empire: An Interpretation of American Expansion, 1860-1898 (1963) Walter La Feber found Mahan to be a perceptive analyst of the American dilemma of his time. Perceiving how the past and the future collided in the present, Mahan concluded that America's plight and her assets--resources and institutions--were inextricably associated with the fate of the world. Further, he prescribed the path that the nation should follow in achieving what he considered to be its destiny; and, according to Frank Freidel, Franklin D. Roosevelt was Mahan's greatest disciple. More recently, in The Naval Aristocracy: The Golden Age of Annapolis and the Emergence of Modern American Navalism (1972) Peter Karsten has viewed Mahan as the epitome of a breed of ideologue publicists promoting a vision of American greatness based on the projection of commercial and political exploitation abroad through the instrumentality of maritime preeminence. While Mahan has been the subject of numerous sympathetic studies (for example, W. D. Puleston's Mahan: The Life and Work of Captain Alfred Thayer Mahan, U.S.N. [1939]) and critical analyses (for example, William E. Livezey's Mahan on Sea Power [1947]) as historian, strategist, tactician, and polemicist, his writings still command attention if for no other reason than that he expressed ideas which found favor in government circles among the great powers that have dominated international affairs for nearly a century.

These handsomely bound and printed volumes of letters and papers provide insights into the personal, professional, and intellectual life of this highly controversial figure. The bulk of the early correspondence consists of detailed accounts of Mahan's experiences at the Naval Academy. They reveal a spirited, fun-loving young man, impatient with the formal learning process and anxious to have done with school and get to sea. "If I were not in the Navy," he wrote in 1858, "but in some profession that would require continual book-worming I should go nearly crazy and shoot myself I am sure" (1:38). There are no letters for the Civil War years when Mahan served in the blockading squadron, but his correspondence while in Asiatic waters during 1868-69 contains superb descriptions of the customs, practices, and political turmoil of Japan. Quite different are his introspective reflections in a diary kept during this period, when Mahan was worried, in fact almost obsessed, about his excessive smoking, drinking, and eating habits. He read extensively in theological works, with an occasional novel for relaxation, and assiduously studied Greek and French. His diary, which fills nearly two hundred pages of the first volume, reveals fits of depression, irritation, uncontrollable temper, unpleasant relationships with subordinates and colleagues, and general dissatisfaction with his life. Just how Mahan recovered from this malaise is not explained, and none of his correspondence--before, during, or after this episode--reflects a similar experience.

As commanding officer of the U.S.S. Wasp on the South Atlantic station, 1873-74, he reported on political developments in Latin America and vented to Samuel A. Ashe, a lifelong friend, his displeasure at "the ignorance and oppression of Congress," although he acknowledged that "naval policy throughout the world is at present in a very unsettled, transition, state--and doctors differ greatly on the courses they advise" (1:434). Mahan made his first detailed criticism of American naval policy to Washington C. Witthorne, chairman of the House Committee on Naval Affairs, in March 1876. Promotion, retention, and retirement practices were castigated, as was the bureau system, which Mahan though should be replaced by a board of admiralty. The following year he expressed an interest in writing a book about a region in France but found publishers' responses discouraging. Speculating in 1880 on the effect of an isthmus canal, he felt it "may bring our interests and those of foreign nations in collision--and in that case--which it is for statesmen to forecast--we must without any delay being to build a navy which will be at least equal to that of England" (1:482). Seventeen years later he was to write Theodore Roosevelt that "the real significance of the Nicaragua Canal now is that it advances our Atlantic frontier by so much to the Pacific, & that in Asia, not in Europe, is now the greatest danger to our proximate interests" (2:506). In 1883 he submitted the manuscript of The Gulf and Inland Waters and admitted, "of course I don't pretend to believe that I have no bias; I only claim I did my utmost to speak the truth: (1:555).

Writing to his daughter, Mahan described his methodology and presented a formula for scholarship that he followed in subsequent works.

> When papa wrote his book a year ago he said; first I will be careful to have everything right, no mistakes; next that everything shall be very clear, the sentences arranged that the reader shall easily understand; and then I will cut out all the big words I can and put short strong English words in their place. To do this papa had to write over and over again, and keep changing words he had written; what a good thing it would have been for him had he had such a habit that he would have written right at first. . . . Papa can write well but with pain (1:575-76).

The years 1884-85 saw Mahan expressing opinions on American and international affairs, and he wrote that "the very suspicion of an imperial policy is hateful; the mixing our politics with those of Latin republics especially" (1:574). In 1885 he expressed one of his classic epigrams, that is, "the surest way to maintain peace is to occupy a position of menace," followed by the uncharacteristic statement "that our geographical position will make war with us unlikely but the surest deterrent will be a fleet of swift cruisers to prey on the enemy's commerce." More consistent with his later position, he urged a "close sympathy, based on common ideas of justice, law, freedom and honesty, with England" (1:593). The correspondence with Rear Admiral Stephen B. Luce regarding Mahan's appointment to the Naval War College reveals the gestation of the sea power thesis as Mahan recounted the impact of Theodore Mommsen's History of Rome and discussed lectures and courses. In preparing himself for his new academic role and the use of the historical approach, he observed, "Of course the question thrust itself forward under all the changed conditions of naval warfare of what use is the knowledge of these bygone days. Here I am frankly a little at sea how to point any moral" (1:623). And to his friend Ashe he confessed, "How to view the lessons of the past so as to mold them into lessons for the future under such differing conditions, is the nut I have to crack" (1:625). Reporting for duty at the Naval War College in 1886, Mahan was to expound certain principles of sea power and naval strategy that he had discerned in his study of history. These principles, he contended, had been vindicated by experience and were immutable.

As an educator, Mahan soon learned that "when a man has to appear, as he does here, in the position of a teacher, he examines and tests his so-called opinions, he really reasons, in anxiety lest he fall into some statement which he cannot maintain before a critical professional audience" (1:662-63). Soon appointed president of the Naval War

College, Mahan became engaged in correspondence with current and potential American political leaders, including Theodore Roosevelt and Henry Cabot Lodge, a correspondence that continued until Mahan's death. Moreover, in 1890 Secretary of the Navy Benjamin F. Tracy asked him to prepare plans for war with certain nations, including Great Britain, which led to exchanges with Tracy and subsequent secretaries and enabled Mahan to express his views directly to policy makers in various echelons of the government. The publication in 1890 of his lectures under the title The Influence of Sea Power Upon History, 1663-1783 brought him instant acclaim as an authority on military and international affairs, although he wrote ruefully in 1893 that "the lack of recognition in our own country--either official or journalistic--has been painful; not to my vanity for that has been more than filled by the superabundant tribute from all quarters in England, but as showing the indifference to service matters among our people." He further noted that "our own navy--by its representatives [Secretary of the Navy] Herbert and [Chief of the Bureau of Navigation] Ramsay--has rejected both me and my work" (2:105).

Ordered to sea as commanding officer of the U.S.S. Chicago, on station in Europe Mahan was entertained in England and awarded honorary doctorates by both Oxford and Cambridge. During this last duty afloat he became involved in an acrimonious dispute with his superior officer, a rear admiral who submitted critical fitness reports on Mahan. But he continued his scholarly strategic interests, and in 1894 wrote a British associate, "I think that in the 'fleet in being' you fellows have got hold of a perfectly sound general idea, but by overlooking the necessary qualifications they are erecting it into a dogma--a fetish--which involves the danger of becoming 'doctrinaires'" (2:337). Working on his Nelson, he complained that "I find biography, according to my aims and aspirations, far harder work than philosophizing over history" (2:436). Nevertheless, he later reported that he had written 70,000 words of the biography in the space of three months, and he agonized over whether the subtitle should contain the word "exaltation," "fulfillment," or "demonstration" of the sea power of Great Britain (2:480). Ultimately, it appeared as The Life of Nelson, the Embodiment of the Sea Power of Great Britain (1897).

Meanwhile, referring to the dispute with Great Britain over the Venezuela boundary, he thought the incident "indicates, as I believe and hope, the awakening of our countrymen to the fact that we must come out of isolation, which a hundred years ago was wise and imperative, and take our share of the turmoil of the world" (2:441). And he ascribed his popularity with the British to his "sympathy with their past history, and with the great part that they (in the main) are still playing in redeeming the world from barbarism to civilization, from lawlessness to order. . ." (2:503). Writing to Theodore Roosevelt in 1904, Mahan observed that "circumstances almost irrestible are forcing us and Great Britain, not into alliance, but into a silent cooperation, dependent upon conditions probably irreversible in the next two generations," and reiterated his contention that commerce destroying would continue to be "a most important secondary operation. . . but as a primary measure a delusion" (3:113). Another letter to the president in 1906 analyzed the international situation and concluded, "when to Germany are added the unsolved questions of the Pacific, it may be said truly that the political future is without form and void. Darkness is upon the face of the deep. We will have to walk very warily in matters affecting the future ability to employ national force" (3:165).

Throughout his teaching and writing career Mahan emphasized the correlation between force and national policy, with the former the servant and merely an instrument of the latter. In January 1909 he wrote to Roosevelt of reading Julian S. Corbett's England in the Seven Years War: A Study of Combined Strategy (1907), in which Corbett illustrated "that for a military establishment the distinction between a state of war and a state of peace in one of words, not of fact" (3:276). While continuing to publish he maintained contact with others on problems of the day, advising Roosevelt to warn Taft not to divide the fleet and taking issue with a Senate resolution in 1909 to do so; telling the General Board that the navy was incapable of supporting American foreign policies; distinguishing between expansionism and imperialism; commenting on the Orange (Japan) War Plan of 1911; and responding to newspaper editorials. Waging a constant campaign against disarmament agitation, he wrote the New York Times on August 31, 1914, and concluded, "The hackneyed phrase, 'Vital interest or national honor', really sums up the motives that lead nations to war. Armament is simply the instrument of which such motives avail themselves. If there be no armament, there is war all the same" (3:543).

In 1913 Mahan had written, "my vogue is largely over" (3:492), a premature judgment as it turned out, for the outbreak of the European war the following year brought numerous requests for his analysis of the military situation. On the controversial submarine question, he believed that it would not neutralize the battleship and that the undersea craft would confine its activities to "scouting and lookout." But, he added, "I have not ventured so positive an adverse opinion as sometimes I see attributed to me" (3:550,700). Shortly before his death on December 1, 1914, he had observed that "the getting the better of others is one of the large occupations of the human race, in business, in lawsuits, as well as in international affairs" (3:553).

The editors of these volumes have performed their task with diligence and, one gets the impression, a certain amount of affection for their subject matter. While letters to Mahan are not included, footnotes identify correspondents, works referred to, and in some cases the circumstances under which correspondence originated or to what it refers. Letters and the diary constitute the majority of the entries, although a number of miscellaneous papers, some on religious subjects, and reports of interviews are included. Listed with appropriate subject matter identification are letters found but not printed, and manuscript collections are specified, even those searched that contained no Mahan materials. Perhaps of most value to the researcher is a four section index, under the headings of general, ships, bibliography, and judgments and opinions. A companion biography, <u>Alfred Thayer Mahan: A Man and His Letters</u>, by Robert Seager II, is forthcoming.

These volumes are an indispensable supplement to Mahan's published writings in understanding the man, the devoted parent, the naval officer, the historian, the strategist, and polemicist. Further, they reveal a perspective on the times when, as Mahan put it in his autobiography, the navy was moving from sail to steam, and, again in Mahan's words, the United States was looking outward with vital interests expanding from North and South to East and West.

MARITIME DIMENSIONS OF THE AMERICAN REVOLUTION:
Chapter 5

Commentary

Both of these papers are designed to correct erroneous impressions widely shared by historians. Dr. Mevers' paper is a corrective to the conventional implication that the Continental Congress, in its consultative, legislative, and administrative capacities, had little interest in, devoted little time to, or accomplished little in naval affairs. Only by consulting specialized works is one able to find an adequate treatment of the subject, works that historians not concerned primarily with military affairs seldom utilize. Dr. Syrett has endeavored to demolish the myth that American naval activity in the years prior to the French alliance had little or no effect on the course of hostilities or the British efforts to subdue the colonists.

Dr. Mevers, in describing the origins of a Congressional naval policy, may be giving a faulty impression of his own. Was Congress prompted to give attention to maritime ventures by Washington's efforts, the Rhode Island resolution, and the dispatch of two British supply vessels? No doubt these events stimulated Congressional initiative. But it is possible that the action of the Massachusetts Third Provisional Congress on 6 June 1775, appointing a committee that recommended the fitting out of six armed vessels to operate under the control of the Committee of Safety, had an equal or greater effect on Congress than did some of the aforementioned developments.[1] Actually, the first formal act by Congress to encourage the waging of naval warfare was a resolution of 18 July 1775 which exhorted "each colony, at their own expense" to "make such provisions by armed vessels" to protect themselves "against all unlawful invasions, attacks, and depredations from cutters and ships of war."[2]

Dr. Mevers states that "Armed vessels, however, had not been nearly so much of a tradition in America." Perhaps not "so much," but seafaring was endemic to the colonies, and at that time the mounting of guns constituted the main difference between merchant and war ships. As Dr. Syrett points out, "America had a long maritime tradition and was capable of waging a large-scale maritime guerrilla war." It has been estimated that 18,000 colonial seamen served in the Royal Navy during the Seven Years' War, while thousands of others were engaged in privateering. So there was a good deal of experience and expertise for individual ship action

53

if not for fleet engagements, a strategy that, as Dr. Mevers indicates, was scarcely even a gleam in the collective eye of the Continental Congress.

Which leads to the question of the "policy" that Dr. Mevers repeatedly says Congress formulated and implemented. Dr. Mevers has convincingly revealed that the Continental Congress took a good deal of interest in naval affairs during most of the Revolution through deliberations, legislation, and the establishment of administrative agencies. But it is not clear, to this commentator at least, just what the naval policy of the Congress actually was at various stages of the conflict, much less why it took the form it did. Just how and why did an authorization to acquire ships to intercept two British supply vessels escalate from these modest beginnings to the creation of a small fleet, to commissioning privateers, to building frigates and ships of the line? The policy and goals of the first acquisition are stated but the "policy" and "goals" of subsequent Congressional actions are not. Nor is the "well defined policy" that the Board of Admiralty followed in functioning as "an active branch of the Congress." Perhaps the term "harass" which Dr. Mevers uses to indicate much of American naval activity, presumably a raiding or guerre de course strategy, would apply. But again, what was its "goal"? Were the "goals" the "threefold objectives" that Dr. Syrett mentions? And how does Congressional policy fit in with support for land operations, assistance to state navies for the protection of ports and commerce, and, eventually, cooperation with the French Navy? Did the creation of successive administrative agencies--Naval Committee, Marine Committee, Board of Admiralty, Secretary and Agent of Marine--reflect changes in policy, dissatisfaction with the existing organization because of incompetence, concern over increasing costs and delays, the miniscule contributions of the Continental Navy, or the realization that privateering was more effective and cost the government nothing? The Congress, in carefully prescribing rules for commissioning and operating privateers, revealed an acute awareness of the value of these quasi-official raiders, an awareness based on results obtained in the most recent war for empire in North America.

Dr. Mevers, in dealing with the demise of the naval organization, mentions the role of "nationalist," pro-navy forces, and "anti-nationalist," anti-navy forces, in Congress. Since much of the naval legislation was bitterly debated, it would be fruitful to explore more fully the influence of sectional attitudes on naval policies adopted by Congress at various periods in the war. The Marine Committee reflected these considerations in being composed of thirteen members, one from each colony. Resolutions pertaining to naval matters were often debated at great length, and involved local interests, expense, strategy, personalities, and means as well as ends. Not only what should be done was at issue, but how it should be done consumed a good deal of time, and experiments with administrative organization were not always successful. In disputes over the Navy's mission, Robert Morris contended that "our infant fleet cannot protect our own Coasts," and recommended that it "attack the enemies' defenceless places and thereby oblige them to station more of their Ships in their own Countries, or to keep them employed in following ours, and either way we are relieved." John Paul Jones happened to agree with Morris, believing that commerce destroying should be carried out by privateers which were "good for nothing else."[3]

The gradual if not leisurely approach taken by Congress in founding a Navy in contrast to the urgency demonstrated in establishing an army, reflects the nature of the conflict as conceived by the delegates at successive steps in the escalation ladder. In the first session of the second Continental Congress there was a reluctance to take action that might provoke sterner measures to suppress the rebellion and evoke a less compromising attitude in London. Then, as the King revealed his determination to crush the uprising, more desperate measures were invoked and the colonists retaliated.

The committee system of administration was consistent with the uncertain jurisdictional, governmental status of Congress, and was, perhaps, even desirable in the early stages of marine warfare when experience and expertise were lacking and affairs were not so multitudinous. When activities expanded, new problems emerged, and membership changed, the complex decision-making process revealed the shortcomings of the committee system. Sporadic attempts to profit by the British organization did not produce an office comparable to the First Lord of the Admiralty until the Continental Navy had virtually disintegrated. Under the circumstances, bureaucratic inefficiency was certainly understandable, and it was compounded by the inexperience of legislators and administrators as well as the uncertainties of communications by land and sea. Nonetheless, it does appear that naval affairs would have been conducted more effectively and expeditiously if executive authority had been delegated to the most qualified individuals who would be held responsible and report to the Congress or to a committee, as was the case with the board at Boston and, to a lesser degree, the board at Philadelphia. Efficiency in administration did increase, as noted, when Robert Morris became Agent of Marine and was able to make decisions without having to convene a committee or worry about a quorum, each of whose members would have a voice equal to his own in determining on a course of action.

Evidently there was a perennial controversy in Congress between two factions: one which advocated a delegation of responsibility and authority to a central department; the other that advocated retention of authority in Congress and decentralization of responsibility by dispersal through committees, boards, and agents. While the latter prevailed throughout most of the struggle, the unwieldiness of the organizational structure eventually permitted the "concentrative" group to induce Congress to establish several offices including a Superintendent of Finance, a Secretary of War, and a Secretary of Marine.[4] No professional office was ever created equivalent to that of the British First Sea Lord or even to that of George Washington in the Army.

In spite of the criticism leveled at the naval policy of the Continental Congress and its committees by this commentator and others, the seven member committee established on 13 October 1775 made an impressive record. Although initially this "Naval Committee" was enjoined only to investigate the cost of, report on, and supervise the fitting out of armed vessels, its duties were soon expanded to assume responsibility for recommending legislation pertaining to all naval matters, and increasingly the Congress delegated authority to the Committee to issue appointments and sailing orders. In less than three months the Naval Committee purchased, outfitted, and manned the first Continental Navy while providing the necessary directives, rules, regulations, and legislation for the prosecution of naval warfare. Its accomplishments would be considered remarkable under any circumstances. But functioning within the military, political, economic, and administrative chaos that prevailed in the colonies makes its achievements almost unique in the annals of bureaucratic performance. Further efforts toward decentralization were exemplified by the establishment of boards at Philadelphia and Boston whose duties, as Dr. Mevers indicates, were comprehensive. Although functioning under the direction of, and reporting to the Marine Committee and its successors, these boards came to exercise a good deal of autonomy in supervising the naval activities of their districts. Only the board at Boston, however, was allowed to issue sailing orders, and this authority was reluctantly given because of communication difficulties with the Marine Committee. These boards performed valuable services during the period of growth and operation of the Continental Navy. But as the Navy deteriorated in 1780 and 1781 due to inefficiency, financial distress, and losses at sea, the boards were gradually dissolved.

Moving from the landlocked formulation and administration of policy to action on the high seas, Dr. Syrett in his paper broadly interprets the term "American Naval Operations" to include activities of vessels in the Continental, state, and privateering categories. As Gardner W. Allen puts it, "there was to some extent a sort of blending of the three classes of sea service, both as regards ships and personnel."[5] Dr. Syrett points out in a footnote that "During the course of the war, naval and privateer commissions were issued by many different American governmental authorities. Therefore, throughout this essay the American forces are referred to in general terms such as 'American naval forces,' 'American raiders,' or 'American cruisers.'" Among Dr. Syrett's contributions, again in a footnote, is his furnishing data to disprove Sidney G. Morse's contention that after the Congressional resolution of April 1776 few privateers were commissioned by states.[6]

In stressing the British failure to correctly assess American intentions, determination, and, especially, capabilities, Dr. Syrett provokes tempting analogies with similar erroneous assumptions, most recently those of American authorities in the Vietnam conflict. Still, in 1775, the London officials may have counted on more support from colonists loyal to the mother country, and the likelihood that these loyalists would inhibit an effective prosecution of the war. But even if the British had been more perceptive in their estimate of colonial resistance, would it have made any difference? According to Dr. Syrett, the British simply did not possess the naval resources to suppress the American maritime effort and meet commitments elsewhere, especially in Europe. Perhaps a concentration in American waters during the initial phase of domestic insurrection before the colonial maritime mobilization got underway, and before the French and Spanish threat had intensified, would have been successful. To paraphrase Bismarck, there are opportunities that occur in military operations that never come again. So--and this seems to be one of Dr. Syrett's points--British misconceptions of the nature and extent of the revolt may have prevented the government from adopting measures to stifle the uprising at this critical juncture.

In his narrative Dr. Syrett does concede that a naval blockade might have worked if the British had been able to deploy sufficient units of the Royal Navy to accomplish the job. At the time British officials differed on the merits of blockade, and historians in retrospect disagree on whether it could have been effective. As examples of the latter, Don Higginbotham in his The War of American Independence, is more than skeptical. Piers Mackesy, writing on The War for America, thinks otherwise.[8] Again, it would depend on the allocation of British sea power at the proper times and places. Diverting substantial numbers of vessels from European waters and from support of land operations could have provided sufficient warships to interdict seaborne trade and ships engaged in naval and privateering activities. The "myried coves, inlets, and streams from Georgia to Maine" that Higginbotham mentions would permit what amounted to American smuggling ventures, but could not provide facilities for larger vessels or the loading and unloading of substantial cargo. Where Dr. Syrett seems to differ with some authorities is whether the British could afford to make such a deployment. In British circles the views of Sandwich and the Admiralty prevailed over those of Germain and others. Of later writers, Piers Mackesy and Alfred Thayer Mahan are among those who believe that the fear of French and Spanish sea power was exaggerated. So much for brief speculation on a complex issue.

Turning to another subject, Dr. Syrett's analysis of the objectives and achievements of the American cruiser offensive constitutes the central part of his thesis. Consistent with his definition of "American Naval Operations," he does not distinguish between captures of British merchantman by vessels of the Continental or state navies, or by privateers, although his footnotes reveal the number of these private marauders commissioned by the Continental Congress and by the government of Massachusetts. Most of the damage to enemy commerce was inflicted by American privateers, whose depredations constituted the most substantive American maritime contribution to victory. Still, Dr. Syrett does not claim, as does Edgar S. Maclay, in his *A History of American Privateers*, that "It was this attack on England's commerce that struck the mortal blows to British supremacy in America--not Saratoga or Yorktown." Nor, obviously, would Dr. Syrett agree with the view of Carroll Storrs Alden and Ralph Earle that "The 'militia of the sea' was as futile as the militia of the land."[10]

Dr. Syrett has not directed his paper to the outcome of the American Revolution, and he has presented an impressive case for the effect of American cruiser warfare on the course of the conflict and its influence in determining the factors that helped make victory possible. But I see no evidence to indicate that American cruisers in the Atlantic had a decisive effect in altering British military strategy in North America during the period 1775-1778. Regarding logistical support to the armies, Piers Mackesy concludes, "The whole effort across the ocean was unparalleled in the history of the world, and it was successful."[11] In spite of some early notable captures of supplies and equipment, British land campaigns in America were not disrupted by raids on British shipping. These early depredations provided American armies with sorely needed munitions, and the seaborne raiders diverted British patrols that could have interfered with the smuggling of supplies and pulled units of the Royal Navy away from greater cooperation with land campaigns. But it was not the American maritime effort during the first years of the war that kept the colonial resistance alive. Simply put, it was the incompetence of British generals in the field that averted a quick end to the rebellion.

Dr. Syrett cites Mahan as virtually ignoring the activities and contributions of privateers in his *Major Opera-*

tions of the Navies in the War of American Independence, and the same deficiency is apparent in the more than two hundred pages that Mahan devotes to the American Revolution in his The Influence of Sea Power Upon History.[12] As an aside, it is worth noting that Mahan, in a personal letter in 1885, asserted "that our geographical position will make war with us unlikely but the surest deterrent will be a fleet of swift cruisers to prey on the enemy's commerce."[13] Writing to Theodore Roosevelt in 1904, Mahan reiterated his better known contention that commerce destroying would continue to be "a most important secondary operation. . . but as a primary measure a delusion."[14] As Dr. Syrett makes clear, these raiding tactics were the only "naval" operation the Americans could undertake on the high seas. Mahan did not even accord it importance as a secondary operation in his treatment of the American Revolution, and the effects of the cruiser offensive were scarcely a delusion in exercising a primary influence on the fate of the American cause.

To continue using Mahan as a means of addressing Dr. Syrett's theses regarding the repercussions of the American cruiser offensive, I would like to consider its contribution "to the breakdown of diplomatic relations between Britain and France and hasten French entry into the conflict." Not that I question the validity of this statement. My caveat is that Dr. Syrett has not introduced, within the framework of his comprehensive definition of American naval operations, the events that culminated in the Battle of Valcour Island. The presence of General Benedict Arnold's flotilla prevented the British from controlling Lake Champlain during a critical period. This obstruction delayed a British thrust from Canada designed to capture Ticonderoga, advance down the Hudson River Valley to crush Washington, join the army moving from New York, and isolate New England, the hotbed of radicalism, from the other colonies. The postponement occasioned by Arnold's tiny force enabled an American army to regroup and prepare to resist the British offensive that resumed in the spring of 1777 under General Burgoyne, whose surrender at Saratoga on 17 October 1777 prompted British attempts to reach an accommodation with the colonies and spurred the French decision to consummate an alliance with the American nation. The Lake Champlain episode demonstrated two of Mahan's favorite dicta, namely, the influence of a "fleet in being" and the possible decisiveness of control of an inland waterway.

Some might quibble with Dr. Syrett's assertion that the Royal Navy had "command of the sea" in the Mahan sense. Phillip H. Colomb said "The primary aim of naval war is the command of the sea."[15] Both of these strategists conceived of command of the sea as including control of the sea lanes, and Mahan for one criticized the British naval effort during the Revolution for not achieving a control that was within their grasp, only to be lost through a defective strategy.

That the Continental Congress had a strategy or strategies is beyond doubt. Just how well defined these strategic concepts were in the minds of American decision makers is difficult to determine. That they developed as they did is not necessarily evidence that members of the Congress formulated a deliberate long range, farsighted plan and followed it with some degree of consistency. In fact, Congressional naval policy, as revealed in these papers and elsewhere, developed in neither an orderly nor totally haphazard fashion. The Continental Congress acted in response to circumstances and within the constraints imposed by limits of jurisdiction, resources, individual strategic theories, and perceptions of Britain's intentions and capabilities. As for the British performance, Leslie Gardiner may be overstating the case when he says "The conduct of the War of Independence on the naval side was mismanaged at home and half-heartedly undertaken on the spot."[16] In war as in football, the side that makes the fewest mistakes usually wins.

FOOTNOTES

1. William Bell Clark, "American Naval Policy, 1775-1776," The American Neptune, I(1941):27.

2. William Bell Clark and William James Morgan, eds., Naval Documents of the American Revolution, 7 vols. to date (Washington, 1964-), I:916.

3. Quoted in Samuel Eliot Morison, John Paul Jones: A Sailor's Biography (1959; paperback ed., New York, 1964), pp. 92, 125.

4. Charles Oscar Paullin, Paullin's History of Naval Administration, 1775-1911 (Annapolis, 1968), pp. 38-9.

5. Gardner W. Allen, A Naval History of the American Revolution, 2 vols. (Boston, 1913), I:51-2.

6. Sidney G. Morse, "State or Continental Privateers?" American Historical Review, LII (October 1946):68-73.

7. Don Higginbotham, The War of American Independence: Military Attitudes, Policies and Practice, 1763-1789 (New York, 1971), p. 150.

8. Piers Mackesy, The War for America, 1775-1783 (Cambridge, Mass., 1964), pp. 97-102.

9. Edgar S. Maclay, A History of American Privateers (New York, 1899), p. xi.

10. Carroll Storrs Alden and Ralph Earle, *Makers of Naval Tradition* (Boston, 1925), p. 11. The role of commerce raiding as a contribution to the American naval effort is also denigrated in Harold and Margaret Sprout, *The Rise of American Naval Power, 1776-1918*, rev. ed. (Princeton, 942), p. 11.

11. Piers Mackesy, "British Strategy in the War of American Independence," *The Yale Review*, LII (1963):543.

12. A. T. Mahan, *The Influence of Seapower Upon History, 1660-1783* (Boston, 1890), pp. 330-541.

13. Robert Seager II and Doris D. Maguire, eds., *Letters and Papers of Alfred Thayer Mahan*, 3 vols. (Annapolis, 1975), II:593.

14. *Ibid.*, III:113.

15. Quoted in Clark G. Reynolds, *Command of the Sea: The History and Strategy of Maritime Empires* (New York, 1974), p. 1.

16. Leslie Gardiner, *The British Admiralty* (Edinburgh, 1968), p. 173.

THE NAVY ON
THE FRONTIER

Chapter 6

The frontier for the United States Navy was both continental and global.[1] The navy opened, and provided means for maintaining relations with countries bordering the seven seas. While the naval frontier may not have influenced American institutions to the extent that Frederick Jackson Turner claimed for the continental frontier, the navy brought oversea frontiers closer to home and provided reciprocal exchange which has broadened and often modified the character of societies and civilizations. Most of the western hemisphere ceased being a part of the frontier of Europe, as Walter Prescott Webb contended, not simply because of the development of capitalism and democracy, but because the U.S. Navy presented a tangible and at times formidable barrier to continued domination and further exploitation. Essentially, the navy enabled Americans to choose between insularity from or contiguity with other lands. The impact of this freedom of choice with its long term influence on American thinking may have an even more lasting effect on the nation than that envisioned by the Turner thesis.

Aside from the suppression of piracy in the Caribbean, certainly a vital American maritime frontier, the navy contributed to the acquisition of the Louisiana Territory. Its valiant efforts in the Quasi-War with France and against the Barbary Powers helped convince Napoleon that the United States was not a paper tiger. President Thomas Jefferson, however ambivalent his views on the navy, was apprehensive that France might close the Mississippi to traffic. He asked for and received from Congress on February 28, 1803 authorization to build a number of river gunboats to maintain freedom of navigation. Bids were invited to construct vessels at Pittsburgh, Marietta, and Louisville to provide a naval force on the Ohio-Mississippi channels to protect produce and settlers, a force that never materialized as the purchase and transfer of the Louisiana Territory was consummated.

During the War of 1812 the navy performed admirably on the frontier. Alfred Thayer Mahan may have been exaggerating when he stated that naval victories on Lake Erie and Lake Champlain gave the American envoys at Ghent "the preponderance of military argument," and that "Perry and McDonough averted from the United States, without further fighting, a rectification of the frontier."² Many factors contributed to the British decision to modify their original demands. Nevertheless their dropping the sine qua non of an Indian buffer area and "revision of the boundary line between the United States and the adjacent British colonies" was related, at least to some degree, to the military situation resulting from naval successes. Inland water victories further demonstrated to the Indians that their cause was lost, and helped save the Old Northwest Frontier for American pioneers. In the south, an American squadron on Lake Borgne, Louisiana, by its presence and determined resistance, delayed the British attack on New Orleans for approximately a week and enabled General Andrew Jackson to prepare his defenses. The repulse of the British invasion, as Harry L. Coles put it, "settled the future of Louisiana and, ultimately, of Florida as well."³

A naval station had been established at New Orleans in 1804 to protect the lucrative commerce from the Ohio and Mississippi Valleys, and within two years some 20 gunboats were engaged in thwarting the designs of freebooters masked as privateers. In 1816, when settlers in Georgia were being harrassed by Indian raids from Spanish Florida and war with the Creek tribes seemed imminent, the government decided to erect a fort on the Apalachicola River north of the Florida line. Army transports were to proceed up the river through Florida territory carrying supplies and munitions, and Commodore Daniel T. Patterson, at New Orleans, ordered units under his command to provide an escort "up the Appalachicola [sic] and Chatahoochee [rivers], to such point or points as may be required."⁴ The trip involved passing a former British fort that had been taken over by fugitive American Negro slaves and some Indians, who on one occasion attacked a boat's crew. General Andrew Jackson had determined that "this fort must be destroyed," and he directed Brigadier General Edmund P. Gaines to "notify the Governor of Pensacola of your advance into his Territory and for the express purpose of destroying these lawless Banditti."⁵

Two navy gunboats under Sailing-Masters Jairus Loomis and James Bassett arrived at what was known as Negro Fort and coordinated an assault with an army detachment. On June 27, 1816 in a heavy exchange of fire, a hot shot from one of the gunboats struck the fort's magazine, and the resulting explosion destroyed the fort and killed some 270 of the 300 defenders.⁶ Thus what could have been a bloody attack by the soldiers was rendered unnecessary, and a source of irritation to Americans and Spaniards was eliminated. This incident may not illustrate Mahan's dictum about the decisiveness of combat on inland waters, but it made a significant contribution to peace on the Georgia-Florida frontier.

When Jackson invaded Florida in 1818 in pursuit of Indians and renegades who had raided American territory and sought refuge on Spanish land, he received support from naval vessels out of New Orleans operating along the Florida coast. That Jackson appreciated the assistance provided by the navy is revealed in his letter of January 10, 1820 to Secretary of War John C. Calhoun. When Spain delayed ratification of the Adams-Onis Treaty, President James Monroe contemplated occupying Florida by force. Jackson, asked by Calhoun for a war plan, gave a detailed response that called for "A strong Naval escort. . . for the protection of our Transports and [which] may be advantageously employed in the reduction of St. Marks and St. Augustine."[7]

The acquisition of Florida and continued piratical activities in the Caribbean prompted the establishment of a West India squadron in 1822, about the time that Lieutenant Matthew C. Perry, commanding officer of the U.S.S. Shark, raised the American flag over Key West and claimed the territory for the United States. The following year, when Captain David Porter assumed command of the squadron, five flat bottomed barges were acquired, each equipped with 30 oars. Dubbed "the mosquito fleet," the barges were named the Mosquito, the Gnat, the Midge, the Sandfly, and the Gallinipper--"insects," as Maclay put it, "with which their crews were destined to be unpleasantly familiar."[8] (While this mosquito fleet was created to combat freebooters, the name came to be associated with vessels manned by navy crews in the Second Seminole War.) Meanwhile the Florida Legislative Council petitioned for a naval depot at Pensacola to "afford a more complete command over the commerce of the Gulph [sic] of Mexico: and "in time of war give efficient aid in the defence of New Orleans as well as additional security to Louisiana, Mississippi and Alabama by presenting a formidable barrier by which inroads through West Florida would be checked and prevented."[9]

As the new Florida frontier became more attractive to American settlers the government decided to remove the Seminole Indians, and in 1835 a naval vessel was assigned to transport the natives to another homeland in the west. About the same time an army column under Major Francis L. Dade was ambushed and massacred, and a series of coordinated Indian attacks revealed a determined effort to resist the migration. The acting governor of Florida appealed for naval assistance, and in 1836 received a commitment from the navy which would last for some 6 years until the government decided to leave the remaining Seminoles in the Everglades. During this period the navy, operating in shallow water craft including canoes, developed through tortuous experience a strategy of riverine or inshore warfare, and eventually functioned in close cooperation with the army. A diary kept by Passed Midshipman George Henry Preble reveals in considerable detail the hardships and frustrations of a naval expedition into the Everglades in 1842 led by Lieutenant John Rodgers, whose report concluded: "On the 11th of

April, we returned to Key Biscayne, having been living in our canoes fifty-eight days, with less rest, fewer luxuries, and harder work than fall to the lot of that estimable class of citizens who dig our canals."[10] A typical Preble entry read, "Today officers as well as men have been compelled to wade in the mud, saw-grass, and water, and assist the sailors in dragging the canoes."[11] It was scarcely the kind of seafaring life envisioned by the crews of the vessels from which this "landing force" came, although some of the sailors brought this arduous duty on themselves by signing community petitions for naval aid against the Indians in exchange for a "glass of grog."[12] So, again, the navy was directly involved in pacifying the frontier, and performed a task for which the army admitted it was unprepared. Meanwhile the West India Squadron was charged with preventing Indians from raiding the Florida keys from the mainland (a practice that bothered the Floridians and the federal government)[13] and naval officers were accused of interfering in local elections in Florida.[14]

In describing the march of Americans across the continent, historians have listed successive frontiers, those of the trapper and trader, the rancher, and the farmer. On the Pacific Coast the navy helped create a contiguous "sea frontier." The first American warship to round the Horn and enter the Pacific Ocean was the frigate _Essex_ in 1813. Pursuing the British Pacific whaling fleet, the _Essex_, under the command of Captain David Porter, cruised as far west as the Marquesas Islands.[15] Subsequently naval vessels were dispatched to the Pacific in support of American interests, and, as one historian put it: "The realization of Manifest Destiny on the west coast was partly the result of these operations. Indeed, investigation has shown clearly the intimate relationship between the development and westward expansion of the United States and American utilization of the Cape Horn route to the Pacific."[16]

Warships were first assigned to the Pacific Station on a regular basis in 1818. They were placed under a commodore in April 1822. During the Van Buren administration American merchants in California petitioned the government to station a warship in California waters for protection from Mexican injustice. In response to this request, the Pacific Squadron was augmented by additional ships, and the commodore was ordered to assist Americans in California. In June 1840, the sloop _St. Louis_, under Commander French Forrest, proceeded to Monterey and secured legal rights for about 60 American and British citizens who had been arbitrarily imprisoned by the local authorities for allegedly plotting an independence movement.[17] Meanwhile, the expedition commanded by Lieutenant Charles Wilkes, which departed from Hampton Roads on August 18, 1838 reached Puget Sound in 1841 and sent a party overland to rendezvous with the ships at San Francisco. Much information about the country was gathered and its publication stimulated interest in California.

In 1842 a most notorious American initiative took place with the abortive naval seizure of Monterey and the announced occupation of Upper California.[18] While the incident has its humorous aspects, it should be noted that the irrascible Commodore Thomas ap Catesby Jones was acting on the basis of information from a variety of sources indicating that the United States and Mexico were at war and that the British were preparing to attack California. His action was consistent with the responsibilities of a naval officer on distant station when communications with Washington took months to reach their destination, and he would have been derelict in his duty if he had not behaved as he did under the circumstances. His indiscretion demonstrated the military weakness of the Mexicans, and may have convinced authorities in London, Washington, and Mexico City that California was ripe for the picking. Jones was relieved of his command but neither court martialed nor reprimanded, and in 1845 President James Knox Polk wrote him that "there has been no disposition to visit you with punishment of any description for conduct actuated by such elevated principles of duty."[19]

When Commodore John D. Sloat assumed command of the Pacific Squadron his secret orders from Secretary of the Navy George Bancroft read: "Should you ascertain beyond a doubt, that the Mexican Government has declared war against us, you will at once employ the force under your command to the best advantage." In addition, the Secretary said, "If you ascertain with certainty that Mexico has declared war against the United States, you will at once possess yourself of the port of San Francisco, and blockade or occupy such other ports as your force may permit."[20] Arriving at Monterey on July 2, 1846, 2 weeks after the Bear Flag Republic was declared, Commodore Sloat earned the scorn of the leaders of this revolt, of the impetuous Captain John C. Fremont, and of historian Allan Nevins. The latter castigates Sloat for his "inexcusable timidity" and "preposterously belated action" in waiting until July 7 to occupy Monterey and order the commanding officer of the U.S.S. Portsmouth, in San Francisco Bay, to seize Yerba Buena.[21] No doubt the Commodore recalled the embarrasing experience of Commodore Jones, and had reread his instructions to "ascertain beyond a doubt" and "with certainty" that Mexico had declared war. According to historian Robert Wilden Neeser, Sloat "acted with all the required energy and promptitude."[22]

In any event, Commodore Sloat began the conquest of California, which was continued and completed under the forthright direction of Commodore Robert F. Stockton. Years later, Secretary of the Navy George Bancroft, writing of the acquisition of California, said, "As we had a squadron in the North Pacific, but no army, the measures for carrying out this design fell to the Navy Department."[23] Further, it appears that naval activities along the Pacific Coast for nearly 30 years helped convince other nations, especially England and France, that this area was in effect a United States preserve.

In some respects the occupation of California following the conquest proved more of a challenge to the navy than had the war. The first alcalde of San Francisco under the American flag was Lieutenant Washington A. Bartlett, U.S. Navy. But the institution of a new system of law and the preservation of order was rendered virtually impossible by the explosive gold rush. The crews of warships were depleted by desertion to the gold fields, and by the use of the ships' men to control Indians and police settled areas.[24] Even the contentious Commodore Jones, now returned to command the squadron, was unable to halt the exodus in spite of the most repressive measures. At this time Congress was in the process of enacting legislation to prohibit flogging as a punishment in the navy, and Captain Samuel F. Du Pont predicted, "As soon as the abolition order was read on board any ship in the Pacific, the crews would seize the vessel and head for the California gold fields."[25] The Reverend Walter Colton, the Alcalde of Monterey, wrote of a breakfast at his home where, bereft of servants, "A general of the United States Army, the commander of a man-of-war, and the Alcalde of Monterey, [were] in a smoking kitchen grinding coffee, toasting a herring, and peeling onions."[26]

From the time that Commodore Stockton, on August 17, 1846, proclaimed himself Commander-in-Chief and Governor of California, the navy played a prominent role in domestic affairs.[27] The navy assumed primary responsibility for the protection of the territory, participated in its administration, and aided in its development. A naval station was established at Monterey in 1847 and a navy yard was authorized at Mare Island in 1852. As Secretary of the Navy Abel Parker Upshur had said, naval expenditures "gave employment to industry, encouragement to enterprise, and patronage to genius." Warships guarded steamers carrying gold, and at the request of San Francisco merchants Commander Cadwalader Ringgold conducted surveys of the California coast in 1849-50. His findings, published in <u>A Series of Charts, with Sailing Directions. . . To the Bay of San Francisco</u> (1851), and <u>Correspondence to Accompany Maps and Charts of California</u>, proved invaluable to mariners, businessmen, and settlers.[28] During the 1850s vigilante committees sprang up in response to lawlessness in California, and in 1856 the governor asked the military authorities to intervene. The army commander refused, as did Captain David G. Farragut, who claimed it was a matter beyond his jurisdiction. But the captain of the sloop U.S.S. <u>John Adams</u> dropped anchor off San Francisco and by threat of bombardment secured the release of prisoners from the local vigilante group.[29] California's eligibility for statehood was hastened by the navy's efforts, and the continued presence of American warships and their crews served as a constant reassurance to Californians during these troubled days.

To the north in the disputed Oregon Territory, the first naval involvement occurred when John Jacob Astor decided to set up a headquarters near the mouth of the Columbia River to pursue the fur trade. The expedition by sea left New York on September 8, 1810 in a ship commanded by Lieutenant Jonathan Thorn, U.S. Navy, on leave for this purpose. He was escorted early in the voyage by the U.S.S. <u>Constitution</u> to prevent harrassment by the Royal Navy searching for British seamen. Senator Thomas Hart Benton declared that this settlement was "done with the countenance and stipulated approbation of the government of the United States," and that "an officer of the United States Navy. . . was allowed to command his [Astor's] leading vessel, in order to impress upon the enterprise the seal of nationality."[30] In 1813, when Astor learned of an impending British attack on Fort Astoria, the government ordered the frigate <u>Adams</u> to the mouth of the Columbia, only to divert it for other duty. Astor then sold the fort to a British firm, but after the war he sought its return, as did the United States government. On July 18, 1815 Secretary of State James Monroe notified the British charge that the post would be reoccupied. After some two years of delay the sloop-of-war <u>Ontario</u>, James Biddle commanding, was ordered in September 1817 to proceed to the Columbia River and reassert American sovereignty over the territory. These orders were carried out, and although the matter of returning the fort was settled later by negotiation, the <u>Ontario</u> was the first American naval vessel to enter the area. Biddle used this opportunity to explore portions of the Pacific Coast.[31]

The next naval encounter with the Pacific Northwest occurred when the expedition commanded by Lieutenant Charles Wilkes spent nearly four years--August 18, 1838 to July 6, 1842--exploring the Pacific Ocean. Arriving on the northwest coast in April 1841, Wilkes charted harbors and the coastline, sent parties into the interior of the Oregon territory, and discouraged settlers from seeking independence. In his report, Wilkes wrote of "the terrors of the bar of the Columbia," where one of his vessels, the <u>Peacock</u>, was beaten to pieces. By his account of the hazards facing mariners attempting to enter the mouth of the Columbia River and his glowing descriptions of the harbor at Puget Sound and the lush Willamette Valley, Wilkes played a decisive role in establishing the northwest boundary at the 49th parallel and in popularizing the appeals of this area to settlers. "These shores which hitherto were little more than myths in the world's mind,"[32] said Hubert Howe Bancroft, "were now clothed in reality," Because of the impact of Wilkes "praising the agricultural and commercial potential of the Willamette Valley," Geoffrey Smith declared him "a naval apostle of Manifest Destiny."[33]

Mounting interest in this vast but little known area was reflected in 1841 when for the first time the geographical mission of vessels on the Pacific Station was defined. The squadron was to cover "All the west coast of America, and westward from the meridian of Cape Horn to the 180th degree of longitude; and southward between those meridians to the South Pole."[34] This pronouncement neither extended nor restricted what the ships on the Pacific Station had been doing, but it more clearly delineated the area of responsibility, that portion of the globe where the commodore could send his vessels without too much fear of court martial, and it revealed a specific government commitment to the coast and to the Eastern and Central Pacific as far west as Midway Island. In 1845, when the dispute over the Oregon boundary with Great Britain was approaching the crisis stage, the Pacific Squadron was ordered "to display the flag of the United States in the Columbia" and gather more information about the territory. In 1846, responding to orders from the Secretary of the Navy, Commodore Sloat sent the schooner U.S.S. Shark to the Columbia River, where it shared the same fate as the Peacock some five years before. The Oregon Question was settled through negotiation.

One of the navy's more notable contributions in the pacification of the frontier occurred during the Indian War of 1855-56 in the new territory of Washington. The governor appealed for naval assistance, and the sloop-of-war Decatur, anchoring off Seattle on October 4, 1855, furnished shore parties to seek out and destroy the hostiles and garrison the town in anticipation of an attack. The morning of January 26 found some seven or eight hundred armed Indians converging on Seattle, and the battle waged for about 6 hours before the attackers were repulsed with heavy casualties. During the following months the Decatur, along with the steam powered U.S.S. Massachusetts and other vessels that appeared subsequently, was employed in bolstering the defenses of Seattle and visiting other settlements and Indian reservations in the territory.[35] One writer, with pardonable license, wrote that the Decatur "helped in no small way in making the great empire of the West and in rendering possible an immigration unequaled in history."[36] A more judicious appraisal would, nevertheless, assign the navy a significant role in convincing settlers and immigrants that the territories of the Pacific Northwest were reasonably safe for exploitation.

One of the lesser known episodes of the navy's frontier experience is its participation in the settling of Alaska.

NAVY AND FRONTIER

Congress made no provision for the governance of this huge wilderness occupied by Americans, Russians, Indians, and half-breeds, and army troops were withdrawn in 1877 as an economy move. In 1879 fear of an Indian uprising brought frantic appeals from the white residents for protection, and a British warship responded and remained until it was relieved by the schooner U.S.S. Jamestown, under Commander Lester Anthony Beardslee. His somewhat vague orders from the Secretary of the Navy basically placed him in the position of a proconsul representing the United States government to maintain order and administer affairs. For 17 months Commander Beardslee, his crew, and a handful of Marines, worked closely with local dignitaries, restored peaceful relations between the various ethnic groups, prodded settlers into establishing local government, reduced crime, suppressed the production of a dangerous alcoholic beverage, and sponsored elementary education. Beardslee was succeeded by Commander Henry Glass, who continued the policies of his predecessor. Naval administration of Alaska so improved conditions that settlers began to bring their wives and children into the territory. With the passage of the Organic Act of 1884 the navy was relieved of its role in administering affairs. But the psychological and practical stabilizing impact of its presence was not forgotten by the inhabitants of this last American frontier in the Northern Hemisphere.[37]

This brief and scarcely definitive survey reveals that naval activities were not restricted to a maritime or seafaring frontier. The mobility of naval vessels permitted their dispersion to any existing or anticipated trouble spot that could be reached by water, and provided the government with flexibility that often meant the difference between submission to or mastery of circumstances. The navy's frontiers were successive--the unknown, the unexplored, the unsettled, the unpacified. The navy's westward movement was across the Caribbean to the Pacific, where it continued to follow the setting sun and American aspirations. It operated on oceans, lakes, rivers, swamps, and dry land. It brought order where there had been chaos and civilization where there had been barbarism. The highways it traversed led to foreign and continental frontiers, and it served as an all purpose instrument for the expansionist urge that propelled thirteen colonies huddled on the Atlantic to hemispheric dominance and world supremacy.

FOOTNOTES

1. President James Monroe said of the Navy, "Capable of moving in any and every direction, it possesses the faculty, even when remote from our coast, of extending

its aid to every interest on which the security and welfare of our Union depends." Message of January 30, 1824 to the House of Representatives, in American State Papers: Naval Affairs, I (Washington, 1834), p. 907. A convenient summary of the various squadron dispositions may be found in Robert G. Albion, "Distant Stations," U.S. Naval Institute Proceedings, LXXX (March 1954), pp. 265-73.

2. A. T. Mahan, Sea Power in its Relations to the War of 1812, 2 vols. (Boston, 1905), II, pp. 100-101. See also Kenneth Bourne, Britain and the Balance of Power in North America, 1815-1908 (Berkeley, 1967), p. 5; and R. Carlyle Buley, The Old Northwest: Pioneer Period, 1815-1840, 2 vols. (Bloomington, 1951), I, p. 110.

3. Harry L. Coles, The War of 1812 (Chicago, 1965), p. 236. Jones contended that his efforts at Lake Borgne delayed the British advance by ten days. Claim of Master Commandant Thomas ap Catesby Jones To a Pension on Account of a Wound Received in Battle, American State Papers: Naval Affairs, III (Washington, 1860), pp. 895-96. John K. Mahon puts the delay at "about six days" in his The War of 1812 (Gainesville, 1972), p. 356; and a delay of one week is ascribed in U. T. Bradley, "Thomas ap Catesby Jones: A Personality of the Days of Sail," U.S. Naval Institute Proceedings, LXIX (1933), p. 1155.

4. Commodore Patterson to Lieutenant Commandant Crawley, June 19, 1816, American State Papers: Foreign Relations, IV, p. 559.

5. Jackson to Gaines, April 8, 1816, edited by John Spencer Bassett, Correspondence of Andrew Jackson, 7 vols. (Washington, 1928-1935), II, p. 239.

6. Report of Sailing-master Jairus Loomis, August 13, 1816, in American State Papers: Foreign Relations, IV, pp. 559-560; and Application for Prize Money on the Destruction of a Fort, Communication to the House of Representatives, March 24, 1818, in American State Papers: Naval Affairs, I, p. 502. A good account of the incident is John Spencer Bassett, The Life of Andrew Jackson, 2nd ed. (New York, 1916), pp. 238-39; and Marquis James, The Life of Andrew Jackson, 1 vol. ed. (Indianapolis, 1938), p. 275.

7. Jackson to Calhoun, January 10, 1820, Correspondence of Andrew Jackson, III, pp. 2-6. The quote is on page 4.

8. Edgar Stanton Maclay, A History of the United States Navy From 1775 to 1898, 2 vols. (New York, 1898), II, p. 30.

9. Memorial to the President by the Legislative Council, September 2, 1822, in Clarence Edwin Carter, ed., Territorial Papers of the United States, XXII, Florida, 1821-1824 (Washington, 1956), pp. 521-528.

10. Quoted in George Henry Preble, "A Canoe Expedition Into the Everglades in 1842," Tequesta, no. 5 (January 1946), p. 32.

11. Ibid., p. 35.

12. George E. Buker, Swamp Sailors: Riverine Warfare in the Everglades, 1835-1842 (Gainesville, 1975), p. 51, footnote 5. This comprehensive account of the navy's role in the Second Seminole War elaborates on strategic and tactical innovations and draws some parallels with the Vietnam War. See also John K. Mahon, History of the Second Seminole War, 1835-1842 (Gainesville, 1967), who concludes, "The navy also gained valuable training" and "played a larger role in this than in any other Indian war." p. 322.

13. The Secretary of War to the Governor of Florida, September 10, 1840, in Carter, ed., The Territorial Papers of the United States, XXVI, Florida, 1839-1845 (Washington, 1962), pp. 213-14.

14. Ibid., p. 325, footnote 96. For navy purchases and attempts to purchase timber land in Florida and Louisiana see American State Papers: Naval Affairs, III (Washington, 1862), pp. 917-958.

15. David F. Long, Nothing Too Daring: A Biography of Commodore David Porter, 1780-1843 (Annapolis, 1970), pp. 80ff.; Patrick W. Strauss, "Captain David Porter: Pioneer Pacific Strategist," U.S. Naval Institute Proceedings, 93 (February 1967), pp. 158-160.

16. Raymond A. Rydell, Cape Horn to the Pacific: The Rise and Decline of an Ocean Highway (Berkeley, 1952), p. viii.

17. Robert Erwin Johnson, Thence Round Cape Horn: The Story of United States Naval Forces on Pacific Station, 1818-1923 (Annapolis, 1963), p. 57; Dudley W. Knox, A History of the United States Navy (New York, 1936), p. 159; Hubert H. Bancroft, The History of California (San Francisco, 1884-1890), IV, p. 36.

18. George M. Brooke, Jr., "The Vest Pocket War of Commodore Jones," Pacific Historical Review, XXXI (1962), pp. 217-233; James High, "Jones at Monterey, 1842," Journal of the West, V (April 1966), pp. 173-186.

19. Quoted in ibid., p. 175.

20. Quoted in Johnson, Thence Round Cape Horn, p. 72.

21. Allan Nevins, Fremont: Pathmarker of the West (New York, 1939), p. 272.

22. Robert Wilden Neeser, "The Navy's Part in the Acquisition of California, 1846-1848," U.S. Naval Institute Proceedings XXIV (1908), p. 268.

23. Quoted in Nevins, Fremont: Pathmarker of the West, p. 246. One writer concludes, "Strangely enough, the conquest of California by the United States could not have been accomplished when it was had not these naval forces been present." Oakah L. Jones, Jr., "The Pacific Squadron and the Conquest of California, 1846-1847," Journal of the West, V (April 1966), p. 187. Josiah Royce contends that Commander John B. Montgomery, commanding the U.S.S. Portsmouth, is the unsung hero of the seizure of California. Josiah Royce, "Montgomery and Fremont," Century Magazine, XIX, New Series (November 1890 to April 1891), p. 780. The lack of enthusiasm for land operations is revealed by one sailor, who upon return to his ship wrote, "Here we are at last and God grant we may never have to go ashore soldiering again." Joseph T. Downey, The Cruise of the Portsmouth, 1845-1847: A Sailor's View of the Naval Conquest of California, edited by Howard Lamar (New Haven, 1963), p. 235.

24. One expedition was dispatched to defend Sutter's Fort from a rumored Indian attack. Fred Blackburn Rogers, Montgomery and the Portsmouth (San Francisco, 1958), pp. 77-78.

25. Harold D. Langley, Social Reform in the United States Navy, 1798-1862 (Urbana, 1967), p. 175. Jones himself was not immune from the gold fever or land speculation. C. Norman Guice, ed., "The 'Contentious Commodore' and San Francisco: Two 1850 Letters from Thomas ap Catesby Jones," Pacific Historical Review, XXXIV (August 1965), pp. 337-342.

26. Walter Colton, Three Years in California (New York, 1850), pp. 247-48, excerpt in The American West: A Source Book, edited by Clark C. Spence (New York, 1966), pp. 165-66.

27. For the impropriety and illegality of Stockton's establishment of a civil government, see K. Jack Bauer, The Mexican War, 1846-1848 (New York, 1974), pp. 168, 174, 176.

28. Allan Westcott, "Cadwalader Ringgold," Dictionary of American Biography, edited by Dumas Malone, 22 vols. (New York, 1946), XV, p. 617.

29. Johnson, Thence Round Cape Horn, pp. 107-8.

30. Thomas H. Benton, Thirty Years View, 2 vols. (New York, 1854), I, p. 109.

31. Hubert Howe Bancroft, History of the Northwest Coast, 2 vols. (San Francisco, 1884), I, pp. 143-44, 201-2; II, pp. 290-94; J. B. McMaster, A History of the People of the United States from the Revolution to the Civil War, 8 vols. (New York 1883-1913), IV, pp. 472-74.

32. Bancroft, History of the Northwest Coast, I, p. 684. But Bancroft is critical of Wilkes for not making the most of his exploring opportunities.

33. Geoffrey S. Smith, "Charles Wilkes and the Growth of American Naval Diplomacy," in Makers of American Diplomacy, From Benjamin Franklin to Henry Kissinger, edited by Frank J. Merli and Theodore A. Wilson (New York, 1974), p. 148. "Recent scholarship. . . has accorded Wilkes a crucial role in determining the 49th parallel as our Northwest boundary." William H. Goetzmann, Exploration and Empire: The Explorer and the Winning of the American West (New York, 1966), p. 238. See also Geoffrey S. Smith, "The Navy Before Darwinism: Science, Exploration, and Diplomacy in Antebellum America," American Quarterly, XXVIII (Spring 1976), pp. 41-55. Wilkes "demonstrated the 'Pacific consciousness' that characterized so many antebellum navalists, an attitude that in Wilkes' words underlined the destiny of 'this western coast' to 'fill a large space in the world's future history.'" Ibid., p. 45.

34. Quoted in Johnson, Thence Round Cape Horn, p. 58.

35. For participant accounts see Gardner W. Allen, ed., The Papers of Francis Gregory Dallas, United States Navy: Correspondence and Journal, 1837-1859 (New York, 1917). The portion of Dallas' journal relating to the Decatur's experience in Washington Territory is on pages 199-211. An account by the then Passed Midshipman Thomas S. Phelps is included as an appendix, pages 266-299.

36. John H. Brandt, "The Navy as an Indian Fighter," U.S. Naval Institute Proceedings, LVI (1930), p. 691. See also Truman Strobridge, "When the Navy Fought the Indians," ibid., XCI (1965), pp. 156-58.

37. Ted C. Hinckley, *The Americanization of Alaska, 1867-1897* (Palo Alto, 1972), pp. 131-38; Jeannette Paddock Nichols, *Alaska: A History of its Administration*, reprint (New York, 1963), pp. 131-38; Henry Glass, "Naval Administration in Alaska," *U.S. Naval Institute Proceedings*, XVI (January 1890), pp. 1-19; Mel Crain, "When the Navy Ruled Alaska," *ibid.*, LXXXI (February 1955), pp. 198-203. "This rule," says Crain, "which directly influenced the course of Alaska's turbulent political history, furnishes one of the most unusual chronicles in Navy annals." *Ibid.*, p. 198.

ORIGINS OF THE NAVY "GENERAL STAFF" Chapter 7

In 1951 the Navy General Board was dissolved. Established in 1900 and often referred to inaccurately as the Navy "General Staff," the General Board had represented the latest of numerous attempts to provide for more effective professional guidance and administration of the United States Navy. An inquiry into its origins reveals another dimension of the "New Navy" which emerged in the final decades of the nineteenth century.

In its formative years the Navy was controlled and managed entirely by civilians. But in 1815, following the war against Great Britain, a Board of Navy Commissioners was established, consisting of three officers, which was to assist the Secretary of the Navy in the administration of the service.[1] The actual jurisdiction of the Commissioners was restricted to supply and equipment, while policy formulation and control remained with the Secretary. Criticized primarily because it eliminated individual responsibility, the Board was abolished in 1842 and the "bureau system" was inaugurated. This action created five separate bureaus in the Navy Department (increased to eight in 1862), each controlling one branch of naval activity and headed by an officer who was directly responsible to the Secretary.[2] The major defect of the new bureaucratic organization was lack of professional coordination. Each of the autonomous bureau chiefs took his business directly to the Secretary, and thus presented him with but one aspect of the overall problem of naval affairs. No competent career individual or body exercised coordinating jurisdiction or provided the civilian head with the advice and knowledge necessary to administer properly the affairs of the Navy.

The weaknesses of the multifarious bureau system were revealed by its inadequate response to the increased demands imposed on the Navy Department during the Civil War. Yet measures introduced in Congress to establish a Board of Naval Administration and a Board of Admiralty failed to receive Congressional approval. Secretary of the Navy Gideon Welles opposed any permanent body that might deprive his office of control, and he was content to convene informal, temporary boards to resolve the more perplexing questions confronting the Navy.[3]

As successive secretaries made futile efforts to grapple with the complexities of Navy Department administration,[4] a series of incidents exposed the inability of the existing organization to cope with emergencies. When the blockade runner <u>Virginus</u> was seized by Spanish officials in 1873 and American members of her crew were executed, the Department was thrown into confusion because war threatened and no staff existed to plot a campaign.[5] The <u>Baltimore</u> incident of 1891, which almost brought Chile and the United States to blows, stimulated a burst of activity in Washington. Captain Alfred Thayer Mahan, now acclaimed for his <u>Influence of Sea Power Upon History</u> (1890), was ordered to duty in the Navy Department to prepare war plans and to be available for consultation. But this brief emergency, which again laid bare the inadequacies of the bureau system in time of peril, provoked no modification of the prevailing organization.[6]

Serious agitation for a reorganization of the bureau-bound Navy Department was begun in 1878 by Admiral Stephen B. Luce, first president of the Naval War College and author of the standard treatise, <u>Seamanship</u> (1863). Struck by the failure of the navy to capture Charleston during the Civil War, he concluded that bungling administration was largely responsible and resolved to expose the pitfalls of the bureau system.[7] Luce urged that the Department be divided into two sections, the military and the civilian. A group of naval officers should be "attached to and made a part of" the secretary's office, with the sole responsibility of "preparing plans for naval campaigns and of directing under the Secretary of the Navy the military operations of our fleets and squadrons." Naval administration in France and England demonstrated the wisdom of such a proposal, Luce contended, and he thought it immaterial whether this body be called "a Board of Naval Commissioners, a Board of Admiralty, a Strategy Board, a General Board or a General Staff."[8]

The red-taped inadequacies of the bureau system were also apparent to the Secretary of the Navy, Louisiana lawyer William H. Hunt. In 1881 he felt obliged to convene what was called the First Naval Advisory Board under Rear Admiral John Rodgers, leader of the assault on Korea in 1871, to determine the number and types of vessels needed for the navy.[9] Surprisingly, the existing organization made no provision for the consideration of such basic requirements. Four years later Secretary William C. Whitney, who was to be one of the architects of the New Navy, complained that the bureau system burdened his office with so many executive duties that he was unable to furnish the counsel and guidance that his position demanded. He therefore asked Congress for a separation of "the work of direction and deliberation from the details of execution,"[10] and he was supported by President Cleveland in this unsuccessful effort at reform.[11] The basic need for coordinating bureau activities was being painfully revealed even in the everyday peacetime functioning of the Navy Department. But the preparation of war plans and the direction of the fleet units during time of conflict made it imperative, in the thinking of many naval officers, that a body of professionals be created specifically to handle these problems.

The Navy Department continued its purblind policy of appearing to prepare for all contingencies—except war—until the outbreak of the Cuban insurrection in 1895. Spurred by public clamor, Secretary Hilary A. Herbert telegraphed the Naval War College to begin immediate preparation of plans for a conflict with Spain and the winning of independence for Cuba. The resultant plan of operations was circulated within the Department for criticism and debate for the next three years, but no staff existed to submit alternative proposals. When Congress declared war in 1898, the Navy Department was obliged to adopt the War College plan because it was the only one available.[12] Yet three months before the outbreak of hostilities Secretary John D. Long shortsightedly complained that his energetic assistant, Theodore Roosevelt, did "bore him" with plans of naval and military movement, and the necessity of having some scheme of attack arranged for instant execution in case of emergency.[13]

Dissatisfaction with the existing system became more pronounced as the New Navy emerged during the 1890's. Criticism was concentrated on the lack of an agency to formulate war plans and on the unwieldiness of the bureau system, which required the appointment of temporary boards to find answers to routine questions.[14] Denounced within the service as an "organization of unsurpassed crudity,"[15] and from without as "an absence of system,"[16] the bureau structure tottered but did not fall. Moreover, in the absence of centralized professional authority, the Bureau of Navigation, which was charged with the control of ship movements and personnel, began to exercise a wider administration of the military functions of the Department. This encroachment aroused the resentment of other bureaus and made cooperation even more difficult.[17]

The problem of a more centralized professional administration in the Navy Department was attacked by the Naval War College in 1893. Studies were made of patterns of business organization, the British Admiralty, and the German army General Staff. A modification of the latter was considered most suitable for the United States, with a nucleus to be formed by combining the Naval War College and the Office of Naval Intelligence.[18] But the proponents of this plan were well aware of the obstacles that lay between them and their objective. Captain Henry C. Taylor, who was president of the College when the studies were begun, reported an "overwhelming opposition" in Washington to the creation of a general staff, which, he thought, "would probably have to grow slowly by a process of natural evolution in the Bureau of Navigation." The officer whom he and Luce thought best qualified to head such a body--presumably Commodore George Dewey--was inclined to favor the innovation but was too busy to take much interest in the project.[19] Assistant Secretary Theodore Roosevelt enthusiastically supported the proposal, but neither he nor Captain Taylor was able to obtain Secretary Long's approval of a staff organization. The plan, Taylor sadly concluded, evidently could be adopted only in the event of war.[20]

The failure to establish a professional body to fill the administrative vacuum that existed between the Secretary and the bureau chiefs is not hard to understand. E. L. Godkin, the redoubtable editor of the Nation, claimed that it was due to public ignorance of the workings of the Navy Department and the caution of civilian Secretaries who were awed by their own professional incompetence.[21] The lack of unanimity among the naval officers themselves contributed to the inertia. In a lecture before the Naval War College in 1897, Rear Admiral G. E. Belknap contended that "commissions and boards are a snare," and he likened a Navy Department containing an intermediary body between the Secretary and the bureau chiefs to a ship with more than one captain.[22] On the other hand, according to Paullin, "The Secretaries during the period 1881-1897 were jealous of their powers, and naturally opposed any measure calculated to increase greatly the influence and control of naval officers within the department."[23] No doubt all of these factors, as well as "centrifugal forces of the department,"[24] contributed to the failure to eliminate what many considered an administrative bottleneck.

As the crisis with Spain over Cuba became more acute, Assistant Secretary Roosevelt urged Secretary Long to appoint a senior naval officer as his "chief of staff" to handle the exclusively military operations. War should be waged by professionals, he maintained, not by amateurs.[25] But Long was not convinced. He believed that the absence of a rival military head was one of the reasons why the Department functioned so smoothly.[26] Although the Secretary was reluctant to place authority in the hands of any individual or group, shortly before the outbreak of hostilities he did ask Roosevelt and three officers to act as a Naval War Board.[27] Roosevelt, who soon dashed off to fight, was replaced as senior member by Rear Admiral Montgomery Sicard, and Mahan was ordered to duty in the Navy Department to serve on the Board. Designed to provide the Secretary with professional advice on strategic, tactical, and technical problems, the Board exercised no authority, and existed only informally under a verbal directive from Secretary Long.[28] Throughout the war the members consulted with Long and prepared dispatches and directives for his approval. Mahan argued vigorously for the appointment of a chief of staff to coordinate and direct military operations, but Secretary Long could not be convinced that such an appointment would be an improvement over the existing organization.[29] Long acknowledged that the service of the Naval War Board "was invaluable in connection with the successful conduct of the war,"[30] but when hostilities ceased he dissolved the group. It was strictly an emergency body which was, presumably, neither necessary nor desirable in normal times. In the opinion of Secretary Long, the routine operations of the Navy Department were best coordinated and directed by civil, not naval, authorities.

But the persistent Admiral Luce would not be denied, and he took advantage of the Spanish-American War to accelerate his campaign. Writing to Senator Henry Cabot Lodge, the venerable Admiral criticized the organization of the Navy Department, denounced the civilian administration of affairs, and argued for a general staff.[31] Lodge agreed that "there ought to be a chief of staff in the Navy Department and I have thought so for years."[32] When the war ended a few months later, Luce thought the time ripe to move for the establishment of a permanent professional body along the lines of the Naval War Board. To this end, he suggested that Mahan present his views to Secretary Long, apparently unaware of the earlier clash between the two men over a similar project.[33] A small group of officers, made more acutely aware of existing shortcomings by the inadequate preparations for the recent war and by the valuable work of the now defunct War Board, sought to obtain a staff organization through Congressional action. But they were thwarted by the bitter opposition of the bureau chiefs and Senator Eugene Hale of Maine, chairman of the powerful Senate Committe on Naval Affairs.[34]

Some two years after the clash with Spain, the earlier studies of the Naval War College and the persistent efforts of Admiral Luce and his cohorts began to bear fruit. Captain Taylor, who had commanded the _Indiana_ at the battle of Santiago, was more than ever convinced of the need for a reorganization of the Navy Department. In response to a request from Long, Taylor and his colleagues marshalled the arguments for a general staff and presented them in a memorandum to the Secretary.[35] Realizing that the plan would fail if it did not make provision for the bureau that controlled personnel and ship distribution, they suggested that the nucleus of the proposed staff consist of the Chief of the Bureau of Navigation together with representatives from the Naval War College and the Office of Naval Intelligence.[36] But according to Long, "the navy was not quite ready for such a comprehensive change as would occur in case of the adoption of the full general staff system," and he resolved the dilemma by effecting a compromise.[37] In fact, without the perplexing problem of an appropriate assignment for Admiral Dewey, the hero of Manila Bay, a modification of the existing organization probably would not have been made.[38]

The Navy General Board was established by Secretary Long's General Order No. 544, dated March 13, 1900. It was to consist of nine members: Admiral Dewey as president; the Chief of the Bureau of Navigation; the Chief Intelligence Officer and his principal assistant; the president of the Naval War College and his principal assistant; and three other officers of or above the grade of lieutenant commander. "The purpose of the Department in establishing this Board," the order announced, was "to insure efficient preparation of the fleet in case of war and for the naval defense of the coast." The Chief of the Bureau of Navigation was to have custody of war plans, direct the War College and the Intelligence Officer to furnish information desired by the Board, and act as presiding officer in the absence of Admiral Dewey. Meetings were to be held at least once each month, twice a year the sessions should last a week, and a quorum would consist of five officers.[39]

The duties of the Board were then amplified by the Secretary. He directed that it consider the role of the naval reserve and the merchant marine in national defense, consult with the army in order to effect "a full and cordial cooperation of the two services in case of war," and be ready to advise the Secretary on fleet dispositions. Plans should be prepared for the defense of the nation and its dependencies, and for any theatre in which war might occur. The selection and preparation of naval bases was to be considered and recommended, foreign navies were to be evaluated, and other topics for investigation were to be determined. Specifically, the Board was to begin an urgent study of plans for the defense of dependencies, the location of naval bases to implement this defense, and the "numbers and kind of ships" needed for this purpose. Members were cautioned to confine their work to a consideration of the broader problems and avoid the "technical questions of material and manufacture," which were handled by the bureaus and the Department. For, Long added, "It is not with the construction, manning, arming and equipping of the ships that the General Board is concerned, but with recommendations as to the proper disposition of the Fleet." While the activities of the Board were limited, it was not to lack for assistance, and officers could be ordered to appear before the Board to give information or advice when required.[40]

At the first meeting, on April 16, 1900, the pertinent directives were read, an Executive Committee was appointed, and it was agreed that sub-committees would be designated as required.[42] The cautious Long, while apparently recognizing the value of this deliberative body, was ever alert to prevent it from exercising authority, and he insisted that all business with the bureaus or other branches of the government be conducted through his office. He was determined that it should remain an advisory body only, directly responsible to the Secretary.[43]

The adherents of the Board regarded it as the nucleus of a general staff that would have the responsibility for planning, coordinating, and controlling the fleet. Admiral Dewey referred to the Board as the "general 'staff,'"[44] but Captain Taylor felt that "the reactionary element in the Navy" would prevent an early realization of this objective.[45] The problem was made more difficult by the fear that such a move presaged service encroachment on civilian supremacy.[46] Taylor urged that the General Board be confirmed by act of Congress in order to ensure its permanence, and that steps be taken toward the development of a general staff. But he could get no support for these proposals from the Secretary.[47]

The stubborn Long was out of office scarcely a month when Admiral Dewey presented President Roosevelt with a five page memorandum recommending the formation of a navy general staff. "To assure complete and well-organized preparation for war," he maintained, "experience has shown that the existence of a general staff in any military or naval service is absolutely necessary." The General Board was a start in the right direction, Dewey added, but a general staff, operating under the jurisdiction of a chief of staff as the senior naval officer, would make for an even more efficient and effective navy. President Roosevelt thought that the argument was "conclusive,"[48] but his efforts to secure legislation establishing a general staff were not successful.[49]

The creation of the General Board, in the words of Captain John Hood, cast the "first glimmerings of light on a true naval policy" for the United States.[50] Assigned no administrative functions or responsibilities, the Board was able to devote its energies to a consideration of the problems of defense and the implementation of foreign policy within the broad framework of national interests. The Board was a response to a long-felt need for planning and coordination within the Navy Department, for the experience of the war with Spain had emphasized the defects of a system not geared to the exacting demands of modern sea power. Existing largely because of the determined efforts of Rear Admiral Henry C. Taylor, the Board's early success was made possible by his activities as Chief of the Bureau of Navigation during its formative years, and also by the prestige and moderate leadership of the Board's first president, Admiral Dewey, who held the position until his death in 1917. The studies and reports prepared by the Board furnished a guide for the Administration in the formulation and execution of naval policy, and provided the tactical and strategic data necessary to cope with the broadening responsibilities of an America that was sensationally emerging as a major power.

The Navy General Board never became a true general staff, for it did not acquire the status or the authority that was envisioned by its proponents. It did not centralize the control of the Navy Department, eliminate the autonomy of the bureaus, or relieve the Secretary of any responsibilities. Yet the weight accorded the Board's recommendations enabled it to play a major role in the development of American sea power throughout the first half of the twentieth century. Formed at a time when America's commercial and expansionist forces were bursting from their continental barriers, and staffed by the most seasoned officers, the Board was to serve as the "thinking organ" for a navy that was both the first line of defense and a major instrument of foreign policy. Although the Board was a belated and not wholly satisfactory response to the extensive mission that had been assigned the navy, it provided a unity and consistency in planning and policy that marked a new era in naval adminstration.

FOOTNOTES

1. See Charles Oscar Paullin, "Early Naval Administration Under the Constitution," U.S. Naval Institute Proceedings, XXXII (1906), 1001-1030; Paullin, "Naval Administration Under Secretaries of the Navy Smith, Hamilton, and Jones, 1801-1814," ibid., XXXII (1906) 1289-1328; Paullin, "Naval Administration Under the Navy Commissioners, 1815-1842," ibid., XXXIII (1907), 597-642; Leonard D. White, The Jeffersonians: A Study in Administrative History, 1801-1829 (New York, 1951), pp. 277-278.

2. Paullin, "Naval Administration, 1842-1861," U.S. Naval Institute Proceedings, XXXIII (1907), 1438 ff.; Leonard D. White, The Jacksonians: A Study in Administrative History, 1829-1861 (New York, 1954), pp. 216-219.

3. Charles H. Davis, Life of Charles Henry Davis, Rear Admiral (Boston, 1899), pp. 117, 134; Lloyd Milton Short, The Development of National Administrative Organization in the United States (Baltimore, 1923), pp. 302-303; Richard S. West, Jr., Mr. Lincoln's Navy (New York, 1957), pp. 50-55, 101-104.

4. Robert W. Neeser, "The Department of the Navy," American Political Science Review, XI (1917), 62-63; Charles Oscar Paullin, "A Half Century of Naval Administration

in America, 1861-1911," Part V, U.S. Naval Institute Proceedings, XXXIX (1913), 1262-1266; Leonard D. White, The Republican Era: 1869-1901 (New York, 1958), pp. 162-171.

5. Stephen B. Luce, "Naval Administration, II," U.S. Naval Institute Proceedings, XXVIII (1902), 845.

6. W. D. Puleston claims that "An informal Naval Strategy Board was formed, consisting of Assistant Secretary Soley, Captain Mahan, and officers from the Office of Naval Intelligence." The Life and Works of Captain Alfred Thayer Mahan, U. S. N. (New Haven, 1939), p. 114. Mahan says "there was no board known to me . . . Mr. Tracy [Secretary of the Navy] kept matters in his own hands, consulted when he wished to consult, and acted without consultation as he chose." Mahan to Luce, September 3, 1901, printed in Albert Gleaves, Life and Letters of Rear Admiral Stephen B. Luce, U.S. Navy (New York, 1925), pp. 324-325.

7. Ibid., p. 227.

8. Stephen B. Luce, "Naval Administration," U.S. Naval Institute Proceedings, XIV (1888), 586-587. For additional criticism of the bureau system at this time, see A. P. Cooke, "Naval Organization," ibid., XII (1886), 492-494; Paullin, "A Half Century of Naval Administration in America, 1861-1911," Part V, 1259-1261; White, The Republican Era, pp. 162-171; Robert G. Albion, "The Administration of the Navy, 1798-1945," Public Administration Review, V (1945), 294.

9. Proceedings and Report of the Advisory Board (Washington, 1882); George T. Davis, A Navy Second to None: The Development of Modern American Naval Policy (New York, 1940), pp. 36-37.

10. Annual Report of the Secretary of the Navy, 1885 (Washington, 1885), I, xxxvii, xli.

11. In Cleveland's first message of December 8, 1885. James D. Richardson, comp., A Compilation of the Messages and Papers of the Presidents, 1789-1897 (New York, n.d.), X, 4936.

12. Rear Admiral W. L. Rodgers, "Memorandum Regarding the History of the U.S. Naval War College," typescript, with notation in ink "(Filed here:) October 1, 1921." Navy Department, General Board File No. 425. Taylor attributes the plan to "the alarm produced by the President's [Cleveland's] Venezuelan message." to Congress in 1895. Henry C. Taylor, "The Fleet," U.S. Naval Institute Proceedings, XXIX (1903), 803. See

also C. H. Stockton, "Notes Upon the Necessity and Utility of the Naval War College in Connection with Preparation for Defence and War," ibid., XIX (1893), 407-413; and Henry C. Taylor, "Naval War College, Closing Address, Session of 1895," ibid., XXII (1896), 205.

13. Journal of John D. Long, edited by Margaret Long (New Hampshire, 1956), p. 213.

14. French E. Chadwick, "Naval Department Organization," U.S. Naval Institute Proceedings, XX (1894), 501-502; William McAdoo (Assistant Secretary of the Navy), "Naval War College, Openinig Address, Session of 1896," ibid., XII (1896), 441; Ira N. Hollis, "A New Organization for the New Navy," Atlantic Monthly, LXXX (1897), 318-319.

15. Chadwick, "Naval Department Organization," p. 499.

16. The Nation (New York), March 2, 1893, p. 155.

17. A. W. Johnson, "A Brief History of the Organization of the Navy Department," (Washington, 1933), Mimeographed, pp. 84-85.

18. Taylor, "The Fleet," pp. 802-803.

19. Taylor to Luce, January 13, 1896, Stephen B. Luce Papers, Manuscript Division, Library of Congress. Dewey was then president of the Board of Inspection and Survey. Taylor refrained from mentioning the name of their candidate, but he remarked that "his mind is upon other things at the present such as the plans and preparation of the material details of the new war ships, in which matters he is, as you know, a master." Ibid.

20. Taylor to Luce, January 22, 1896, Luce Papers; Roosevelt to Taylor, May 24, 1897, The Letters of Theodore Roosevelt, edited by Elting E. Morison (Cambridge, Mass., 1951-1954), I, 617; Roosevelt to Captain Caspar Frederick Goodrich, November 19, 1897, ibid., I, 718.

21. The Nation (New York), March 2, 1893, p. 154.

22. Rear Admiral G. E. Belknap, "Some Aspects of Naval Administration in War, with its attendant Belongings of Peace," U.S. Naval Institute Proceedings, XXIV (1898), 272-273.

23. Paullin, "A Half Century of Naval Administration in America, 1861-1911," Part V, p. 1262.

24. Neeser, "The Department of the Navy," p. 62.

25. Roosevelt to Paul Dana, April 18, 1898, Roosevelt Letters, II, 816-817.

26. The Journal of John D. Long, p. 225.

27. John D. Long, The New American Navy (New York, 1903), I, 162.

28. Ibid.; Mahan to Dewey, October 29, 1906, Navy Department, General Board File No. 401; Report of the Naval War Board, Annual Reports of the Navy Department for the Year 1898 (Washington, 1898), pp. 33-34.

29. America of Yesterday, as Reflected in the Journal of John David Long, edited by Lawrence S. Mayo (Boston, 1923), p. 194; Mahan to Dewey, October 29, 1906, Navy Department, General Board File No. 401.

30. Long, The New American Navy, I, 163.

31. Luce to Lodge, May 24, 1898, Luce Papers.

32. Lodge to Luce, May 27, 1898, ibid.

33. Luce to Mahan, August 25, 1898, ibid.

34. Taylor, "The Fleet," p. 803; Gleaves, Life and Letters of Rear Admiral Stephen B. Luce, p. 237.

35. Taylor to Long, January 30, 1900, printed in Papers of John Davis Long, 1897-1904, selected and edited by Gardner W. Allen (Massachusetts Historical Society Collections, vol. 78) (Boston, 1939), p. 306; Captain Henry C. Taylor, "Memorandum on General Staff for the U.S. Navy," U.S. Naval Institute Proceedings, XXVI (1900), 441-448.

36. Taylor, "The Fleet," p. 803.

37. Long, The New American Navy, I, 123. For his arguments against a navy general staff, see ibid., II, 182-185.

38. Testimony of Rear Admiral C. McR. Winslow, House Naval Affairs Committee, Hearings on Estimates Submitted by the Secretary of the Navy, 1916, I, 1401.

39. General Order No. 544, General Orders and Special Orders, U.S. Navy (Washington, n.d.), p. 6.

40. Long to Dewey, Serial 211305 of March 30, 1900, General Board Letterbook, I, 17-19, Navy Department, General Board Files. This letter was probably prepared by

Captain Taylor after consultation with Admiral Dewey and others. See unsigned Memorandum, initials "HCT" on front, pencilled date "March 29/00," General Board File No. 401.

41. "Proceedings of the General Board," I, 1, Navy Department, General Board Files.

42. Ibid., I, 3-4; Memorandum, undated, prepared by H. C. Taylor, with forwarding letter, Dewey to Crowninshield, dated April 11, 1900, General Board File No. 401.

43. Long, The New American Navy, I, 124; Dewey to Long, December 19, 1900, General Board Letterbook, 1, 127-128; Long to Dewey, December 21, 1900, General Board File No. 401-1.

44. Dewey to Taylor, Wednesday (no date, but probably in 1901), Henry C. Taylor Papers, Manuscript Division, Library of Congress.

45. Taylor, "Memorandum on General Staff for the U.S. Navy," p. 442.

46. Boston Herald, March 23, 1900, editorial. The Nation hailed the appointment of the Board as an essential and overdue reform. March 22, 1900, p. 214.

47. Taylor to Long, June 8, 1901, Papers of John Davis Long, p. 368; Taylor to Long, August 12, 1901, ibid., p. 387.

48. Roosevelt to Dewey, June 4, 1902, stapled to typewritten "Memorandum for the President, from Admiral Dewey, Concerning the Proposed Formation of a General Staff for the Navy," dated June 3, 1902, General Board File No. 401.

49. Actually, a bill was introduced to establish the General Board by Congressional authority. This was defeated in part by the hostile testimony of Assistant Secretary of the Navy Charles H. Darling and certain bureau chiefs who contended that it would weaken the power of the secretary and eliminate the autonomy of the bureaus. Hearings Before the Committee on Naval Affairs, House of Representatives, on Appropriation Bill for 1905 Subjects and on H. R. 15403 for General Board. 58 Cong., 2 sess., 1903-1904 (Washington, 1904). The Hearings on H.R. 15403 were held in April 1904, and are contained in pp. 909-991.

50. John Hood, "A General Naval Policy," The Navy, VII (1913), 181.

THE GREAT ABERRATION OF THE 1890's   Chapter 8

THE DAYS OF MCKINLEY. By Margaret Leech. New York: Harper Brothers. 1959. $7.50. **IMPERIAL DEMOCRACY**: The Emergence of America as a Great Power. By Ernest R. May. New York: Harcourt, Brace & World. 1961. $6.75. Thomas A. Bailey, "America's Emergence as a World Power: The Myth and the Verity," Pacific Historical Review, XXX (1961), 1-16. **THE SPLENDID LITTLE WAR.** By Frank Freidel. Boston: Little, Brown & Company. 1958. $8.50. **THEODORE ROOSEVELT AND THE RISE OF AMERICA TO WORLD POWER.** By Howard K. Beale. New York: Collier Books. 1962. $1.50. Raymond G. O'Connor, "Force and Diplomacy in American History," Military Review, XLIII (March, 1963), 80-89.

In his textbook on American diplomatic history, first published in 1936, Professor Samuel Flagg Bemis characterized the acquisition of the Philippine Islands as "The Great Aberration."[1] Oddly enough, the term "aberration" was not used in the sense of a deviation from a usual or normal course but to indicate a mistaken action. Professor Bemis, speaking of what he called "those years of adolescent irresponsibility," condoned all the territorial acquisitions made by the United States directly or indirectly through the war with Spain except for the Philippines.[2] In a more accurate sense, then, it would appear that the term "aberration" could appropriately be applied to the entire movement for overseas colonies which prevailed in the 1890's and marked a new trend in American expansion. The widening of national boundaries through the absorption of contiguous territory which had occurred in the first half of the nineteenth century was replaced by a European type of imperialism, not aimed at settlement or the rounding out of "natural" geographical limits, but designed to enhance commercial opportunities, provide additional military security, fulfill missionary zeal, promote national "interests" and contribute to the nation's prestige.

There is something almost unreal about the circumstances surrounding this radical departure in American foreign policy, and somehow the period lends itself more to fantasy than to history. Perhaps this helps account for the numerous attempts to explain what happened and why it happened, among them the racy best seller, The Martial Spirit by Walter Millis published in 1931 during the "debunking" era of American historical writing. In 1936 Professor

Julius W. Pratt produced his scholarly <u>Expansionists of 1898: The Acquisition of Hawaii and the Spanish Islands</u>, which devoted considerable attention to the expansionist tendencies displayed in the abortive attempt to annex the Hawaiian Islands in 1893, an attempt frustrated by the rectitude of President Grover Cleveland. More recently, Margaret Leech reassessed the period in the Pulitzer Prize-winning study, <u>The Days of McKinley</u>, and the latest full-length account is <u>Imperial Democracy: The Emergence of America as a Great Power</u>, by Professor Ernest R. May of Harvard, published in 1961. The title of the latter work is notable for the use of the term "Great Power," since it has been customary for historians to conclude that the United States became a "world power" as a result of the victory over Spain in 1898. In his stimulating presidential address before a meeting of the Pacific Coast Branch of the American Historical Association in 1960, Professor Thomas A. Bailey dealt with "America's Emergence as a World Power: The Myth and the Verity," and concluded that the historical profession had been misreading the American record. In his opinion, the United States became a world power in 1776 with the Declaration of Independence, but by the 1890's the nation ranked sufficiently high in those elements which determined power relationships to merit the superlative "great." The humbling of Spain merely added the final ingredient of prestige. Though appellations designating distinctive epochs in a nation's past are often inexact and misleading, it appears that this recent clarification will reduce the confusion that prevails among a generalization-starved generation which is attempting to understand the past.

Of perennial interest to students of the period is the responsibility of President McKinley for the coming of the war with Spain. Professor May presents a detailed account of the multiple events and forces which, he finds, led a reluctant McKinley to accept war rather than risk personal unpopularity and possible disaster for his party in forthcoming elections. Though maintaining that Spain actually had not agreed to and would not accept American demands for a solution to the Cuban problem, May contends that the President could have preserved peace by exercising leadership. "McKinley," however, "was not a brave man. In his whole political career, there had been no act of boldness. And the one resource which he did not employ in 1898 was courage." [159] This criticism of the President's failure to halt the war fever or guide it in another direction is shared by Margaret Leech, who concluded that "The President had conummately failed, not in the conduct of his diplomacy, but in restraining the belligerence of Congress and the American people."[180] Thus Leech and May agree that McKinley was a follower rather than a leader of opinion, and neither approves of the President's pursuing a course which resulted in war. They find the true tragedy of McKinley not in his failure to make up his mind but in the fact that he made it up in the wrong way.

GREAT ABERRATION

To move from the outbreak of war to the gathering of the fruits of victory, the President again emerges as the crucial element. The annexation of the Philippines revealed that "The executive branch rather than the Congress had become the source of decision in foreign affairs."[3] But May believes this decision was not made on the basis of a mandate from the Almighty as indicated by McKinley's oft-cited statement. On the contrary, "The sole concern of the President was with the mood and whim of public opinion," which demonstrated that "not just McKinley himself, but the United States as a nation, seemed to have chosen imperialism as its policy."[4] Professor Paolo Coletta, in a recent article, also holds the President responsible for acquiring the Philippines but he cites other motivations, including Cabinet unanimity and the imperatives of "dollars, duty, and destiny."[5] In any event, it appears that in his efforts to resolve the Cuban and Philippine questions, the vacillating McKinley was overwhelmed by a complexity of pressures which he either would not or could not resist.

Certainly, the attempt to determine the motives of statesmen is one of the most difficult and hazardous feats of the historical profession. As human beings they are, no doubt, able to find reasons for doing what they want to do, and again, as human beings, they may seldom be sure just why they did what they have done. In choosing one course of action in preference to available alternatives they undoubtedly use a variety of criteria which may be moral, personal or rooted in the nebulous "national interest." One authority, speaking of the agitation over the annexation of the Philippines, observed that "the same motive, in accordance with varying interpretations of an issue, impelled different individuals in opposite directions. Both morality and national self-interest impelled some to expansionism, others to anti-expansionism."[6] Each decision is also a prediction, i.e., the individual is predicting that a particular course of action will prove to be more satisfactory (in terms of criteria) than any of the alternatives. Furthermore, a statesman cannot divorce his actions from the pressures and attitudes of the period, both abroad and at home. How far can any leader go, whether he is the elected representative of the people or a military dictator, in emancipating himself from the prevailing winds of his age? Does he become a leader because he is tossed up by, represents, or lends himself to the predominant forces, or at least what he and his advisers believe these forces to be? Was McKinley, for example, a victim of the "psychic crisis of the 1890's"[7] or the instrument of "crusading morality" stemming from "the reform element in the population"?[8] It may be impossible to determine public opinion on any given subject, but an elected representative, aware of the need for winning votes in order to remain in power, realizes that he must espouse popular policies on crucial major issues. In fact, it might be more important to try to determine what the executive

91

WAR, DIPLOMACY, AND HISTORY

believed public opinion to be rather than what it actually was. In this way a clearer insight into motivation could probably be obtained.

In assessing the American temper concerning the annexation of the Philippines, much has been made of the election of 1900. The Republican victory was hailed by some as an endorsement of imperialism, though it has been pointed out that the issues in the campaign were so complex that such a conclusion is unwarranted. Perhaps, however, one should consider the election of 1896 and the plight of the Republican Party. Too often the Democratic Party had served as the party of expansion, and in the political world actions speak with a stentorian voice. The Republican platform of 1896 jumped on the expansionist bandwagon by advocating the acquisition of Hawaii, the construction of a Nicaraguan canal and the purchase of the Danish West Indies. The Monroe Doctrine was reasserted, along with the stated hope for the eventual withdrawal of European powers from the Western Hemisphere. Sympathy was expressed for the Cuban rebellion, and it was advocated that the United States use its good offices to make Cuba independent. As an aid to a vigorous foreign policy, the continued enlargment and modernization of the navy was approved. On the other hand, the Democratic platform declared for the maintenance of the Monroe Doctrine and expressed sympathy for the Cubans in their struggle for independence. With the choice so clearly presented, could McKinley resist this directive from his party and, presumably, from the people who elected him on such a platform? An election may not be a mandate for any particular policy, but it is one of the most eloquent indications of the public will that an official can find. The election of 1896, therefore, and not that of 1898 or 1900, might well have been interpreted as a mandate for imperialism.

Another aspect of this "great aberration" deserves attention. Ever since World War II there has been frequent mention of Clausewitz' dictum that "War is a continuation of state policy by other means." When the diplomats have exhausted their bag of tricks the generals and admirals are called in to furnish the means for enabling the nation's will to prevail. But the Clausewitz axiom does not fully account for the annexation of the Philippines. The original objective of the war with Spain, namely, to effect the freedom of the Cuban people, was altered by the very course of the hostilities. The electrifying victory at Manila Bay which sparked American popular interest in the islands and provided justification for their retention is linked with the new American navy that began to emerge in the 1880's. This steel and steam fleet that was created in the final decades of the nineteenth century was spurred by factors other than mere technological change. The rapid naval growth of this period was a response to the pressures emanating from several elements in the population, and it in turn served as a catalyst for an acquisitive national impulse. If, for example, the modern navy had not existed, would the nation have been so eager to promote hostilities? At that it was a risk, calculated or not, for certain European experts thought the American navy no match for the Spanish fleet. Moreover, even if the old navy were thought capable of protecting American troops en route to Cuba and guarding their supply lines, not even impetuous Assistant Secretary of the Navy Theodore Roosevelt would have dared send the antiquated post-Civil War vessels into Manila Bay.[10] So it is possible that without the modern navy there would have been no war, and probable that if war had occurred there would have been no victory in the Philippines and no compelling reason to acquire the islands. Perhaps this aspect of the interaction of force and diplomacy has been too often ignored by historians.[11]

There is a constant temptation to indulge in what might be called the "want of a nail" type of speculation in dealing with momentous events. It is clear that not one but a great many nails, shoes and horses combined to make the United States a colonial power. On the other hand, the want of any one of a number of these components could have averted or delayed McKinley's agonizing decisions. But the central figure of the great aberration remains the President, for while the impetus to change the direction of American foreign policy came from many quarters, the final decision came from the White House. It is evident that the one man in the right place at the right time who exerts a profound influence on the course of history need not be a dynamic leader or a commanding personality. McKinley rode the crest of a wave instead of struggling against it, and as a result the United States assumed the assets and liabilities of an empire in the Pacific. The outcome of this departure from tradition is another story.

FOOTNOTES

1. Samuel Flagg Bemis, A Diplomatic History of the United States (New York, 1936), Chapt. XXVI.

2. Ibid., 474-475.

3. May, Imperial Democracy, 262.

4. Ibid., 255, 262. Miss Leech asserts that "McKinley was wont to evade the bleakness of constraint by dwelling on the moral mission of America," and concludes that "The President's political instinct was never more sure than in adorning territorial acquisition with the bright leaf of duty and the rose of spiritual salvation."[344, 345]

5. Paolo Coletta, "McKinley, the Peace Negotiations, and the Acquisition of the Philippines," *Pacific Historical Review*, XXX (1961), 345.

6. Albert K. Weinberg, *Manifest Destiny: A Study of Nationalist Expansion in American History* (Gloucester, Mass., 1958), 281-282.

7. Richard Hofstadter, "Manifest Destiny and the Philippines," in Daniel Aaron, ed., *America in Crisis* (New York, 1952), 173.

8. Freidel, *The Splendid Little War*, 6.

9. Thomas A. Bailey, "Was the Election of 1900 a Mandate on Imperialism," *Mississippi Valley Historical Review*, XXIV (1937), 43-52.

10. Speaking of Theodore Roosevelt, his anxiety for fleet action in the Philippines in the event of war and the celebrated telegram of February 25 ordering Dewey to attack the Spanish fleet in the Philippines should war erupt, Howard K. Beale says: "The Assistant Secretary had seized the opportunity given by Long's absence to insure our grabbing the Philippines without a decision to do so by either Congress or the President, or least of all the people. Thus was important history made not by economic forces or democratic decisions but through the grasping of chance authority by a man with daring and a program."[70] The perpetuation of this myth is difficult to understand in light of the evidence that such a plan had been formulated for war with Spain and had been discussed with the President and other authorities the year before. See William R. Braisted, *The United States Navy in the Pacific* (Austin, Texas, 1958), 22-24, and May, *op. cit.*, 244.

11. O'Connor, "Force and Diplomacy in American History," 80-89.

PEACE MAKING AFTER THE FIRST WORLD WAR:
Chapter 9

Commentary

Mr. Trask has presented us with an account of a man of strong convictions experiencing the frustrations and disappointments of the give and take atmosphere of a diplomatic conference. Though Bliss' approintment as a delegate to the Conference was a surprise to some, his experience as a member of the Supreme War Council should have prepared him for the dissension and compromise at Versailles. Yet the single minded objective of winning the war forced a degree of cooperation which might have been deceptive, though writing after the war on "The Evolution of the Unified Command," Bliss observed that "Unified command came in 1918 at the first moment that it could possibly come. Opposition gave way only when it was manifest that every other course had been tried - and had failed. Unified command was then accepted, not for the purpose of winning victory but to prevent irretrievable defeat." In making the peace treaty at Versailles there was no such imperative, and Bliss should have been prepared for the kind of compromise that usually prevents complete fulfillment of the best laid plans.

In dealing with certain of the General's proposals for a lasting peace, Mr. Trask emphasizes that "General disarmament was the very essence, the health-giving principle of the peace settlement." Trask goes on to point out that Bliss believed the United States should provide world leadership in promoting the rule of law and "make the world safe for civilization by establishing adequate safeguards against suicidal total war." Yet this commentator, at least, was unable to discover how disarmament and law were going to preserve peace. Implicit in Bliss' proposals is a belief that weapons cause wars, and by reducing, controlling or eliminating weapons, the likelihood of war in turn would be reduced. On the other hand, Bliss appears to be conscious of the national rivalries in Europe and the need to restore Germany and limit French aspirations. Missing from his program is the method of implementing this rule of law, either through collective security, the use of sanctions, or the like. One is left with the impression that American leadership should be imposed unilaterally by appeals to world opinion or the use of economic or other pressures, as he suggested when the powers resisted American proposals at the peace conference. Presumably, these methods were to be used in order to induce the nations to observe the rule of law, and these, apparently, were to be the "adequate safeguards against suicidal total war."

At the same time that the General appeared to be advocating American leadership and control in "forcing the world to be free," and in preserving the peace, he urged the United States to limit its commitments and avoid entanglement in world affairs. We were told that Bliss could not divorce himself from a traditional American distrust of Europe, and it also seems that he could not emancipate himself from a heritage of hostility toward entangling alliances. Consistency may be the hobgoblin of little minds, but in this case Bliss not only wanted to have his cake and eat it too, he wanted to preserve the ingredients in their pristine state without even mixing the batter.

Some other questions occur to this commentator. It is my understanding that Bliss advocated an unconditional surrender of the German army and a conclusive admission of its defeat. This is difficult to reconcile with his subsequent resistance to what Trask calls "French rapacity." Bliss' reasons for wanting a strong Germany after the war are clearly indicated in this paper, but this seems inconsistent with his previous desire for unconditional surrender and abject humiliation of the German army. Such a development would have set the stage and provided the proper state of mind for a truly punitive peace, and have ruled out even the concept of "peace without victory." A complete defeat of Germany would have destroyed any bargaining power that she had, eliminated any need for the conditions under which the armistice was concluded, and made still more difficult any attempt to insure that "Germany would become a strong secure democratic bulwark in Central Europe."

Throughout this paper I am constantly reminded of Bliss' limitations in relating ends to means, in his "blunt" and "uncompromising" attitude on complex issues, in his simplistic approach to history through broad analogy, and in his myopic view of world affairs through the twin lenses of the United States and Europe. I am also aware that he was the only non-civilian member of the American Commission, that he was a product of West Point, and that he had served in the Army during his entire adult life. There is a temptation to attribute Bliss' limitations to his background and experience as an officer in the military service of his country. Perhaps certain of his limitations can be attributed to what has been called the "military mind," and here we have an example of such a mind at work in an alien element, namely, peace making as distinct from war making. Of course, as Holmes said, no generalization is worth a damn including this one, and here we have in effect a case study which an intrepid commentator can investigate.

Bliss, in his new role of diplomatist, was outside his element. He was trying to extend his field of competence from combat to ideology and the mulifarious aspects of international rivalry and negotiation. As a military expert

PEACE MAKING

dedicated to the winning of any war in which his nation might become involved, Bliss was on pretty firm ground. As a statesman who must recognize that military power was only one element of national security, Bliss was uncertain and confused. His insistence on disarmament as a "condition precedent" to peace revealed a certain monomania that could be attributed to his background. His refuge in dogmatic, absolutist positions could reveal an insecurity in the face of conditions beyond his knowledge and comprehension. It might also reveal a military approach to problems that insists on clear cut solutions, unhampered by doubts and questions which impede execution. Without belaboring the point, the characteristics which I have mentioned might stem from the fact that the military establishment has had its function as an instrument, not as an end, and its use has been instrumental, not ultimate. Trained and conditioned in such an atmosphere, Bliss was constitutionally unfitted for the role of peacemaker, and his frustrations at Versailles were largely due to a mild schzophrenia resulting from the attempt to accommodate a military mind to the methods and objectives of a diplomatic settlement. Mr. Trask may be appalled at my assessment, and he may be distressed at my using his material for this purpose, but he did ask if we have faced up to the impact of proliferating militarization throughout American life since World War I. It seems that his paper is a contribution to this study.

Mr. Buckley's paper is not directly related to the peace settlements following World War I, though it certainly is related indirectly. Japan had taken advantage of the war to consolidate her position in Asia and thereby pose a greater threat to American and British interests. The naval competition which flourished after the armistice and the treaty of Versailles reflected a conflict in aspirations that stemmed from the outcome of the war. In this sense, then, the Washington Conference could be regarded as a continuation of the negotiations begun in 1919.

The subject matter of Mr. Buckley's paper is in many respects broader than that of Mr. Trask, and therefore it is much more vulnerable to criticism. There is a great need for a new interpretation of the Washington Conference and we should all be grateful for this effort. But I am sure that Mr. Buckley would not expect to satisfy everybody. To begin with a minor point, we are told that "Most contemporary writers approved of the Washington settlements." This is followed by a quote from 1934 and the statement that "It was not until after the Japanese attack on Pearl Harbor that popular journalists, searching for explanations of the rapid Imperial Japanese advance in the Pacific, began to attack the conference treaties." Actually, Raymond Leslie Buell in his scholarly study of The Washington Conference published in 1922, concluded that "the American Delegation might have secured a number of additional concessions if it had been more bold." He criticized the non-fortification agreement on the grounds that "Without such bases, a naval attack on Japan is practically impossible unless the attacking power possesses a navy two or three times as strong as the Japanese Navy." Because the treaty limited only capital ships and aircraft carriers, Buell concluded that "From the strictly tactical viewpoint, naval competition has not been destroyed. Its objects have been merely changed," changed, that is, to aircraft and so-called auxiliary vessels. He also declared that "Peace at Washington was purchased at the sacrifice of the Open Door." Dudley W. Knox, whose views may be suspect because of his association with the Navy, in a book published in 1922 concluded that "America resigned to Britain the predominance in Sea Power, and gave up also her power to defend the Philippines and to accomplish our policies toward China and Russia." As to the popular journalists writing after the Japanese attack, John Chalmers Vinson in 1955 asserted that the Senate in approving the treaties believed peace could be assured through agreements and "moral force," and encouraged the settlement at Washington that relinquished naval supremacy. "In the twentieth century," Vinson concluded, "this proved to be a parchment peace." Well, I don't want to belabor the point, and I'm not sure how many examples it takes to weaken a generalization, but it is clear that all contemporary responsible accounts of the treaties were not favorable, and all post-Pearl Harbor criticisms were not the product of "popular journalists."

All this may have little bearing on the basic question which Mr. Buckley has set out to answer, namely, "Did or did not the Washington Conference sacrifice American national interests to an idealistic concept of disarmament?" As I understand the paper, the main thesis is that the United States benefited from each of the three agreements. The Four-Power Treaty ended the Anglo-Japanese Alliance which had posed an implicit threat to the United States; the Nine-Power Treaty gained formal acceptance of the Open Door principle long espoused by the United States; and the Naval Limitation Treaty preserved a favorable balance of military power which would have been lost if competition had continued. Mr. Buckley also insists that these treaties be considered in relation to each other, and that they cannot properly be evaluated separately. This is fine as far as it goes, but there is another essential step. The Naval Limitations Treaty must be judged in terms of its relationship with all American interests, that is, the Cardinal American policies which the navy had to be prepared to defend.

The fundamental problem at any disarmament conference is that of security. No responsible statesman is going to agree to a position of relative military power that will place his nation at the mercy of a potential or extant rival. And this security extends to the protection and promotion of the national interests, at home and abroad.

There were a number of basic American policies which the navy had to be capable of supporting, among them:

1. The Monroe Doctrine, that is, the protection of the Western Hemisphere. Great Britain was the only nation possessing a navy sufficiently powerful to threaten this American preserve, and with parity achieved in battleships and aircraft carriers, the former considered the "backbone of the fleet," the Doctrine could be defended.

2. The protection of American possessions in the Caribbean and the Central and Western Pacific. The warships authorized by the treaty were sufficient to defend Puerto Rico and the Hawaiian islands, but Samoa, Guam, and the Philippines were dangerously close to Japan, the third ranking naval power, which also posed a threat to The Open Door in China. To support this latter policy and to defend possessions in the Western Pacific the United States needed both fighting strength and sufficient force to provide a deterrent to any violation of American interests.

The naval experts concluded that if the Anglo-Japanese Alliance were discontinued, the United States would need parity with Great Britain and a two-to-one superiority over Japan in order to have an equal opportunity in a conflict with either nation. As a result of the conference, a 2 to 1 superiority was not secured and the important island bases were sacrificed. As Elihu Root acutely perceived, the outcome of the conference was "the complete negation of naval policy."

What the Naval Limitation Treaty did, then, was to deprive the United States of the ability to enforce unilaterally its policies in the Far East. This agreement was made at a time when the United States had renounced the principle of collective security. And even if our military position relative to Japan was improved over what it would have been without the treaty, as Mr. Buckley contends, it is one thing to recognize a situation, but it is another thing to agree to it and perpetuate it by treaty. Also, the naval limitation at Washington helped create an atmosphere in the United States that discouraged building and prevented the nation from trying to keep up with Great Britain and Japan in auxiliary vessels. This attitude was aided and abetted by the report of the American delegation which concluded that "The limitation of capital ships, in itself, substantially meets the existing need, and its indirect effort will be to stop the inordinate production of any sort of naval craft." Furthermore, I doubt that Japan could have afforded a naval race with the United States at that time for her resources were considerably less than those of this nation. This last observation is highly questionable because of the experience of other countries, but an analysis of Japan's financial state at that time would provide some support for this argument.

Under the circumstances, the restrictions placed on Japan by these several treaties rested solely on her good faith, for her military position in the Far East was made virtually impregnable. She extended her building in the auxiliary craft, she violated the terms of the Limitations treaty by laying down cruisers which were allegedly under 10,000 tons but actually displaced up to 14,000 tons, and when she violated the Nine-Power Treaty in 1931 and 1937 the United States was militarily incapable of stopping her. Mr. Buckley correctly states that "As a result of the Five-Power Treaty none of the signatories could easily attack, and carry on offensive warfare, against a vigilant home territory of the other. Each was supreme within its own defensive sphere unless faced by a combination of the other two." In other words, the United States could protect itself, the Western Hemisphere, and certain of its possessions, but it could not defend its holdings in the Western Pacific or its interests in China. Moreover, the treaties constituted a further involvement in Asia, for they committed the United States to a concerted effort to maintain the territorial integrity of China, a commitment which was formalized by a duly ratified agreement. Previously, America's responsibility had been confined to a unilateral declaration of policy that had never received Senate approval. Certainly, as Mr. Buckley observes, all treaties are based on a large element of faith, but experience demonstrates that faith is an unreliable factor in national survival.

Mr. Buckley mentions that critics have deplored the absence of enforcement procedures in the treaties, and explains that the United States probably would not have accepted the treaties if coercive sanctions were included. Although he is undoubtedly correct, this failure to provide for multilateral enforcement placed ultimate responsibility on that nation whose ox happened to be gored.

Finally, Mr. Buckley quotes Secretary of State Hughes to the effect that "this country would never go to war over any aggression on the part of Japan in China." As a historian who relishes hindsight I find this statement to be merely another example of Mr. Hughes' shortsightedness. The Stimson-Hoover Doctrine was based on Japan's violation of the Kellogg-Briand Pact and the Nine-Power Treaty, and its adoption by Franklin Roosevelt had a great deal to do with our involvement in World War II.

The American delegation failed to understand the relationship between military power and national objectives. The ratio which it advocated was not based on commitments and responsibilities but on the numbers of capital ships which each nation possessed or was in the act of building. The delegates were anxious to reach an agreement and they did, but the equilibrium of naval power that had been established was deceptive. Based on prestige and mathematical factors, the ratios bore no relationship to the policy commitments, binding or assumed, of the United States. Forgotten was the Clausewitz dictum that "The most important single judgment a political or military leader can make is to forecast correctly the nature of the war upon which the nation is to embark. On this everything else depends." The agreement at Washington provided America with the naval power to wage a successful war against her least likely antagonist, Great Britain, and deprived her of the ability to check her most probable foe, Japan.

THE "YARDSTICK" AND
NAVAL DISARMAMENT
IN THE 1920's

Chapter 10

On April 22, 1929, Ambassador Hugh S. Gibson, chairman of the American delegation to the League of Nations Preparatory Commission on Disarmament at Geneva, proposed that a formula, or "yardstick," be used to evaluate the characteristics of naval vessels in an effort to reconcile the differing needs of the naval powers. The proposal was hailed both by diplomats and by the public as the answer to the problems that had beset disarmament negotiations since the Washington Conference of 1921-1922, and it spurred the conversations that culminated in the London Naval Conference of 1930. But the yardstick neither began nor ended at Geneva, and its origin, meaning, and outcome help clarify some of the issues that made naval disarmament so difficult.

In the first decade of the twentieth century the Navy Department possessed a number of ships that were approaching obsolescence, and it sought an equation that would determine whether a ship should be scrapped or repaired and modernized.[1] This search resulted in an attempt to develop a formula by which combat vessels could be compared as to military value. The Naval War College assisted the Navy General Board in the quest, but their efforts were unsuccessful because of the complexities of the problem and the various imponderables involved. The Board recommended that "twenty per cent of the total cost of a vessel be the upper limit of the cost of repair or modernizing and this only in cases when the vessel after being repaired is equal at least to her original value in battery, speed, fuel endurance and protection, thus giving her a military value approaching that possessed when first commissioned."[2] In a later study of ships built after 1882, the Board found that, "so far as any rule can be established," the life of naval vessels was about twenty-four years for capital ships, twenty years for destroyers and scouts, and fifteen years for torpedo boats.[3] The navy professionals were reluctant to reduce battle efficiency to computations that could not encompass the realities of war, but age was a tangible factor that could be measured.

The Washington Conference of 1921-1922 provided the impetus for another search for a formula that would determine equivalent naval strength, although in this case for the purpose of limiting armament. Secretary of State Charles E. Hughes, who headed the American delegation, presented the problem and employed the term that later was to catch the popular imagination. "One of the difficulties by which I am confronted," he wrote to the Secretary of the Navy, "is that of determining what I can perhaps best describe as a 'yard stick' by which to measure existing armaments and which can also be applied as a standard of measurement in any general plan of reduction. If you have reached any conclusions on this particular point, I would be most grateful to have your views."[4] In response to this request the Navy's elder statesmen, calling on the experience of their predecessors, replied: "The General Board can not define a 'naval unit' in such a way as to make it an accurate measure of strength of the navies of the world. It is not practicable to commute the combatant value of one class of ships into combatant value of another class for purposes of comparative measurement, even in the case of our own navy."[5] Hughes later acknowledged that the Board supplied the formula which, "slightly modified," was the basis for agreement on limitation at the Washington Conference,[6] namely, the use of capital ships as a measure of strength. Such a simple standard was a far cry from the "yard stick" that Hughes wanted, but it did provide a basis for comparison.

The Board's reluctance to commit itself to paper equations based on selected statistical data cannot be attributed solely to the traditional intractability of the military mind, although the admirals probably resented this civilian effort to penetrate the screen that enveloped their technical and specialized domain. More important, the Board, conscious of its responsibilities and steeped in the vagaries of naval history, refused to bind itself to an abstract computation that ignored the realities of national defense and the unpredictability of maritime warfare. Conflict over this issue was to put an additional strain on the relations between the civilian and naval branches of the government.

The agreement at Washington established ratios between the major naval powers for capital ships and aircraft carriers but placed no restrictions on ships under 10,000 tons. A subsequent outburst of building in so-called auxiliary craft, especially cruisers, led to the abortive Geneva Conference of 1927. This meeting, dominated by professional naval officers, failed because of Britain's refusal to concede parity to the United States and her preference for smaller 6-inch-gun cruisers, as opposed to America's desire for 10,000-ton ships armed with 8-inch batteries.

The League's Preparatory Commission on Disarmament, which had been in adjournment, was scheduled to meet for its sixth session on April 15, 1929. The continental European nations were reluctant to continue efforts to formulate plans for a general disarmament conference until the naval powers had reached a solution to their problems.[7] The instructions issued to the chairman of the American delegation to the Commission, Hugh S. Gibson, ambassador to Belgium, were comprehensive but general. They reiterated the American contention that limitation by tonnage by categories was "the simplest, fairest and most practical method." Nevertheless, in order to facilitate agreement, the United States was willing to consider a method suggested by France at a meeting of the Commission in 1927, whereby total tonnage was combined with tonnage by categories, with a provision for a change between categories through proportionate increase or decrease. America was firm in its belief that limitation, in order to be effective, must be made in all types of combat vessels, and that the aim should be reduction in existing armament, not merely control.[8] President Hoover took advantage of Gibson's presence in Washington to join in drafting a speech that the latter was scheduled to deliver at Geneva. The President was anxious to "inject life" into the Commission's deliberations by offering a "bold and unexpected proposal,"[9] and Ambassador Gibson sailed for Europe carrying Hoover's answer to the dilemma that had stalled five previous sessions of the Preparatory Commission.

The Commission met at Geneva on April 15, 1929, and Gibson learned that the German delegate intended to propose that a special committee of the five principal naval powers be formed to consider naval disarmament. He was to contend that the naval problem was the main obstacle preventing the Commission from proceeding with methods of land and air reduction, and that naval reduction was of concern to the naval powers alone.[10] The British delegation, realizing that agreement with the United States was essential to further progress, was anxious to prevent any public discussions that might tear open old wounds.[11] On April 22, as the delegates settled down to resume their hitherto barren activities, the American chairman rose to address the assemblage.

Gibson began by emphasizing that America's defense was primarily a naval problem, and that the United States was content to allow land disarmament to be handled by those nations most concerned. He reaffirmed the belief that limitation by tonnage by categories was best, but he conceded that the French proposal combining total tonnage and tonnage by categories would be acceptable as a basis of discussion. He then presented what came to be known as the "yardstick" formula.

> My Government [he said] will be prepared to give consideration to a method of estimating equivalent naval values which take account of other factors than displacement tonnage alone. In order to arrive at a basis of comparison in the case of

categories in which there are marked variations as to unit characteristics, it might be desirable in arriving at a formula for estimating equivalent tonnage to consider certain factors which produce these variations such as age, unit displacement, and caliber of guns. My Government has given careful consideration to various methods of comparison, and the American delegation will be in a position to discuss the subject whenever it comes before the commission.

Continuing, Gibson maintained that results were more important than method, which was secondary. He pointed out that the pact renouncing war as an instrument of national policy should "advance the cause of disarmament by removing doubts and fear which in the past have constituted our principle obstacle." The United States was willing to agree to the most drastic limitation of armaments so long as all types of combat vessels were included, for a nation's naval strength was determined by that of other nations. Gibson concluded that "what is really wanted is a common-sense agreement, based on the idea that we are going to be friends and settle our problems by peaceful means," an agreement possible only through a "change of attitude toward the use of force in the settlement of international disputes."[12]

Hoover's desire to inject life into the discussion of the Commission was realized. The British, Japanese, French, Canadian, and Italian delegates made cordial replies, and Gibson reported that the reception of his speech was more favorable than he had hoped. In fact, he feared that it might give rise to "a degree of optimism that may be difficult to sustain."[13] The following day London formally endorsed both the spirit and the letter of Gibson's address, and expressed the belief that efforts should proceed along the lines indicated.[14]

Press response in the United States was enthusiastic in its approval of the proposals, which the New York World considered an effort to "cut across" the "vicious circle" in which discussion of naval limitation had become involved. The New York Herald Tribune regarded it as evidence of American good will and desire to disarm, and the New York Times found "doubt and depression" giving way to hope for success at Geneva. The Brooklyn Daily Eagle thought that Gibson had challenged the other naval powers to "stop quibbling and go forward" with reduction, and to the Washington Star the speech meant that "statesmanship as opposed to seamanship must be the controlling factor." The address received widespread and generally favorable publicity throughout the United States,[15] although criticism was expressed by Representative Fred A. Britton, chairman of the House Naval Committee, who called the speech a "complete surrender" and "another naval victory for British Diplomacy."[16]

THE YARDSTICK

The British press abandoned its traditional calm in welcoming the proposals. The London Times thought that the United States had "taken the initiative that belongs to it," while the Daily Telegraph termed the speech "frank" and "radical." The Daily Express considered it "the most important thing that has happened in connection with disarmament since Mr. Hughes . . . rose to address the Washington Conference," and the Daily News hailed it as a "magnificent peace opportunity which British statesmanship cannot possibly ignore." The speech had come as a "great surprise" to the British, who regarded it as a friendly gesture by Hoover.[17] Perhaps the substance of Britain's response was summed up by the British Review of Reviews, which claimed that Gibson's offer "amounted to an--albeit conditional --American declaration of peace to Great Britain."[18]

French reaction was in a similar vein. The independent, semi-official Le Temps, of Paris, felt that Gibson's effort had "completely modified the dangerous atmosphere prevailing at Geneva," while the conservative Figaro found it "cause for optimism." The Republican Journal des Debats said that the initiative, which could only come from the United States, had been taken by Hoover, and the Socialist Populaire approved the speech, although attributing it to the pressure of public opinion. Only the Communist Humanite cynically observed that it was a clever speech aimed at upsetting the "Franco-British naval arrangement which is so odious to the White House."[19] On the whole, this was a surprising degree of unanimity from a press noted for its partisanship.

Newspapers in Italy expressed a difference of opinion that may not have reflected the public reaction. The Osservatore Romano, published by the Vatican, considered Gibson's proposals a "step in [the] advancement of peace." The Fascist L'Impero caustically observed that America's willingness to make concessions on land armaments was comparable to Switzerland making concessions on naval armament, and no more commendable. Gibson's contention that no other nation should have a navy larger than that of the United States was an "insincere doctrine."[20] Since all newspapers published in Italy were organs of the government, except for the Osservatore Romano, a greater divergence of press response was unlikely.[21]

Japanese editorial comment was unrestrained in expressing approval. The Jiji Shimpo hailed the American attitude "with joy, for it means a chance for a compromise," and the Kokumin Shimbun regarded the Gibson offer as the removal of the "first obstacle to discussion at a main conference." The Osaka Mainichi Shimbun thought the speech showed "how earnest the American Government is for the actualization of disarmament," and the Hochi Shimbun found that "The moral courage and straightforward statesmanship of Mr. Hoover evoke our heart-felt admiration."[22] The statesmen of Japan could look forward to newspaper support in their quest for the reduction of armaments.

Undoubtedly, most of the enthusiasm was evoked by Gibson's suggestion of a formula that would assess the equivalent value of ships in terms of combat effectiveness instead of relying exclusively on tonnage and gun dimension. Even the proponents of integrated disarmament, after six unproductive sessions of the Preparatory Commission, were reluctantly admitting that the dispute over methods of naval limitation was delaying the activities of the Commission, and that it was a dispute which only the naval powers could resolve. It could be further reduced to a conflict between the British desire for 6-inch-gun cruisers in sufficient quantity to satisfy her needs and the American demand for 8-inch guns and mathematical equality in ships with Britain. The formula offered hope for a solution of the cruiser problem and a new approach to the question of parity. Obviously, the next move would have to be made by the two major naval powers, and the Commission adjourned on May 6, 1929, apparently reconciled to awaiting the outcome of future Anglo-American conversations.[23]

The formula that Hoover and Gibson suggested at Geneva was soon universally referred to as the "yardstick," a term that caught the imagination of statesmen and public alike. It became the magic word that would bring an end to naval competition, make general disarmament possible, and dispel the atmosphere of mistrust between nations that remained in spite of the Pact of Paris. The response indicated a belief that the yardstick actually existed, and that it had been worked out by the President and his aides with the mathematical exactitude expected of a highly successful engineer. Unfortunately, such was not the case. Hoover and Secretary of State Henry L. Stimson seem to have been even more astonished than Gibson by the reception accorded an idea designed to stimulate activity at Geneva. Confronted by a request from the British Ambassador nearly two weeks later for clarification of the proposal, Stimson could only lamely explain that it was a "suggestion, which was not in any way completed," intended "merely to provide for the elaboration of a formula" that would permit a comparison of the "strategic usefulness" of different types of naval vessels. He offset his vagueness by stressing that the "fundamental proposition" which was "absolutely necessary" to agreement between Britain and the United States remained the issue of naval parity.[24]

The failure of the administration to consult the Navy General Board prior to offering the proposal at Geneva indicates that it had not been explored too carefully.[25] A formula capable of equating the fighting strength of men-of-war would of necessity be highly technical in nature, and involve a consideration of the qualities constituting combat effectiveness. It would demand an expert knowledge of ship construction, gunnery, operational efficiency, naval tactics, and grand strategy. The Navy General Board, by training and experience, was qualified to devise such a formula. Hoover, subsequently, may have regretted that the Board's views were not obtained before he sent Gibson to Geneva.

An earlier public suggestion of a yardstick had been made by Allen W. Dulles, who had served with the American delegation to the Geneva Conference in 1927. In an article in Foreign Affairs, Dulles asked that combat strength rather than tonnage alone be considered in determining parity. He cited the French proposal to the Preparatory Commission in 1927, which had recommended that the age of naval vessels be made a factor in arriving at an evaluation of naval power. Such a formula, he claimed, would make it possible for the United States and Britain to have the type of cruisers each wanted and arrive at an agreement.[26] The publication of this article coincided with a speech by the British Foreign Secretary, Sir Austin Chamberlain, in which he urged that an "equation" be worked out by which the conflicting aims of the two nations could be reconciled.[27] The extent to which Hoover was influenced by these suggestions is not known, but it is clear that while the idea of a formula did not originate with the President, he was responsible for its official proposal in a form that offered the possibility of its acceptance, and at a most propitious time in the deliberations of the Preparatory Commission.

Prior to the meeting at Geneva, Britain and the United States had agreed that talks on naval questions through diplomatic channels were prerequisite to the success of any formal conference.[28] Then, on May 3, the British government proposed "a private and confidential exchange of views" on naval disarmament between the two countries. They were confident that a settlement could be reached, based on the Gibson overtures and their impression "of the mind and purpose of the President." Such conversations could establish a "broad line of agreement" that would offer hope of a settlement with other naval powers, but they should be postponed until after the forthcoming general election in England.[29] Preparations for the talks were not neglected, however, for Stimson and Sir Esme Howard, the British ambassador, decided that negotiations would be conducted by civilian statesmen rather than naval experts, because the latter would approach the problem on the basis of war between the nations, whereas the civilian "might be able and willing to take chances which the professional service man could not take."[30] The United States, which accepted the British suggestion, was to be represented by General Charles G. Dawes, the new ambassador to Great Britain, who was scheduled to arrive in London after the general election.[31] It was also decided to present the American plan first in

109

order to place Britain in the more difficult position of having to prove the United States wrong.³²

Lunching at the White House with Hoover and Dawes on the eve of the General's departure for London, Stimson presented an agenda that was approved by the President:

(1) The President and I will try to produce such a yardstick which we favor from our naval advisers;

(2) We will then try to persuade the heads of the governments of Great Britain and Japan to do the same independently with their naval advisers. Each Government will then produce a yardstick from the efforts of their civilian representatives, using the Navy only as advisers;

(3) Civilian representatives of the Governments will then compare the three yardsticks and attempt to get an agreement upon a common one, the naval experts of all parties acting only as advisers in this attempt at agreement.³³

The time had arrived for calling in the admirals, but due caution was to be exercised to prevent their intrusion into matters of policy. The margin of error had been reduced.

The luncheon must have concluded in a happy vein. Britain and America were already in agreement on so many fundamentals that it seemed as though only details needed filling in. The mutual desire for bilateral negotiation, the moral force of the Kellogg-Briand Pact, the prospects of a formula to reconcile the cruiser dispute, the relegation of the naval officer to a subordinate position, and the atmosphere of good will and high intention that prevailed, all tended to dispel doubts and encourage confidence. The results of the general election in England, which placed a Labour government in power, offered even greater hope of success, for the new Prime Minister, Ramsay MacDonald, had long been the foremost spokesman of a party that stood for peace and the reduction of armament. The President and his Secretary of State must have contemplated the future of Anglo-American relations and the prospects for naval limitation with considerable optimism.

General Dawes arrived in London amid the plaudits of the British press, which claimed the story "no longer a secret" that he brought with him the formula that would make possible the reduction of naval armaments.³⁴ The story remained a secret only to the General, who was to find the matter a continual source of embarrassment. When he spoke on June 18 at a banquet of the Society of Pilgrims of Great Britain, he could only suggest that "each Government might separately obtain from their respective naval experts their definition of the yardstick and then the inevitable compromise between these differing definitions, which will be expressed in the final fixation of the technical yardstick, should be made by a committee of statemen of the nations." He blamed the failure of the Geneva Conference of 1927 on the fact that there was "a mixed commission of statesmen and naval technicians," a "method adjusted to human reasoning, but not to human nature." Dawes concluded by reiterating the principle of equality of naval strength between the United States and Great Britain, and by appealing to the English-speaking people to lead the way to world peace.[35]

Meanwhile, the President and his advisers were attempting to devise the yardstick that Dawes was supposed to have brought with him to London. The General Board was first asked for its comments and recommendations on the Gibson proposals more than a month after they had been advanced.[36] The Board's reply was discouraging. The admirals considered it highly improbable that an accurate computation of the combat value of a naval vessel could be made, or that agreement could be reached on the weight to be assigned to the factors involved. If such a formula was absolutely necessary, the Board recommended that it should include only age and displacement of ships, because the introduction of other factors would make for complexity and disagreement on evaluation.[37]

Hoover apparently was not satisfied with this response, for he asked that Rear Admiral Hilary P. Jones, who had participated in numerous disarmament negotiations, furnish him with a "purely confidential and personal note" on an equivalent British cruiser strength based on American existing and authorized cruisers, keeping in mind "a possible conflict of the two fleets."[38] Admiral Jones submitted a lengthy, detailed study of America's naval defense problems that emphasized the critical lack of modern cruisers and the advantage that Britain enjoyed by virtue of her numerous overseas bases and her vast merchant marine. He argued that the United States could achieve parity in sea power only by possessing a preponderance of combat vessels.[39]

Evidently this information offered no satisfactory solution, for a few weeks later Stimson suggested a yardstick that assigned a percentage evaluation to large ships as compared to smaller vessels. One ton of a cruiser of less than 5,000 tons would be rated as the equivalent of nine tenths of a ton of a cruiser that displaced from 5,000 to 10,000 tons, and a ton of a destroyer would be equal to nine tenths of a ton of a small cruiser.[40] The General Board response, which was incorporated in its entirety in Secretary of the Navy Charles Francis Adams' reply to Stimson, rejected the plan and recommended against any solution based on the assumptions contained in Stimson's letter. Destroyers could not be compared with cruisers in combat value, the Board contended, for their tasks and functions were entirely different. Furthermore, it was not desirable to divide cruisers into two categories, because the United States would then be required to build ships unsuited to her needs. Any computation of equivalent combat strength was impossible, for it would be based on arbitrary evaluations of factors that could not take into account the actual conditions that might arise during conflict.[41]

The formula contrived by the General Board was prepared at the direction of the Secretary of the Navy after it had repeatedly rejected the principle of a yardstick. In arriving at a formula the Board considered three factors: displacement, age, and gun caliber. Using "E" for battle efficiency, "D" for displacement, "A" for age, and "G" for gun caliber, the equation read, $E = D \times A \times G$. To express the equation in numbers, "D" was the ship's displacement in standard tons. The factor "A" was determined by a formula that established an arbitrary maximum age for each type of vessel and measured the age of a particular ship against a numerical constant. Factor "G" was determined by the gun caliber, e.g., 8-inch equaled 1.00, 7.5-inch, .99, 6-inch, .96. This in turn could vary by a hundredth of a point depending on whether it was an "equitable," "acceptable," or "unacceptable" value. The Board insisted that the formula could not be used to evaluate the fighting quality of ships in different categories, such as destroyers and cruisers, because their function and purpose were so different. Moreover, the factor "G" could not be used in comparing the efficiency of submarines or destroyers because the gun was not the primary weapon on these ships. Admiral Jones devised a formula that assigned a different age factor and included the size of the vessel in one part of the equation, but the result was little different from that obtained by the General Board formula.[42] The problems involved were considerable and it was apparent that any yardstick would ignore or distort many imponderables. Armor, speed, maneuverability, and the number of guns mounted were significant items that could be decisive in battle, but they lay outside the formula. The introduction of future tonnage presented other problems, for all computations were based on the end of the period that the agreement was to cover, namely, December 31, 1936.

The conversations in London between Dawes and MacDonald continued, with the British government under the impression that the President and his advisers were evolving a formula that would change the problem of limitation "from one of tonnage to one of points."[43] After much prodding the Prime Minister did accept the principle of parity,[44] thereby formally acknowledging Britain's acquiescence to the American claim to equality in naval strength. This voluntary surrender of control of the sea was fundamental to a successful outcome of the negotiations. At the Washington

THE YARDSTICK

Conference of 1921-1922, parity had been conceded in battleships and aircraft carriers, but its denial in cruisers at Geneva in 1927 had made agreement impossible. MacDonald's acceptance of this principle was probably the most significant concession made by any statesman during the negotiations that preceded the London Naval Conference of 1930.

Encouraged by this development, the President and his Secretary of State offered some specific suggestions pertaining to the scope of a formal conference. They suggested: (1) that the agreement should cover all classes of combat vessels; (2) that the categories should consist of capital ships, aircraft carriers, cruisers, destroyers, and submarines; (3) that the "right of limited transfer between these categories" should be permitted in accordance with an agreed yardstick; (4) that capital ships and aircraft carriers, already limited by the Washington Treaty of 1922, should be considered only as to the deferment of replacements; and (5) that "In measuring relative combatant strength we should consider the elements of such yardstick to be (a) displacement; (b) guns; (c) age. Our general view is that protection, speed, habitability, etc., are entirely relative to the other factors and do not require special consideration."[45] The transfer of tonnage between categories would permit each nation to build the type of ship it preferred, utilizing tonnage allotted in another category.

These decisions apparently had been made without consulting the Navy Department, whose views were contained in the letter from Adams to Stimson dated July 15, which strongly advised against such proposals.[46] In Washington the initiative had been taken by the civilian statesmen, who were probably impatient with and somewhat nettled by the dilatoriness and intractability of the naval experts. But the proposal furnished the Prime Minister with a more specific indication of America's intentions, and it provided him with a framework within which he and his advisers could formulate the British program.

A few days later MacDonald summarized the situation by declaring the two nations in agreement on all issues except the yardstick, and he urged that it be hurried.[47] Washington retorted that "drastic action with regard to cruisers by the British" was imperative, and that the determination of a yardstick to measure the relative value of ships was best left to the conference.[48] The Prime Minister was disappointed at the failure to get a yardstick, and he feared that the question of tonnage was being raised "in its old absolute form." He had hoped that they could "examine the present conditions, [work] our parity within it, total the results and see what happens." MacDonald summarized the two cruiser fleets, built and building, as follows:

113

WAR, DIPLOMACY, AND HISTORY

> Eight-inch-gun cruisers: Great Britain, 15 ships, 146,800 tons; 3 projected, 30,000 tons; total 176,800 tons. United States, 13 building, 130,000 tons; 10 projected, 100,000 tons; total, 230,000 tons.
>
> 7.5-inch-gun cruisers: Great Britain, <u>Hawkins</u> class, 4 ships, 29,400 tons. United States, none.
>
> Six-inch-gun cruisers: Great Britain, 40 ships, 179,270 tons; United States, 10 ships, 70,500 tons.

He claimed that the 7.5-inch-gun cruisers, built in 1916, were comparable in effectiveness to 6-inch-gun cruisers, and that certain of Britain's 6-inch-gun cruisers were inferior in both guns and tonnage to the more recent American ships in that class.[49]

The introduction of figures into the negotiations was to make the Prime Minister more dependent on the Admiralty and less able to rely on his own judgment, which tended toward uncluttered generalities. His First Lord of the Admiralty, Albert V. Alexander, was a political appointee, and although he was loyal to his party leader he was not versed in the technicalities that surrounded naval problems.[50] MacDonald had intended to employ the professionals solely for the purpose of arriving at a formula that would enable the civilian statesmen to dispense with their services. The American desire to exchange figures and reach an understanding on totals prior to the acceptance of a yardstick was to drive him into the arms of his experts. This eventuality he had neither foreseen nor prepared for.

The Prime Minister finally revealed his government's conception of parity in cruisers. The United States was to be allotted eighteen 8-inch-gun and twenty 6-inch-gun cruisers to Britain's fifteen 8-inch and forty-five 6-inch, with the 7.5-inch <u>Hawkins</u> ships included in the latter group until replaced by ships mounting the smaller caliber guns.[51] This information was received with dismay in Washington, for it envisaged a disparity of twenty-two cruisers totaling approximately 80,000 tons, a gap of impossible "yardstickability."[52] A brief exchange of correspondence was followed by an American suggestion that cruiser parity be set at 250,000 tons, to be attained by 1936, with a proviso that if world conditions should warrant, Great Britain could request an additional 60,000 tons, with the United States having the same option.[53]

The reaction in Washington apparently had a beneficial effect, for the Prime Minister became more conciliatory and less categorical in his demands.[54] He was willing to allow the United States a "material preponderance" of 8-inch-gun

114

THE YARDSTICK

cruisers in order to make parity possible, and he indicated a readiness to permit the construction of as many of these ships as America wanted so long as it did not upset the balance between Britain and other countries, notably Japan.[55] He outlined the current cruiser dispositions and explained that the ships were in a "police category" rather than a "fighting category," and revealed a plan whereby Britain would maintain a strength of fifty cruisers, ten less than he had previously insisted on as a minimum. Not all was concession, however, for he reiterated the necessity for a yardstick. His information revealed that the large cruisers were "worth in a fight almost an infinity of smaller craft and guns," and Britain's geographical position posed obligations greater than those faced by the President.[56] Stimson thought that this marked "great progress toward agreement," but he questioned MacDonald's contention as to the relative value of the 8-inch-gun, 10,000-ton cruisers. It appeared that the naval experts in the Admiralty were giving the Prime Minister information different from that given the President by the experts in the Navy Department. Under these circumstances, a yardstick, even if agreed to, might be more of a hindrance than a help in bridging the gap that separated the demands of the two nations.[57] At this point Hoover and Stimson had realized the impossibility of reaching an agreement that would permit a reduction in existing American naval strength. But they believed that a settlement based on parity of fleets would remove ill feeling and suspicion between the United States and Great Britain, and create an atmosphere of good will that might promote a desire for reduction at a later date.[58]

Soon afterward, the Secretary of State wired Dawes that it would be unwise for the two nations to attempt to reach agreement on a yardstick at that time. Such technical discussions would become prolonged, other countries would become involved, and the public would learn of the issue. The resultant controversy would be harmful to the projected conference.[59] Dawes reluctantly agreed, and voiced the fear that agreement on the formula might lead to a "yardstick drawn up to fit the settlement . . instead of the settlement fitted to the yardstick."[60] The much heralded yardstick had been reduced to the dimensions of a foot rule,[61] a far cry from the part it was expected to play in reconciling the different cruiser needs of the two nations. The issue was not dead, for Stimson continued to refer to it in computing the relative tonnage of the two fleets,[62] and its discussion was to continue into the subsequent conference. The failure to communicate the formula to MacDonald was a blow to him and to the sympathetic General Dawes, both of whom had considered it indispensable to the success of the negotiations. It was an affront to the British government, and its continued use by the United States, while keeping it a secret from Britain, was scarcely consistent with the assertions of frankness and good will that emanated from Washington.

Stimson, on August 28, proposed that the United States be allowed twenty-three 8-inch-gun cruisers to offset Britain's preponderance in 6-inch-gun ships, and concluded that if the tonnage of the proposed fifty British cruisers as of December 31, 1936, were 330,000 tons "we could go into a conference."[63] MacDonald objected, for on the basis of a 5:5:3.5 ratio Japan would be granted sixteen of the large cruisers, or one more than Britain. If the United States were to accept twenty, Japan would receive fourteen, a figure that the dominions would reject. A total of eighteen was suggested. This would give Japan 12.6, or thirteen, which she might be persuaded to reduce to twelve.[64] The British Prime Minister also asked that the proposed 330,000-ton limit be raised to 339,000 tons, but the 7.5-inch-gun cruisers would be scrapped by 1936, thereby eliminating a consideration of them in the settlement.[65]

In Washington, these changes appeared to be so extensive that the entire situation needed reappraising. The proposal to scrap existing vessels and add new ones threw off the previous American figures that had allowed for age, and the additional 9,000 tons upset parity more than the actual weight involved. Time was needed for the Navy General Board to digest and evaluate this new offer, which made "the difficulties seem greater today than they have for a long time."[66]

The Board presented a detailed analysis of the latest British position. It reiterated the belief that the cruiser category should not be divided, that total tonnage and not numbers of ships should be limited, and that the 8-inch-gun ship was best for the United States. The yardstick should not be used in determining parity, and Britain's bases and merchant marine gave her "an enormous preponderance" in sea power over America. After this forthright assertion of principle, the Board recommended acceptance of the figure of 339,000 tons of cruiser tonnage and of the proposal to scrap the 7.5-inch-gun ships. In order to attain parity, the admirals were willing to accept a total of twenty-one 8-inch-gun, 10,000-ton cruisers in lieu of the twenty-three previously demanded, but they were unwilling to settle for the eighteen that MacDonald proposed. In addition, the existing ten _Omaha_ class 6-inch-gun cruisers, totaling 70,500 tons, would be retained, and eight ships mounting guns of not more than 6 inches and totaling 58,500 tons were requested.[67] Thus the Board wanted identical tonnage with Britain and three more 8-inch-gun ships that the British thought the United States should have.

On the morning of September 11, the American statesmen met with their naval advisers at the White House. Present were Hoover, Stimson, Secretary of the Navy Adams, Undersecretary of State Joseph P. Cotton, and all of the members of the General Board. The purpose of the meeting was to

THE YARDSTICK

arrive at a figure that represented America's concept of parity in cruisers based on the figures submitted by the Prime Minister.[68] A portion of the Board's report was read, and it was revealed that no yardstick had been used in arriving at the figures recommended, as the Board understood that it had been abandoned. The President pointed out that this was not so, for the yardstick was necessary and the Board had agreed to use the one that they had worked out.[69] Hoover then asked for figures based on the yardstick, and was given an amount based on a formula using displacement and age factors, which reduced the number of new 6-inch-gun cruisers from eight to five. The President then asked for a computation that included the gun-caliber factor, which effected a reduction of one-half a ship in the new 6-inch-gun class.[70] After receiving this information, Hoover stated that the yardstick established parity at an American strength of "21 large ships, 10 Omahas and 4 new 6-inch cruisers," and he was assured by several Board members that this was correct.[71] The meeting then broke up at 12:45.

At two o'clock, the General Board convened to discuss the new problem posed by the reintroduction of the yardstick. During the course of this discussion, the Secretary of the Navy entered with a dispatch to Dawes that had been prepared by the State Department. It stated that the General Board, computing parity on the basis of displacement, age, and gun factors, had arrived at an American requirement of twenty-one 10,000-ton, 8-inch-gun ships, ten of the <u>Omaha</u> class, and four new 7,000-ton, 6-inch-gun ships--a total of 315,000 tons. The Secretary stated that he wanted to be sure that this was the Board's opinion as to what constituted parity. He was told that it was not. The members had understood that the President had asked if this was the correct figure in applying the formula, and they had agreed that it was. They had not agreed that this was their conception of parity with Great Britain. The Secretary left, saying that he would have to see the President. Later, Stimson arrived and discussed the matter with members of the Board for approximately an hour, during which time it was decided that five new 6-inch-gun ships would be satisfactory. Undersecretary of State Cotton then arrived with the dispatch that Adams had read to the Board earlier in the day, and it was changed to include the figure arrived at during the afternoon discussion.[72]

The misunderstanding that occurred at the White House was the source of considerable irritation to the President, who, after being advised of the Board's rejection of the original figures in the dispatch, wrote a letter to Stimson giving his version of the conversations and professing his inability to see any cause for confusion.[73] The reason for the misunderstanding is clear, for while Hoover understood that the figures were computed using a formula conceived by the Board, he failed to recall that the Board did not agree

117

with the formula as a means for determining parity. On the other hand, the admirals, probably resentful of the criticsm that had been directed at them by the statesmen in public and in private, made no effort to clarify their position. There was no meeting of minds during these exchanges between the civilians and the naval officers. Their training and point of view often made it difficult, and their responsibilities and prerogatives often made it impossible. This was the only occasion on which Hoover met with the General Board.

The narrowing of the gap that separated the demands of the two nations brought an invitation to the Prime Minister to visit the United States for a meeting with the President.[74] The conversations between MacDonald and Hoover were carried on in an atmosphere of informality and amicability from October 4 to October 8. No agenda had been prepared for the meeting, and each of the participants presumably intended to confine the discussion to a consideration of naval limitation and the improvement of Anglo-American relations.[75] Although no agreement was reached on the cruiser problem, a modified British proposal was considered by the President, who applied both the General Board formula and the one provided him by Admiral Jones in finding MacDonald's offer unsatisfactory.[76] A member of the Prime Minister's delegation made a determined effort to discover the American yardstick by comparing the detailed proposals of the two nations, but he could discern only a comparative tonnage ratio similar to that previously suggested by Stimson and rejected by the Navy Department.[77]

Meanwhile, the Japanese statesmen had welcomed the Gibson proposals, but they were under the impression that the United States would develop the formula. After prodding by America and Britain, efforts were made to work out an equation, but the Tokyo naval experts were skeptical of the yardstick and believed that differences over technical details would make its acceptance unlikely.[78]

Invitations to a formal naval disarmament conference were finally issued by the British government. The American delegates met beforehand in Washington, where Stimson warned that there was little possibility of reaching agreement on a yardstick because it involved so many imponderables that only adroit bargaining could bring about its acceptance.[79] At a pre-conference meeting with MacDonald the Secretary of State discussed all aspects of the disarmament problem but the question of a formula was not raised.[80] The agenda for the conference, as approved by the heads of delegations, failed to mention the matter of an equation.[81] By February 3 Stimson and MacDonald "had come to the conclusion that it was impossible to find a scientific yardstick which would be agreed upon by the Admiralties of both sides,"[82] and the following day Stimson expressed his views on the "futility

THE YARDSTICK

of the so-called 'yardstick'[83] to the American delegates and his two top naval advisers. The issue was now dead, and subsequent agreements were reached by negotiations outside the framework of any formula.

There is little doubt that the removal of the yardstick from the arena of naval limitation was a relief to some statesmen and most naval officers. The former had become skeptical of its effectiveness and the latter had never believed in it. Admiral Jones later told the Senate Committee on Foreign Relations: "I said all the time, sir, that the yardstick was a certain amount of camouflage."[84] The President and his advisers were probably sincere when they suggested a formula to resolve the differing needs of the various nations. As they became aware of the complexities of the problem and the hostility of the experts their enthusiasm diminished, but by that time the differences separating the demands of the major naval powers were so slight that an equation would have been of little assistance. The real significance of the yardstick was psychological. It caught the popular imagination and helped dispel the aura of gloom and disillusionment that had developed from the repeated failures at Geneva, and it put the statesmen and the public in a frame of mind that made possible a treaty in which, for the first time, all of the naval weapons of three great nations were limited and a relative position of naval power was established.

FOOTNOTES

1. General Board No. 420-2 of May 27, 1909, General Board Files (Navy Department, Washington), Letterpress, VI, 65.

2. General Board No. 420-2 of September 28, 1910, ibid, VII, 88.

3. General Board No. 420-2 of December 7, 1912, General Board Files.

4. Charles E. Hughes to Edwin Denby, September 1, 1921, in binder, "The General Board and the Conference on the Limitation of Armament," General Board Files.

5. General Board No. 438, Serial 1088, of September 12, 1921, ibid.

6. Hughes to Rear Admiral William L. Rodgers, February 10, 1922, ibid. The formula to which Hughes referred was the following statement: "In estimating the relative strengths of navies today, the General Board has, as

always, used displacement tonnage of capital ships (battleships and battle cruisers) as the basis of its estimate." General Board No. 438, Serial 1088-A, of September 17, 1921, ibid.

7. Telegram, Hugh R. Wilson to Frank B. Kellogg, February 9, 1929, Papers Relating to the Foreign Relations of the United States, 1929 (3 vols., Washington, 1943-1944), I, 67. Hereinafter cited as Foreign Relations.

8. Kellogg to Gibson, March 23, 1929, ibid., 75-77.

9. Herbert Hoover, The Memoirs of Herbert Hoover: The Cabinet and the Presidency, 1920-1933 (New York, 1952), 340.

10. Telegram, Gibson to Henry L. Stimson, April 16, 1929, Foreign Relations, 1929, I, 86.

11. British Foreign Office Memorandum of June 10, 1929, Documents on British Foreign Policy, 1919-1939, edited by Ernest L. Woodward and Rohan Butler, 2nd Series, Vol. I (London, 1946), 3. Hereinafter cited as British Documents.

12. Foreign Relations, 1929, I, 91-96.

13. Telegram, Gibson to Stimson, April 22, 1929, ibid., 96; British Foreign Office Memorandum of June 10, 1929, British Documents, p. 5.

14. The British Ambassador (Sir Esme Howard) to the Secretary of State, April 23, 1929, Foreign Relations, 1929, I, 96-97.

15. Telegram, Stimson to Gibson, April 24, 1929, Folder, "Instructions, Telegrams, 6th P. C.," General Board Files. The quotations are given in this source at greater length. According to the Literary Digest (New York), May 4, 1929, p. 9, "scores of American papers approve the Hoover-Gibson declaration of policy without reservations."

16. Literary Digest, May 4, 1929, p. 9.

17. Telegram, American Embassy, London, to Secretary of State, April 24, 1929, Folder, "Instructions, Telegrams, 6th P. C..," General Board Files.

18. Review of Reviews (London), May 15, 1929, clipping in Naval Record Group 45, Box No. 488 (National Archives).

THE YARDSTICK

19. Telegram, American Embassy, Paris, to Secretary of State, April 24, 1929, Folder, "Instructions, Telegrams, 6th P. C.," General Board Files.

20. Literary Digest, May 11, 1929, p. 17.

21. Walter H. Mallory (ed.), Political Handbook of the World: Parliaments, Parties, and Press, as of January 1, 1930 (New Haven, 1930), 105-106.

22. Quoted in Tokyo Trans-Pacific, May 21, 1929, p. 9.

23. Telegram, Gibson to Stimson, May 6, 1929, Foreign Relations, 1929, I, 104; British Foreign Office Memorandum of June 10, 1929, British Documents, p. 5.

24. Telegram, Stimson to Gibson, May 6, 1929, Foreign Relations, 1929, I, 101.

25. That the Board was not consulted is affirmed in a Memorandum by Captain Alfred W. Johnson, Director of Naval Intelligence, dated June 8, 1929, General Board File 438-1.

26. Allen W. Dulles, "The Threat of Anglo-American Naval Rivalry," Foreign Affairs (New York), VII (January, 1929), 180.

27. London Times, January 28, 1929, p. 7.

28. Memorandum, British Embassy to Department of State, March 28, 1929, Foreign Relations, 1929, I, 79-80; Memorandum, Department of State to the British Embassy, April 4, 1929, ibid., 81.

29. Memorandum, British Embassy to the Department of State, May 3, 1929, ibid., 99-100.

30. Stimson, Memorandum of a conversation with the British Ambassador (Sir Esme Howard), May 9, 1929, State Department Records, File No. 500.A15A3/1 (National Archives).

31. Telegram, Ray Atherton (Counselor to the Embassy) to Stimson, London, May 27, 1929, Foreign Relations, 1929, I, 109-10; Editorial comment, British Documents, pp. 6-7.

32. William R. Castle, Jr. (Assistant Secretary of State), Memorandum of a conversation with Secretary of the Navy Charles F. Adams, May 4, 1929, Foreign Relations, 1929, I, 100.

33. Stimson, Memorandum of Conversation with President and General Dawes, June 6, 1929, State Department Records, File No. 500.A15A3/21½.

34. London Daily Telegraph, June 14, 1929, p. 1.

35. Foreign Relations, 1929, I, 127-128.

36. Adams to General Board, Serial 1427, May 31, 1929, General Board File 438-1.

37. General Board No. 438-1, Serial 1427, of June 10, 1929, ibid.

38. Hoover to Adams, June 14, 1929, Hilary P. Jones Papers (Manuscript Division, Library of Congress). The President specified that he wanted to avoid "troubling the whole of the Navy until we have something more formal to submit," probably a not too subtle effort to by-pass the General Board.

39. Jones to Adams, June 18, 1929, ibid. This letter is eleven pages in length and contains three pages of charts.

40. Stimson to Adams, July 9, 1929, General Board File 438-1.

41. General Board No. 438-1, Serial 1437, of July 13, 1929; Adams to Stimson, July 15, 1929, ibid.

42. General Board No. 438-1, Serial 1427, of June 10, 1929; General Board No. 438-1, Serial 1430, of August 1, 1929, General Board File 438-1. Also, Jones to Adams, June 18, 1929, Jones Papers. For a comparison of the respective merits of the formulas submitted by the General Board and Admiral Jones, see Department of State Memorandum, Division of Western European Affairs, October 29, 1929, State Department Records, File No. 500.A15A3/358.

43. Telegram, Arthur Henderson (British Foreign Secretary) to Howard, June 24, 1929, British Documents, p. 9.

44. Telegram, Dawes to Stimson, June 28, 1929, Foreign Relations, 1929, I, 139.

45. Telegram, Stimson to Dawes, July 11, 1929, ibid., 141-43.

46. General Board File 438-1.

47. Ramsay MacDonald to Dawes, July 18, 1929, Foreign Relations, 1929, I, 148-49.

48. Telegram, Stimson to Dawes, July 21, 1929, ibid., 149-52.

49. MacDonald to Dawes, July 25, 1929, ibid., 160-61.

50. Telegram, Dawes to Stimson, July 23, 1929, ibid., 157. Drew Pearson and Constantine Brown, in The American Diplomatic Game (New York, 1935), p. 84, claim that Alexander was "won over" by the naval officers.

51. Telegram, Dawes and Gibson to Stimson, July 29, 1929, Foreign Relations, 1929, I, 165.

52. Memorandum, Division of Western European Affairs, Department of State, July 30, 1929, State Department Records, File No. 250 Proposals/1, Record Group 43 (National Archives).

53. Telegram, Joseph P. Cotton (Undersecretary of State) to Dawes, August 5, 1929, Foreign Relations, 1929, I, 181-82.

54. Dawes claims that MacDonald began to take the initiative away from the Admiralty, thereby making progress again possible. Charles G. Dawes, Journal as Ambassador to Great Britain (New York, 1939), 49.

55. Telegram, Dawes and Gibson to Stimson, August 6, 1929, Foreign Relations, 1929, I, 183-85.

56. MacDonald to Dawes, August 8, 1929, ibid., 186-88. Alexander said the reduction to fifty cruisers was agreed to by the Admiralty because of the Kellogg-Briand Pact and "improved world relationships." 238 House of Commons Debates, 5th Sess., p. 2196. MacDonald had evolved a formula of his own in which only the size of the vessel was considered, and one large ship was rated the equivalent of 2½ to 4½ small ones. This was rejected by the American negotiators. Hugh Gibson, Memorandum of Conversation, August 6, 1929, Charles G. Dawes Papers (Northwestern University Library, Evanston).

57. Telegram, Stimson to Dawes, August 15, 1929, Foreign Relations, 1929, I, 190-95.

58. See record of conversation between Stimson and the British Ambassador, in telegram, Howard to Henderson, August 21, 1929, British Documents, pp. 46-47.

59. Telegram, Stimson to Dawes, August 28, 1929, Foreign Relations, 1929, I, 209-10.

60. Telegram, Dawes to Stimson, August 30, 1929, ibid., 211-13.

61. R. L. Craigie (Head of the American Department of the British Foreign Office), Memorandum of a conversation with F. Lammont Belin (First Secretary of the American Embassy), August 26, 1929, British Documents, p. 53.

62. Telegram, Stimson to Dawes, August 28, 1929, Foreign Relations, 1929, I, 210.

63. Telegram, Stimson to Dawes, August 28, 1929, ibid., 203-207.

64. MacDonald to Dawes, August 30, 1929, ibid., 213-14.

65. MacDonald to Dawes, August 31, 1929, ibid., 214-16.

66. Telegram, Stimson to Dawes, September 3, 1929, ibid., 217-18.

67. General Board No. 438-1, Serial 144-A, of September 11, 1929, General Board File 438-1.

68. Note attached to ibid.

69. Hoover to Stimson, September 11, 1929, State Department Records, File No. 500.A15A3/329.

70. Memorandum, dated September 11, 1929, General Board File 438-1. This account of the meeting, unsigned, was probably prepared by Captain Robert L. Ghormley, who was secretary of the General Board.

71. According to the President, he repeated this question three times, and received confirmation from three admirals. Hoover to Stimson, September 11, 1929, State Department Records, File No. 500.A15A3/329.

72. Ghormley Memorandum, September 11, 1929, General Board File 438-1.

73. Hoover to Stimson, September 11, 1929, State Department Records, File No. 500.A15A3/329. Dawes gives an account of Stimson's version of the incident in his Journal as Ambassador to Great Britain, pp. 95-96, and cites it as evidence of Hoover's "constant struggle to get fair play from the Naval Board."

74. Telegram, Stimson to Dawes, September 11, 1929, Foreign Relations, 1929, I, 223.

75. MacDonald, Memorandum concerning conversations with Hoover, British Documents, p. 113; Hoover, The Cabinet

and the Presidency, 342. Official notes and documents on the meeting are contained in Foreign Relations, 1929, III, 3-33; and British Documents, pp. 106-26. The latter are often more revealing as to motives.

76. Memorandum by President Hoover, October 6, 1929, Foreign Relations, 1929, III, 25-26. Prior to the meeting Hoover had suggested that parity be based on 10,000-ton cruisers with 8-inch guns, and that 20 per cent additional tonnage be allowed for ships under 7,000 tons with 6-inch guns, as well as for ships depreciating from age. Lawrence Richey (Secretary to the President) to Stimson, October 1, 1929, No. 1F-600, Henry L. Stimson Papers (Yale University Library, New Haven).

77. Craigie's Memorandum of October 6, 1929, ibid., 27-29.

78. Stimson to Edwin L. Neville (Charge in Tokyo), June 24, 1929, Foreign Relations, 1929, I, 131-32; telegram, Sir J. Tilley (Tokyo) to Arthur Henderson, July 12, 1929, British Documents, p. 21; telegram, Henderson to Tilley, July 16, 1929, ibid., p. 24; telegram, Tilley to Henderson, August 12, 1929, ibid., pp. 38-39.

79. Memorandum of the First Meeting of Delegates to the London Naval Conference, December 11, 1929, State Department Records, File No. 110.001/3, Record Group 43.

80. Stimson, Memorandum of a Conference with the Prime Minister of Great Britain, January 17, 1930, State Department Records, File No. 110.001/19, Record Group 43.

81. "Agenda as Finally Approved by the Heads of Delegations, January 28, 1930," Proceedings of the London Naval Conference of 1930 (Washington, 1930), 59-60.

82. Memorandum, Department of State, Division of Western European Affairs, May 28, 1930, State Department Records, File No. 500.A15A3/910½.

83. "Resume of Daily Occurrences," prepared by Admiral Hilary P. Jones, copy in Commander Harold C. Train, "Daily Log," II, under date of February 4, 1930, General Board Files.

84. Senate Foreign Relations Committee, 71 Cong., 2 Sess., Hearings on Treaty on the Limitation of Armaments (Washington, 1930), 128.

THE INFLUENCE OF DISARMAMENT UPON TECHNOLOGY:
Commentary

Chapter 11

Professor Hughes has presented an interesting account of, as he puts it, "research and development in a major and dynamic field of technology" in Germany "between 1918 and 1930." The industrial demands of modern warfare had stimulated German scientists and technicians to greater efforts, and the example chosen demonstrates one way in which war can accelerate technological change. Professor Hughes also points out that in this period "Germany was denied an armament program and therefore research and development that had expanded under wartime conditions needed to find [an] outlet under conditions of disarmament." Though it is likely that a normal peacetime reduction in military effort would have required the same type of conversion, the sublimation may not have been so drastic. Yet the transition necessary in this industry to adapt it to peaceful use involved only a few technological problems that scarcely absorbed the creative talents of the engineers and scientists, which were diverted to developing the large-scale production of two synthetics, namely, wood alcohol and gasoline.

The impact of disarmament on a nation's economy has been the subject of much controversy, and after World War I authorities differed perhaps as much as they do today. In regard to Germany, some felt that disarmament might prove to be a blessing in disguise, for hundreds of thousands of young men whose lives would be "wasted" in the service or in the "unproductive" task of turning out armaments could be available for "productive" work. It seems that Professor Hughes is suggesting that the industrial advances he speaks of would not have taken place if the industry had remained geared to armament production. In other words, that this "technological creativity" was due to the restrictions imposed on the manufacture of war material by the Treaty of Versailles. One is appalled at the thought of how this creativity might have been expressed under other circumstances, conceivably in the development of a propellant that would have given Germany an earlier rocket capability and altered the course of the second world war.

As for "the challenge of developing a synthetic auto fuel for a peacetime German market," Professor Hughes has not indicated any correlation between this effort and German rearmament. Perhaps there were military connotations in two respects. First, as an attempt to promote a self-sufficient economy in light of the successful allied blockade in the recent war. Second, as an effort to provide fuel for the machines that would be the backbone of mechanized warfare. The restrictions imposed on the size of the German army placed a premium on the tactical use of machines rather than masses of soldiers, and the theories of armored land combat coincided with the imperatives of disarmament. The ingenius methods employed by both the German military and civil authorities to evade the strictures imposed by the allied victors are well known. But the renamed "General Staff" established an "Economic Staff" which organized a number of "black" production centers for war materials inside Germany, encouraged the creation of subsidiaries abroad to manufacture weapons, and helped establish plants in Russia to manufacture aircraft parts, poison gases, shells, and the like. Money from the military budget was used to subsidize these industries and the German army was promised a share of the products. The Reichswehr also maintained study and research projects in all fields, including those pertaining to branches of the service which had been prohibited by the Treaty. The main center of military technical and experimental research within Germany was the Charlottenburg Politechnic School (<u>Technische</u> <u>Hochschule</u>). All of this activity took place under the Weimar Republic, which thereby nurtured the technological creativity that was to find it greatest opportunities under the Nazi regime.

Turning to Professor Scamehorn's paper, I must confess that I am confused. He does not deal with disarmament in the conventional sense, that is, the limitation, reduction, or elimination of military forces by treaty. Apparently he uses the term to mean an American reduction in expenditures for military aircraft from that which had prevailed in the first world war. Also, he does not deal with the specific technology of aircraft design and performance but with the factors which impeded the development and production of military aircraft. These factors appear to be the Air Service's stress on research and development under military supervision, the emphasis on experimentation and improvement of equipment at the expense of production, and the refusal of Congress to provide sufficient funds. The <u>bete</u> <u>noire</u> in this case is not quite clear. But evidently the alleged Yankee ingenuity that flourished in a free enterprise atmosphere was not given carte blanche, in part because it was denied government subsidies without strings.

One of the main problems during this period was that of deciding which tasks the planes should perform. The tactical and strategic function of aircraft had not been determined, nor was there agreement on their effectiveness in land or sea warfare. Until these matters had been decided it was virtually impossible to know the types or numbers of planes that should be ordered. Professor Scamehorn quotes from the report of the American Aviation Mission on this question. But, as he says, it was "written during the convulsion of demobilization." Subsequently he cites the recommendations of the Morrow Board, although the portions quoted have nothing to do with the basic problem. Actually, by 1934 some 14 principal boards and committees had made studies devoted to "the efficient development of aviation as an element of national defense." And after December 7, 1941, General Billy Mitchell became the consensus martyr of air power. So, as I implied earlier, an investigation of the correlation between mission and performance in terms of technology would be fruitful. The factors mentioned in this paper seem primarily political and economic.

As a former naval person I found Professor Woodbury's paper of consuming interest. His apology for the "lack of the customary documentation" did not deter me, for I, too, possess "first-hand knowledge," having served on both pre-disarmament treaty and post-treaty cruisers. As a personal aside, I might add that the latter was a hell of a lot better in every respect, although the improvement could be attributed to factors other than the strictures of the treaty.

Professor Woodbury addresses himself directly to the subject of his paper, and claims that the Naval Limitation Treaty of Washington was one of the "political and other factors," presumably the former, which forced the naval designer to "accept solutions which were from the naval standpoint unsound or even disastrous." To support his thesis he cites the case of the U.S.S. Quincy, one of a number of so-called "treaty cruisers" built under the restrictions imposed at Washington. It should be noted that the London Naval Treaty of 1930 did not alter the armament or the displacement of these vessels, nor was "each of the signatory navies . . . free to divide its total allowed cruiser tonnage into as many ships of the different classes as it desired." Each contracting party was allocated so much tonnage in the 8-inch gun category and in the 6-inch gun category. In fact, the relative fighting quality of ships mounting the different caliber of guns was a matter of considerable controversy among American naval experts as well as those of other nations, and efforts to arrive at a formula or equation to measure their value were unsuccessful. Be that as it may, the validity of Professor Woodbury's argument rests on his contention that the navy was forced by disarmament treaty to build ships that it would not otherwise have built. In my opinion, the record does not support this conclusion.

When the first world war ended the United States was far behind the other great naval powers in cruiser construction. Great Britain had the HAWKINS class, ships mounting 7.5 guns, displacing about 8,000 tons, and capable of 30 knots. Japan was expanding her force of 6,000 ton, 5.5 inch gun cruisers which speeds in excess of 30 knots. The United States, in 1916, had laid down ten ships of about 7,000 tons, with eight 6-inch guns and a hopeful speed of more than 30 knots. But when the war ended the United States possessed not a single cruiser that could exceed 24 knots. In December of 1919 the Navy General Board urged immediate authorization of "increased numbers and improved types" of cruisers. The Board stated that it did "not believe that in our Navy we should immitate the light cruiser abroad but should proceed at once to vessels of about ten thousand (10,000) tons displacement, high speed and long cruising endurance in all weathers, together with heavy armament." In March 1920 it was publicly recommended that twenty ships mounting 8-inch guns and displacing 10,000 tons be authorized, and later that year it was announced that the Navy Department desired to lay down thirty ships of this type within the next three years. Consequently, the naval limitation treaty concluded at the Washington Conference of 1921-22 was not responsible for the American adoption of the 10,000 ton, 8-inch gun cruiser. In fact, there is evidence to suggest that the reverse is true, namely, that Secretary of State Hughes suggested this ceiling when his efforts to place limits on all naval construction failed, and he followed the advice of the navy planners in separating the capital ship and cruiser categories. This cutoff was designed to conform with what the American naval leaders had wanted and did want.

It is certainly possible that cruisers designed some years later might have had a heavier displacement if the treaty hadn't been in effect, because of experience and technological change. But it is interesting to note that as late as 1939, when restrictions had been removed, the General Board recommended that 8-inch gun ships displace 12,000 tons, not to provide more armor but to increase the rate of fire, add anti-aircraft weapons, and give more speed. In 1942 the General Board recommended a displacement of 13,600 tons for 8-inch gun cruisers and 11,000 tons for 6-inch gun cruisers, again for pretty much the same reasons. As of this date the Board wanted a new 8-inch gun, rapid firing, mounted on the heavy cruisers, and this accounted for much of the added weight. So it appears that the treaty limitations had no significant effect on the design or the capabilities of these cruisers.

As for armor, it is my understanding that the Japanese emphasized speed and sacrificed even more protection than did the United States. The Japanese heavy cruiser ATAGO, completed in 1930, designed for a top speed of over 34 knots, had turret face-plates less than 2 inches thick, compared with 5 or 6 inches on the turret faces of America's PENSACOLA class. The performance at the "battle" of Savo Island is, in my opinion, no sound basis for concluding that the Japanese cruisers could "take it" better than the American, for the number and location of hits must be considered. In this department there was a woeful disparity, and without going into the details of the engagement there is little doubt that the Japanese came out ahead in every respect.

Regarding the removal of the torpedo tubes from these cruisers, it was ordered by the General Board not for the purpose of saving weight but to provide additional platforms for anti-aircraft guns. Many authorities have concluded that this was a wise exchange, for while Japanese cruisers were more effective in close surface naval engagements because of the added fire power they were extremely vulnerable to air attack.

The seaworthy qualities of these vessels have been questioned, by Professor Woodbury and others. Certainly they rolled more than the earlier OMAHA class but they pitched less, although I might add that firing from a rolling platform is much better than firing from a platform that pitches. Also, the stern post cracked on the shakedown cruise, but these ships represented a new type and this flaw had nothing to do with tonnage limitations. The fracture of deck plating suffered by the QUINCY in a heavy gale six years after commissioning did not occur in her sister ships, and they experienced some pretty rough weather in their careers. One example may suffice for a generalization in certain contexts but I would hesitate to accept it here.

In sum, I have many reservations about the desirability of the naval limitation treaties, and there is some truth in Elihu Root's statement that the outcome of the Washington Conference was "the complete negation of naval policy." But this was not so in regard to the displacement and armament of cruisers.

NAVAL POLICY BETWEEN WORLD WARS:
A Review Article

Chapter 12

NAVAL POLICY BETWEEN THE WARS: THE PERIOD OF
ANGLO-AMERICAN ANTAGONISM, 1919-1929

By Stephen Roskill. London: Collins, 1968. Illus. 639 pp.

The first of a projected two-volume study of naval policy during the interlude separating the world wars, this work by the eminent British naval historian is based on an intensive perusal of British sources, both official and private, previously closed to researchers. In addition, the author consulted American materials in the National Archives and the Office of Naval History in order to provide an authoritative foundation for his inquiry into the reasons why the Western democracies failed in their efforts to deter totalitarian aggression by the application of seapower without recourse to hostilities.

Beginning with an introduction covering the entire period, the author declares that this volume is devoted to the naval aspects of Anglo-American rivalry, "the fundamental causes of which lay in the challenge, by the United States, to the long-standing maritime and mercantile predominance enjoyed by Britain." Initially, at least, "the broad motives of the United States were as strongly mercantilist as those of the British authorities," in spite of the fact that "overseas trade played a comparatively small part in the maintenance of American prosperity throughout our [sic] period." The American General Board, he finds, was "as strongly navalist as the British Sea Lords . . . markedly anti-British," and dedicated to the primacy of the battleship, although more perceptive than its British counterpart in regard to the role of aircraft. The naval aspects of the Versailles Treaty "produced the first serious clash between Britain and the United States in the field of naval policy," and by 1921, "the threat of an Anglo-American naval building race had become serious, and the policy of the British government was to strive for an agreement on the relative strength of the two nations' navies." In the controversy over a Fleet Air Arm, "Trenchard and his disciples were entirely wrong to cling to the concept of unified control over aviation."

Brief but incisive portrayals of American and British naval and civilian figures enliven the narrative. Secretary of the Navy Josephus Daniels and Chief of Naval Operations Rear Admiral W.S. Benson receives scathing treatment, while

Admiral Hilary P. Jones, "without doubt the most difficult character that the British civil and naval authorities had to contend with since Benson's day," is held largely responsible for the breakdown of the Geneva Naval Conference of 1927. Rear Admiral William A. Moffett is given much credit for advances made in American naval aviation, and Secretary Charles F. Adams is commended for contributing "to the softening of Anglo-American antagonism in the late 1920s." Admiral William V. Pratt was regarded in British circles "as one of the most intelligent and attractive American sailors of the period between the wars, perhaps because he was singularly free of the rigidly dogmatic outlook of so many of his colleagues." One candidate for the post of First Sea Lord failed to be selected in part because of his addiction to polo and his superior's belief that he would be "insufficiently amenable to political requirements." In general, British figures are assessed in more moderate language, although the author does not hesitate to judge their performance. The leaders of both nations are found wanting with the conclusion that "the London Treaties of 1930 and 1936, like the Anglo-German naval agreement and the American Neutrality Acts, operated strongly in favour of the dictatorships." The extent to which the responsibility for these events can be ascribed to the personality, ability, or point of view of the naval and civilian leaders, is questionable. Functioning within the framework of domestic and international realities, these people helped fashion a seapower relationship designed to maintain an acceptable peace.

The main narrative opens with an account of naval affairs during World War I Armistice negotiations and the making of the treaty of Versailles. The author states that:

> It was obvious to the American naval planners that if the war-time alliance between Britain, France and Italy were continued, and the Anglo-Japanese alliance of 1902 was extended when it fell due for renewal in 1921, the United States might be faced by an overwhelming preponderance at sea.
>
> The British authorities stated that whilst regarding war with the United States as 'unthinkable,' could see no reason why that country should need a large navy, and was determined to oppose the emasculation of the means whereby the British Empire had come into being and its wealth had been accumulated.

Admiral Benson protested armistice terms providing for the surrender of German battleships rather than their internment, ostensibly on the grounds that it would precipitate a German rejection of the armistice. But the author feels that the Benson's real motive was to prevent these ships from being added to the British fleet. With regard to the mandates granted Japan, "the truth was that the Wilson administration had virtually surrendered to Japan the dominance of the central and western Pacific." This opinion is difficult to reconcile with the fact that "in February 1917 Britain had secretly agreed to Japan acquiring those islands as the price of helping in the campaign against enemy submarines in the Mediterranean." One might more easily conclude that Wilson, by insisting on the mandate status, had contributed somewhat to a curtailment of Japanese strength in the Pacific by invalidating the British offer. And it should be noted that the General Board had recommended internationalization of these former German possessions in order to prevent their being used as bases.

The President's grand design for collective security had a direct bearing on postwar naval strength, for:

> Lloyd George made it plain that British support for the League Convenant was conditional on a naval agreement with the United States, [and] the Americans were totally unwilling to accept any agreement which left their navy inferior to that of Britain.

Wilson, in turn, used the threat of impending American naval superiority to induce the British to support the Convenant. Apparently, both statesmen felt that their bargaining by the application of force without violence had been successful, and Wilson used the influence of both existing and projected naval power. But, in presenting the American case for parity in naval strength, the author could have been more understanding, if not more charitable, by considering other aspects of the postwar international situation.

With the defeat of England's great commercial rival, Germany, it seemed likely that the most formidable successor would be the United States, and such rivalry often had led to war. The naval authorities of both nations had to "think about the unthinkable," for their primary obligation was to be prepared to win any war in which the nation might become engaged. Moreover, the American Navy was responsible for the protection of the Western Hemisphere under the dictum of the Monroe Doctrine, and, after the German menace had been eliminated, the only nation capable of endangering this basic principle of American defense was Great Britain. The enforcement of the Convenant posed another challenge, for American naval strength equal to that of any other power was deemed necessary in order to have a comparable voice in League councils. After membership in the League was rejected, it became even more imperative that Britain not be granted naval supremacy. The only means by which the United States could resist the imposition of League dictates, especially those pertaining to Latin America, was by possessing a navy capable of standing up to that of Great Britain. Yet, in spite of American efforts, "British supremacy at sea was not seriously impaired by the agreements of 1919." Although another two years were to pass before the struggle for an equilibrium of naval power was to resume at Washington, in post-war projections, "determination to achieve parity with the British Navy was the cardinal point in American naval planning," while "rivalry with the United States Navy [was] an important element in the formulation of Admiralty policy."

A confused situation also prevailed in the Near East in 1919-23, where the scene is set against the ambitions of the major powers, the complications of secret wartime accords, and the anomalous position of the United States, which had not been at war with Turkey but was anxious to promote commercial interests in the area. Rear Admiral Mark L. Bristol, who commanded the American naval detachment and became a High Commissioner, is favorably depicted for opposing American participation in the intricate political and military maneuvering. Repeated warnings from the military authorities of the dire consequences of their activities were ignored by the Supreme War Council and the Allied governments, and, as in the Russian venture, a diversity of aims impeded the operation. The Greek Anatolian invasion is characterized as "surely one of the most ill-conceived adventures of all times."

During the Near East involvement, the British government was more belligerent than the generals and admirals, which, the author contends, "should help to dispel the view, of which Lloyd George himself was the chief protagonist, that in issues of war, or when peace hangs in the balance, the judgment of politicians is necessarily sounder than that of military and naval men." Collaboration between the British Army and Navy was "quite admirable," although the lesson of inter-service co-operation seemed to have been forgotten in the subsequent decades.

Reverting to the theme of naval rivalry, the author points out that the cabinet gave the Admiralty a budget figure within which it was expected to operate, and Winston Churchill, as Chancellor of the Exchequer, is revealed as one of the most vigorous opponents of requests for additional funds to develop the Singapore base or build ships. His zeal for economy even derided the notion of Japan as a probable enemy. Not until the 1930s was the Admiralty able to institute a regular replacement schedule to retire older vessels and retain the qualified people necessary to design and build modern warships. The General Board's proposals of 1919 are held to have been contrary to the understanding at the Versailles Conference, and, though Congress refused to approve the program, it did create dismay and bitterness in the Admiralty. The First Lord reported in 1919 that his department felt "the only Navy for which we need have regard . . . is the Navy of the United States," for France, Italy, and Japan were looked upon as British allies. The Board of the Admiralty estimated that a continuation of the American 1916 program with no additional building by Britain would result in the United States becoming the primary naval power, and the Board recommended efforts to reach an agreement on the basis of parity or a revival of British construction. News of the projections in Britain and the United States helped prompt the Japanese government to embark on a similar expansion and "thus did the closing months of 1920 strongly indicate a trend towards a new naval building race." An early clue to the Admiralty's concept of parity is revealed by its definition of the "One Power Standard," i.e., that Britain should possess a navy equal to that of the strongest other fleet. These dimensions of protection were to haunt efforts to arrive at an understanding of equality in warships between the two major naval powers for the next decade.

A thorough account of the naval aviation controversy in Great Britain finds the debate largely concerned with the issue of the battleship versus the airplane and the relative merits of a separate, independent air force. Views of the leading protagonists are presented, and the author is critical of the British failure to recognize the role of aircraft in fleet operations, as he is of the denial of a naval air arm. The major stumbling block proved to be General Hugh Trenchard's single-minded adherence to the doctrine of the strategic air offensive and the government's espousal of his theories. Since the American experience was not quite so drastic:

> It thus came to pass that whereas the disputes and disagreements of the early 1920s over naval aviation had the result of projecting the thinking of many American naval men into the future, the British Admiralty's thinking was directed more to the causes of the Royal Navy's lack of success at Jutland than to the question whether such lessons had any validity for the future.

With so much of its effort devoted to the struggle to regain control over its aviation branch, the Admiralty neglected a thorough study of the tactical and strategic application of air power. The Japanese, with the advice and technical assistance of the British, began to develop their own naval air capability and soon surpassed that of their mentor.

The strategic imperatives of Empire defense are dealt with at some length, with careful attention being given the considerable logistic problems. Official reports reiterated the need to develop a major base at Singapore, which the Admiralty regarded as "the western gateway to the Pacific."

A continuance of the Anglo-Japanese Alliance was thought by the Admiralty to be "neither necessary nor desirable," on what the author calls the "somewhat illogical" basis of not having the force "to support a strong policy involving possible coercion of Japan." But plans for a conflict with Japan were formulated by the naval strategists consistent with Empire interests in the Far East.

In preparing for the Washington Conference of 1921-22, the British delegation was advised to appeal for a numerical limitation of capital ships, avoid total tonnage restrictions, and strive to abolish submarines. The specific proposals of Secretary of State Charles Evans Hughes for a drastic reduction in ship strength brought vigorous protests from the Admiralty, which felt that America would be permitted to retain more modern vessels than Britain and that the limiting of cruisers, destroyers, and submarines would impair Britain's ability to meet her world-wide defense commitments. Ships in these latter categories, which came to be known as "auxiliary vessels," were not included in the naval limitation treaty, and the Admiralty views also prevailed on aircraft carrier restrictions and the upper limit of 10,000 tons on cruisers. The British naval experts were overruled by the total tonnage agreement on capital ships, and, the author claims, neither they nor their American counterparts were consulted regarding the non-fortification of specified possessions in the western Pacific. The Washington treaties temporarily checked Anglo-American rivalry, stopped battleship construction in the two countries, and left everyone free to build cruisers, destroyers, and submarines. Both the British Naval Staff and the American General Board warned that the treaties had decreased the amount of influence that either nation could exert in the Far East, where Japan was the most probable antagonist.

Naval developments in the period following the Washington Conference found the British authorities endeavoring to devise and implement a defense policy in the framework of the new agreements, budgetary exigencies, Dominion resistance to centralization of control, the peril of French air power, the intransigence of Trenchard, and the significance of a base at Singapore, where the possibilities of a successful land assault were discounted. They tended to ignore submarine lessons of World War I by stressing the need for cruisers to protect merchant ships from surface raiders. Moreover:

> . . . whereas the Admiralty consistently took the strength of the Japanese Navy as the standard for assessing British needs, the General Board measured those of the US [sic] Navy solely in relation to British naval strength. This of course accorded with the ratios agreed at Washington and with the navy 'second to none' dogma; but it seems fair to remark that in the General Board's eyes

parity with Britain outweighed the strategic considerations involved in a possible conflict in the Pacific.

Here, it seems, the author is not being "fair" on several counts in his appraisal of the American position.

The General Board papers, the nature of the games at the Naval War College, and expressions of naval opinion clearly reveal that Japan was regarded as the most probable enemy and that planning was primarily concerned with such an eventuality. The "dogma" to which the author refers was more effective in gaining support for a larger navy than an appeal based on a hypothetical war with a nation that posed no significant threat to what many considered America's fundamental interests. Then, too, building against Britain actually constituted building against Japan, for the former was the greater naval power. The selection of a <u>bete noire</u> for practical reasons also clarifies the activities of the Navy League, which the author finds perplexing. The persistent British refusal to accept a numerical parity with the United States is more open to question, and it can be explained primarily on the grounds of pride, far-flung responsibilities, and the possibility, if not the likelihood, of war between the two nations.

The reappearance of a naval race in the categories not covered by the Washington treaty, especially cruisers, brought about a conference of the three major naval powers at Geneva in 1927. British proposals included a demand for 70 cruisers, 25 for fleet operations and 45 for sea lane patrol, with the United States and Japan allotted 47 and 21, respectively. Anxious to curb the American predilection for 10,000-ton, 8-inch gun vessels (for reasons of economy, according to the author), the British delegation advocated two classes of cruisers, and American agreement to construct smaller, 6-inch gun vessels, and a total tonnage greatly in excess of what the American delegation was prepared to accept. Efforts at a compromise were unavailing, and the author, after assessing various explanations for the conference's failure, concludes that:

> . . . although it would certainly be unfair to place the whole responsibility for the debacle of 1927 on that body [the General Board], it does seem fair to attribute it mainly to American mishandling of the initiative and excessive rigidity in negotiation.

Here, again, the reviewer must take issue with the author's use of the word, "fair," and with his conclusion as well. Essentially, the British wanted a great many more cruisers than they possessed; they refused to allow the United States to build the kind of vessels it wanted, and they insisted that their "special circumstances" warranted special concessions. The absence of naval bases in the western Pacific explained the requirement for larger vessels with a greater cruising radius, and the British tacitly admitted the superiority of 8-inch guns by attempting to persuade the Americans to adopt 6-inch weapons. No doubt the need for cruisers by the two services differed, but it does seem unfair to censure one nation for not submitting to the program of another. Nor does the author indicate that even if Great Britain and the United States had been able to reconcile their differences, the conference probably would have foundered over the Japanese demands, despite the fact that "the Japanese delegates strove hard to produce an acceptable compromise." Unlike the situation that prevailed six years earlier, the Americans were not in a position to apply the threat of naval dominance to coerce the other nations into accepting their terms. While many factors influenced the outcome at Geneva, the strategic doctrines that determined the minimum security requirements of each nation made agreement impossible; there was certainly enough blame to go around.

The author again reveals a degree of myopia when he asserts:

> In retrospect Anglo-French compromise [of 1928] certainly seems entirely reasonable; but the big navy propagandists in the United States chose to use it as a means of spreading mistrust of Britain and France--especially the former.

Regardless of an apparent inconsistency in denouncing the "big navy" propagandists in one portion of the narrative and, in another, criticizing the United States for not building more effectively against Japan, it is difficult to see how an agreement to place limitations on the type of cruisers desired by the United States, while exempting the type desired by Britain and France, could be considered "entirely reasonable." The fact that the compromise was made without consulting the United States, and that it involved a British concession on the exclusion of French Army reserves in land disarmament discussions, casts further doubt on the propriety of the accord and makes one wonder why the author should be so appalled by the vigorous American reaction.

Nonetheless, it would be a mistake to judge this impressive, heavily documented work on the basis of what this reviewer considers an occasional oversimplification or distortion of the American position during naval limitation negotiations. This shortcoming may be partially explained by the allocation of the major portion of the narrative to British naval activities, considerably less to American and virtually none to those of other nations, including the

Japanese. Also, the author could be faulted for excessive detail in treating controversies between the Admiralty and other branches of the government or for dealing insufficiently with the international and domestic circumstances which influenced the formulation of naval policy and within which it was developed. But in spite of what some might view as a narrow approach to the subject, the author is writing his own book and it should be evaluated within the context of his purpose. In stirring up some old controversies, providing new insights, and illuminating facets of civil-military relations, Captain Roskill has produced another outstanding contribution to naval history.

U.S. AMPHIBIOUS DOCTRINE AND NAVAL POLICY IN THE 20th CENTURY

Chapter 13

The Oxford English Dictionary gives as the first definition of amphibious, "Living both on land and in water." It further cites the use of the term in a book published in 1654, in which the author said: "The . . . admiral . . . being scanted in Mariners . . . was enforced to take in two thousand two hundred land men, who should be amphibious, serving partly for seamen, and partly for land soldiers." The American College Dictionary says that "amphi-" means "on both sides," and comes from the Greek "amphibios" meaning "living a double life." Whether this applies more aptly to sailors or marines is debatable, but the term "triphibious" might be more appropriate in light of the added dimension of air activity, and Alfred Vagts has used "tri-elemental." Yet here we are faced with, as they say, a situation, not a theory, and the three services have agreed on a definition as stated in the publication, <u>Doctrine for Amphibious Operations</u>, dated 1 August 1967, namely, "An amphibious operation is an attack launched from the sea by naval and landing forces embarked in ships or craft involving a landing on a hostile shore. It normally requires extensive air participation and is characterized by closely integrated efforts of forces trained, organized, and equipped for different combatant functions." Still, in America it was relatively late in the game before "amphibious" succeeded "expeditionary," "landing party or force," "combined operations," and "advance base," although the English term, "conjunct," meaning joint fleet and army activity seems never to have come into common usage in this country.

When the problem of sea-shore operations became increasingly important to American naval planners they were in the midst of grappling with the technological innovations that promised to revolutionize warfare. Thus the evolution of amphibious doctrine must be analyzed and described within the context in which it emerged. Amphibious doctrine appeared in response to a need, and this need was determined by the tasks assigned the Navy. These tasks were specified in the war plans formulated by the Departments of War and

---

Reprinted from MILITARY AFFAIRS, October, 1974, pp. 97-103, with permission. Copyright 1974 by the American Military Institute. No additional copies may be made without the express permission of the author and of the editor of MILITARY AFFAIRS.

Navy and coordinated after 1903 by the Joint Army-Navy Board, to be approved by the service secretaries and occasionally by the President. The war plans, in turn, were developed in response to the "probable enemy" concept, which was based on an assessment of those nations most likely to pursue a course of action that would conflict with fundamental interests of the United States. Amphibious doctrine therefore evolved, not in a vacuum, but within the broad framework of national policy, international rivalry, and accelerated technological change.

The final decades of the nineteenth century found the Navy in the birth pangs of modernization, not only in ships and administrative organization but in tactical and strategic doctrine and the clarification of its mission. Mahan provided a theory, what Elting E. Morison has called "a great, ruling, general idea," within which the "Modern American Navy" could develop in response to those forces--domestic, international, and technological--that were altering the course of history. And this New Navy developed according to doctrines hammered out in the forge of controversy, doctrines which themselves became a source for new disputes. The focal point of these doctrinal disputes beginning in 1900 was the Navy General Board, established by Secretary of the Navy John D. Long as a compromise with those who agitated for the creation of a Navy "general staff" to centralize professional control of the department and reduce the autonomy of the bureaus. Exercising no jurisdiction and strictly advisory to the Secretary, the General Board served for fifty years as the "thinking organ" for the Navy and was presided over by Admiral George Dewey from 1900 to 1917. Writing in U.S. Naval Institute Proceedings in 1928, Colonel J. C. Breckinridge, USMC, then Commanding Marine Corps Schools, Quantico, said his research "convinced me that that body [the General Board] alone is responsible for the concentration of men and material into homogeneous units of organization, which, in ordinary conditions, are ready to move instantly as units, either on routine expeditionary duty, or to establish an overseas base for the fleet."

Colonel Breckinridge's findings and the convenient chronological coincidence of the Board's creation with the beginning of the twentieth century--the focus of this study --make it appropriate to start with that august body. General Order No. 544 dated 13 March 1900 established the Board, indicated its composition, and specified its duties. "The purpose of the Department in establishing this Board," the order announced, was "to insure efficient preparation of the fleet in case of war and for the naval defense of the coast." Outlining duties in more detail, the order included the preparation of plans for the defense of the nation and its dependencies, for any theater in which war might occur, and a consideration of the selection and preparation of

AMPHIBIOUS DOCTRINE

naval bases. In accordance with this directive, one of the first orders of business for the Board was to provide for the new commitments assumed by the nation. Traditionally the Navy had been expected to defend the American coastline and the Monroe Doctrine, and support commercial interests abroad. Within two short years the Navy assumed responsibility for the protection of an island empire in the Pacific and the possible enforcement of a vague principle known as the "Open Door" in China. The vital interests of the United States were no longer overwhelmingly North and South; a new dimension of vulnerability had been added.

Undaunted, the Board, thoroughly committed to the fleet concept of control of the sea, devoted much of its time to disputes over the design and characteristics of warships, and somewhat belatedly, how they should conduct themselves in battle. But Mahan, who paid little attention to the tactical aspects of amphibious attack, was not alone in emphasizing the importance of overseas bases to support operations in distant waters, and among the first problems considered by the Board was the need to deny certain bases to the enemy and secure bases for the American fleet. On 21 May 1900, the Board began making plans to thwart an attempt by Germany to occupy a portion of South America and advance into the Caribbean. Representatives of the Army were called in the following day to discuss specifically the joint occupation (Army and Navy) of the island of "Hayti-San Domingo." In June the Board dropped consideration of this problem to take up "the present war situation in Asia," and emerging from this study was a recommendation that "a force of 1,000 marines be detailed and held in readiness for the defense of an advanced base, which would be required by the fleet in the event of war in Asiatic waters."

The Board, while cooperating with the Army, came to realize in 1901 that the Navy should be able "to meet all demands upon it for services within its own sphere of operations," and asked that the Brigadier General Commandant of the Marine Corps consider the requirements "for garrisoning such points in our insular possessions, in addition to the various home stations, as are now or may in the future be established for coaling stations or for other purposes . . ." It went on to recommend the organization of a battalion of four (4) companies of 104 enlisted men each, "and have provided for such battalion and stored at Philadelphia, ready for instant use, a complete equipment for expeditionary field service for such force." Certain training was recommended, nothing was mentioned about landing on beaches or the intricacies of amphibious assault, and stress was placed on holding existing bases. The Commandant gave a detailed response which indicated that a school would be established and pointed out that "the question of the landing of troops, guns, and other military stores, at the base of operations, is a problem deserving of much consideration." He mentioned that the Naval War College had prepared a "complete scheme" dealing with the problem. Of course the Marine Corps over the years had participated in the relatively simple process of debarkation from naval vessels "from the shores of Tripoli to the halls of Montezuma" with excursions to many other points of the compass, and most recently in the landing at Guantanamo during the Spanish-American War, a successful venture which the Commandant proudly described in a letter to the General Board. Obviously the Board members were well aware of this experience, and, evidently, of Admiral Dewey's belief that if he had had a few thousand marines aboard his vessels he could have captured Manila with little delay and possibly prevented the Philippine Insurrection. So virtually from its inception the Board was recommending that expeditionary forces of Marines with appropriate equipment be established for emergency advanced base duties, although the emphasis was on defense of existing facilities rather than offensive action to acquire new facilities.

Yet the logic of fleet operations compelled the Board to contemplate the use of "invading and defensive mobile forces," whether Army or Marine Corps, and on 16 July 1902, Secretary of the Navy W. H. Moody directed the Commandant to assign a battalion of Marines to participate with the North Atlantic Squadron in exercises in the Caribbean. The following year the General Board approved a plan for the seizure of a base on the island of "Haiti-San Domingo" by the fleet and a force of Marines, "pending the landing of an army for the occupation of that island." The same year, 1903, on the recommendation of the General Board, the Joint Army-Navy Board was established by the two service secretaries to provide for greater cooperation in planning, and subsequently the role of the Marine Corps in the defense or capture of bases was more clearly defined. Essentially, the defense of existing facilities became an Army responsibility, and the capture or recapture of bases became a Navy and Marine Corps function, after which the Army would take over. This clarification of respective tasks is a story in itself, but in September 1905 the Board wrote, "It must be borne in mind that an expeditionary force dispatched at the outbreak of war to seize and defend an advanced base would probably be composed wholly of Marines." Readiness for immediate action was constantly emphasized by the Board in its exhortations to provide battalions for use in the Atlantic and Pacific, for as the Board wrote on 3 February 1905, "all the war plans made by the General Board demand an advanced base of operations . . ." Again, the bases were considered valuable only insofar as they contributed to the operations of the fleet, which would provide the final and ultimate ingredient for victory.

Debate over the most effective type of warship consumed much of the Board's time, and the appearance of the British dreadnaught and the experience of the Russo-Japanese War led to the conclusion that the all-big gun battleship was truly "the backbone of the fleet." In its recommendations on the building program in 1904 the Board said: "The greater accuracy at long ranges of heavy guns as compared with lighter ones, their relatively as well as positively increased rapidity of fire, their greater collective effectiveness against armored ships, and the evidence furnished by the war in the East that naval battles will be most often fought at long ranges--all point to increasing the number of heavy guns at the expense of the intermediate battery. . . . There should be no needless multiplication of calibers," concluded the Board. But a decision on ships' characteristics was not accompanied by agreement on how they should be used.

After the Board had spent approximately five years in trying to arrive at some principles of tactics, a sub-committee reported in 1906: "There can be no better illustration of the fact that our officers have vague ideas how one fleet should be maneuvered against another in action than that furnished by the eight officers who responded to the request for their individual solution of the three tactical problems stated in the letter of June 4, 1904. No two gave the same solution, and no one gave the same solution as that proposed by the Board of Admirals." In sum, the sub-committee caustically observed, "All of the various solutions could surely not be the best." The Board also studied the potentialities of aircraft, and in 1907 reported that it "does not deem that the science of aeronautics has as yet sufficient importance in its relation to naval warfare to render advisable at the present time the establishment of an Aeronautical Division of the Navy nor the assignment of any officers to duty in connection therewith."

Meanwhile the Board had been trying to cope with the changes taking place on the international scene and their impact on defense plans and priorities. The Anglo-Japanese Alliance of 1902 raised the possibility of a two-ocean war against formidable antagonists; the acquisition of rights to a Panama canal in 1903 promised the opportunity for a single fleet but imposed additional demands for security in the Caribbean; the outcome of the Russo-Japanese war presented a threat to American interests in the Far East and the San Francisco School Board crisis in 1906 added to the prospect of war with Japan. Involvement in the Algeciras Conference of 1906 seemed to bring the United States further into the European cockpit with implications that assumed frightening proportions.

In the midst of juggling these various contingencies the Board became even more emphatic about the need for ready Marine Corps expeditionary forces. A major problem related to equipment, which had to be provided by the respective bureaus. Since no single bureau had funds for this purpose the General Board asked that they be included in the budget requisitions of the various bureaus, including the Marine Corps, but in 1906 the Board plaintively noted that such requests were not incorporated in the Department budget request and of course were not approved by Congress. The Board pointed out that "Under present circumstances a completely equipped expedition such as contemplated [to seize and defend bases] could not start from the United States for months after receiving orders to do so." And, the Board stressed, "In the Russo-Japanese war there were a number of instances of advanced bases occupied by the Japanese, the most notable of which was the base at the Elliot Islands from which the fleet blockading Port Arthur operated, another the base at Mesampho, Korea, where Admiral Togo awaited the arrival of Admiral Rojestvensky's [sic] fleet." This report, signed by Admiral Dewey, observed that, "In the Philippines the need for an advanced base outfit in reserve is even more imperative than in the Atlantic . . . In both the Atlantic and the Pacific the inability to promptly establish an advanced base might be the means of delaying, or of compelling a change in, important strategic operations by the U.S. fleet, and the whole course of the war might depend upon the promptness and the security with which our advanced base is established." In this "for want of a nail the shoe was lost" approach, the Board was faulting the organization and indirectly the obfuscation over the function of the Marine Corps.

A perennial question agitating the Department during the early years of the twentieth century was whether Marines should continue to serve aboard ship. Their traditional role of keeping mutinously inclined sailors in line seemed no longer necessary, and modern ships no longer came close enough for effective rifle fire or for coming alongside for boarding and hand-to-hand fighting. Not until the Commandant was made an ex officio member of the General Board in 1915 did friction over this matter cease, but in 1908 President Roosevelt signed an Executive Order "Defining the Duties of the United States Marine Corps" that clarified certain items and contained several phrases relating to the garrisoning of advanced bases and providing for expeditionary forces. The autonomous bureau system was attacked during the Taft administration by the establishment of the Aide system, which was designed to coordinate budget preparation, expenditures, and other activities within the Department. Though the Marine Corps had no representative on the General Board from 1905 until 1915, that body continued to urge attention to the preparation and training for advanced base activity, including a continuance of the joint exercises that had begun at Culebra in 1902.

Almost nothing seemed to be out of the province of the General Board as it recommended the acquisition of the Danish West Indies from 1901 on, prepared plans for war with

AMPHIBIOUS DOCTRINE

Mexico beginning in 1911, wrestled with building programs, unsuccessfully tried to acquire two electric fans for the meeting room (they got only one), and admitted defeat on the question of eliminating unnecessary paperwork. In 1909 the Board reiterated that, "In the majority of cases an advanced base will be solely for naval convenience, established for the supply and maintenance of a battle fleet. . ." The Board added, "there may be instances where a point on the mainland seized at first by the Navy as an advanced base may be used at a future time as a point of landing and the principal base for operations of an Army, but this fact would materially alter its character. . ." In the next few years the Board repeatedly urged further development in the training, outfitting, and organization of advanced base units, and in 1913 referred to the "spasmodic efforts during the last ten years" to do something about the problem. That same year the Aide for Inspections, W. F. Fullam, wrote a scathing letter about advanced base training and preparations, saying in part, "In short, considered from the view point of real efficiency for war purposes, it may be said that practically nothing has been accomplished during the past thirteen years," and he blamed most of the trouble on the organization of the Marine Corps. The Commandant vigorously defended the Corps structure but admitted that "the Naval service, at present time, is not in a state of preparedness to do efficient Advance Base work. . ." Striving to rectify the situation, in 1912 transports were incorporated in the Board's recommendation for the 1914 building program, transports to carry 1,250 troops and have "An adequate number of boats and launches for landing men and supplies," and "some specially designed lighters or scows for landing guns, mounts, animals and stores." On 24 January 1913, the Board recommended that the Marine Corps participate in maneuvers with the Atlantic Fleet to "exercise in actual landing." This was done in 1913, and after the subsequent maneuvers of January 1914, the General Board wrote: "The results are gratifying, and the General Board recommends that these advanced base exercises be held each year as a matter of routine training. . ." But events of the next few years were to find the Marines engaged in activities that prevented full participation.

War plans, of course, continued to occupy much of the Board's time and these were constantly being reassessed, especially those for Germany (Black), Japan (Orange), and England (Red). By 1909 both Army and Navy planners were convinced that in the event of war with Japan the Philippines would fall, and Guam and Pearl Harbor seemed to be the farthest outposts that might be held. Captain Bradley A. Fiske, Aide for Operations, contended that planes could attack the Japanese transports and prevent troops from landing, but the Board felt that aircraft in their current stage would not be effective. In 1910 the Secretary of the Navy, commenting on plans for a campaign against Orange, observed that "in the past, such plans have rarely gotten farther than taking the fleet and its auxiliaries to the scene of hostilities, and have not indicated the course to pursue after reaching that point. It is desirable," he added, "that the plan include the strategic plan recommended after arrival of the fleet near the scene of hostilities." As William Braisted points out, "West of Pearl Harbor. . . the Navy's outlook was extremely uncertain during the four years after 1909. . . The Navy's track to the Philippines simply disappeared in the waters of the broad Pacific west of Pearl Harbor."

The Board, in reporting on its activities during the fiscal year ending 30 June 1913, stated that while 250 subjects had been considered, constantly in the foreground were plan portfolios and "the preparation of logistic plans for the movement of the Fleet to the different theaters of war and for its maintenance after arrival." Again, events in the Caribbean, Mexico, and Europe were to provide a set of priorities that prevented a fuller development of advanced base techniques and the elaboration of a Pacific strategy. Resources, human or material, simply were not adequate to permit the kind of attention that every possible eventuality deserved. But the General Board had refined and elaborated on the role and composition of an advanced base, asserting that it "should be self-supporting and contain within itself all the elements for an efficient defense," and that none of the real fighting units of the fleet should be "sidetracked to defend a base," but should be "employed in their legitimate role of finding and destroying the enemy." Following up this report in 1913 the Board presented a "Comprehensive plan for work of Advanced Base expedition from date of embarkation to completion of work," a plan that covered practically everything except for the sticky business of landing on a hostile shore.

The outbreak and course of World War I found the General Board faced with the prospect of an Allied or Central Powers victory and the threat posed to the United States by either. Completion of the Panama Canal with its defense assets and liabilities, ventures in support of President Wilson's missionary diplomacy, and Japan's capture of German holdings in the Far East and her twenty-one demands on China all placed added burdens on the naval planners. The grass roots preparedness movement which Wilson finally supported culminated in the Navy Bill of 1916 designed to provide the United States with a navy "second to none" by the mid-1920s, based on the decisive fleet action principle. When America entered the war it was the submarine menace and not the German High Seas Fleet that occupied the Navy, and the Marine Corps fought on the battlefields of Europe instead of the islands as some had contemplated.

AMPHIBIOUS DOCTRINE

The treaty of Versailles furnished new problems for the navy planners, who had urged that German possessions in the Pacific be internationalized to prevent their use as bases. Yet in a secret treaty of February 1917, Britain had promised these islands to Japan, and Wilson could do no more than have them placed in a mandate status which the General Board believed would not keep them from being developed to support the Japanese Navy. The non-fortification of bases provision in the Naval Limitation Treaty of 1922 further upset the Board, and coupled with the ratio of strength established in capital ships and aircraft carriers, seemed to render Japan's position in the Western Pacific virtually impregnable.

Naval competition with Great Britain surfaced at the Versailles Conference in the context of enforcement of the League Convenant, for Wilson and Secretary of the Navy Daniels wanted to prevent Great Britain from ruling the world through the League. When the treaty was rejected by the Senate, a strong navy seemed equally imperative to resist the imposition of League dicta, especially in regard to Latin America, since the elimination of German sea power left England as the only nation that could threaten the Monroe Doctrine. Disarmament, or actually the limitation of armaments, was the major problem facing the naval planners during the decade of the 1920s as the experts quarreled with each other and the civilian authorities over ratios, the relative fighting value of ships, and the slicing of an ever-smaller budget pie.

Service controversies were exposed to the public as Congress investigated Admiral W. S. Sims' charges that the Navy was not prepared for war in 1917, and everyone became involved in the debate over the role of aircraft, which brought intra-service and interservice rivalry to a new high.

Meanwhile, the Marine Corps was performing its usual troubleshooting role in the Caribbean, Nicaragua, and China while participating in landing exercises with the fleet. Japanese control of the mandated islands and the non-fortification of bases agreement placed greater emphasis on the ability to secure footholds to support the fleet. According to Admiral Robert E. Coontz, CINCUS and later CNO, "The participation of the Marine Corps Expeditionary Force with the Fleet in the winter maneuvers of 1924 afforded the first real opportunity for determining the value of such a force to the Fleet." Advance base techniques were the subject of numerous articles in the <u>Naval Institute Proceedings</u>, in service papers, and lectures at the Naval War College. In fact, Fleet Admiral Chester W. Nimitz was to write with some exaggeration that his course at the Naval Was College from 1922 to 1923, "was so complete that when the war in the Pacific actually started, nothing that happened surprised us at all except the kamikaze attacks."

The Naval War College from its inception in 1884 had played a major role in the examination and formulation of naval doctrine, and during the 1920s considerable attention was given to the abortive British Dardanelles expedition of 1915. One study, completed by Captain W. D. Puleston, was published by the Naval Institute in 1926 and became for some a virtual "Bible" of amphibious doctrine. While Puleston questioned the wisdom of the venture and thought that most authorities would agree "that Great Britain and France should have concentrated their efforts in one theater of war," much of the book was devoted to the tactical dimensions of the operation which were more relevant to the American planners. Puleston concluded that "The eternal question of whether or not ships can fight forts is apparently answered by an emphatic negative in this engagement," but "in justice to ships it must be added that there is but one Constantinople in the world, and in other places ships would have a better chance." Actually, naval gunfire was quite effective and mines and submarines primarily hampered support, while improper unified command contributed to the failure. Puleston did emphasize the contributions of British aircraft in reconnaissance and felt that "Air superiority would have turned the scales in favor of the attackers," although, he concluded, "In general the submarine and airplane appear to assist the defense more than the offense in sea warfare."

So a superficial reading of Puleston's study could have had an adverse effect on the prospects for success in amphibious operations, but a careful perusal opened new vistas for the protagonists. Contributing to further efforts were the perennial disarmament preparations and negotiations. On 11 February 1922, the Commandant wrote to the General Board on the subject of "Future Policy for the Marine Corps as influenced by the Conference on Limitation of Armament." "The primary war mission of the Marine Corps," he asserted, "is to supply a mobile force to accompany the Fleet for operations on shore in support of the Fleet," and he recommended "The discontinuance of the use of the term, 'Advanced Base Force,' as now applied to organizations of the Marine Corps." Following the London Naval Conference of 1930 where Japan was granted a ratio in so-called auxiliary vessels more favorable than that secured at Washington for capital ships, the General Board declared categorically that, "The present fundamental function of the Marine Corps as laid down by the Planning Section of Operations is to seize and defend bases." Just how this function was to be carried out was a problem that engaged the attention of many planners, but the most substantive work appears to have been done at the Marine Corps Schools, Quantico, in the early 1930s.

Evolving from the Advanced Base School established in 1910 or the earlier embryo organization, the Schools at

AMPHIBIOUS DOCTRINE

Quantico around 1930 engaged in the preparation of a <u>Landing Operations Manual</u> to serve as a guide for a true amphibious operation as distinct from the simple navy landing force method of placing a few armed sailors ashore. Relying on historical examples, a knowledge of the instruments of modern warfare, intelligence and imagination, a dedicated group of Marine and Naval officers investigated virtually every dimension of the subject and produced specific recommendations on the problems to be met and how to overcome them. Suggestions came from all quarters, and one young officer, H. K. Hewitt, who had served as Fleet Gunnery Officer, submitted detailed studies on Ships Gunfire Support to Landings which, one participant later wrote, "for the first time (of record) explored the subject that became so vital to the success of Landing Ops in WWII. . ." These studies contributed to the formation of the Fleet Marine Force in 1933 and its participation in landing operations in connection with Fleet exercises in 1935. In this and subsequent joint training activities many problems were detected and steps were taken to solve them. The size and composition of the attacking force, the proper vessels for landing of men and material on reef-encrusted beaches, the most effective caliber and proximity for supporting gunfire, and the role of aircraft were explored and clarified as efforts were made to transform theory into doctrine.

In an early draft of a portion of the <u>Landing Force Manual</u> written by Charles D. Barrett, USMC, even the mission of the bases as solely a vehicle adjunct to ship operations was questioned, for, in Barrett's words, "territory within the theatre of operations of the two fleets, which otherwise might have no strategic or tactical value, assumes an important role as a possible aircraft base. For this reason, landing operations may be conducted solely for the purpose of securing or denying landing fields to land-based aircraft." Bases to permit the strategic bombing of the enemy homeland evidently had not entered into the calculations of the naval planners prior to this time.

As of 1932, Navy Department plans called for an expeditionary force of 18,000 to be available within thirty days after mobilization, and the General Board made it clear that "The Marine Corps should be so organized as to be capable of performing its mission in the seizure of an advanced base and in providing for its <u>initial</u> defense. The Army would in general relieve the Marine Corps of the permanent defense, thereby permitting the latter to resume operations with the Fleet for further expeditionary work." This same year, 1932, Navy Regulations Change No. 15 eliminated all ex officio members of the General Board, including the Commandant of the Marine Corps who had been serving in that capacity since 1915. During this period the future of the Marine Corps as an entity was in jeopardy as both President Hoover and Admiral William V. Pratt, Chief of Naval Opera-

153

tions, appeared to favor its incorporation into the Army as an economy measure, but for various reasons the Marine Corps survived as a component of the Navy. One reason for its survival may have been ignorance of its actual condition, for on 16 June 1932 the Director, Division of Operations and Training, USMC, wrote to the Major General Commandant saying in part, "Actually, the Marine Corps today has no organized and trained emergency force in readiness."

Meanwhile events on the international scene had been contributing to the problems haunting statesmen and military authorities. The relative calm of the 1920s where only the smaller, weaker nations seemed to get out of line was destroyed by the Japanese invasion of Manchuria in 1931, Hitler's successive unilateral steps to revise the Treaty of Versailles, the Italo-Ethiopian War, and the Spanish civil conflict. Neither the League of Nations nor military pacts proved effective in halting these efforts to change the status quo; the World Disarmament Conference at Geneva brought no agreement on the limitation of arms; and the London Naval Conference of 1935-36 produced a treaty providing for "qualitative" and not "quantitative" restrictions without Japan. By 1938 unbridled naval competition was underway and President Roosevelt's attempts to build the fleet to treaty strength by relief funds and the implementation of the Vinson-Trammel Act of 1934 were augmented by Congressional approval of his special request of January 1938 for additional appropriations, which provided for a 20 percent increase, and later by the "two-ocean" Navy bill of 1940. Fleet action continued to be the criterion for construction, with battleships, carriers, cruisers, destroyers, and submarines consuming most of the budget, and their design and employment much of the Navy planners' efforts. But as Japan loomed more and more as the "probable enemy" with its resumption of war with China in 1937 and its negative reaction to President Franklin Roosevelt's Quarantine Speech and the Brussels Conference, the Navy intensified landing exercises in the Caribbean and the West Coast. The islands of Culebra and San Clemente bore the brunt of these mock assaults, and General Holland M. Smith has written, "If the Battle of Waterloo was won on the playing fields of Eton, the Japanese bases in the Pacific were captured on the beaches of the Caribbean."

There has been a good deal of criticism about the Navy not being prepared to combat the submarine when the United States entered both world wars, and at one point when President Roosevelt was submitting memos urging the development of escort vessels, he is said to have remarked that trying to get the Navy to do anything was like punching a pillow. In regard to landing craft, from the first exercises in 1902-1903, every evaluation stressed the shortcomings of regular ships' boats for the delivery of troops and equipment to hostile beaches, and a few experimental craft were

AMPHIBIOUS DOCTRINE

improvised sporadically. Then on 12 January 1937 the Secretary of the Navy established a continuing board in the Navy department for the development of landing boats. The story of a few individuals functioning in unorthodox and even illegal fashion to create the vessels that were indispensable to the amphibious operations in World War II is well known. But it has been estimated that the funds allocated to landing craft research and development in 1935 amounted to $40,000 and even in the affluence of 1940 to only $400,000.

The European war that erupted in September 1939 provided the navy planners with additional vicarious experiences, initially in commerce raiding and minor naval engagements. The feared effectiveness of the German pocket battleship was somewhat mollified by the defeat of the <u>Graf Spee</u> by three British cruisers, one mounting 8" and two 6" guns, although the <u>Exeter</u>'s difficulties resulted in frantic emphasis on damage control techniques in the American Navy. Of greatest significance for amphibious doctrine was the Norwegian campaign in the spring of 1940. As the Admiralty historian, P. K. Kemp, put it, the "lack of air cover was to prove in the end too great a handicap to the Allied forces and was to reveal, for the first time in history, the complete dependence of effective operations, both by sea and by land, on efficient air cover." Thus fuel was added to the arguments of the aviation exponents in the Navy Department, although the British carriers had not been able to operate effectively against land based planes and submarines. A second lesson of the campaign, according to Stephen Roskill, was that "special craft needed by combined operations could not be extemporized, nor could trained men be produced at short notice." Among other factors responsible for the German success was the element of surprise, seizing and maintaining the initiative. The operation also was well planned and well executed, with excellent coordination among the services. It appeared to some that the British could not have been more inept, and American observers had plenty of grist for the mill in which they were grinding out amphibious doctrine. The fall of France in June 1940 removed the land barrier to German expansion westward, and with England the only remaining bulwark between Hitler and the Western Hemisphere, defense measures in the United States took on even greater meaning. A more convenient site for amphibious training was secured at New River, North Carolina, and the First Joint Training Force was established within the Atlantic Fleet under the command of Major General H. M. Smith, USMC.

In an effort to juxtapose a topical with a chronological treatment of this complex subject I have slighted the preparation of war plans, which obviously had a significant relation to the activities of the Navy. The revisions of war plan ORANGE between 1924 and 1938 found the Army often in disagreement with the Navy over operations west of Hawaii, with the Navy constantly urging an offensive strategy that called for movement into the mandated islands to support the fleet that would end the war by the defeat of the Japanese forces and a blockade of the home islands. The Hepburn report of December 1938 strongly advised that Guam be fortified as a key to the defense of the Philippines and the projection of the fleet into the Central and Western Pacific, but Congress refused to authorize what some viewed as a provocative act toward Japan. Yet the annual fleet problems continued to be held in the Pacific in spite of Japanese protests, and that of 1937 involved a simulated attack on Oahu that proved successful beyond most expectations. In 1939 the Caribbean was the center of activity, but in 1940 the problem was held in the Pacific and on its completion the President ordered the fleet retained at Hawaii as a deterrent to Japanese expansion in Asia. The British authorities wanted American units sent to Singapore, and as the Royal Navy encountered more trouble with the Reichsmarine, Roosevelt, in May 1941, weakened the Pacific fleet by transferring a division of battleships and a division of cruisers to the Atlantic. The security zone or "chastity belt" established by the American nations escalated into an undeclared war on German U-boats. The destroyer-bases exchange was consummated and the old adage that assets create liabilities was borne out as American planners sought to transform ORANGE and BLACK into RAINBOW, and PLAN DOG became the order of the day. The American professionals acquired a new antagonist in doctrinal debates as they were joined by British authorities for multilogues that made some yearn for the good old days of simple interservice rivalry.

With formal American entry into the war and the alarming Japanese success in the early months, amphibious preparations accelerated drastically. To return to General Smith and his First Joint Training Force, landing maneuvers conducted at Cape Henry in January 1942 produced a report highly critical of the Navy on the grounds that it failed to provide suitable transports; combatant vessels had not practiced shore bombardment in a year; naval aircraft were untrained for cooperation with ground troops; and troops were not landed on designated beaches. He also specifically recommended unity of command under the Commander of the landing forces. Soon thereafter the amphibious forces were established and reorganized in the Atlantic and Pacific fleets, and on 9 April 1942, General Joseph T. McNarney, as acting Chief of Staff wrote to Admiral Ernest J. King complaining about a "lack of progress in our combined efforts in amphibious training." He suggested a different training approach for operations in the Pacific and the Atlantic, the former being a Marine Corps responsibility and the latter Army since it would be a prelude to prolonged land operations. In June an Amphibious Warfare Section (F-26) was added to the Readiness Division in Cominch headquarters, and a crash program in the final half of 1942 produced nearly 250,000 tons of landing craft and in the first half of 1943 nearly a third of a million tons.

In the Pacific the "defensive-offensive" strategy, i.e., tactically offensive, strategically defensive, provided practical experience in amphibious operations, and by the time a purely offensive strategy became practicable techniques had become so refined that the Kwajalein assault became what has been called the model of a "perfect invasion." In the European theater Admiral Hewitt, as General Eisenhower wrote to Admiral King, came to know "just about all there is to know concerning the landing of troops on a hostile beach. . ." The question of command relationships during the successive phases of an amphibious operation became more acute as General "Howling Mad" Smith and Admiral "Madman" Richmond Kelly Turner were central figures in this "doctrinal dispute" and the prosecution of the war against Japan. Pretending no expertise on this matter I refer you to Admiral Dyer's study of Richmond Kelly Turner for what might be called an "antidote" to some existing literature on the subject.

Essentially, the war in the Pacific vindicated the role of the advance base and the Marine Corps in fighting Japan as espoused by the General Board from its inception, with the possible exception of their function in providing airfields for the strategic bombing of the Japanese homeland. Techniques of amphibious warfare were developed to the point where what has been called the most intricate problem of modern warfare became both a science and an art, a science in its planning and an art in its execution. In this context, it was revealed most emphatically that a maritime strategy can permit the choice of time and place for ground intervention, with the usual tactical advantages that accrue from such an operation. Furthermore, in this conflict the need for inter-service cooperation was more imperative than at any previous time in history. Technology and experience had contributed to the refinement of amphibious operations, and some changes included Tactical Air Control Parties, Air and Naval Gunfire Liaison Companies, Underwater Demolition Teams, Joint Operations Centers, Logistic and Beach Control, and improved systems of communications.

In this greatest of multidimensional wars one can say without unreasonable partiality that in the war in the Pacific, control of the sea and the air was necessary to provide for the landings to secure bases that permitted the further extension of control of the sea and the air to the point that the homeland of Japan was vulnerable to destruction and defeat was insured. The situation in Europe was similar but not identical, for England provided the airfields and the staging area for the cross-Channel invasion. In the Mediterranean the situation was more analogous to that in the Pacific, for North Africa made possible Sicily, which permitted Italy, which helped on Southern France. Without the previous forty years of effort to develop amphibious doctrine and techniques, the road to victory, difficult though it was, might well have been impassable.

Within the context of so-called limited wars of the past twenty-seven years, amphibious operations have assumed great importance, and in directives and legislation the Marine Corps has been assigned the mission of developing landing force tactics, techniques, and equipment to conduct amphibious or land operations. Naval doctrinal disputes have continued, and after the surrender of Japan the General Board could report that "the high offensive and defensive qualities of the battleship, including its inherent power of survival, are likely to make it the final arbiter in any engagement between fleets which are well matched. . ." While that particular issue has vanished along with the General Board, arguments over the relative merits of surface ships, submarines, and aircraft carriers continue, although the Navy appears to be in agreement on the necessity for maintaining the capability to land on a hostile shore. Since imitation is said to be the highest form of flattery, it is reassuring that our Soviet rival in sea power seems to be developing its own amphibious force.

What is the present and immediate future of amphibious operations? Helolifted assault forces, nuclear weapons, and other devices for placing troops ashore and increasing firepower are in existence and more are on the drawing board. Being a historian and not a prophet I shall predict only that the advance base expeditionary force has a great future in naval doctrine, national defense, and in the preservation of the peace of the world. The heroes of the past, sung and unsung, who contributed to what became a determinant factor in warfare can view their efforts with great satisfaction, and those who benefitted from these efforts can be eternally grateful. And no doubt one of the most closely guarded secrets in the Defense Department today is the preparation for Marine Corps units to undertake the first astrophibious operations in the annals of man.

BIBLIOGRAPHY

The main primary sources for this paper are located in the Naval History Division, Department of the Navy, Washington, D.C., particularly the records of the Navy General Board. Also invaluable were materials acquired by the late Professor Richard S. West from the Marine Corps archives in Washington and Quantico, used in preparing a lengthy unpublished manuscript on amphibious operations commissioned by

AMPHIBIOUS DOCTRINE

the Director of Naval History. Studies of various aspects of amphibious warfare, typewritten or mimeographed, may be found in official files. Numerous primary and secondary sources have been published in the Annual Reports of the Secretary of the Navy, the U.S. Naval Institute Proceedings, and the Marine Corps Gazette. Among the many secondary accounts that have proved useful in providing historical background are Alfred Vagts, Landing Operations: Strategy, Psychology, Tactics, Politics, From Antiquity to 1945 (Washington, 1946); Jeter A. Isely and Philip A. Crowl, U.S. Marines and Amphibious War, Its Theory and Its Practice in the Pacific (Princeton, 1951); Frank O. Hough, Verle E. Ludwig, and Henry I. Shaw, Jr., Pearl Harbor to Guadalcanal: History of U.S. Marine Corps Operations in World War II (Washington, 1958); Holland M. Smith and Percy Fuch, Coral and Brass (New York, 1959); George C. Dyer, The Amphibians Came to Conquer: The Story of Admiral Richmond Kelly Turner (2 vols., Washington, 1972); and Robert Debs Heinl, Jr., Soldiers of the Sea: The U.S. Marine Corps, 1775-1962 (Annapolis, 1962).

DID FDR WANT WAR IN 1941 ?

Chapter 14

Franklin Delano Roosevelt has furnished posterity with a battery of questions that offer a major challenge to the historian, and controversial though his domestic program may be, both his critics and his apologists are often inclined to judge him on the basis of his foreign policy. In 1941 a confused and divided nation wondered whether peace or war would best serve American interests, and the people sought an answer from the leader who nine years earlier had promised redemption from economic chaos. The sudden attack on Pearl Harbor, which terminated the most intricate and epochal diplomatic negotiations since independence, put an end to speculation and uncertainty. But the solution uppermost in the mind of the President remained a mystery.

Roosevelt was not neutral from the moment that Hitler invaded Poland. Yet it was only with the sudden and unexpected collapse of France that he became fully aware of the real and immediate danger of the Nazi menace. The pressure of events in Europe accelerated his efforts to educate and awaken American public opinion to the threat of Hitlerism and secure support for a policy calculated to insure the defeat of Germany. At the same time the President took steps which led the United States from a professed neutrality to non-belligerency, cobelligerency, and finally a formal declaration of war. While he maintained that his actions, however far removed from neutrality, were designed to keep the country out of war, the United States exchanged destroyers for bases, patrolled the Atlantic sea lanes, enacted Lend-Lease, tracked German submarines, escorted vessels, occupied British and neutral territory, formulated joint war plans, and coordinated foreign policy with the enemies of aggression. Must we take the President at his word? Must we assume that he meant what he said when he insisted again and again that every move was planned to avoid hostilities? I think not.

In the first place, Roosevelt believed that Nazism was a direct threat to the security of the United States, as well as to that of the rest of the world, and therefore the European conflict could not be considered a "foreign war." Secondly, he was convinced that Britain, and later Russia, could not defeat Germany without American military assistance, and both FDR and Hitler knew that any delay in all-out participation against Germany was to the advantage of the Axis powers. Thirdly, he was confident that an allied victory in Europe would put an end to Japan's aggressive policy in the Far East. And finally, the President felt that the United States must have an equal voice in the formulation and preservation of the peace that followed, which would be possible only in the event that the nation became a full partner in the war effort.

Franklin Roosevelt was never a simple person, and he defied understanding by his friends, his associates, and even his family. Yet some conclusions about him are possible and they help clarify his position in 1941. FDR loved a challenge. For him, obstacles, whether polio or politics, were created for the purpose of being overcome, and he was exhilarated by the prospect. Also, he usually knew where he wanted to go but he was not too particular about how he got there. Roosevelt could be, as James M. Burns asserts, both a lion and a fox, varying his means and his tactics in order to attain his objective. Furthermore, he was enough of a realist to settle for less than the ideal and adjust his sights to the possible. These qualities were constantly displayed as the President countered the problems that emerged during the troubled year of 1941.

Roosevelt's peacetime strategy demanded a balance of power both in Europe and in the Far East in order that no single nation or group of nations would be free to threaten the safety of the Americas. He did not regard Japan as a buffer to protect the United States from a hostile China or an aggressive Russia, nor, apparently, did he share Admiral Harold R. Stark's belief that an equilibrium in the Far East was possible only if Japan had a foothold on the continent. The President's opinion was probably influenced by the existence of the Japanese Fleet, which posed the only immediate military threat to the United States in the Pacific.

By 1939 Roosevelt realized that the Atlantic Ocean was no adequate barrier against attack. Meeting with the Senate Military Affairs Committee in January of that year, he warned that America's first line of defense was those buffer states which stood between Hitler and the Atlantic. The French army and the British navy preserved the balance of power in Europe and permitted the United States the luxury of a one-ocean fleet. With the crushing defeat of France in the spring of 1940 the land barrier that protected the Western Hemisphere was eliminated, and the American military buildup shifted from the Pacific to the Atlantic as FDR redoubled his efforts to support America's last line of defense in Europe.

The President pounded home his theme with persistence and skill. At press conferences and in meetings with congressional committees he asked if the United States should defend the Philippines or Alaska, and received a ready affirmative because they were American possessions. He then extended his questions to embrace Canada and Mexico and the countries of South America as he pointedly illustrated the danger of isolationism, and, by clear implication, America's vital interest in the European conflict. In his message to Congress on January 6, 1941, FDR declared: "At no previous time has American security been as seriously threatened from without as it is today," and in May he warned that "the war is approaching the brink of the Western Hemisphere itself. It is coming very close to home," for "the attack on the United States can begin with the domination of any base which menaces our security--north or south." At this time he agreed to occupy the Azores in the event of an attempted German invasion, and he considered a declaration placing West Africa within the compass of the Monroe Doctrine. By September the President was sufficiently sure of his domestic audience to announce that "The Nazi danger to our Western World has long ceased to be a mere possibility. The danger is here now--not only from a military enemy but from an enemy of all law, all liberty, all morality, all religion." Thus FDR finally admitted publicly what he had denied saying or believing a year and a half before--that America's first line of defense was on the Rhine; and now the initial bulwark had been destroyed.

Roosevelt's strategy was clear. All of the hostilities were part of a world conflagration but Hitler was the head and Germany the heart of this force of evil which threatened free institutions and the safety of America itself. Japanese aggression, while jeopardizing allied interests in the Far East, was contingent on Axis success in Europe, which tied the hands of those nations dedicated to the maintenance of the status quo in Asia.

The President responded to the German challenge with all of his resourcefulness and ingenuity. The Lend-Lease Act expressly denied authority for the use of convoys to deliver goods to Britain or the sending of American ships into designated combat areas. FDR merely substituted "patrol" for "convoy" and authorized his cabinet officers to plead publicly for the employment of naval escorts. On April 10, 1941, he circumvented Congress by removing the Red Sea area from those combat zones denied to American vessels by a previous presidential proclamation. In the same month he told a press conference that the naval patrol would extend "as far on the waters of the seven seas as may be necessary for the defense of the American hemisphere." The attack on Russia, although adding a valuable ally to the Nazi resistance, weakened Roosevelt's contention that the conflict was being waged to preserve freedom and probably caused the President to move more slowly in the face of an intensified domestic opposition. But by September he was ready to announce that American warships and planes would protect friendly vessels "in our defensive waters," which included, according to Cordell Hull, "the shipping lanes across the North Atlantic, as well as the waters to the South." In order to bolster Britain's shaky defenses in the Far East, Roosevelt provided navy ships and crews to transport British soldiers to Singapore, and in November he was able to secure the repeal of those sections of the Neutrality Act which prevented the arming of merchant vessels and sending them to belligerent ports. Basil Rauch contends that by this act Congress authorized the President to wage a naval war and did "absolve him of his implied promise to commit no 'act of war' under Lend-Lease." Actually, however, Roosevelt admitted that hostilities already existed in the Atlantic, so this new law was no more than an ex post facto authorization at best.

Following the October torpedoing of the destroyer Kearny, the President proclaimed that "America has been attacked," and, he added, "We are pledged to pull our own oar in the destruction of Hitlerism." Early in November he declared that "The American people have made an unlimited commitment that there shall be a free world," and "Upon our American production falls the colossal task of equipping our own armed forces, and helping to supply the British, the Russians, and the Chinese. In the performance of that task we dare not fail." Yet at this very time Britain was stripping herself of badly needed armaments to supply Russia, and the previous month she had offered to provide the weapon-starved American army with artillery for target practice. Only two four-engine bombers came from American factories in July, and just over 200 were scheduled for the remaining five months of the year. During 1940 China received $9,000,000 worth of military equipment, and the $7,000,000,000 appropriated for Lend-Lease seemed pitifully inadequate when compared with the estimated need for $150,000,000,000 in supplies by 1943 to support the war effort of the European allies. Nor was the problem merely a matter of funds. Production simply could not even begin to meet requirements until the nation's economy was placed on a war basis. Business was unwilling to convert factories from the manufacture of consumer goods and labor refused to curtail its organizational activities. The spirit of urgency and sacrifice was lacking and only a great national crisis could supply it. In the meantime the self-styled "arsenal of democracy" was not supporting its end of the struggle against the Axis, and the desperate appeals of Britain, Russia and China warned that aid might be too little and too late.

Roosevelt's ultimate objective in desiring a successful conclusion of the European war is revealed by his words and actions in 1941. He announced to Congress on January 6 that "In the future days, which we seek to make secure, we look forward to a world founded upon four essential freedoms," the fourth being, in his words, "freedom from fear which, translated into world terms, means a world-wide reduction of armaments to such a point and in such a thorough fashion that no nation will be in a position to commit an act of physical aggression against any neighbor--anywhere in the world." At a press conference on April 25, he declared himself "agin" dictatorships and said "We will fight for the Democratic process." The following month, in a letter to Harold Vanderbilt, FDR wrote: "It seems so clear that the ultimate choice is between right and wrong that smug inaction on our part is in effect an aid to wrong. Even if our continental limits remain intact I, personally, should hate to live the rest of my days in a world dominated by the Hitler philosophy." During August he joined the British Prime Minister in a statement which called for, after "the final destruction of the Nazi tyranny," the establishment of "a peace which will afford to all nations the means of dwelling in safety within their own boundaries." And in a radio address two days after the attack on Pearl Harbor, he announced: "We are now in the midst of a war, not for conquest, not for vengeance, but for a world in which this Nation, and all that this Nation represents, will be safe for our children. . . . We are going to win the war, and we are going to win the peace that follows." America's entry was an essential step in the attainment of this goal.

In the fall of 1941, as the clouds in Europe darkened, events in the Pacific moved toward a climax. Contrary to the opinion shared by the British and some of his advisers, Roosevelt believed that if Japan were pushed too hard she would fight. He wanted to be firm enough to prevent any action that would threaten Great Britain or Russia and interfere with their struggle against Hitler, but he was reluctant to deprive Japan of an alternative to war.

This, then, was Roosevelt's dilemma. On the one hand he was anxious to avoid a conflict in the Pacific because it would impede the war effort in Europe. On the other hand he had to keep enough pressure on Japan to prevent the collapse of China, the severance of the British Empire lifeline, or an attack on Russia. The President was plagued by the knowledge that the American contribution to the war was falling far short, but a forthright stand in Asia was the equivalent of many divisions and much material.

Following months of tortuous negotiations, a crucial set of proposals was received from Tokyo on November 20. Although Hull considered the offer an ultimatum, the American statesmen began formulating a reply which would delay the clash that many of them believed inevitable. To add to the tension, a Japanese message intercepted on November 22 revealed that if a satisfactory reply to the earlier dispatch was not received by November 29, "things are automatically going to happen." The Secretary of State and the President were agreed that efforts should be made to prevent a break in negotiations, and with this in mind a modus vivendi was prepared which offered Japan some raw materials in exchange for certain concessions and guarantees.

In clearing this proposal with the friendly nations Hull received vehement protests from the Chinese and British envoys. He attempted to mollify the former by observing that there was only one chance in three that the Japanese would accept the terms, and to the latter he "pointed out the utter impracticability of requesting a suspension of further (Japanese) military advances in China." That same evening, November 25, a strong telegram arrived from Chruchill reaffirming Chiang Kai Shek's objections to the proposed note and stressing the common danger of a collapse of China, which, the Prime Minister asserted, could be hastened by the terms of the modus vivendi. After a hasty discussion with his advisers, Hull, on the following morning, recommended to the President that the modus vivendi be dropped and a ten point note be substituted containing the basis for a permanent settlement of the Far Eastern crisis. Roosevelt agreed, and on November 26 the Japanese envoys were handed the note which, in Churchill's words, "not only met our wishes and those of the associated Governments, but indeed went beyond anything for which we had ventured to ask."

The controversy surrounding the modus vivendi illustrates the two schools of thought concerning the best method of stopping Japan. The British Prime Minister and some of Hull's advisers maintained that a firm and positive warning would be most effective. The President did not share this belief, and he refused to take such a step until November 26. Because of the intercept of November 22, both Hull and Roosevelt knew that the only possibility for continued negotiations lay in the provisions of the modus vivendi. By its rejection they knowingly, albeit reluctantly, made the decision for war. Moreover, the moral aspect of the situation was apparently a minor factor in their deliberations. Primarily, they were intent on keeping China in the war because of her restraining effect on the Japanese, whose troops could otherwise be freed for action against the British or the Russians and thereby weaken resistance to Hitler. "We wanted peace," Hull later protested. "We wanted nothing to interrupt the flow of our aid to Britain, Russia, and other allies resisting Hitlerism," and the note of November 26 was designed to promote this resistance. It was a calculated risk and a matter of some controversy as to whether the European war effort would best be furthered by the modus vivendi or the ten point note.

A further clue to Roosevelt's intentions is found in his extreme sensitivity to public opinion. Even in his press conferences he was frank in admitting that he could not state publicly certain harsh aspects of the world situation because the people were not ready to accept them. FDR well knew that any public repudiation of his convictions or his policies could jeopardize his entire program of American assistance to Hitler's enemies. When the President warned the Senate Military Affairs Committee in January 1939 of the potential threats to America's safety, he prefaced his remarks with the statement that "it may come as a shock and it should not be talked about out loud because the country would not understand it in those terms." A few days later he branded as a "deliberate lie" the allegation that he had claimed America's first line of defense was on the Rhine, and he denied sharing such an opinion. In April, 1940, he admitted to having been evasive in answering a question as to whether Greenland was included in the Monroe Doctrine because of his fear that the American people would not support such an interpretation. The following month FDR told members of the press that "We have to look ahead to certain possibilities. If I had said this out loud in a fireside talk, again people would have said that I was perfectly crazy," and he followed these prefatory remarks with a warning of the danger of a Nazi victory to the United States.

Both Secretary of War Henry L. Stimson and Secretary of the Navy Frank Knox were openly hostile toward Hitler and outspoken in their pleas for aid to Britain. In their official position as civilian heads of the departments charged with defense, they advocated warlike actions in speeches read and approved beforehand by the President. Obviously they were expressing the opinions of their chief, whose position was much more vulnerable and more open to criticism. These officials and many others in the administration, including the military leaders, were convinced that Hitler could be destroyed only by America's all-out participation in the war. The necessary weapons could not be produced by a peacetime economy, they could not be delivered by the British navy, and the Axis military might could not be defeated by the armed forces of England and Russia alone. Furthermore, time was running out. The Allies needed help immediately to forestall the German successes and prevent a disillusionment that would lead to a negotiated peace. Such a contingency was quite possible in the case of ravaged Russia, and conceivable in the case of battered and war-weary Britain. China had already reached the stage of exhaustion and the Soviets were no longer in a position to provide her with equipment or moral support.

Perhaps Admiral Stark best summed up the attitude of many of FDR's advisers in a memorandum to the President in October, 1941. "I have assumed for the past two years," he wrote, "that our country would not let Great Britain fall; that ultimately in order to prevent this we would have to enter the war and . . . I have long felt and often stated that the sooner we get in the better." According to Robert

Sherwood, this memorandum was "highly refreshing to the President," presumably because he agreed with it. Writing of a conference held on the afternoon of the Pearl Harbor attack between the President, Secretary Stimson, Secretary Hull, Secretary Knox, Admiral Stark, and General Marshall, Harry Hopkins observed that "all of us believed that in the last analysis the enemy was Hitler and that he could never be defeated without force of arms; that sooner or later we were bound to be in the war and that Japan had given us the opportunity."

Roosevelt was avowedly dedicated to the destruction of Nazism. At one time he may have believed that this could be accomplished without American intervention, but after the fall of France he realized that Britain alone could not do the job, and his words and his acts soon belied any pretense of neutrality. He moved as fast and as far as he could to help the British within the limits of law and public opinion. He freely interpreted the phrase "aid short of war" to mean "short of declared war," and he stretched his constitutional prerogative as Commander in Chief of the Army and Navy to permit him to wage war without Congressional approval. Yet this was not enough. The American effort was far short of the mark, and, as Sherwood observes, FDR had exhausted his bag of tricks. He could not get the authority to implement his program, or the war spirit to provide the necessary sacrifices. Only the mobilization of America's industrial might and military manpower could do what FDR considered essential for the safety of the Western Hemisphere and the free world.

Other questions occur to the student of this period. Why did Roosevelt refuse to ask Congress for a declaration of war? What made him so sure that he was right? To what extent was he influenced by the experience of his former chief, Woodrow Wilson? No doubt he was haunted by his repeated assertions that he was not going to send American boys to fight in foreign wars, and many people placed the struggle against Hitler in this category in spite of the potential threat to the Americas. Then, too, he feared that debate over the issue would drag out for weeks or months and divide the nation, regardless of the outcome. FDR wanted the support of a united people who could not accuse him of having led the country into war. His profound dedication to the overthrow of Hitlerism was probably associated with his belief in himself as a "man of destiny," placed in the position to exercise a decisive influence at a crucial period in world history. In the fulfillment of this mission he was determined to avoid the mistakes of Wilson, both as a national leader and as the architect of a new world order. Yet the joint objectives of Axis defeat and postwar collective security seemed impossible of realization unless the United States joined in the conflict. Roosevelt's influence on the war or the peace that followed could not be fully exerted unless America's sacrifices and contributions to victory were commensurate with those of other nations.

A president is able to circumvent the constitutional requirement that only Congress can declare war by so conducting foreign affairs that war is unavoidable. No doubt FDR could have pursued a policy that would have postponed hostilities for an indefinite period, but he chose not to do so because the stakes were too high and he believed it would be an unwarranted gamble with national security. If asked whether any responsible statesman ever wants war, Roosevelt, it seems clear, would have answered: "Yes, if he believes that an imperative objective cannot be achieved in any other way." In 1941 there was no alternative consistent with his obligations and his purpose.

NAVAL STRATEGY IN WORLD WAR II

Chapter 15

According to an official Navy Department publication, "Naval power is the capacity of naval forces to establish, maintain, and exploit control of the seas and to deny their use to the enemy in furtherance of national power and objectives." Today I shall use the term "naval strategy" in this sense, with the substitution of the word "utilization" in place of "capacity," and "defeat of the enemy" for "furtherance of national power and objectives." For the defeat of the enemy forces was the military objective of every nation involved in this greatest of all wars.

The second world war began in September 1939, and the naval strategies of the major antagonists were clearly defined. Great Britain was committed to an essentially defensive strategy in what was deemed the initial period, for a three year conflict was assumed and it was believed that time was on her side. A significant portion of the British navy was deployed in the Mediterranean in anticipation of Italy joining Germany as an ally, and command of this area was considered imperative. The remainder of the British naval forces was deployed to protect the isles from a German invasion, which was considered a possibility; to blockade Germany; and to protect British commerce on the high seas, commerce without which the nation would collapse in a matter of weeks. And protecting commerce involved, in the thinking that prevailed, cruiser protection against surface raiders, not escorts for convoys. As one Admiralty historian puts it, "The convoy lessons of 1917 had never been fully digested, indeed to some extent had been forgotten." Also, the fleet air arm had been weakened by having it placed under the Air Ministry until 1937, and even then the Admiralty was not given control of research and development. The British Navy was also affected by what might be called the "Jutland syndrome." As Stephen Roskill puts it, during much of the inter-war period "The British admiralty's thinking was directed more to the causes of the Royal Navy's lack of success at Jutland than to the question whether such lessons had any validity for the future."

The German navy, with little in the way of surface forces, could not dream of a Jutland-like engagement. Admiral Raeder had hoped to follow an attrition strategy by piecemeal destruction of major British naval units and by the forced dispersal of the British-Home Fleet through

German far-ranging commerce raiding. Oddly enough, in 1939 the German undersea force consisted of only ten 750 ton long range ocean-going submarines, twenty 500 ton vessels, plus some small coastal U-boats. Essentially, Hitler had engaged the nation in a war with Great Britain before his Navy was prepared, but Germany did deploy raiders and submarines to interdict commerce when Britain declared war.

France and Italy concentrated their efforts on preparing for war in the Mediterranean with shore based aircraft, heavily gunned high speed cruisers and destroyers, submarines, and virtually unsinkable battleships. Neither expected to establish control of the area, and Italy's primary objective was to prevent a superior seapower from exercising maximum command of the Mediterranean.

The first six months of the war saw no major naval operations, although minor engagements such as the Battle of the River Plate had significant overtones. The GRAF SPEE incident revealed that the vaunted German pocket battleship was vulnerable to a well planned and vigorously executed attack by cruisers. It also created in Hitler a sensitivity to the utilization--and risk-- of his major naval units. The Royal Navy, in countering the German commerce raiders, organized merchant convoys to the extent of its supply of escorts. But spurred by Winston Churchill and others, it also wasted time and effort on hunter groups. Samuel Eliot Morrison has observed that a lesson of World War I was the necessity of escorting merchant shipping, and the folly of trying to cope with submarines by hunting them all over the place, "looking for a needle in a haystack" as Alfred Thayer Mahan had put it many years before. After a big fleet carrier, HMS COURAGEOUS, had fallen victim to a U-boat while engaged in one of the hunts, the British halted this practice, and when the United States formally entered the war Admiral Ernest J. King set his face sternly against this type of operation. With the aid of the land-based Coastal Command of the Royal Air Force, now under Admiralty control, the Royal Navy did well against U-boats in 1939-1940. German moored magnetic mines and surface raiders proved more destructive than submarines in this period, and while the Royal Navy learned to cope with these dangers, hydrostatic or pressure mines were never mastered.

The first major naval operation of the war was in connection with the Norwegian campaign, which also marked the end of what was known as the "phony war" on the continent of Europe. Both the British and the Germans were aware of the strategic value of the Norwegian ports and the Norwegian coastline. The ports could provide bases for German submarines, while the coastline permitted Germany to secure iron ore primarily from Sweden. In March 1940 when Britain resolved to lay minefields in Norwegian territorial waters to interrupt the iron ore trade, Hitler decided to occupy Denmark and Norway by force utilizing almost the entire German Navy. The German ships were sighted going up the Jutland coast but an attack by British bombers failed to do any damage, and the Admiralty failed to perceive the purpose of the operation, thinking it a maneuver to pass raiders out to the Atlantic trade routes. By the time the German purpose became apparent, the Allies were in the position of having to wage a defensive battle at sea, beyond the range of their shore-based aircraft, unlike the Germans who moved air squadrons to newly acquired fields in Denmark and Norway. As an Admiralty historian puts it, "This lack of air cover was to prove in the end too great a handicap to the Allied forces and was to reveal, for the first time in history, the complete dependence of effective operations, both by sea and by land, on efficient air cover." A second lesson of the campaign, according to Stephen Roskill, was that "special craft needed by combined operations could not be extemporized, nor could trained men be produced at short notice." Other factors responsible for the German success were the element of surprise, seizing and maintaining the initiative. The operation also was well planned and well executed, with excellent coordination among the services. British aircraft carriers covered the evacuation of those troops that had been landed, although two of the carriers were lost in this salvage venture. With the Norwegian coast in German hands, the sea ring around Germany had been pierced, and the harbors and airfields were available for the battle against Britain.

Meanwhile, the United States, while modifying the Neutrality Act to permit cash and carry and thereby aid the Allies, had established a Neutrality or Security Patrol in cooperation with the Latin American Republics which was designed to preserve a neutral zone extending some hundreds of miles off the American coastline, except for Canada, a zone in which the belligerents were forbidden to conduct military operations. None of the belligerents accepted this restriction, and both Britain and Germany felt that the zone was to their disadvantage. The United States also accelerated the naval construction program and began applying pressure on Japan to desist from aggression in the Far East. The fleet problem of 1940 was held in the Pacific in the face of vigorous protests from the Japanese presses, and the fleet was retained at Pearl Harbor in order to, as the Chief of Naval Operations put it, act as a deterrent to Japan. With the German victory in Europe in June 1940, what Roosevelt considered America's first line of defense against the European Axis powers, namely, France, had been destroyed. Furthermore, it appeared unlikely that Britain alone could prevail. On the recommendation of the Navy General Board, Roosevelt asked for legislation providing for the construction of a two-ocean navy, and other steps, including selective service, were taken to prepare the nation for possible war with the Axis powers. It should be noted that the President kept trying to get the Navy to build escort vessels, and his memoranda on this matter reveal irritation and frustration. At one point he observed that trying to get the Navy to do anything was like punching a pillow. But one of the Navy Department arguments was that it took time to build the larger ships, whereas smaller vessels could be turned out rapidly when and if the United States went to war. In the summer of 1940 Roosevelt, in response to a desperate plea from Churchill, exchanged 50 destroyers for bases, and some American authorities believe these ships saved Britain in its fight against the U-boats. British authorities are not so effusive, but the gesture did much to enhance British morale.

With the passage of the Lend Lease Act in the spring of 1941 the matter of insuring delivery of supplies to Britain began more acute, and the American Navy became engaged in the escort of convoys and the hunting of German submarines. In May 1941 the President authorized the transfer of major units from the Pacific to bolster British efforts in the Atlantic, and shortly before he had relieved Admiral Richardson as Commander in Chief of the Pacific Fleet for insisting that the fleet should be returned from Hawaii to the more adequate California bases. The President, committed to Britain's survival, was also determined to resist Japanese expansion in the Far East.

As Germany's successes mounted in the European and North African theaters, her Axis partner Japan continued aggression in China and coerced the French Vichy Government into allowing her to occupy portions of French Indochina. Roosevelt countered each Japanese move by increasing economic sanctions, until in the summer of 1941 he placed an embargo on the export of oil. Up to this time the Japanese army leaders had been at odds with their navy counterparts over the desirability of action that might involve a war with the United States, but the oil embargo and the American naval construction program convinced the Japanese naval authorities that war must come soon or never. After considering four separate military strategic concepts, a compromise was reached which incorporated proposals by the two services. This plan called for simultaneous attacks against the Philippines and Malaya to be followed by an advance on the Netherlands East Indies. By September 1941 agreement was reached on details except for Admiral Yamamoto's bold plan to attack the American fleet at Pearl Harbor, an operation which many of his colleagues thought too risky. Yamamoto, against almost unanimous opposition from naval planners, remained adamant and even threatened to resign. Finally, in mid-October, his proposal was approved.

The Japanese "grand design" envisioned an attack on the United States fleet at Pearl Harbor to neutralize American sea power. Japanese forces would then occupy territory, establish bases, and create a veritable "fortress area" in the Southwest Pacific containing all the resources necessary to sustain military and civilian activity. Some Japanese naval leaders had wanted to allow or induce the American fleet to enter the Western Pacific and engage the Japanese navy within the shelter of its land based planes, with destruction of the enemy virtually assured. The Japanese had been preparing for just such an encounter for a generation. Also, in regard to possible alternatives, Fleet Admiral Chester W. Nimitz later observed that it was fortunate that the United States did not know of the approach of the Japanese task force toward Hawaii. The American fleet would have steamed forth to meet it, and in Admiral Nimitz's words, "The Japanese would have sunk every one of our ships in deep water," primarily because of superior carrier air power. When, or whether, the United States would have recovered from such a disaster in order to wage war effectively against Japan, while at the same time providing the effort necessary against Germany, is conjectural. The Japanese hope that America would decide that the task was too great and agree to a compromise peace settlement may have been realized, and of course they counted on Axis success in Europe. So in some respects the attack at Pearl Harbor may have been advantageous to the United States, for it unified the nation for an all-out war effort and saved enough of the fleet to wage a defensive action in certain areas, to prevent the Japanese from gaining control of the Western and Central Pacific, and to provide the nucleus of subsequent dominant naval power.

Japan, flushed with her early successes, succumbed to what has been called the "victory disease." Instead of consolidating their impressive conquests of the early months of the war and concentrating on a defensive strategy, the Japanese embarked on a new program of conquests. First, to capture Tulagi in the Solomons and Port Moresby, the capital of Papua, New Guinea, in order to dominate the Coral Sea and threaten Australia. This attempt was thwarted by the first naval engagement between carriers, and the Battle of the Coral Sea was a tactical draw but a strategic defeat for the Japanese. The second venture was more ambitious: to capture Midway Island and the Western Aleutians, enlarge the defense perimeter, and draw what remained of the American fleet into battle to destroy the last effective resistance in the Pacific. This enterprise, which if successful would have compelled America to alter its global strategy, was frustrated by the "incredible victory" at Midway.

There are a number of "without whiches" that could have changed the course of events in this crucial battle. If the Japanese code had not been broken Admiral Nimitz would not have had his carriers available. If Japanese search and reconnaisance activity had been adequate the disaster might have been avoided. One Japanese authority has attributed this shortcoming to the Japanese Navy's over-emphasis on attack, which resulted in little attention being given to training or specialization in aerial surveillance. Admiral Raymond Spruance, who directed the American forces, in commenting on the engagement has used terms such as intuition in explaining a decision, and has remarked on the role played by good fortune or luck in tactical combat. He also has been criticized by armchair strategists for retiring to the eastward instead of following up the attack of the Japanese task force. But his primary mission was to prevent the capture of Midway and his decision was based, as his biographer says, on "a thorough weighing of all the factors, not the least of which was the admonition of [Admiral Nimitz] that cruisers and carriers were not to be unduly risked."

This crucial repulse of the Japanese fleet gave Admiral King a chance to press for more support for the Pacific theater. Although King was in agreement with the "Europe first" strategy, he waged a constant struggle to obtain sufficient resources to maintain pressure on the Japanese. As for the Japanese, the Midway defeat caused them to drop their plans for the conquest of Port Moresby, Fiji, New Caledonia, and Samoa. The Americans created a new fleet to advance from Rabaul into the Southwest Pacific, and King was able to secure approval for a move on Tulagi and Guadalcanal. The Joint Chiefs of Staff had finally accepted his arguments for, as he put it, a defensive-offensive strategy, namely, tactically offensive, strategically defensive. Thus the Solomons were invaded to prevent a Japanese advance to the southeast against the United States-Australia communication line.

The battle for Guadalcanal was in every respect a "cliff-Hanger," and the Japanese made two fundamental errors. First, in their attempt to recapture the island they did not realize the magnitude of the task and they committed too few forces. Second, their plan violated the sea-control-land-control order of conventional strategy. During the Solomons campaign that followed, the Japanese Naval Air Force lost 3,000 land and carrier based planes and 70 per cent of its experienced pilots. The Imperial Navy never recovered from this loss, and the Combined Fleet had to abandon the Central Pacific and withdraw behind a new Defense Line, the island chain running from Tokyo southeastward through the Marianas and Truk. The American strategy now moved to the purely offensive phase, both because of the Solomons victories and because the two-ocean navy had become a reality. Admiral Nimitz now had the most formidable naval force in history structured around the fast carrier task force.

At this point a debate among the service branches over the most desirable strategy reached a crescendo. Army leaders thought Japan would have to be invaded, and that Luzon and Okinawa would be needed as staging areas. The Navy felt that defeat of the Imperial Navy and a blockade of the home islands would bring capitulation. The Army Air Force contended that strategic bombing would be sufficient, with the Marianas and possibly Okinawa needed as bases for the B-29s. Fortunately, by 1944 the United States possessed the resources to combine all three strategies. Deciding on a parallel advance, the Southwest Pacific Forces continued their thrust along the southern axis, while the Fifth Fleet struck westward across the Central Pacific from Pearl Harbor. Conditions were ideal for the carrier task force, with its striking power, its reach, its mobility, its sea-keeping capacity, and its ability to surprise.

Profiting by experience, notably that at Tarawa which revealed the dangers of inadequate preparatory bombing and bombardment, the Kwajalein assault became the model of a "perfect invasion," and this landing, as Stephen Roskill says, "punched a hole right in the center of the 'defensive perimeter' which the Japanese had hoped to hold." In mid-1944 the Fifth Fleet assault on the Marianas brought the Japanese fleet out of the Java Sea area, and the Battle of the Philippine sea found the Imperial Fleet repulsed with significant losses from submarine and carrier attacks. The capture of the Marianas gave the B-29s the opportunity to bomb the home islands and provided bases for submarines to step up their campaign. The interdiction of shipping by submarine attack and the laying of mines in home waters became so effective that it promised to paralyze the Japanese nation. To return to the Battle of the Philippine Sea for a moment, it should be noted that American submarines gave accurate and timely reports of the enemy's preliminary movements and also sank two big carriers; that although Admiral Spruance has been criticized for not pursuing and attempting to destroy the Japanese fleet, his primary objective was to protect the landings. As he wrote in 1952, "we were at the start of a very large and important amphibious operation and we could not gamble and place it in jeopardy. The way Togo waited at Tsushima for the Russian Fleet to come to him has always been in my mind. We had somewhat the same basic situation."

The campaign for the recapture of the Philippines was in many ways a MacArthur ploy and President Roosevelt journeyed to Pearl Harbor to decide between the General's position and that advocated by the Navy. Involved were not only political and morale considerations but the Army conviction that the Philippines were needed as a staging area for the invasion of the Japanese home islands. Significantly, at least one top naval commander who opposed the venture at the time later said he thought MacArthur was right. One controversial aspect of this operation relates to Admiral Halsey's activities during the Battle for Leyte Gulf, when he broke off protecting the landing operations to pursue what turned out to be a decoy Japanese task force. When Admiral Spruance was President of the Naval War College after the war he was asked what he would have done if he had been in Halsey's place. After a moment of deliberation, he replied, "I would have reread my instructions." Actually, Halsey's orders were somewhat ambiguous. He was directed by Nimitz to "cover and support forces of the Southwest Pacific in order to assist in the seizure and occupation of objectives in the Central Philippines, to destroy enemy naval and air forces in or threatening the Philippine area, and to protect air and sea communications along the Central Pacific axis." But, Nimitz added, "in case opportunity for destruction of a major portion of the enemy fleet offer or can be created, such destruction becomes the primary task." As Lord Nelson once said, "it is at best but a guess, and to him who guesses right goes victory." But a decision in war is an educated guess, and it is a composite of those factors in a human being which represent his professional training and his native abilities. Success or failure also depends on how much the commander knows about the situation and what the enemy does.

Regarding the Philippine campaign, Admiral of the Fleet Lord Keyes has observed that "the success of the battle for the Philippines was only made possible because the U.S. Navy had been free to develop its own naval aviation. It has been done with an amazing skill and enterprise and on a gigantic scale. Furthermore, it has shown that in the complex business of waging war on the seas, it cannot be set down as a maxim that any one factor can be exclusively decisive." Admiral Sherman has noted that at Leyte, "Unlike other battles in the Pacific, no previous radio interception had given any inkling of enemy intentions." So during the war of the Pacific the American naval leaders enjoyed certain advantages, informational, technological, and quantitative. While each may have proved decisive in specific engagements, no one would want to ignore the fighting qualities of the Americans or the brilliance of their leaders.

To return to the European scene, the major tasks assigned the Allied navies, which meant essentially those of Great Britain and the United States, were to blockade western Europe, maintain the sea lanes to permit shipping to reach the Allies, and provide the massive logistical and bombardment support for landing operations in North Africa, Sicily, Italy, and finally France. The blockade was not too difficult, although the Axis powers controlled enough of the continent of Europe to be freed from critical dependence on outside sources of material. The protection of shipping was another matter, and some of the ineffectual methods employed by the British early in the war have been mentioned. This most intensive _guerre de course_ that any navy ever faced found an Allied loss of 5,150 merchantmen totalling 21½

NAVAL STRATEGY

million tons, with the German U-boat accomplishing most of the destruction. During the war Germany turned out 1,162 U-boats, and the strategic bombing campaign on submarine bases and yards had virtually no effect on the Atlantic battle until the autumn of 1944, when it did delay completion of the new type vessels. By far the most effective anti-submarine instruments were the sea and air convoy escorts, who thus reinforced the old lesson that the escort-of-convoy strategy provided the best means for defending merchant shipping and destroying raiders of all types. As for landing operations, Roskill points out, "What is beyond doubt is that every offensive step which led to the Italian surrender was based on our command of the sea, and that the Mediterranean campaigns as a whole provide a wonderful example of the successful application of a predominantly maritime strategy."

In some respects one of the most impressive developments of the war was, as the British put it, what the Americans call "logistics." In fact some British authorities believe that the creation and successful employment of the "fleet train" ranks with the effective utilization of the carrier task force as the greatest American innovations of the naval war. Of course the British do say that Americans were very inefficient in the use of the merchant marine. Unlike other countries the United States could almost afford that luxury.

To conclude with a few observations, as Admiral Gretton has noted, in World War II "strategical thought in Britain and America returned to the maritime strategy which had been forgotten in 1914." Also, the carrier emerged as the successor to the battleship as the "backbone of the navy," its most powerful striking force, and its successful employment revealed a degree of flexibility and resourcefulness rare in military annals. In this sense alone the old adage that each war is fought with the weapons of the last is inaccurate. Moreover, techniques of amphibious warfare were refined to the point where what has been called the most intricate problem of modern warfare became both a science and an art, a science in its planning and an art in its execution. In this context, it was revealed most emphatically that a maritime strategy does permit the choice of time and place for ground intervention, with the usual tactical advantages that accrue from such an option. Furthermore, in this conflict the need for inter-service cooperation was more imperative than at any previous time in history. Not only was such unity imperative because of the multi-faceted dimensions of warfare, but it was necessary in order to present a solid front against the importunities of civilian authorities. In fact, Roskill and Schofield are among those British authorities who attribute the failure of British seaborne operations to disagreement between soldiers and sailors over strategic issues, and the inability of the civilian government to understand or support either. Cooperation between allies was fundamental to success, and although I have slighted the British contribution the command relationships were generally excellent in spite of some feeling of Anglophobia on the American side. General George C. Marshall thought the British were less suspicious of the Americans, although, as he said, "They may have just felt we weren't smart enough to cause them trouble."

To summarize the role of seapower in this gigantic struggle, control of the Pacific was essential in order to defeat Japan, and control of the Atlantic and the Mediterranean was necessary to defeat Italy and Germany. So without arguing which was the predominant factor in each case, there is no question that without a victory at sea there would have been no victory on land or in the air. To quote Field Marshal Viscount Montgomery of Alamein in his A History of Warfare, "The lesson is this: in all history the nation which has had control of the seas has, in the end, prevailed."

STRATEGY FOR VICTORY IN THE PACIFIC:
Chapter 16

Commentary

Commenting on these papers presents a challenge almost as great as that faced by American leaders in December 1941. Historians traditionally find fault not only with those who make events but with each other as well. Today we have heard analyses of the strategy of the four architects of victory in the Pacific by historians whose credentials are impeccable, and who, functioning under rigorous time limitations, have provided insights into the complex problems that faced the planners and the solutions provided by the decision-makers. Some reputations have been enhanced; at least one, by consensus, has been diminished. These papers represent no attack on the "cult of the individual" but on what one individual advocated and what he did. The challenge facing this commentator is that, unlike opinions of American strategists in December 1941, these papers represent agreement with each other on most issues that overlap.

Fortunately, the program and the speakers have placed their subjects in the proper perspective. In comparing and contrasting the strategic positions of each of these commanders, one is aware that King and Marshall were waging a global war against a host of enemies; MacArthur and Nimitz were contending with the Japanese and the greater Pacific Ocean. The disparate outlooks are understandable, and while Nimitz is not revealed as suffering from localitis, MacArthur seems myopic to a degree that almost defies credibility. Perhaps each theater commander should regard his area of operations as the most significant. After all, it is his primary responsibility and he must stress its importance in order to get the support he needs or thinks he is entitled to. Admiral King, as Clark Reynolds points out, tilted more toward the Pacific than did his colleagues on the Joint Chiefs of Staff or the Combined Chiefs of Staff, and the battle for the allocation of resources was often more intense than inter-service and intra-service rivalry or disputes over strategy and tactics. The outlook from Washington was different from that of any other post, and it appears that Marshall, as well as King, was the right man in the right place at the right time. The statesmanship of overall command demanded a combination of abilities found rarely in any individual, for each had to fight his opposite numbers, his bosses, and at least one difficult subordinate. We may conclude that King had as little trouble with Nimitz as Marshall did with Eisenhower. But of King's five main obstacles as enumerated by Clark Reynolds, only one was the official enemy. General Marshall felt obliged to remind MacArthur that the Navy was on the same side. But as Yossarian observed in the novel CATCH 22, the enemy is whoever might get you killed.

Each of these four papers necessarily incorporates the subjects of the others, for command relationships were closely intertwined. The personalities of MacArthur and King were such that cooperation under any circumstances would have been difficult, and while only Clayton James and Clark Reynolds emphasize the intractibility of their subjects, some characteristics of the others are revealed. The multifarious dimensions of coalition warfare placed considerable strain on the Washington commanders, which, coupled with the sea, air, and land collaboration required to prosecute the war against Japan, made it even more essential that unity of purpose and effort be maintained. Within this context the similarities and contrasts between the waging of war in Europe and that in the Pacific are notable, and at least the heads of state seldom intruded into the strategy and tactics of Pacific operations. Some observations on the relationship between the wars in the Pacific and in Europe would include an early acknowledgment that amphibious operations in the Pacific were to be a Marine Corps responsibility and those in Europe were to be an Army responsiblity since it would be a prelude to prolonged land combat. Also of interest is the impact that the delay in the anticipated ending of the war in Europe had on planning in the Pacific.

Admiral King and the American Navy, we are told, had been preparing to fight Japan, the "most probable enemy," for more than a generation. Conversely, of course, the Japanese Imperial Navy had been preparing for war against the United States. The composition of the fleets and their disposition, the development of bases, the annual exercises, and the war plans of each of the potential adversaries were designed for this eventual encounter, and each synchronized with the other in regard to capabilities and intentions. The bold attack on Pearl Harbor, whatever its merits, violated the traditional Japanese approach. Predicated on an encounter with the American fleet in the Western Pacific, a fleet weakened by submarine attrition, the Imperial Navy had anticipated the advantages of proximate logistic support and land based aircraft. The strike at Pearl Harbor upset the American timetable, and frantic efforts in Washington to retrieve the situation and devise a new strategy to save the Philippines were frustrated by a reaffirmation of the Europe First decision and a reluctant acceptance of Japanese control of much of the area west of Midway. Resources were to be allocated to the Pacific as necessary to preserve communications with Australia and follow a defensive strategy, while efforts would be concentrated in the European theater. But the repulse of the Japanese force at Midway altered this outlook. The British felt that the immediate threat in the Pacific had been alleviated and more resources should be committed to Europe. Admiral King, disagreeing, urged that the Midway success be exploited by following up with what he called a defensive-offensive strategy: strategically defensive and tactically offensive. King earlier had defined this term in a letter to the Secretary of the Navy on 8 February 1942: "The defensive-offensive may be paraphrased as hold what you have and hit them when you can." Prior to the outcome of the Midway battle, however, this strategy consisted of sporadic raids and the Coral Sea and Midway interdictions of Japanese initiatives. On 2 July 1942, less than a month after Midway, the Joint Chiefs authorized a more vigorous effort to improve the defensive posture in the Pacific, an effort that was to evolve into the purely offensive strategy. In April 1942, King had submitted a plan to Admiral Nimitz for a thrust across the Central Pacific that eventually was followed, with certain modifications resulting from changing circumstances and differing opinions of strong-willed associates.

These differing opinions on certain issues make up the substance of these papers. The merits of the various proposals and their rationale are not, to this commentator, always clear. To what extent were strategic predelictions determined by service affiliations? Did Marshall support King's strategy in the Pacific because King deferred to him on the European theater? Faced with options and the unpredictability of the enemy, what were the criteria that determined whether one course of action should be followed rather than another? Clayton James reveals how MacArthur deviated from instructions, wasted resources and time in pacifying the Philippines, seemed more interested in conquering territory than in defeating Japan, and virtually wanted to wage his own private war. King, Marshall, and Nimitz wanted to get the war over as expeditiously as possible, and, to take issue with Clark Reynolds, it seems that these three leaders were more addicted to the "direct" strategic approach in contrast with MacArthur's espousal of the peripheral or indirect strategy. The dramatic meeting at Pearl Harbor where President Roosevelt supported MacArthur's assault on the Philippines illustrated the divergent views, although King later said he thought the decision was correct in light of subsequent events. According to an old football adage, the team that makes the fewest mistakes usually wins. But in the last two years of the Pacific war the Americans had such an overwhelming preponderance of resources that errors of comission or omission could have little effect on the final outcome.

But Ned Potter and Forrest Pogue have introduced a factor that is often ignored, namely, the impact of casualties on strategic choices. It may seem odd that 1,000 dead in one campaign should so disturb the decision makers when casualties in the hundreds of thousands were commonplace on the European fronts. Although Luzon appeared a less formidable obstacle than Formosa, the bloody Tarawa experience was followed by the masterfully executed invasion of Kwajalein that demonstrated the art and science of amphibious operations. Okinawa came as a shock to almost everyone, even though the huge losses occurred after successful landings. The role, then, of sustained and anticipated casualties, while always a consideration in military planning, evidently was a major factor at times in altering the strategy of the Pacific war. Which brings up the question of the desirability or undesirability of Russian entry into the war against Japan and the use of atomic bombs. Militarily, the issue was simple: to defeat the enemy get whatever help was available and use the most effective weapons at your disposal. On unconditional surrender, from the announcement of this "doctrine" at Casablance it was made clear on numerous occasions that it pertained to the armed forces and did not mean a total capitulation by the people or the nation. Consistent with this repeated assertion, the three nations singled out--Germany, Japan, and Italy--signed documents submitting unconditionally only to the surrender of their armed forces.

To continue, one gets the impression from these papers that Nimitz, unlike King, Marshall, and MacArthur, had little to do with the formulation of strategy and confined himself to implementing directives from Washington. Nimitz' somewhat hasty endorsement of MacArthur's proposal for a southwest strategy casts doubt on his judgment and earned him a deserved if brutal rebuke from King. Professor Potter, in his forthcoming biography of Nimitz, undoubtly will reveal the Admiral's contributions as a tactical and strategic innovator. Contrary to the old cliche that each war is fought with the methods of the last, the fast carrier task force, sophisticated logistic support, and refined amphibious techniques, characterized the most revolutionary changes in naval warfare.

A story current in the Pacific had General MacArthur and Admiral Nimitz floating on a raft that began to sink. Nimitz said, "Doug, I have a confession to make; I can't swim." MacArthur replied, "Chester, I, too, have a confession to make; I can't walk on water." Conflict and cooperation were endemic as each service, convinced of its own decisive role, sought priority status. As successive Japanese defense perimeters were penetrated each service became more certain that it held the key to surrender: the Navy by blockade, the Air Force by bombardment, and the Army by invasion. At each level of the command structure, most importantly at the top level where the war was managed, the concept and general practice of unified command in its broadest sense prevailed, and revealed a commitment to the joint effort that made victory possible.

THE EUROPEAN SECOND FRONT IN WORLD WAR II: Commentary

Chapter 17

Among the oft-quoted and frequently inaccurate cliches is that each war is fought with the weapons of the last. Parenthetically, if this were so the fist hatchet would still be employed as the major weapon. A similar and possibly more accurate observation might be made of historians, who so often engage in rewriting each other or seem bent on demonstrating that the explanation of the past is difficult, complex, and, previously, incorrect. The historiography of World War II promises to rival, if it has not surpassed, the textual criticism of the Bible, with exegesis only awaiting eschatology. But indulgence in cynicism is a luxury that only the young can afford, and my assigned task is to deal with the papers you have heard.

Professor Steele has tried to grapple with one of the knottiest problems confronting the historian, namely, the influence of public opinion on a military/political action. In so doing he must establish: first, what public opinion is; second, what it happened to be on the issue; and third, the causal connection with the decision. The sources cited for his information are polls conducted for the Government, using sampling techniques not indicated in the paper. So what we have is the reaction of an undisclosed segment of the population, and reports whose results were made available only to certain individuals or groups within the Government. My observations here are not for the purpose of denigrating the nature of the information or the methods by which it was acquired. Most important are (1) the fact that this data was not furnished to the communication media and the general public, which in itself could have had an impact on that nebulous entity "public opinion"; and (2) that the "decision makers" were directly exposed to the sentiments revealed in these private polls. Professor Steele says the President was sensitive to the public mood which he divined from many sources, but this other material is not documented in the paper. So, for the purpose of Professor Steele's paper, the question of what public opinion happened to be is irrelevant; what the decision makers (and in this case the President) <u>thought</u> it was is crucial, for what Professor Steele is investigating is a causal relationship. Still, I believe that the title of this paper should be changed to indicate more precisely what is being attempted.

To continue, I heartily agree that "The President's approach to grand strategy was never entirely or even predominantly military." Here Professor Steele takes issue with conventional interpretations, although unfortunately he does not have (or take) the opportunity to develop this thesis. He then contends that "For Roosevelt the politics of victory meant two things: first the creation and maintenance of a harmonious alliance against Hitler, and second an American 'home front' which provided unstinting support of the war effort." This second statement, it seems to me, contradicts the former assertion, for if Roosevelt's grand strategy was not essentially military then the "politics of victory" would embrace other than military considerations. On the other hand, perhaps Professor Steele divorces grand strategy from the politics of victory, the latter dealing solely with the military aspects of the war. If this is so, then again I must fault Professor Steele. Roosevelt was not only concerned with maintaining the alliance and domestic support for the prosecution of the war--he wanted the war fought in the most efficient and expeditious manner possible. In saying this I am not referring to the effect that the military strategy might have on negotiations for postwar settlements, even though I believe it to be a crucial factor and one which Roosevelt recognized better than some others, including Winston Churchill.

Roosevelt's concern for creating a "martial spirit" and his "passion for 'unity' or 'high morale'" is certainly understandable. As an amateur but avid student of American history he was aware of the problems his predecessors had encountered in waging wars without widespread support, and prior to the attack on Pearl Harbor his efforts to garner sufficient public enthusiasm for more direct participation in the European conflict seemed unsuccessful. Even after Pearl Harbor, as Professor Steele points out, the administration was not convinced that the public was behind the President in his proposed strategy. Proximity to the conflict was a factor in creating enthusiasm for its prosecution, and most Americans simply were not directly affected by the violent aspects of the war. Perhaps as Professor Steele says, "few took the Japanese seriously in December 1941," but polls revealed, as he indicates and as other data supports, that most respondents believed that prosecution of the war against Japan should be given top priority. Yet Roosevelt stuck to the Europe first strategy, which gives support for Dean Rusk's observation that "The difference between the world of decision and the world of opinion is a vast difference." Still, circumstances do alter cases, and there is no agreement on how many examples are necessary for a generalization. At least Roosevelt's perception of the "public mood" did not alter his decision to give major attention to the European theater, nor did the series of defeats suffered by the Allies in the Far East. Whether victories or defeats create greater public enthusiasm and support for war efforts is another question.

EUROPEAN SECOND FRONT

To shift slightly to another topic, it seems strange that, as Professor Steele reports, ". . . many Americans didn't really understand why they had been thrust into war. More than 45% of those polled admitted that they had no clear idea of what the United States was fighting for." Strange, I say, because the President had been expounding his aims since January 1939. His Four Freedoms address, his persistent warnings against aggression and world anarchy, the Atlantic Charter, the Declaration of the United Nations, all had revealed prescriptions for the postwar world in terms more specific than was usual either before or after entering a conflict. Ordinarily the "causes" are expounded at great length but the conditions of peace are not. Of course the President's objectives were couched in somewhat general language as would befit a nation engaged in a coalition effort, where the ambitions of allies often are not in harmony. In this momentous struggle the Allies were pretty much agreed on what they were fighting against; detailed expositions of postwar settlements could well have had an adverse effect on the task at hand.

Nevertheless, the American public had been apprised of the President's objectives. First, to destroy the governments of the Axis nations, whose activities jeopardized the safety of the United States, the Western Hemisphere, and the entire world. Second, to establish a peace to demonstrate that aggression did not pay. Third, to create some system of collective security to enforce common standards of conduct among nations and halt aggression at its source. According to Professor Steele, it was not a matter of the people disagreeing with Roosevelt's aims; most of the respondents simply did not know what they were. Perhaps better understood by the public was the need to defeat the enemy, and here the Congressional resolutions and the President's repeated exhortations for "victory" were understood. Under these circumstances it may have seemed even more imperative that American troops engage the German forces on a major scale and reverse the trend of Axis successes in virtually every theater.

Yet the arguments for and against a "second front," when and where, embraced considerations other than a desire to mollify domestic opinion, and some are indicated by Professor Steele as he describes briefly the shifts in Anglo-American planning in regard to the nature and timing of the land assault against the Nazis. British reluctance to invade the Continent involved, among other considerations, the enormity of logistics problems, an addiction to the peripheral or indirect strategy, and a fear of huge casualty lists reminiscent of abortive World War I campaigns. But to deal with what I gather is Professor Steele's main thesis, has he demonstrated that the decision to embark on the North African venture was dictated by the President's desire to satisfy American "public demands."?

Not at all, in the opinion of this commentator. Too many other factors were involved, and even though Professor Steele may be correct the evidence is not apparent. The causal connection between public opinion and the decision to invade Africa simply is not revealed.

The processes of decision-making have been subjected to numerous studies by scholars in recent years, although these processes often are divorced from motivation. On the one hand there are the steps or methods by which decisions are made; on the other hand there are the reasons why a particular decision is made. The decision-maker, in facing various alternative courses of action, usually finds that a multiplicity of factors must be considered. He also, consciously or unconsciously, assigns various weights to each of these factors, and though they may not be numerically quantifiable some are obviously more important than others. In dealing with the question of the European Second Front it seems highly unlikely, to put it mildly, that a monocausal explanation would suffice. Certainly the President wanted and needed domestic support for the war effort, and the lapse of one year without American troops engaging the German Wehrmacht could not fail to create dissatisfaction at home. Yet how much greater the displeasure of the Soviet Union which was suffering the brunt of the Nazi onslaught and being bled white. Professor Anderson, in his paper "The Second Front is Europe: the Soviet View," reveals the Kremlin's anxiety for some action that would draw a significant number of German divisions from the Eastern Front, and both the British and American governments had made what in Soviet eyes were commitments to do just that. The Western Allies simply were not carrying their share of the load and the implications for the future of the alliance were ominous. Aside from suspicions of bad faith, and accusations of ulterior and base motives, it was not inconceivable that Russia might collapse or reach a compromise peace with the Nazis. The events of August 1939 were fresh in the minds of Washington and London officials, who were compelled to consider possibilities as well as probabilities.

The most significant aspects of Professor Anderson's paper, which I only received at this meeting although he did phone me last week to outline his thesis, are the motives he introduces in explaining Stalin's anxiety and his sincerity in urging for a second front in Europe. No national leader can be completely impervious to public opinion--after all, the Kremlin controlled the nation's effort but the people suffered, fought, and sustained the resistance. Then, too, Stalin could not allow the professional soldier to gain too much prestige and power. Political commissars were a luxury that could not be afforded when the survival of the government and the nation depended on thwarting the Nazi blitzkrieg, and military coups are not unique in the annals of the past and present. Professor Anderson's paper tends to invalidate the contention that the Soviets did not want the Western Allied forces on the continent of Europe, although even the recent breed of Kremlinologists is often at a loss to know what is going on or what has gone on in Moscow. Perhaps they have acquired a degree of humility from the experience of a former Kremlin leader, Nikita Khrushchev, who in spite of his vantage point was unaware of his pending removal.

Well, the role of a commentator is not to answer questions but to raise them. The controversies undoubtedly will continue, and, hopefully, bring more light to bear on the darkened areas of the past.

REFLECTIONS ON THE CHARACTERISTICS OF A COMMANDER

Chapter 18

Probably one of the more difficult problems for the historian is the discernment of those personal qualities and characteristics that bear on the performance of the successful military commander. Mahan, in analyzing types of naval officers, found they "by natural characteristics arrange themselves in pairs--presenting points of contrast, in deficiencies and excellencies, which group together, not by similarity chiefly, but as complementary."

This observation certainly applies to the six leaders that are discussed in this paper. In fact, one is tempted to conclude that there are no absolute qualifications necessary for successful leadership, no scientific formula, no universal criteria or statistical profile by which to measure an individual's potential or existing ability to exercise command. Those of us who have struggled with courses designed to train young men in the complexities of leadership are aware that the subject scarcely merits the designation of an "inexact science," and the simple enumeration of glib generalizations may be useful only as an exercise in demonstrating the exceptions. Nonetheless, all military personnel are constantly being evaluated by their superiors in terms of leadership qualities, and they are being judged by the men they command in terms of their effectiveness.

Each of these officers possessed an image which had an impact that was directly related to his success in command. Beatty, King, and Halsey gave the impression of boldness, aggressiveness, dash, dynamism, toughness, and flair. They had, in Madison Avenue parlance, STYLE. Their physical appearance, including dress, visage, and physique, their speech and their mannerisms, all contributed to the effect. On the other hand, Jellicoe, Spruance, and Nimitz were quiet, modest if not self-effacing, conventional in dress and conduct, each the very antithesis of flamboyance. Yet their cool exteriors exuded confidence and they had that indefinable quality, PRESENCE. These three officers used their power quietly, and which of these stereotype groups was most effective in exercising leadership could well depend on the circumstances and the requirements of the particular job.

The more than casually curious person, seeking to discover how these people got that way, would surely find himself involved in the age-old argument over heredity and environment. Some authorities contend that leaders are born not made, although the services stress education, indoctrination, training, and experience. But in regard to the image, does the individual assiduously cultivate an exterior designed to project in a particular way, which he deliberately creates as suited to his personality, his aspirations, and his assessment of the qualities needed for success in his chosen profession? Probably most have some sort of model, a Nelson or a Lord Hornblower, to which they try to conform; and evidently none of the men considered made strenuous efforts to disabuse others of their convictions in attributing to them distinctive qualities, however inaccurate. Halsey later could protest, "Now that I am sitting down to my autobiography it is Bill Halsey whom I want to get on paper, not the fake, flamboyant 'Bull.'" Yet it is clear that he came to take pride in the nickname, and he selected El Toro to be used as his TBS code call. His boastful statements about a quick end to the war, dictating the peace in Tokyo, riding the Emperor's horse, and exhorting everyone to kill more Japs made headlines and contributed to his image. At the same time it helped restore the morale of a fleet reeling from a succession of defeats. In his thesis written as a student at the Naval War College, Halsey enumerated the characteristics he considered necessary in a fleet commander. Stressing what we would call the "charismatic" qualities or "star appeal," he felt the commander should inspire the men and insure that his will permeated and dominated the entire force. To continue briefly with the cultivation of an image, King protested about certain legends concerning his toughness, but in his autobiography he quotes with pride stories of his shaving with a blowtorch. Beatty's vanity was manifest in his six-button coat, which he did not inflict on others. King insisted that the slate-gray uniform replace the summer khaki, and while eventually it did not prevail, a number of us bought the damned things only to find that they were not permitted in the Pacific.

In contrast with King, Halsey, and Beatty, the other three leaders appeared uninterested in any type of unique or distinctive projection, with the possible exception of Nimitz' propensity for having his photograph taken pitching horseshoes with enlisted men. Jellicoe's biographer described him as that "great little man," and Nimitz referred to Spruance as "this reserved and self-effacing man." As for temperament being part of the image, King had a reputation of engaging in name-calling with his subordinates; Halsey's rages were legend, and both of these men had acquired reputations for being harsh and outspoken in their criticism of shortcomings in their subordinates. Probably these outbursts were not contrived, but they contributed to the image and may have contributed to an efficiency of performance. Conversely, the "iron hand in the velvet glove" approach, as illustrated in the stories about Nimitz' firmness, could have been just as effective. The relative merits of the carrot and the stick, the pat on the back rather than the kick in the posterior, are hotly debated. But it appears that none of these "types" had significant problems with morale, loyalty, dedication, or performance.

Still, one should resist the tendency to assume that the commander who wins has made no mistakes, or the other extreme, which one might conclude after reading a number of war books, that nothing that anyone did was right. Perhaps the most essential factor in exercising command is good judgment, and this dimension of leadership deserves a good deal more attention. Liddell Hart has concluded that "The most successful of the Allied commanders enjoyed such immense quantitative advantage that the qualitative value of their own performance cannot be gauged." But such was certainly not true during the early years in the Pacific, and, in any event, the commanders had to make a number of hard decisions which, for their forces and at times for the nation, were "moments of truth." There is a story about a wise man being asked how one avoids making mistakes, and he replied that one does so by exercising good judgment. When asked how one develops good judgment, he replied "by making mistakes." Both Alfred P. Sloan and Henry Ford II have been quoted to the effect that a successful executive should be right at least half of the time, which may be satisfactory in the automobile business. But military leaders and physicians bury their mistakes, and a single major defeat can have catastrophic consequences.

C. P. Snow defines good judgment as "the ability to think of many matters at once, in their interdependence, their relative importance, and their consequences." Significantly, Spruance was dubbed as the man with a computer brain, and we are all familiar with the current stress on systems analysis, which I define as a more efficient method for considering all the factors involved in making a decision. But without engaging in the controversy over "computers versus judgment" I would like to deal with this ultimate test of a commander's talents.

As to the process, it appears that judgment involves both logical, rational thought and intuition based upon imagination and experience. "The intuitive process or factor," says Henry Eccles, "is the creative or artistic element of military thinking," and Justice Brandeis thought judgment involved "the almost instinctive correlation of a thousand imponderables." Mahan extolled "the intuitive ability which practice gives to size up a situation. The French call it coup d'oeil--at a glance." Spruance, in explaining why he had followed a particular course of action at Midway, called his reason "a feeling, an intuition perhaps." His biographer points out that the decision "was actually based upon sound logic [and a] thorough estimate of the situation and orderly thought." Spruance, "the thinking man's naval officer," has ever been aware of human fallibility, and recently he attributed much of his success at Midway to "luck." He is quoted as saying that "I am more than ever impressed with the part that good or bad fortune plays in tactical engagements. [We have been given] credit, where not credit is due. . ." He would probably agree with Machiavelli, who surmised that human beings exercise control over about 50 percent of their activities (he was not so foolhardy as to specify which half). Spruance also has stressed the value of imagination, "tempered and guided by common sense and reason," which he thinks necessary to, as he puts it, "discipline the imagination." So the commander must consider a multiplicity of factors and weigh their significance, but before deciding he must endeavor to anticipate the outcome. Every decision is a prediction, and the operator is selecting from alternative courses of action that which is most likely to be successful in light of the objective. The situation is often such that a lengthy appraisal, "due deliberation," would be impracticable, in which case he must rely on an intuitive or "gut" reaction. While this area of investigation may more appropriately be the province of the psychologist, a bit of conjecture may provoke discussion if not dissention.

Freud maintained that the "unconscious mind" was more reliable in certain matters than the conscious mind, i.e., that intuition can be more effective than reason as a guide to action. We are reminded of the saying that women are wiser than men because they know less but understand more. Be that as it may, this intuitive ability which I have emphasized is developed by the individual in his own professional field through experience, both directly and vicariously. Mahan quoted Napoleon to the effect that on the field of battle the happiest inspiration--again coup d'oeil--is often only a recollection. And Mahan went on to observe that:

> This is a testimony to the value of historical illustration, which is simply recorded experience; for, whether the recollection be of what some other man did, or whether it be of some incident one's self has been and recalls, it draws upon the past and that, too, not in a general way, but by specific application to an instant emergency, comprehended at a glance, just because it is familiar.

Numerous military figures have commented on the value of history, not only for what to do but for what to avoid doing, and the best way to escape what Marx called the "dead hand of the past controlling the living" is to study history.

COMMAND CHARACTERISTICS

At this point I take the opportunity to introduce the role of the Naval War College. Nimitz remarked, "I regard the course I had here in 1922 to middle '23, an 11 months course, as the best training I could conceive of for command at sea," and of the Pacific war game, "the course was so complete that when the war in the Pacific actually started, nothing that happened surprised us at all except the kamikaze attacks." Being forewarned he was forearmed, and he recognized the contingencies as they arose. Spruance's biographer says the admiral "himself attributes his later successful war operations in large measure to the training received at the Naval War College," and Spruance says of the College "this is where I got my education." Halsey learned strategy and tactics "with emphasis on the problems of logistics." But, as noted earlier, he was required to deal with the knotty question of command qualities. "The duty," Halsey wrote, "was pleasant, stimulating because of the instruction, the exchange of ideas, the chance to test your pet theories on the game board, and the opportunity to read up on professional publications." King found the months at Newport "refreshing and valuable." "What he learned of Pacific strategy," he said, "proved its usefulness in due time," and his first thesis, "The Influence of the National Policy on the Strategy of a War," submitted on 7 November 1932, contained, in King's words, "passages that were to be confirmed by developments of nine years later."

Well, I'm not engaged in a public relations venture for my temporary institution, but these examples demonstrate one of the most effective means of developing judgment. King has observed that:

> Any man facing a major decision acts, consciously or otherwise, upon the training and belief of a lifetime. This is no less true of a military commander than of a surgeon, who, while operating, suddenly encounters an unsuspected complication. In both instances, the men must act immediately with little time for reflection, and if they are successful in dealing with the unexpected it is upon the basis of past experience and training.

No doubt a critic would feel that King is slighting what is called native ability, or that the opponent by his ineptitude might contribute more to victory than the superior decisionmaking of the victor. But the cumulative effect of exposure to situations, real or imaginary, actual or vicarious, cannot be discounted.

Of course there were a great many factors operating in the favor of the American naval leaders and some have been noted in passing. At the highest level, as Walter Millis observed, the war was not fought, it was administered. But administration has always constituted a large part of the commander's responsibilities, and successful administration demands the resources of a scientist and the talents of an artist. King often maintained--as he says only half in jest--"that he has never done anything for himself that he could get someone else to do for him." The delegation or decentralization of <u>authority</u> is almost a maxim among organizational theorists, but the man at the top can never absolve himself of <u>responsibility</u>. Halsey expressed a strong opinion on the subject of overcentralization in his Naval War College thesis. "A commander," he wrote, "may become so fascinated and engrossed in his planning, that he assumes the initiative rightfully belonging to his subordinate. His plans may become so complicated, so detailed, and so manifold, that it is a practical impossibility to follow them." Yet chaos must be avoided, and the successful commander usually adopts the adage of telling subordinates what to do but not how to do it, only to be faced with the prospect of losing control over the segments of his command, destroying essential cohesiveness of purpose, and creating a situation of virtual anarchy. Conversely, one of Jellicoe's defects was his tendency to become absorbed in details, to devote his energies to the trees rather than the forest. Such a situation could be remedied, it seems, by a change in the commander's habits or interests and the selection of a competent staff in which he had confidence. In practice the former may be more difficult than the latter, and many a good staff officer has been wasted by serving under an overconscientious commander. The problem is to provide leadership and guidance without stifling responsibility and initiative, and success in command is often directly related to the amount and caliber of work that can be secured from subordinates. The authoritarian personality has its place in a military organization, although persuasion and manipulation may prove more effective than arbitrary dictatorship.

Of the four American leaders discussed, only two faced actual battle situations. It is of some interest to note their reactions to emergencies and disappointments. Halsey tells us that after an operation had been launched he worried and fretted, smoked numerous cigarettes, drank quantities of coffee, read trashy magazines, and was completely miserable. On the other hand, we are told that after an operation had been set in motion, "Spruance relaxed. He had though things through so thoroughly that his mind was free of unnecessary worry about improbable contingencies." As for disappointments, Halsey to the day of his death never stopped torturing himself about his absence at Midway and what he considered his "hardest and wrongest decision," namely, to turn away from his pursuit of the Japanese carrier force and heed Kinkaid's request to protect the ships in Leyte Gulf. Spruance, at one time notified that he had been denied an opportunity to engage a Japanese force because of a failure in radio communications, replied quietly, "That's too bad, isn't it?" He gave no indication of wasting time in regrets or recriminations.

COMMAND CHARACTERISTICS

To pursue another tack in this impressionistic commentary, Spruance emphasized the significance of a change in war planning by stressing the enemy's capabilities rather than his intentions. Of course any commander in his estimate of the situation must consider both factors, but the order of priority is crucial. In the Pacific war the American leaders enjoyed a considerable advantage over their opponents because they could read the Japanese code and their ships were equipped with radar. This advantage could prove decisive, and Midway is the most notable but far from the only example of the contribution made by intelligence to the outcome of a battle. Admiral Sherman, in his <u>Combat Command</u>, says with some exaggeration that at Leyte, "<u>Unlike</u> other battles in the Pacific, no previous radio interception had given any inkling of enemy intentions." This superior knowledge was usually available to the commander not only during the initial maneuvering and disposition of the fleets but to a significant degree after the engagement began. General Marshall has observed that battlefield decisions are made in an atmosphere of "chronic obscurity," but the American naval leaders enjoyed the benefit of many "eyes of the fleet." Still, it is frightening to consider the amount of incorrect information that was received by these commanders, and the armchair critic must often contemplate the relevance of the Tolstoyian view of warfare. Of course many participants find out what happened only after the event, and in trying to reconstruct the details of an engagement we might ask whether anyone would submit a battle report that contained information to warrant his court-martial.

One writer has asserted that leading forces in battle is "possibly the most complete human activity, since it involves all the intellectual, physical and moral power in a man." Modern war accentuates the intellectual dimension, for adapting technology to strategy, or the reverse, the awesome logistic problems, and the intricate command relationships in theaters of war covering thousands of miles of land, sea, and air, imposed demands which seemed almost impossible of human resolution. The Navy that these men represented and the forces they led were the product of the most highly industrialized society known to man. These leaders embodied, and in action realized, many of the ideas and processes of thought which characterized the period. They should be viewed as both products and molders of their times, times characterized not only by mechanization but by a closer association of disparate nations. In the latter connection one discerns qualities necessary to function with opposite numbers in coalition warfare and, from the Navy's point of view, the situation in Washington required a leader who would not be dominated by the forceful personality of General Marshall, overwhelmed by the labyrinthian system, or intimidated by the British. Forrest Pogue has observed that King and Marshall "never succeeded in developing the warm affection Marshall and Stark had for each other," and they had what the Chief of Staff described as "one or two pretty mean fights, but each gained the other's respect and made honest efforts to reach agreement when it seemed that further controversy would interfere seriously with the conduct of the war." That each made significant contributions to the American position on strategy is indicated by Lord Alanbrooke's notes on 1 November 1943 after the Quebec Conference. "I realized only too well how far I have failed," he wrote. "If only I had had sufficient force of character to swing those American Chiefs of Staff and make them see daylight." Of course some of us regret that the American strategy regarding Europe was not implemented at an earlier date, but the joint chiefs had a formidable antagonist in the British Prime Minister whose addiction to the indirect approach amounted to an obsession.

On the matter of interservice relationships, Louis Morton has related how the commanders in the Pacific argued among themselves over the role of their respective arm in contemplated operations, both on the strategic and tactical level. The alleged "military mind" was subdivided as the professional prism reflected air, land, and sea points of view. Admiral "Mary" Miles recently has described his frustrations in dealing not only with the Army but with the sinister cloak and dagger OSS representatives, from all of which we may reach the obvious conclusion that a commander should be able to get along with and handle people at all levels and in all dimensions of activity. The extent to which "getting along" involves concession and compromise is fundamental, and the successful commander must see that his views prevail a good part of the time. That he need not be a "personality boy" is apparent, although the complexities of modern warfare and the need to deal with so many people outside the service environment seem to emphasize "operator" techniques.

One quality that appears common to these leaders is related to one of the generally accepted principles of war, namely, concentration of force. But in their case it may more appropriately be called "concentration of purpose." Not that these men were necessarily monomaniacs, but they had a dedication and singleness of purpose which colored their outlook and channeled their energies in such a way that they brought to bear on their professional tasks a degree of cumulative and intensive effort unusual in human activity. The casual, part-time naval officer is seldom found in the annals of history.

There is a desperate need for more analyses in depth of the command, leadership, administrative, and decision-making qualities which positions of authority have required, of the ways in which men have met specific challenges, of the extent to which individuals have controlled events, and of the common or unique characteristics which are most valu-

COMMAND CHARACTERISTICS

able. And we should try to understand how and why these men got that way, how they came to possess the personality, character, and ability to succeed in this ultimate test of human resources.

THE FOREIGN RELATIONS PAPERS, 1940-1943: A Review Article

Chapter 19

The eighteen volumes under review contain documents relating to the events of the critical years 1940-1943, years in which the Roosevelt administration sought first to promote American security by negotiation, moral suasion, material aid, and covert military assistance. Later, when the United States became an official belligerent, the emphasis shifted to the complexities of coalition warfare on a global scale. Diplomacy for victory imposed an enormous strain on state department officials as customary political and economic activities were replaced by the strategic and tactical imperatives of modern warfare. The predominantly military character of relations with the allies altered not only the subject matter of negotiations but often found civilians replaced by uniformed personnel. Finally, in 1943, the diplomats returned to a position of prominence as planning for a postwar world assumed greater importance in the deliberations of government leaders. Thus these volumes illuminate both the unity and the diversity of American foreign policy during this chaotic, transitional period.

The first volume opens with the mission of Under Secretary of State Sumner Welles to Europe in the spring of 1940 during the short-lived "phony war."[1] Meeting with the political heads of the major belligerent nations, Welles was able to furnish the president with a clear picture of their attitude toward the war and the conditions they demanded before peace could be concluded. While at the time the administration denied that Welles was being sent abroad to seek means of ending the war in Europe, he began his conversations by saying that he had been "directed by the President to report to him upon the present possibility of the establishment in Europe of a stable and lasting peace. . ." (p. 23). Then, successively, the documents deal with the invasions of Norway and Denmark, the Netherlands, Luxemburg, Belgium, and finally the collapse of France. One is able to read of the shocked reaction at the startling German successes and the utter inability of the government leaders to comprehend the magnitude of the disaster, let alone to cope with the situation. The despatches of Ambassador William C. Bullitt in Paris shift from factual reports to the state department to desperate pleas for military equipment addressed directly to the president.

201

The next section contains material bearing on the Russo-Finnish war. The reader is struck by the contents of a memorandum of a conversation between the Finnish minister and Secretary of State Cordell Hull on January 22, 1940, in which the latter ruled out the possibility of Finland's purchasing arms in the United States on the grounds that "the one matter of concern in this country is that this Government does not engage in acts or utterances that might materially endanger its peace and safety by causing it to be drawn into war" (p. 279). The events of the succeeding six months were to bring about a drastic change in this policy, which few in the administration were able to foresee. The role of the United States in promoting a peaceful solution to the conflict is revealed in a series of communiques between the state department, the minister to Finland, and the ambassador to Russia, which reports in detail conversations with the respective foreign ministers. The move toward a Finnish-German understanding following the peace treaty irritated the Soviet Union and brought expressions of concern by the Finnish foreign minister lest this development prejudice the United States against his government.

Measures taken by the Soviet Union to occupy the Baltic countries and establish puppet governments are described in despatches from the American ministers to Latvia, Lithuania, and Estonia. The nonrecognition of the forcible acquisition of these states was emphatically reaffirmed by Hull in a conversation with the British ambassador on October 14, 1940. Nevertheless, the purpose of the United States in improving relations with Russia, namely, to "move in our common direction with respect to axis countries" (p. 439), is clear throughout the negotiations with the Soviet Union during this period.

Volumes V and VI for the year 1940 and Volume VII for 1941 consist largely of materials relating to efforts to promote Western Hemisphere security, including additional steps to implement the Good Neighbor policy such as the efforts to settle differences between the Bolivian and Mexican governments and United States firms.[2] The activities of the inter-American neutrality committee are covered, as are negotiations with Latin American nations designed to eliminate Axis financial interests in those countries.[3]

The year 1941 also found the United States more intensively involved in attempts to stem aggressive moves in other parts of the world, both unilaterally and in closer co-operation with Great Britain. Volumes on the Far East, the British Commonwealth, the Near East and Africa[4] cover these activities in detail. The former contains material on the Japanese move into French Indochina, apprehension about the security of southeast Asia and the southwest Pacific, and evidence of increasing pressure from the British government to secure American assistance in halting the Japanese advance. The latter volume is filled with documents pertaining to lend-lease arrangements, although there are some interesting memoranda speculating as to whether the United States should urge Great Britain to accord dominion status to India.

The first volume for 1942 begins, appropriately enough, with the declaration of the United Nations, and contains some enlightening information on its formulation.[5] President Roosevelt's ideas are revealed in a letter to Hull commenting on an early draft of the declaration, wherein he urged changes to make the document more acceptable to certain nations, including the Soviet Union and China; directed that the "Free French" be eliminated from the text; expressed hope that Great Britain would consent to the inclusion of India; and ordered that this "supplement [to] the Atlantic statement" reflect more adequately "the real purposes for which we fight" (p. 13). Other items cover lend-lease agreements, negotiations for the establishment of the United Nations relief and rehabilitation administration, postwar economic planning, and the future status of Korea. Efforts to secure the co-operation of the Chinese government in promising independence began as early as December 22, 1941, and involved, among other considerations, tactful dealings with various factions in exile claiming to speak for the Korean people.

Europe is the subject of two volumes for 1942, numbered II and III.[6] Among the topics included in the former are American efforts to dissuade Finland from continuing the war as an ally of Germany; negotiations concerning France, highlighted by the diplomatic break with the Vichy government; attempts to secure French aid in the North African invasions; and relations with the Free French forces. The president's continued anxiety lest Great Britain enter agreements with its allies over postwar territorial settlements and the British willingness to avoid such commitments are revealed in a memorandum by Welles dated October 21, 1941, in Volume III. A lengthy selection of documents is devoted to American interest in the Polish government and the future status of that nation. Other items include the concern over the maintenance of Spanish neutrality, relations with the Soviet Union, and American efforts to persuade the Pope to denounce Nazi atrocities. In one despatch the assistant to the president's personal representative to Pope Pius XII observed that ". . .possibly the controlling [motive] behind the Pope's disinclination to denounce Nazi atrocities is his fear that if he does so now, the German people, in the bitterness of their defeat, will reproach him later on for having contributed, if only indirectly, to this defeat" (p. 777).

Volumes V and VI for 1942 cover relations with the American republics.[7] Both deal primarily with hemisphere defense, military cooperation, and the procurement of essential raw materials. Volume V contains documents pertaining to the establishment of the inter-American commission for territorial administration of European colonies and possessions in the Americas and negotiations with Argentina, including United States efforts to induce Argentina, through exhortations and a curtailment of trade, to sever its ties with Axis nations.

The year 1943 found many of the earlier threads being drawn together, for previous plans began to take form. Volume I treats the tripartite conference at Moscow in some detail, and includes drafts of the proposed agenda and a joint four-power declaration which the United States was anxious to have issued at the close of the conference. The president, prior to Secretary Hull's departure, emphasized the need to include China in the declaration. Aware of the difficulties of securing British and Russian consent because "Churchill does not like China" and Russia might object to the implications regarding Japan, Roosevelt concluded that "China is too important a factor, both now and in the future, both because of herself and because of her influence over British India, to be alienated" (pp. 541-542). The president also "stated categorically that he favors partition of Germany into three or more states," and he indicated his hope that eventually he could persuade Stalin to conduct another plebiscite in the Baltic countries and eastern Poland after the war (p. 542). A British aide-memoire on postwar Europe brought objections from the president on the grounds that "it smacked too much [of] 'spheres of influence' policies, the very thing which it was supposedly designed to prevent" (p. 544).

Secretary Hull, who headed the American delegation to the conference, hoped to avoid a discussion of military affairs. But the Soviets insisted on a full exploration of "measures for shortening the war against Germany and its allies in Europe," specifically the long-promised cross-channel invasion (p. 534). Hull studiously refrained from commenting on the subject, and allowed Major General John R. Deane, secretary of the combined chiefs of staff and chief of the United States military mission to the Soviet Union, to speak on these matters. Molotov persistently demanded a firm commitment for the opening of a second front, urged that pressure be applied on Turkey to enter the war, asked that one-third of the Italian fleet be turned over to Russia, and resisted, until the end of the conference, the American desire to include China in the final declaration. Soviet fears of British efforts to create a cordon sanitaire in Europe against Russia were somewhat assuaged by British Foreign Secretary Anthony Eden's assurances that his government "was not interested" in doing so (p. 639).

FOREIGN RELATIONS

On the whole the conference went extremely well, and these documents give the impression that Molotov was a congenial, co-operative host. Making numerous concessions, he appeared to convince Hull that the prospects for future Russian-American co-operation were bright. Obviously, American good will was extremely important to the Soviets at this time and they could afford to be generous when no significant postwar adjustments were under consideration.

Volume II for the year 1943 contains a great deal of material on the tortuous question of relations with French resistance groups, especially the problems over General de Gaulle. Roosevelt, unwilling to recognize any group, wrote Churchill that "The people of France will settle their own affairs after we have won this war. Until then we can deal with local Frenchmen on a local basis wherever our armies occupy former French territory. And if these local official won't play ball we will have to replace them" (p. 23). Hull, on several occasions, complained to the British ambassador about de Gaulle's political ambitions, which appeared to interfere with the prosecution of the war in North Africa, and Great Britain's toleration if not encouragement of the French general's activities (pp. 27-28, 29-30, 59-60). In turn, de Gaulle bitterly denounced what he called American "plots" and "duplicity" in attempting to undermine his position (p. 43). Anthony Eden, striving to blunt the American protests, recounted his own difficulties with the general and expressed his own "doubts of de Gaulle's stability" (p. 64).

Roosevelt's exasperation over the situation is clearly revealed. In a memorandum to Churchill, wherein he referred to de Gaulle as "the Bride," he observed that the French leader's "course and attitude [were] well nigh intolerable," pointed out that his activities were financed by the British government, urged that he be removed from the French national committee, and concluded by saying, "I do not know what to do with de Gaulle. Possibly you would like to make him Governor of Madagascar" (pp. 111-112). Subsequently, the president wrote Churchill, "I am fed up with de Gaulle and the secret personal and political machinations of that Committee in the last few days indicates that there is no possibility of our working with de Gaulle," and went on to state why "we must divorce ourselves from de Gaulle" (pp. 155-156). But neither the president nor the prime minister was able to remove from his neck what Churchill referred to as "the Cross of Lorraine." The general's own position is somewhat clarified by memoranda of conversations between him and the American representative to the political-military commissions at Algiers (cf. pp. 188-192, 199-200). Among other topics included in this volume are the surrender of Italy and its acceptance as a co-belligerent, continued efforts to maintain Spanish neutrality, and concern over disunity among Yugoslav resistance forces.

United States relations with China during 1943 are the subject of a separate unnumbered volume.[10] Numerous reports from the embassy at Chungking are very critical of the Chiang regime, which is characterized as inefficient and corrupt. Some American observers gained the impression that the Nationalist government was content to rely on the United States to win the war against Japan and save its troops to destroy the Communist forces. Chinese suspicions of Great Britain and the Soviet Union are revealed, and a few conversations are reported in which General Joseph Stilwell is criticized by Kuomintang representatives for not being sufficiently co-operative. No doubt a subsequent volume will relate the Stilwell controversy in greater detail.

The visit of British Foreign Secretary Anthony Eden to Washington in March is the initial topic of the third volume for 1943.[11] Ostensibly to discuss matters relating to the war, the trip was made actually to exchange views on postwar problems. In the course of the conversations, the foreign secretary frankly admitted to the president that "England would probably be too weak to face Russia alone diplomatically" (p. 13), and, having recently spoken with Stalin and Molotov in Moscow, he accurately outlined Soviet demands in Europe (pp. 13-17, 22-24). Roosevelt reiterated "that he wanted no negotiated armistice after the collapse; that we should insist on total surrender with no commitments to the enemy as to what we would or would not do after this action" (pp. 34-35). The president's attitude toward China is further revealed by his observations that it could help "police" the Far East (p. 35), and that "China, in any serious conflict of policy with Russia, would undoubtedly line up on our side" (p. 39). In a press conference after Eden's departure, he emphasized that the conversations regarding postwar settlement were "exploratory" only, and were intended to avoid the experience of World War I, when the conflict ended with very little planning for peace (p. 42). This volume also contains an extensive collection of documents dealing with relations between the Polish government in exile and the Soviet Union, with the United States in the delicate position of trying to effect a reconciliation. The issue of Korean independence reappears with consideration of a trusteeship, warnings of Soviet ambitions, and a vigorous request from Syngman Rhee that the provisional government of the Republic of Korea, of which he was chairman, be recognized.

Much of Volume IV for the year 1943, The Near East and Africa, is devoted to the furnishing of military supplies to the various nations.[12] But it contains documents pertaining to the governing of Greece following liberation, the political situation in Iran, the American attitude toward the Arab-Zionist controversy over the future status of Palestine, and the question of Turkey's becoming a co-belligerent.

Volume V, The American Hemisphere, deals primarily with defense and trade matters.[13] The circumstances leading to the recognition of the Ramiriz government in Argentina are contained in the depatches exchanged between the American ambassador and the secretary of state, as are subsequent efforts to induce the government to break diplomatic relations with the Axis nations.

The summit meetings of 1943 at Cairo and Tehran are the subject of a volume in the special series on World War II conferences.[14] Numerous sources were tapped for this selection, including the files of the joint chiefs of staff and private papers of participants. But in spite of searching so far afield, "the record of Conference proceedings is far from complete, even for some high-level discussions" (p. xii). Part of the explanation for the need to utilize other materials lies in the fact that Secretary Hull did not attend these meetings, although the predominance of military matters also accounts for the paucity of documents in the state department files. In the absence of a high-ranking official from the state department, the political aspects of strategy and postwar settlement were handled by the president and Harry Hopkins.

This volume furnishes evidence for those historians who wish to challenge the widely accepted viewpoint that Roosevelt, unlike Churchill, did not understand the correlations between force and diplomacy. Early in May the president wrote Stalin that "There is always the possibility that the historic Russian defense, followed by taking the offensive, may cause a crack-up in Germany next winter. In such a case we must be prepared for the many next steps. We are none of us prepared today. Therefore, it is my belief that you and I ought to meet this summer" (p. 4). Later, en route to Cairo, he voiced two objections to Churchill's suggestion that Great Britain occupy the northwestern portion of Germany and the United States occupy the southern portion south of the Moselle River: first, that France was Britain's "baby" and the United States did not want the task of reconstruction in that country; second, that American ships could best use the northern German ports and the United States should occupy Germany as far as Berlin, with the Soviet Union having the territory to the east (pp. 253-254). "There will definitely be a race for Berlin," the president observed, adding that "We may have to put the United States divisions into Berlin as soon as possible" (p. 255). If the President had not acceded later to the prime minister's insistence on his allocation of occupation zones the entire course of subsequent relationships with the Soviets might well have been altered.

British efforts to delay the cross-channel invasion, usually on the grounds that increased activity in the Mediterranean would be more deisrable, are amply documented in this volume (pp. 409, 547-552, 555-563). Apparently it did not occur to the British leaders, civilian or military, that the sooner OVERLORD was mounted the farther east the Anglo-American troops would be when the war ended and the greater would be the influence that could be exerted on the Soviet Union to accede to the demands of its allies. In fact, had the invasion of western Europe begun in 1942 or 1943 as Roosevelt and his military advisers had urged, many of the problems that arose over the fate of eastern Europe and the eventual partition of Germany probably would have been avoided.

Winston Churchill's complicity in the so-called "rape" of Poland is clearly indicated. In the course of a conversation with Premier Stalin and the president, Churchill confessed that "he personally had no attachment to any specific frontier between Poland and the Soviet Union; that he felt that the consideration of Soviet security on their western frontiers was a governing factor," and "remarked that it would be very valuable if here in Teheran [sic] the representatives of the three governments could work out some agreed understanding on the question of the Polish frontiers which could then be taken up with the Polish Government in London." He added that "as far as he was concerned, he would like to see Poland moved westward in the same manner as soldiers at drill execute the drill 'left close'. . ." (p. 512). At a later meeting of the three leaders the Prime Minister provided a rationale for imperialistic land-grabbing that, if publicized, would have brought anguished cries from the victims of Axis aggression. As recorded in the minutes of the conversation kept by Charles Bohlen

> The Prime Minister then said that it was important that the nations who would govern the world after the war, and who would be entrusted with the direction of the world after the war, should be satisfied and have no territorial or other ambitions. If that question could be settled in a manner agreeable to the great powers, he felt then that the world might indeed remain at peace. He said that hungry nations and ambitious nations are dangerous, and he would like to see the leading nations of the world in the position of rich, happy men (p. 568).

Such an open invitation to territorial acquisition rendered doubly difficult later attempts to induce the Soviet authorities to accept a border based on the "Curzon" line and other proposals based on the declaration of the United Nations.

At Tehran the president outlined his proposals for the world organization and the body composed of what he called "the Four Policemen," consisting of the United States, the

FOREIGN RELATIONS

Soviet Union, Great Britain, and China, which "would have the power to deal immediately with any threat to the peace and any sudden emergency which requires this action" (p. 530). In response to Stalin's questioning of the inclusion of China, Roosevelt replied that he realized that nation's present weakness. But, he noted, it was better to have a country of four hundred million people "as friends rather than as a potential source of trouble" (p. 532). Although he did not say so, the President may well have felt that with Japanese power destroyed no other nation would be able to counter Soviet influence in the Far East.

In this volume the state department historical section has done more than its normal share of work for the historian. In addition to a list of persons mentioned, there is a calendar of the individual papers, a bibliography of sources and special secondary works bearing on the conferences, and generous footnotes quoting material not in these documents that help clarify the record. Photographs of the participants and a reproduction of the map of Poland's eastern frontier on which Stalin marked with a red pencil are among the other unique features of this book.

Historians of all nations have come to rely heavily on the foreign relations series, which stands alone as the most complete, authoritative, and up-to-date source for a study of modern diplomatic history.[15] It is to be hoped that sufficient support will be forthcoming from the congress and the top officials in the state department to permit the publication of volumes dealing with the even more recent past.

FOOTNOTES

1. U.S. Department of State, Foreign Relations of the United States: Diplomatic Papers, 1940, I, General (Washington, Government Printing Office, 1959).

2. Ibid., 1940, V, The American Republics (Washington, 1961); VI, The American Republics (Washington, 1963).

3. Ibid, 1941, VII, The American Republics (Washington, 1962).

4. Ibid., 1941, V, The Far East (Washington, 1956); III, The British Commonwealth, The Near East and Africa (Washington, 1959).

5. Ibid., 1942, I, General, The British Commonwealth, The Far East (Washington, 1960).

6. Ibid., 1942, II, Europe (Washington, 1962); III, Europe (Washington, 1961).

7. Ibid., 1942, V, The American Republics (Washington, 1962); VI, The American Republics (Washington, 1963).

8. Ibid., 1943, I, General (Washington, 1963).

9. Ibid., 1943, II, Europe (Washington, 1964).

10. Ibid., 1943, China (Washington, 1957).

11. Ibid., 1943, III, The British Commonwealth, Eastern Europe, The Far East (Washington, 1963).

12. Ibid., 1934, IV, The Near East and Africa (Washington, 1964).

13. Ibid., 1943, V, The American Hemisphere (Washington, 1965).

14. Ibid., 1943, The Conference at Cairo and Tehran (Washington, 1961).

15. For a thorough appraisal of the series, see Richard W. Leopold, "The Foreign Relations Series: A Centennial Estimate," Mississippi Valley Historical Review, XLIX:4 (March, 1963), pp. 595-612. For a foreign appreciation which favorably contrasts the series with the shortcomings of similar publications by other governments, see D. C. Watt, "Restrictions on Research--The Fifty-Year Rule and British Foreign Policy," International Affairs, XLI:1 (Jan.), pp. 89-95.

THE POLITICS OF STRATEGY AND PEACE IN WORLD WAR II

Chapter 20

The subject today is concerned with the Allied coalition, and the first American experience in coalition warfare occurred during the revolution in which this nation won its independence through association with France. Altercations over strategy and peace negotiations prompted John Adams to write from Paris in 1782 that "History shows that nations have generally had as much difficulty to arrange their affairs with the allies as with their enemies." In more recent times, Winston Churchill noted that the only thing worse than fighting with allies is fighting without them--a somewhat more positive approach.

The <u>Oxford</u> <u>English</u> <u>Dictionary</u> defines a coalition as "A temporary alliance of distinct parties for a limited purpose," and adds the date "1645." Going along with this definition, certainly in World War II the parties were distinct, namely, the Big Four: the United States, Great Britain, the Union of Soviet Socialist Republics, and China. The latter must be included, if for no other reason than its impact on the relations of the other three powers.

To continue with the quoted definition, a problem arises concerning the "limited purpose." Militarily, an agreed upon purpose was the defeat of the Axis nations, although the method and the means for doing so was a constant source of disputation. As to war aims, a divergence in purpose becomes more marked. Assuming that wars are not waged for their own sake, and accepting the Clausewitz dictum that they are a continuation of state policy, the peace objectives of the major allies were not always compatible. Therefore we have a situation in which the coalition agreed on the military end but not always on the means; and each had a concept of "victory" that shared a degree of commonality along with fundamental and at times basic differences. The reconciliation of differences in military strategy and the conditions of peace were resolved by the heads of state, each of whom perceived of victory as the cessation of armed conflict under circumstances satisfactory in terms of specific objectives.

What I hope to do in this brief time is to explain how the basic problems of this coalition--problems that were strategic, logistic, political, and economic--were dealt with and resolved by the ultimate decision makers in consultation with their advisors and with each other through messages, emissaries, and in conference.

The collaboration between the United States and Great Britain began with surreptitious naval conversations in 1937, accelerated rapidly after the fall of France in June 1940 and the adoption of paragraph "Dog" of the Chief of Naval Operation's memorandum of November 12, 1940, which urged a "Germany first" strategy, and culminated in the ABC-1 staff agreements of March 1941. Plans for joint action were confirmed by the military staffs of the two nations at the Argentia conference in August 1941, which also produced the Atlantic Charter declaration of war aims by Roosevelt and Churchill.

The road for collaboration with the Soviet Union was somewhat rocky in light of the Nazi-Soviet Pact of August 1939, the partitioning of Poland, the Soviet-Finnish War, and the absorption of the Baltic states of Latvia, Esthonia, and Lithuania. In spite of these events, the President and Secretary of State Cordell Hull continued to believe that German and Russian interests were basically opposed, and that eventually Russia would side with the Allies. So the United States followed a policy of caution and restraint to avoid pushing the Soviets irretrievably into the Nazi camp. Roosevelt and Hull felt that Soviet aggression was motivated primarily by a desire to bolster the defense perimeter against Hitler, who was bound to attack Russia. They also considered the Soviet Union useful in containing Japan in the Far East. When their prophecy was fulfilled by the German invasion of the Soviet Union on June 22, 1941, the United States soon joined Britain in extending material aid to the hard pressed Russians.

Meanwhile, the United States continued to exert pressure on Japan to refrain from further aggression in China or elsewhere. This pressure escalated from diplomatic protests to the institution of economic sanctions and the retention of the Pacific Fleet at Hawaii as a deterrent. These coercive methods were brought to bear primarily in an effort to prevent Japan from taking action that would be detrimental to the Allied war effort in Europe; specifically, moving south to cut the British lifeline or north to assault Russia from the rear. Each of these moves had been contemplated, and, as a recent study demonstrates, the Japanese naval high command was instrumental in pushing the nation into war in 1941 because it realized that by 1943 the American Navy would reach overwhelming strength.

But a dispute over peace aims took place within the Coalition even before America's formal entry into the war. In spite of American protests, Great Britain, anxious for an alliance with Russia, was preparing to sign a treaty acknowledging Soviet territorial gains resulting from the pact with the Nazis. Roosevelt vigorously opposed the agreement on the grounds that it was premature; the United States had not been consulted or allowed to participate; it violated the principles of the Altantic Charter; its provisions would become known and have an adverse effect on morale; and it was reminiscent of the secret treaties that had created trouble for Woodrow Wilson at the end of the first World War. Although Churchill intended to sign the treaty and incur Roosevelt's wrath, the Russians finally relented because, as Soviet Foreign Minister Molotov said, the President did not want the territorial clauses included. I cite this incident as an example of Churchill's willingness to make concessions to the Russians; Roosevelt's desire to postpone peace settlements until the military situation had improved and until he had an opportunity to participate in the deliberations; and as early evidence of a cleavage among the Allies in regard to postwar goals.

Soon after the attack on Pearl Harbor, the Western Allies reached agreement on the strategic control of military operations. The United States assumed principal responsibility for the entire Pacific area and China, while Great Britain was assigned the Middle East and Far East except for China. The Combined Chiefs of Staff were placed in charge of grand strategy in both zones and all operations in the Atlantic-European area. But to reiterate, the heads of state made the final decision on all major operations. It was not a simple matter of the President saying to the Joint Chiefs of Staff, "I got us into this war, now it's your job." Involved were the allocation of vast but limited resources in men and material, the needs and aspirations of other allies, the morale of home populations, and the impact of military operations on the negotiations for peace. The implications and ramifications of campaign strategy were such that the professionals were simply not capable of making these decisions.

The "common" military objective of the Allies was the defeat of the Axis powers, and the Declaration of the United Nations signed in Washington on January 1, 1942, pledged the signatories "not to make a separate armistice or peace with the enemies." Yet early agreements in principle on the overall strategy for waging war against the common enemy did not solve specific campaign issues, and differences led to disputes and recriminations that at times threatened to split the coalition. Complicating the joint military effort was the fact that the United States and Great Britain were fighting a global war, while the Soviet Union was fighting a one front war. Each nation had its own concept of priorities, which on occasion were at odds and created deep seated resentment and suspicion. Further, the British and American leaders were opposed in their views on the strategy that should be followed to defeat Germany and Italy. The Americans favored a direct approach, namely, to concentrate on an early landing on the continent of Europe to engage and defeat the main enemy forces in cooperation with the Russians. The British favored an indirect or peripheral approach, virtually a war of attrition, nibbling away at the edges of the Nazi stronghold supplemented by bombing and the activities of resistance groups.

Conversations in early 1942 found the British accepting the direct cross-channel invasion strategy, with SLEDGEHAMMER planned as an emergency landing in 1942 if the Russians seemed in danger of collapsing on the eastern front, and ROUNDUP, the massive assault scheduled for 1943. Then the British had second thoughts, and their opposition provoked General Marshall and Admiral King to recommend to the President that if the British would not adhere to the original plan, the United States should divert its major effort to the Pacific. But the President, anxious to maintain Anglo-American unity and convinced that the European theater deserved priority, refused to issue such an ultimatum. Efforts to persuade the British to relent were unavailing, and TORCH, the invasion of North Africa in late 1942, was substituted for the cross channel venture. Churchill volunteered to travel to Moscow to explain why the Western Allies were not going to meet their commitment for an early second front, and a second postponement occurred after the successful North African campaign, when at Casablanca in January 1943 Marshall and King again strove for a return to a continental invasion strategy but were overruled in favor of the Sicily-Italy campaign.

So on two occasions the Soviets were disappointed in not securing the relief that had been promised, and they continued to vigorously protest the delay until a firm commitment was made at Tehran in December 1943 for a spring 1944 second front in Europe. Adding to their grievances was the announced cancellation of the Murmansk supply run due to heavy losses of shipping. Under the circumstances, and remembering the attitude displayed by the United States and Great Britain toward the Soviet Union during the 1920's and 1930's, the Kremlin leaders not unreasonably suspected that the Western Allies were plotting to bleed the Russians to the point where their government might collapse or at least would be so weakened as to constitute no threat in the postwar world.

To switch to a related subject, most accounts of World War II diplomacy contend that Roosevelt was excessively concerned with the military aspects of the war and tended virtually to ignore the political objectives of the peace; that Churchill was acutely aware of the correlation between force and diplomacy; and that if the President had followed the Prime Minister's policies the Soviet Union would not have emerged in such a strong position.

My contention is that the opposite is more nearly true, and the delay of the second front is merely one example. If the cross channel invasion had taken place a year earlier, as originally scheduled, the Western Allies would have been in a much stronger position when postwar settlements were first discussed in a substantive way at Tehran in December 1943, and when they were finalized at Yalta in February 1945. The concentration of the Anglo-American effort on clearing the Mediterranean allowed the Russians to occupy vital territory in Eastern and Central Europe and gave them a significant advantage in bargaining on territorial and political issues. As Secretary of State Kissinger put it last year, "It is not easy to achieve through negotiation what has not been achieved on the battlefield."

Further evidence of Churchill's shortcomings is revealed in the question of occupation zones in Germany. Roosevelt had wanted the United States to occupy a northwest, wedge-shaped section that would include Berlin. The Prime Minister had other ideas, and after a somewhat lengthy exchange of differences he reached agreement with the Soviets and in effect presented the United States with a *fait accompli* and the southwestern zone. In spite of Anglo-Soviet unity on the issue, Roosevelt held out for seven months until he finally acceeded to the division. Conceivably, if Churchill had supported the original American proposal it might have been accepted by the Soviets, and the later cancerous Berlin altercation would have been avoided.

Churchill continued his bilateral diplomacy in "stabilizing" the Balkan situation. His well known deal with Stalin took place in Moscow on October 9, 1944, but as early as May of that year he notified the President that the Soviets were willing to give Britain control of Greece in exchange for Russian hegemony in Rumania. Roosevelt protested on the grounds that this would divide the Balkans into "spheres of influence," and he urged consultative machinery to avoid such a development. Churchill reacted vehemently, denounced a "committee approach," and cautioned against consultation and "a set of triangular or quadrangular telegrams." The President finally consented to the proposal on a short term basis, only to find it extended to other Balkan nations by the Moscow agreement. Of course the Russians negotiated the terms of surrender with most of these countries, and later Churchill claimed that the proportionate allocation of control did not apply to the postwar situation. But there is no evidence, and Churchill did not claim, that this proviso was explicit--merely, in his opinion, it was implicit. Subsequent developments in these nations found Communist elements dominating their governments and the Western Allies unable to influence events.

The Prime Minister's charitable attitude toward the Soviets is, perhaps, best revealed in the Polish issue. As previously mentioned, Chruchill, early in 1942, was willing to agree to Russian retention of much Polish territory in order to get an alliance. At Tehran, a conference intended to concentrate on military planning, the Prime Minister introduced the question of Poland's boundaries and urged that the nation be moved westward to absorb part of Germany and give land in the east to Russia. This arrangement was confirmed at Yalta, though by that time Churchill had become concerned about Soviet ambitions and he protested the establishment of Poland's western boundary at the Oder-Neisse. The question surfaced at Potsdam, and finally, in November 1970, the West German and Polish governments signed a treaty acknowledging the frontier, although I understand the treaty has not been ratified by West Germany. Discussions at the summit conferences of Poland's boundaries found Roosevelt playing a minor role, apparently content to allow Churchill to present the Western Allies' viewpoint. The President did urge, however, that Poland be allowed to retain Lvov and some oil fields; that the government contain non-communist elements; and that free elections take place.

Generally, Roosevelt followed Churchill's lead in regard to European settlements, often, as previously indicated, only after much altercation. He resisted early territorial agreements, bitterly opposed the Balkan deal, fought against the British occupation zone allocation in Germany, refused to recognize the de Gaulle government until after the landing in France, and strove to avoid a discussion of postwar settlements at Tehran in hopes that the Western Allies' military position would be stronger when these matters came up for decision. But he realized that British interests and involvement on the continent were greater than those of the United States, and he believed that the American people and the Congress would not tolerate a long-term commitment in Europe.

Related to much of the foregoing and to the military-political role of America in the war is the highly controversial Unconditional Surrender policy. Again, contrary to the mythology perpetuated by many writers, this was not a spur of the moment inspiration of the President; nor, in my opinion, was it a mistake. Roosevelt, as Assistant Secretary of the Navy during World War I, was among many who disagreed with Wilson's negotiated armistice, including General Pershing, Theodore Roosevelt, and Senator Henry Cabot Lodge, all of whom specifically advocated "unconditional surrender." He was also aware that the armistice provisions created many problems in making a peace treaty at Versailles, and that the legend that Germany had not been defeated aided Hitler's rise to power, exacerbated conditions in Europe during the 1920's and 1930's, and contributed to the outbreak of World War II. In May 1942 the President was notified by Norman Davis, chairman of the Subcommittee on Security Problems of the Advisory Committee on Post-War

Foreign Policy, that the members were unanimous in recommending that unconditional surrender be demanded of the major Axis powers with the possible exception of Italy. Davis reported to the Subcommittee that the President expressed agreement with this recommendation. Just prior to the Casablanca conference he brought the subject to the attention of the Joint Chiefs of Staff but there is no record of his asking their opinion. At Casablanca, Churchill cabled his War Cabinet on the question and it responded with the suggestion that Italy be included with Germany and Japan. Churchill thought the declaration should be a part of the communique to be issued at the conclusion of the conference, but evidently it was decided that an announcement by the President to the press corps would be more effective. The Soviet Union formally adopted the doctrine at the Moscow Conference in October 1943 where Hull represented the United States.

In my opinion the unconditional surrender policy was desirable if not essential in maintaining the Grand Alliance and winning the war.

1. It helped compensate for the deferred second front by reassuring the Russians that the Western Allies were committed to a complete military victory.

2. It postponed debate over peace aims that could have split the coalition and inhibited the prosecution of the war.

3. It reassured those who had been disturbed by the deal with the proto-fascist Admiral Darlan in North Africa.

4. It bolstered morale in the Western nations, at least, by providing a specific military goal in lieu of the generalities of the Atlantic Charter that had been incorporated in the Declaration of the United Nations.

5. It offered a simple formula for terminating the fighting and minimized enemy and allied bickering over terms and negotiations.

The major objection voiced to the unconditional surrender doctrine is that it lengthened the war, especially in regard to Germany, by furnishing the Nazi government with propaganda to exhort the people to greater effort in order to avoid extinction, and prevented resistance movements from overthrowing Hitler. In response I offer the following: First, it should be noted that Roosevelt in his declaration said that unconditional surrender "does not mean the destruction of the population of Germany, Italy, or Japan, but it does mean the destruction of the philosophies in those countries which are based on conquest and the subjugation of other people." Second, the only effective resistance in Germany capable of overthrowing the government was the army, and it was committed to demands that were unacceptable to the Allies. Third, one must look at the way in which surrenders were effected. Italy was the first, negotiations were protracted, conditions were included in the terms, unconditional surrender was required only of the armed forces, and even that clause was later cancelled. With Germany, the armed forces surrendered unconditionally under the authority of Grand Admiral Karl Doenitz, Hitler's successor, and the Allies simply took over the nation. Japan unconditionally surrendered its armed forces, maintained the Emperor, submitted to the stipulations of the Potsdam Declaration, and acknowledged that "the authority of the Emperor and the Japanese Government to rule the state shall be subject to the Supreme Commander of the Allied Powers." The Axis satellite nations and Finland negotiated surrender instruments with the Soviet Union that contained many conditions. Interestingly, the United States did not consider Finland an Axis power, as it did Hungary, Rumania, and Bulgaria, all of whom had signed the Tripartite Pact.

Having brought the war in Europe to a conclusion, let me shift to the Pacific and the Far East before taking up the question of whether we won the peace. The Japanese strategy had envisioned the creation of a virtual fortress area in the Western Pacific in which they would consolidate their conquests, the United States would become discouraged, and finally agree to a peace that would recognize Japanese domination of the Greater East Asia Co-Prosperity Sphere. Then Japan, flushed with her early successes, succumbed to what has been called the "victory disease," moved into the Central Pacific and was repulsed at Midway. Admiral King was able to embark on a defensive-offensive strategy, namely, tactically offensive, strategically defensive. No doubt you are familiar with the tortuous path followed by American forces across the Pacific, and the interservice and intraservice rivalries and disputes that occurred over strategy and tactics. Further, I do not intend to fight the Pacific War, but I do want to make some observations about the use of the atomic bombs.

The employment of these nuclear weapons has brought heavy criticism from distinguished military and political figures, historians and others on the grounds that they were unnecessary and immoral. But in my opinion the war would not have ended when it did and in the way it did if the bombs had not been used. To oppose the anticipated invasion of the Japanese islands some 2,000,000 troops and 8,000 aircraft of all types had been mobilized, and the fanaticism that had characterized previous Japanese resistance, including the dreaded kamikazi suicide attacks, could be expected to intensify in defense of the homeland. The loss of American and Japanese lives would have been considerable, aside from the material destruction and dislocation of population that would have posed an enormous task of reconstruction. Further, any delay in surrender would have enabled the Soviets to progress in their war against Japan and have a more forceful argument for a share in the occupation. The first bomb was dropped on August 6, Russia entered the war on August 8, and the second bomb was dropped on August 9. Prompted by these events, the Premier and the Cabinet met with the Emperor on August 9 and August 14, who, on both occasions, sided with the moderates and "decided" for peace. This unusual action by the Emperor could have occurred only under the impact of the atomic weapons, although the repercussions of the Soviet declaration of war undoubtedly had an influence on the extreme measures taken by the Japanese government. So far as the morality of using these bombs is concerned, the fire raids on Tokyo and the raids on Hamburg and Dresden had, in each case, killed more civilians than did either of the atomic attacks. As General Marshall once said, an industrial civilization provides more efficient methods for killing people, which is a criterion for successful warfare.

While on the subject of the Far East it seems appropriate to make some observations on China. Roosevelt had supported the Nationalist government actively from 1939 through 1941 in large part to keep Japanese troops tied down and reduce the likelihood that Japan would act in a way to interfere with the war against Hitler. After the attack on Pearl Harbor, Chiang kai shek assumed that he would have an equal voice in the councils directing Allied activity. Yet he was soon disillusioned by the Anglo-American agreement on a Europe first strategy, by the denial of membership in the Combined Chiefs of Staff, and subsequently by being excluded from meetings of the three heads of state. These frustrations combined with minimal American assistance and his difficulties with General Stilwell led him to conclude that China was conceived of as a second class ally, a conclusion that was confirmed when Roosevelt acceded to Russian demands for certain rights in China without consulting Chiang.

Yet the treatment accorded China must be seen in its total context. The President was waging a global war with Europe and the Pacific Ocean simply higher on the list of priorities, and some evidence revealed that Chiang was more interested in saving his troops to fight the Chinese communists than he was in pursuing the war against the Japanese. Still, the United States was responsible for persuading the Soviet Union and Great Britain to allow China to be a signatory of the Declaration of Four Nations on General Security that emerged from the Tripartite Conference of foreign ministers at Moscow in October 1943, and Roosevelt and Churchill joined with Chiang to issue the Cairo Declaration on December 1, 1943, "restoring" to China territory occupied by Japan.

There were many reasons why the President insisted on treating China as a great power, often over the objections of his British and Russian associates. Speaking to British Foreign Secretary Anthony Eden in March 1943, he expressed the opinion that China could help "police" the Far East after the defeat of Japan, and that "China, in any serious conflict of policy with Russia, would undoubtedly line up on our side." Issuing instructions to Hull before the Moscow conference of October 1943, Roosevelt said, "China is too important a factor, both now and in the future, both because of herself and because of her influence over British India, to be alienated." And at Tehran he observed that it was better to have a country of four hundred million people "as friends rather than as a potential source of trouble." Perhaps Roosevelt, aware that little military aid had been given to China, may have tried to assuage her feelings by securing formal acceptance as a "great power," although undoubtedly he realized that with Japanese power destroyed no other nation would be able to counter Soviet influence in Asia. But it does seem likely that Roosevelt understood he would have to make some concessions to the other allies in order to get their support for his China policy, not necessarily specific concessions, more an awareness that they had acceded to his request and would expect something in the nature of a quid pro quo. At Yalta he was prepared for the Russian demands on China, he knew they could impose them easily, and he wanted to assure Stalin's support for Chiang's government and abandonment of the Maoist communists. These "concessions" were not made simply to induce the Soviets to join in the war against Japan, and the fact that Chiang was not consulted or notified immediately was due to the lack of security in his government.

The Stilwell mission to China is another controversial issue that surfaces periodically. Barbara Tuchman's Pulitzer prize winning Stilwell and the American Experience in China, 1911-1945, is a stout defense of the General that emphasizes the corruption and inefficiency of the Nationalist government. Chin-tung Liang's General Stilwell in China, 1942-1944: The Full Story, based on archives in Taiwan, is a spirited indictment of American and British policy which assigned a low priority to the China-Burma-India theater. Stilwell is portrayed as an incompetent strategist who did not understand the Chinese and was insubordinate as Chiang's chief of staff. Foreign service officers on the scene, what the author calls the "Davies-Service group," are accused of being pro-communist and of distorting the situation in reports to Washington, reports which influenced the decision-makers in an adverse way. My own impression is that the Tuchman version is more nearly correct, and I've cited only these two recent works to illustrate diverse interpretations of extremely complex and emotionally charged events.

STRATEGY AND PEACE

Among the many charges directed against Roosevelt, perhaps the most serious is his alleged willingness to compromise on basic postwar issues in order to gain British and especially Soviet concurrence for the United Nations organization. It should be recalled that the Atlantic Charter, later incorporated in the Declaration of the United Nations, mentioned "the establishment of a wider and permanent system of general security." The President's early tentative concept of the "Four Policemen" to maintain peace was dropped in favor of a "wider and permanent system." By August 1943 the State Department had completed a draft "Charter of the United Nations," and the Moscow Declaration of Four Nations, issued November 1, 1943, confirmed "the necessity of establishing at the earliest practicable date a general international organization" open to all states. From August 21 to October 9, 1944, at Dumbarton Oaks the three major allies hammered out details, and after the Soviets left the Chinese were brought in to approve the document. The final version of the Charter was completed at San Francisco by delegates from allied nations including Latin America working steadily from April 25 to June 26, 1945.

Meanwhile Roosevelt had had to persuade Stalin and Churchill that the organization should be formed prior to the ending of the war, and that it should provide not only for the maintenance of peace and the solution of international disputes but concern itself with social and economic issues. Among other obstacles the President had to overcome were Stalin's demand for separate representation for each of the Soviet Republics and his recalcitrance on a veto compromise. While it is not clear what Roosevelt sacrificed specifically in order to get agreement on the world organization, it seems likely that he pushed certain issues less vigorously than he would have otherwise.

On the other hand, it is doubtful that Roosevelt could have altered significantly any of Stalin's territorial demands, the composition of the Polish government, the conduct of "free elections" in that war torn country or in the Baltic states, the Russian influence in the Balkans, spoils from Japan, or rights in China. Churchill's early generousity and proclivity for introducing postwar issues when the military position of the Western Allies was weakest, the delayed second front, and Russian military occupation of vital areas, all deprived the President of bargaining power on matters that the Soviets considered essential to their national interest. Deserving further consideration is the fact that the Soviet Union had suffered a great deal more than the other allies and had carried the main burden of the war against Germany for a long time. If contribution to victory should be commensurate with the voice a nation has in determining the peace, then Stalin was in a very strong position to make his views prevail. Also, one must recall that Roosevelt was not at all optimistic about the degree of involvement in European affairs that the American people would permit after the war.

On the coalition politics of the military dimensions of the war, there was close collaboration between the United States and Great Britain on strategy; consultation with the Soviet Union on planned offensives and massive material aid; little collaboration or consultation with China. To add a footnote on the "Free French," begrudgingly little in the way of collaboration or consultation--much less official recognition--until implementation of the cross channel invasion. But all members of the coalition knew what they were fighting against, and this common sense of purpose added an adhesive quality that helped overcome many obstacles.

On the politics of peace, most of the diverse war aims were evident at an early stage but they were kept from surfacing until later, and the Grand Alliance held until the war was won. It was not a matter of subordinating peace goals to the winning of the war, for if the war were lost nothing could have been achieved. However, the way a war is waged can influence the terms of the peace, and you have heard some observations on what I consider Churchill's obstructionism and bad judgment.

To summarize the basic objectives of the three major allies, Roosevelt wanted to destroy the governments of the aggressor nations, whose actions jeopardized the safety of the United States, the Western Hemisphere, and the entire world; to establish a peace that would demonstrate that aggression did not pay and eliminate injustices that create disequilibrium; and to institute an international organization that would enforce certain standards of conduct among nations and promote a new political, social, and economic order throughout the world. Churchill, aware that Britain went to war not to save Poland but to prevent Germany from dominating Europe, wanted collective security but seemed more inclined to place faith in alliances and spheres of influence for the major powers. Having asserted that he had not become the King's first minister to preside over the liquidation of the British Empire, he realized that the principle of self-determination of peoples incorporated in the Atlantic Charter and Roosevelt's anti-colonial policy held out such a prospect. Moreover, Churchill was less than enthusiastic about having the United Nations engage in the comprehensive activities envisioned by the President. Stalin wanted territorial gains confirmed, security, an atmosphere in which the Soviet Union could prosper and be accepted as a co-equal of other nations and as a leader in world affairs, and have the opportunity to promote national and ideological aspirations. So Roosevelt and Stalin wanted a new order in contrast to Churchill, but they did not want the same order of domestic and international relationships.

STRATEGY AND PEACE

The trials and tribulations endured by the Grand Alliance were phenomenal, and in retrospect one might conclude that the association could not have been maintained or the war have been won. Compromise and concession were almost the order of the day as the politics of military strategy and postwar planning threatened to destroy the unity that brought victory in war and agreement on the basics of peace. These men led their nations through the most grueling of times and held together a tenuous coalition until it prevailed. They were formidable adversaries for the Axis powers and for each other. Each was a practical idealist in his own fashion, and they bequeathed to posterity a host of solutions and problems that promise to endure. They were giants, the likes of which emerge rarely in the course of human affairs.

HISTORICAL DIMENSIONS OF WAR GUILT

Chapter 21

I confess that I was puzzled by the title of this session, specifically by the use of the term "guilt" instead of "crime." The Charter of the International Military Tribunal defined war crimes as "violations of the laws or customs of war." Guilt has a broader connotation with legal, religious, philosophical and even psychological implications. In taking a smorgasbord approach to the question I trust that I won't be doing too much violence to the topic, especially since history embraces the totality of human experience.

Guilt began in the Judeo-Christian tradition in the Garden of Eden with the onus (discovery) of original sin. This does account in at least one mythical sense for the origin of the dualistic concept of good and evil, of right and wrong, of proper conduct in particular situations and under certain circumstances. The precepts embodied in the Ten Commandments were designed to regulate behavior. Perhaps the most absolute of moral imperatives is the dictum "Thou shalt not kill," yet both practice and law have condoned this act within a prescribed context, and the context in this session is war where casualties usually have a direct bearing on the outcome. So the question of guilt embraces (1) the method of prosecuting the war; and (2) the reason for engaging in war.

To deal with the method of pursuing armed conflict, all may be fair in love but all is not fair in war. Certain rules have governed the conduct of armed conflict from time immemorial, namely how and when it was appropriate to try to kill whom. The enemy was fair game on the field of battle and uniforms came to identify those eligible. The means for decimating opponents occasioned some concern and it is likely that the Philistines objected to Samson's use of the jawbone of an ass or David's slingshot. The introduction of new weapons systems brought increased concern over the legitimacy of devices employed to destroy the foe, and in recent times, most notably beginning with the Hague conferences of 1899 and 1907, numerous attempts have been made to codify rules to effect what has been called the humanization of war. Regarded as a contradiction in terms by some, conventions and declarations have emerged relating to aerial bombardment, dumdum bullets, the use of submarine mines and poison gas, the behavior or outlawing of submarines, the treatment of prisoners or a civilian population, and the like. Many nations at various times have subscribed to these rules, although observance in times of war usually depended on the military effectiveness of the action. For example, certain forms of warfare were not resorted to in World War II, including poison gas, because they (1) might not have proved militarily decisive; (2) would have provoked a like or greater reaction from the opponent. Some standards of conduct usually have been observed, and although Winston Churchill claimed that the American Civil War was the last armed conflict fought between gentlemen and chivalry among fighting men allegedly ended with aerial combat in 1918, the armed forces of virtually every modern nation are prohibited by their own regulations from indulging in certain activities on penalty of court martial with punishment designed to fit the crime. The good old days when Wellington would allow his troops 72 hours of rape and pillage after the capture of a town no longer prevail. Atrocities in formalized wars, at least, seem to be the exception rather than the rule, although what constitutes an atrocity can vary. The nations that recoiled in horror from the aerial bombardments of Chinese cities and Guernica in the 1930's formally adopted these methods in World War II, and plane crews were decorated for the amount of destruction they inflicted on the civilian sector. Evidently the impersonality of killing civilians from the air eliminates the element of criminality that resides in the same act if committed on the ground. And even the terrestrial dimension has its qualifications, for shelling from a distance carries the same exemption accorded the dropping of bombs but denied the firing of rifles. In Vietnam, Hanoi initially labeled captured American pilots war criminals and promised a trial, only to drop the charges and treat them in their own fashion as prisoners.

The nature of the armed conflict and the category of combatants often have a direct bearing on the rules that prevail. The behavior of official forces in wars between nations is more carefully circumscribed, but as in World War II when partisan, insurgent, underground groups of civilians operated against the enemy they were denied the amenities of the Geneva Convention. Internal conflicts, such as revolutions, civil wars, guerilla uprisings, or terrorist activities seem to create their own standards, and the point when rebels become eligible for treatment as an honorable foe varies considerably. Complicating the issue is the impact of industrialization, for the battlefield now extends to virtually every segment of activity. Destroying the sinews of war and breaking the will to resist have acquired equal or greater significance than "purely" military operations and almost all of the population qualifies as a combatant. This "total war" aspect is not confined to industrialized nations, for the "developing" peoples wage total war in their own fashion using the resources at their disposal, coupling military efforts with constant political, economic, and ideological activities. Terrorist tactics become conventional and the entire populace becomes the enemy, so when civilians, including women and children, are perpetrating violence the distinction between eligible and ineligible victims becomes blurred. Under these circumstances the infantryman might feel that killing civilians of either sex or any age is as justified as is the killing of the uniformed foe. Even though the taking of another person's life may be abhorent, both legally and morally most of us have been taught that we can do so in order to preserve our own. So the infantryman is observing the letter and the spirit of the law, and while he might suffer remorse, both his conscience and the law absolve him of guilt. Justifications of actions may be rational or emotional, but self-defense is a broadly based motive for drastic measures against those bent on destroying us.

But who decides whether a crime has been committed, or rather, who prosecutes the offender? As mentioned, each nation has its own rules and can and does discipline its own. But in recent times there are examples of what has been called "victor's justice." Article 228 of the Versailles Treaty provided that Germans accused of atrocities be turned over to the Allied and Associated Powers for trial, although it turned out they were tried by German courts. Article 227 arraigned the Kaiser "for supreme offenses against international morality and the authority of treaties," although the Netherlands government refused to release him to the authorities. In World War II, the Moscow Declaration of October 30, 1943, pledged the prosecution of German war criminals, and the Potsdam Declaration provided that ". . .stern justice shall be meted out to all war criminals, including those who have visited cruelties upon our prisoners." The United Nations Commission for the Investigation of War Crimes, established by the Allies during the war, distinguished two classes of war criminals: those whose crimes were directed against the nationals of one state (they were to be tried by national courts or military tribunals), and those whose crimes were international in scope (they were to be tried by special international tribunals organized according to military law). At Nuremberg, the Allies indicted 24 individuals and 8 organizations; at Tokyo, 28 Japanese defendants were tried. The charges included conspiracy to wage war, crimes against peace, war crimes, and crimes against humanity.

But to what extent should anyone involved in the prosecution or support of the war effort be held responsible? What is the degree of guilt, if any, that devolves on the political leaders, the military commanders, or those who act under the orders of superiors who enjoy a certain "privilege" or immunity by virtue of their customary role in warfare? What is the causal connection in regard to responsibility and guilt between the highest and lowest denominator in this juxtaposition of actions, for even civilians who abet military activity in any way have been accused of "vicarious murder." Do we ascribe guilt by association, or apply the legalisms of contributory negligence and diminished responsibility? No doubt there is enough guilt and responsibility to go around, but to what extent can the perpetrator of the crime escape the consequences of his action, assuming that the perpetrator in the one who performs the act?

    Having provided some grist for the mill regarding the method of prosecuting the war, I should like to comment on the second question, namely, guilt as related to the reason for engaging in war. Ordinarily a nation resorts to armed conflict in an effort to alter an existing situation, or, conversely, to prevent an alteration of a prevailing situation. Relating to this matter is the complex subject of the "just war," and most governments contend that their war is "just" whether it meets Augustine's criteria or anyone else's. Resisting the temptation to examine the numerous and persistent efforts over the millennia to prevent war and provide for the peaceful settlement of disputes between nations, I shall mention briefly only recent developments. Since 1950, at the direction of the General Assembly, the International Law Commission and various special committees have been working on a formulation of the principles of international law recognized in the Charter of the Nuremberg Tribunal and in the judgment of the Tribunal; to produce a draft code of offenses against the peace and security of mankind; and to provide an acceptable definition of aggression. The ex officio War Crimes Tribunal, which met in Stockholm in May 1967, had as its purpose an investigation and assessment of the character of the United States' war in Vietnam. Five questions were posed, including acts of aggression according to international law, the use of weapons prohibited by the laws of war, bombardment of civilian targets, the inhuman treatment of prisoners and reprisals against civilians, forced labor camps, and acts amounting "juridically" to genocide. The tribunal invited all parties to present evidence, and while Hanoi and the National Liberation Front cooperated the United States government did not. The tribunal sent more than 30 investigators into battle areas, and it eventually found the United States guilty of specific acts that violated international law.

    Essentially, while there is no enforcing agency, the decision-maker is being placed in a position of greater vulnerability on "statutory" grounds as having violated conventions or treaties whether Hague, Geneva, League Covenant, Kellogg-Briand Pact, UN Charter, or the like; on "precedent" grounds from the Versailles treaty to the Tokyo and Nuremberg trials; and on moral or humanitarian grounds (the conscience of mankind) depending on which principles are violated. Judgment may not be imposed by his peers and the body may not be impartial, but at least the rules of the game are being more carefully defined and the consequences made more clear. The difficulties of reconciling different legal systems and an addiction to generalizations to reach common agreement permit varieties of interpretation on specifics. But efforts are being made as never before on a world-wide scale to ameliorate the horrors of war and humanize this inhumane institution.

SEA POWER IN A MULTI-POLAR WORLD

Chapter 22

The term "sea power" evokes memories of Alfred Thayer Mahan, who analyzed its elements but never provided a concise definition. Every schoolboy knew that the seas cover approximately three fourths of the earth's surface, but few schoolboys or others have been aware of the significance of the seas in contributing to a habitable planet or affecting the destiny of nations and peoples. Apropo of ignorance, as H. J. Mackinder pointed out, "The influence of geographical conditions upon human activities has depended . . . not merely on the realities as we now know them to be and to have been, but in even greater degree on what men imagined in regard to them." Perceptions of the role of the sea, especially by those whose decisions and actions affect our lives, are what really matter. So let me take a few minutes to define these terms as I see them and as some others have seen and do see them.

Seventy-one years ago the then President Theodore Roosevelt spoke in San Francisco at the dedication of a monument to Dewey's victory at Manila Bay. "The seat of power," he said, "ever shifts from land to land, from sea to sea," and "the Atlantic Ocean became to the modern greater world what the Mediterranean had been to the lesser world of antiquity. The empire that shifted from the Mediterranean," he concluded, "will in the lifetime of these new children bid fair to shift once more westward to the Pacific." Today, however, we can say with some confidence that while the Pacific has played a major role in the 20th century it has not produced an "empire" comparable to those of the Mediterranean and the Atlantic, and that the "seat of power" is not confined to any one sea. It is conceivable that the locus of power will skip the Pacific and emerge in the Indian Ocean. But currently and for some time to come it seems clear that the "seat of power" is the World Ocean which borders, and has been to a considerable degree responsible for the fate of, every major nation.

The term "power" has many connotations, a la Humpty Dumpty, and often it is taken to mean both the <u>ability</u> to exercise control and its <u>application</u>. Within the framework of this paper it seems more appropriate to use "power" in the context of the method and implementation of the exploitation of the sea in order to further stated objectives. As for "multi-polar world," the assumption is that the free-world-Communist bloc polarity no longer exists; that the Sino-Soviet split and the emergence of the third world states have fractionated both interests and power with the possibility of creating an equilibrium; and that the Western nations find the hoped for "Year of Europe" has been further dislocated by disagreement over the Middle East, while the President and the Secretary of State have been faced with the task of trying to put NATO together again.

So, to "Sea Power in a Multi Polar World." Here, again we must remember the comprehensive totality of sea power. Alfred Thayer Mahan found the key to much of the history and policy of nations bordering the sea in three factors: production, shipping, and colonies. Further, he enumerated six "principle conditions affecting the sea power of nations," namely, (1) geographical position; (2) physical conformation, including natural products and climate; (3) extent of territory; (4) number of population; (5) character of the people; and (6) character of the government, including therein the national institutions. But he went on to say that command of the sea was essential to the fulfillment of these maritime commercial ambitions, and that command could be achieved only through a superior navy. Without this final ingredient, he contended, the other conditions, no matter how favorable, could not add up to effective sea power.

Mahan viewed sea power as being comprised of many components, not all of which need be equal or even be present in considerable degree, but if properly enmeshed would promote greatness. The greatness to which many nations aspire may take different forms, and the role and substance of sea power may vary. But traditionally the sea has provided protection, transportation, food, and other material resources; and ships have been the vehicle for exploration, migration, trade, intimidation, and war. The vessels on which the exploitation of the sea depends comprise the fishing, merchant, and naval fleets that, apparently, have appeared in that order in the chronology of the past as man has sought to master this awesome barrier/highway in pursuit of whatever benefits were desired. Essentially, then, sea power related to man's use of the sea for whatever purpose he chooses. Today, many of the dimensions of sea power are similar to those of the past, as are many of the national objectives. Yet there are some differences in degree if not in kind which reflect alterations in international relations, technology, ideology, and resources. Let me now go, in pedagogical terminology, from the general to the particular and even resort to that last refuge of a scholar, namely, statistics.

When World War II ended the United States had achieved a domination of the world ocean never before approximated by any nation. Its naval forces and merchant marine literally had no rival, and these two dimensions of sea power served the nation well in supporting the role it had decided to play in the postwar world. The U.S. merchant marine carried about 60% of the world's seaborne commerce and had some 4,500 ships suitable for use. The naval presence, projected in various portions of the globe, influenced governments and provided that control of the sea which permitted military intervention in Korea, Lebanon, and Vietnam. Aside from the combat role of the Navy, the logistics of warmaking and peacekeeping in distant places demanded utilization of the sea, and made it imperative that the United States maintain effective communications everywhere in the broadest sense of the term, that is, the ability to transport men and material anywhere in the world.

Yet the intervening years found the American Navy and merchant marine declining in both relative and absolute terms. As the ships aged, were mothballed, or decommissioned, and as Great Britain, faced with the dissolution of its empire and financial crises, curtailed its Navy, the Soviet Union embarked on a steady comprehensive development of sea power in all of its manifestations, with each element co-ordinated so completely as to evoke the admiration of the most hostile anti-Soviet critic. Never before had a nation developed its maritime potential in such a short period and in such a systematic manner, with each dimension of the entire spectrum synchronized. Icebreakers, oceanographic vessels, fishing fleets, merchant ships, and naval craft have been produced or purchased in a steady flow to complement each other and inaugurate a modern version of mercantilism that integrates economic, political, and ideological objectives with the means for their implementation. The broadening of the geographical foundation, the thrust away from a restrictive continental outlook, the erection of an industrial base, the tapping of natural resources, and a concerted effort to orient a segment of the population toward the sea, all give evidence of the most determined exposition of sea power that the world has ever witnessed.

But before embarking on a more specific comparison of the naval strength of the two super-powers, let me make some observations about the relative state of the merchant marine. In regard to registered merchant fleets, Liberia, Japan, and Great Britain lead, each having over 2,000 vessels with emphasis on freighters, bulk carriers, and tankers, with relatively few passenger cargo ships. Next in order are Norway, Greece, the USSR, and the United States. The Liberian figure is somewhat misleading for many ships owned by nationals in other countries are registered with Liberia or Panama. The most dramatic developments in merchant vessels have been in bulk or container carriers and the huge oil tankers that Japan pioneered with displacement in the hundreds of thousands of tons instead of 10 or 20 thousand tons. While these huge tankers cannot use certain passages such as the narrow Panama Canal, are wary of the shallow Strait of Malacca, and pose difficulties in handling and docking, they are efficient and economical. Further, the merchant ships of Japan, the USSR, and the United Kingdom are relatively new as compared with those of the United States, which has fallen far behind in new construction and in some ways is priced out of the market in respect to ship-building and competition for the carrying trade.

So far as naval vessels are concerned, the United States has no competition in attack aircraft carriers, although the Russians have built one and are building another, and Great Britain made the agonizing decision five years ago to phase out this type. On submarines, diesel and nuclear powered, the USSR is far ahead in totals, but in categories she is about equal to the United States in nuclear and missile armed submarines, ahead in attack and hunter-killer submarines, and is outbuilding the United States two to one. Her surface vessels are much more modern than those of the United States, most of which are over 20 years old and approaching if they haven't reached obsolesence, and the number of ships in the American Navy has been reduced by 44% while the Russian Navy has expanded phenomenally. As for support vessels, the United States Navy has had to concentrate its fund on building combatant ships and rely increasingly on the merchant marine for replenishing type ships. Obviously, the Soviet Union with its ownership and centralized control of all vessels can orchestrate its effort much more effectively than can the United States with its pluralistic and open society approach to the factors of naval and maritime power.

Again, in trying to pursue a multipolar treatment of the problem of sea power, a few words are appropriate in regard to what some of the other nations are doing. Japan possesses a first rank merchant marine as is consistent with her industrial status and lack of raw materials which must be procured from abroad. Her Maritime Self-Defense Force (MSDF) cannot provide for the safety of her homeland or the protection of her sea lanes, but she enjoys the safety furnished by the Security Treaty with the United States and the presence of the Seventh Fleet. In this respect some believe that Japan is the exception to the Mahan dictum, although, of course, someone else is looking out for her and providing the protection that otherwise she would have to furnish. Mainland China has a long way to go before it emerges as a competitor in the contest for the sea, but her overtures to the outside world reveal a greater interest in trade. She has the potential, and it appears that her castoff navy may be joined by nuclear powered submarines in the not too distant future to operate in the Sea of Japan and the China Seas, not to mention prospects for future deployment in the Indian Ocean. As for those nations bordering this enormous sea, India is predominant in naval power, and her strategic location, vast population and natural resources are of concern for the present and hold promise of greater development in the future. Her hostility toward China and the support she secured from the Soviet Union in the 1971 war with Pakistan make India an even more important factor in the question of world sea power. Australia, too, has made vigorous efforts to provide for her security in the face of Britain's curtailment east of Suez and the changes that have taken place in the Far East. Virtually astride one of the two main passages between the Indian Ocean and the Pacific, with her major naval base awkwardly situated at Sydney, she is constructing a station near Fremantle which the previous government had invited the United States to share. Conversely, the present government has denounced an American buildup in the Indian Ocean and decried the limited exploitation of Diego Garcia as an auxiliary facility.

While it is impracticable to give a summary of the maritime or naval status of many nations, and I've tried to mention only some that I think most significant, it would be amiss to ignore the role of the other 14 NATO countries and the small but modern navies they possess. The circumstances under which the United States could count on aid in an altercation, crisis, or clash with the Soviet Union are not clear. The European members of NATO cooperate with the United States in resisting the threat of Soviet aggression by supporting a strategic deterrent and creating a shield against Soviet sea power in a general or conventional war or a post-nuclear exchange situation. In either of these latter cases the military mission of the United States would be to provide reinforcements, men and materiel, to the NATO forces in Europe, and most of these reinforcements would have to come by sea. The mission of the Soviet Navy would be to prevent these reinforcements from arriving, and in this respect, in regard to the Atlantic, would amount to that of "sea denial" rather than "sea control," a point emphasized by some authorities. Whether this means that the Soviet Navy in pursuing this strategy is offensively or defensively oriented is a matter of semantics. But the trend toward huge merchant vessels makes the _guerre de course_ a more effective weapon, and the logarithmic advances in submarine sophistication have created problems for antisubmarine warfare undreamed of in many previous naval philosophies.

Thus a situation prevails in which a nation such as Japan is outstanding in some of the elements of sea power such as industrial productivity and a superb merchant marine, but deficient in natural resources and naval strength. Whereas the United States, once supreme ruler of the seas, has relinquished the trident in merchant shipping, oceanography, fishing fleets, and, as some see it, in naval superiority. While the expenditure of American military resources in Vietnam has diminished, the alleged retreat from a Pax Americana has scarcely lessened the demands on the American Navy under the commitments, formal and/or implicit, undertaken by the nation.

The mission of the United States Navy, according to the recent Chief of Naval Operations, Admiral Elmo R. Zumwalt, Jr., is fourfold:

1. Strategic deterrence, provided by Polaris/Poseidon forces.

2. Sea control--ensure that we have free use of the seas during both peace and wartime. Forces composed of attack submarines, maritime patrol aircraft, ASW forces and strike aircraft operating from carriers.

3. Projections--Strike carrier and amphibious forces provide capability to project power into the Eurasian rimland, supported by the merchant marine which carries over 90% of the logistical burden of supplying our forces overseas.

4. Overseas presence--Our ability to use our forces to enable our national influence and the credibility of our national determination to be known in areas around the world bordered by the world's oceans.

A formidable assignment to be sure, and in many respects more difficult than that faced by any other service. The sea, unlike the earth's land surface or its atmosphere, is exploitable diplomatically, militarily, and materially. Traditionally open to all nations in time of peace, it is most vulnerable to Soviet penetration, and the high seas abound with Russian fishing, oceanographic, merchant, surveillance, and naval craft. Soviet naval deployment has been circumscribed by both capability and opportunity. For example, a significant presence in the Mediterranean coincided with the early stage of the expanded building program and the outcome of the 1956 Mideast war, and port visits in the Indian Ocean began in 1968 following Britain's decision to withdraw from that area and the accelerated United States involvement in Vietnam. An American task force sent to the Bay of Bengal during the 1971 Indo-Pakistani conflict was followed a few days later through the Strait of Malacca by a Soviet contingent, and the October 1973 Arab-Israeli war saw both Russia and the United States bolster their forces in the Mediterranean in support of their clients, with the United States even detaching a task force from the Seventh Fleet and sending it to the Mideast through the Indian Ocean. Each of the two naval super-powers is employing its forces in a similar but not identical manner in conformity with their respective objectives and commitments, and statements emanating from Moscow over the years provide almost a mirror image of the declared mission of the American Navy.

It appears unlikely that either of these navies, with or without their respective allies, could perform all of the missions assigned or assumed. Specifically, I seriously doubt that the sea lanes to Europe could be secured because of Soviet submarines and the present state of anti-submarine warfare. Logistic support to the Far East probably could be sustained, for the Soviets would most likely concentrate their efforts in the Atlantic to weaken the NATO forces. But losses in the Pacific would be considerable and our ally Japan would be in dire straits. The Middle East, known for centuries as the crossroads of civilization, continues to take on added significance for obvious reasons, and here, it seems, the West would simply be outclassed. The Western Mediterranean might remain open with the aid of the NATO forces, although surface communication to support Greece or Israel, for example, would be denied. Obviously, this scenario is controversial because air and land operations would play a vital and perhaps decisive role.

To continue on the Middle East for a moment, we must recall that the Turkish Straits are the "umbilical cord" of Soviet maritime/commercial and naval penetration into the Mediterranean, the Arab lands, and the Indian Ocean. The Russians consider themselves a legitimate occupant of this area while the United States is regarded as an interloper. Moscow's plea for the Mediterranean to be designated a "sea of peace" called for the departure of the Sixth Fleet and the continued presence of the Soviets. The closing of the Suez Canal has seriously inhibited Russian maritime and naval mobility in regard to the Red Sea, Persian Gulf, Indian Ocean, and Siberia, the latter being especially significant because the Trans-Siberian railroad is simply incapable of handling the cargo for that region. The opening of the canal has been estimated to be the equivalent of providing the Soviet Union with an additional 300 merchant vessels. Russian contiguity and vital interest in the Middle East make questionable the feasibility of United States military intervention in an Arab-Israeli conflict even if Russia did so. Analogies such as Hungary and Czechoslovakia, on the one hand, and Cuba, Korea, and Vietnam on the other, seem pertinent. Yet President Nixon ordered a "precautionary military alert," during the October 1973 Arab-Israeli war, presumably to prevent the Russians from sending troops to aid the Egyptians in that conflict. The President ostensibly was threatening general rather than limited or proxy war.

In the event of a general war between the United States and the Soviet Union, with their various allies, the demands on the American Navy would be overwhelming. The Atlantic and the Mediterranean would probably retain first priority to support the NATO allies as previously indicated. In the Far East the tasks would be to attack and blockade the Siberian coast, defend South Korea and Japan and keep open the Western seas, including the Indian Ocean which Admiral Zumwalt recently described as the West's "jugular vein." While the United States has sought Russian agreement to limit naval armaments in this area, in October 1974 Admiral Zumwalt claimed that the Soviets had five times as many warships in the Indian Ocean as did the United States. Geographically, India is in an ideal position to sever the main lines of communication between the Middle East and the Pacific. The Indo-Soviet Pact of 1971, although a friendship treaty, gave evidence of closer ties between these two nations, and the trade transiting this area is vital to the interests of America and her allies, especially Japan. In February 1972 Admiral Zumwalt told the Senate Armed Services Committee that America's increasing dependence on foreign oil supplies and the prospect that the Navy may someday protect hundreds of U.S. bound oil tankers was creating what he called a "new" and "emerging" role for the American fleet.

Although not probable, it is still conceivable that a "limited" naval conflict might occur between the two superpowers with varying degrees of assistance from allies. It could take place in the context of aid to a client state, and while the Soviet Union has avoided overt military involvement in a proxy struggle with the United States, circumstances might induce it to do so in the Middle East or South Asia. Both areas lend themselves to blockade as an effective weapon, and the American luxury of one-sided interdiction in Korea and Vietnam may not be repeated. While strategists debate the possibilty of localizing such a conflict, proxy wars have been contained and the planners must anticipate and prepare for this type of eventuality.

Such a limited war would find the Soviet Union at a distinct disadvantage because of the lack of carrier-based aircraft. It would be denied the mobile airfield from which to launch attacks inland, strike at enemy vessels, provide adequate reconnaissance, or protect Soviet ships from aerial assault. Nor could air cover be furnished for the amphibious landings that the Russians have been practicing assiduously in the Black Sea and the sub-Arctic regions. The two helicopter carriers and naval infantry or marines add some flexibility, and the former are especially useful for anti-submarine patrol. But shortcomings in regard to naval aircraft are well known and are reflected in the completion of one plane-launching carrier and the construction of another. The lack of this important ingredient probably has affected the credibility of the USSR as an active ally in a proxy war waged outside the immediate Soviet defense perimeter. When the Soviet Union acquires this capability its friends may have greater confidence in promises of assistance, and may be tempted to follow more aggressive policies and take greater risks in dealing with stubborn neighbors.

Nor has the Soviet Union neglected what their naval high command calls "the moral-psychological preparation of sailors for modern war." The enemy exists in the form of capitalism and imperialism with the United States representing the embodiment if not the culmination of these two evils. This psychological preparation includes not only readiness for a vigorous response to attack but for "preemptive" or "first" strikes. In the words of Admiral Gorshkov, "the struggle for the first salvo." Thus a favorable climate is being created by the Kremlin hierarchy, and the Navy is being prepared for any action ranging from the "peacekeeping" chores performed by the Army in East Berlin, Hungary, and Czechoslovakia, and American-style intervention in Korea and Vietnam, to the ultimate of total war.

Those who read the U.S. Naval Institute Proceedings and the Soviet Naval Digest (Morskoi Sbornik) would find the writers saying a great deal of the same thing from a different point of view. The Soviets, too, appear to be striving for a balanced force capable of handling any contingency. Yet James Cable, in his book Gunboat Diplomacy, maintains that "Limited war, let alone limited force, finds no place in Soviet political or military doctrine," and the Paul Cohen article "The Erosion of Surface Naval Power," in Foreign Affairs of January 1971, created an uproar by arguing that the submarine was the only effective warship. Still another civilian, Samuel Huntington, contended that American interests demand a new strategy of "counterintervention" against the Soviets, and that naval power, especially naval air power, will be critical for this mission, while stress on the future role of the submarine is not justified.

Many authorities believe that Soviet surface fleets do not have a true world-wide maritime capability for lack of mobile logistic support and carrier borne aircraft, with the latter deficiency compelling them to rely on land based aircraft for both air cover and strike supplemented by surface to air (SAM) and surface to surface (SSM) missiles. Their venture into carrier construction was criticized because the vessel was too small to handle the large, long range aircraft accommodated by the American ships. Now, however, it seems they anticipated a new trend in naval aviation toward small carriers embarking relatively small, supersonic fighter/attack aircraft which possess vertical or short take-off and landing capability. Great Britain is building a "through-deck cruiser" with a flight deck for helicopters and fighter-bombers, and France appears to be going in this direction. New construction in submarines finds the Soviet Delta class, now operational, with the SSN-8 missile having a range of some 4,600 miles, or about

1700 miles more than the U.S. Polaris and Poseidon missiles. The American TRIDENT program, finally authorized after much haggling with Secretary of Defense James Schlesinger and Congress, incorporates the Undersea Long-Range Missile System, (ULMS) but it won't be operational for from five to ten years depending on subsequent appropriations, and the cost of approximately one and a half billion dollars for each craft makes unlikely an ambitious building program such as the ten projected. Budget restrictions have killed the Sea-Based Anti-Ballistic Missile Intercept System (SABMIS) which was submitted to Congress with great enthusiasm not many years ago, and the pressure for economy coupled with the need for surface warship replacement has led to the urging of what amounts to a different naval strategy. Designated the Sea Control Ship Program, it calls for greater dispersion as a basic concept for future naval forces and a shift toward smaller, less expensive vessels. Perhaps, as one authority has intimated, only the Soviet Union will be able to afford the kind of navy that it takes to establish command of the sea in the not too distant future.

As seems evident, while the world may be depolarized in some respects, including maritime commercial power, it is still a bi-polar world in respect to naval power, and the absence of naval power in any of its dimensions can limit options. The current Institute for Strategic Studies report and the editor of Jane's Fighting Ships are in accord in speaking of variables in trying to compare the two navies, but agree that overall the West probably has the edge especially in intervention situations because of American carrier superiority. Certainly, the most effective weapon in any arsenal depends on what you want it to do, and the spectrum of sea power is so broad that the creation of a stable equilibrium is probably impracticable for the foreseeable future. Even less promising is the possibility that there will be anything in the nature of an agreed upon "trade off" on spheres of naval influence so far as the oceans and seas are concerned, although this arrangement tacitly exists in regard to the Caribbean, much of the Pacific, the Baltic and Black Seas, and segments of the Arctic and Antarctic regions.

During the period of alleged detente in a political sense there has been increasing tension in a naval sense. Still, the horrors of modern war and the increasing interdependence of nations lend dramatic emphasis to the need for cooperation in the exploitation of the sea. The demands on resources--raw materials, facilities, manpower and technology--are making for greater unity in a nationalistic, politically and ideologically divided world. The standardization of rules of the road and navigational aids is an example of what needs to be done in defining the law of the sea; to settle the extent of territorial seas where the old three mile limit has been stretched unilaterally to 12, 50 and over 200 miles; to establish the right of free transit in many straits, such as Gibralter and Malacca, where Spain in the first case and Malaysia and Indonesia in the second case are insisting on sovereignty; to regulate the use of the ocean floor, with the United States proposing national economic jurisdiction out to 200 miles or roughly the edge of the continental shelf, and international jurisdiction of other zones of the seabed; to more carefully prescribe sea lanes and control of fishing rights; to combat marine pollution; and to coordinate scientific investigation of the ocean areas.

The seas have served both to separate and unite mankind, and man has used them to his detriment and his benefit. The extent to which the sea will continue to contribute in either capacity is a challenge second only to that of our trying to get along together, and, depending on one's definition of a pessimist or optimist, preserve the human species in what literally is one world.

THE MAYA CULTURE AND AMERICA: A Comparison

Chapter 23

The Rythm of History-Upbeat or Down?

I

The topic of this meeting is devoted to what I consider a major function of history, namely, to utilize the past in order to understand the present and thus avoid repeating mistakes of our predecessors. While I do not endorse the concept that we can only discover what man is by knowing what he has been, I do believe that historians provide insights into human achievement and potentiality that are not otherwise available. History is the record of human experience, what we know about all of humankind's past activities.

Many historians have sought to discover meaning in the past, to find "laws" of human development analogous to those that were thought to exist in the physical world, and I suspect that all of us have, consciously or unconsciously, a "theory" of history. Most theories of the past follow either a linear or a cyclical interpretation, that is, either a steady progression in one direction or a repetitive cycle of growth, peak, and decline. Contributing to the complexity of studying the past is the question of the size and context of our model, what Toynbee called the "unit of intelligible study." Some would call it the microcosmic versus the macrocosmic approach, or as Spengler put it, using an analogy with the solar system, the geocentric versus the heliocentric approach. This conference deals directly with both the problem of interpretation and that of approach, and adds the even more vexing problem of applying them to two specific periods of human development, the Maya and the American, one of which we know very little about and the other about which we may think we know too much.

Before I become specific let me state some of my premises in regard to the theme of this symposium. Using the criteria established by Western man, the course of history has not been constant or always in one direction; linear and cyclical movements are discernable in regard to the changes that have occurred in the past, and in this sense there are some characteristics of "rhythm" if by rhythm we mean no more than movement. But if by rhythm we mean a regular or uniform recurrence, a pattern, then this speaker has not discovered one. Primitive societies, nations, and civilizations or "universal states" have experienced varying degrees of development and durability, and the factors responsible for success or failure often vary in degree and even in kind. The historian tries to determine what happened, how it happened, and why it happened, to discover the reasons for stability or change, and to weigh the factors responsible. The search for "causal connections" poses the great problem for those who try to understand the past, and to separate "primary" from "secondary" or "tertiary" causes of events. Some of us take refuge in a monocausal or deterministic explanation, such as geography, race, or economics. Others, including myself, discern a complexity in human affairs that precludes a single explanation and adopt a "multifaceted" or "multiple causationist" approach that tends to minimize generalizations and enhance the intriguing uncertainties that confront historians. This uncertainty is reflected in the hazards of dealing with historical "parallels," and my outlook of a disordered past and complex causality will be obvious in the following remarks.

Aside from these brief observations on historical interpretation, my assignment tonight, as I understand it, is to compare the factors responsible for the rise of Maya Civilization with those responsible for the development of the United States. The method I've chosen is to deal with those factors individually and discuss their applicability or inapplicability to each or both nations. We must recognize at the outset that the amount of knowledge we possess about these nations is far from comparable, and that most of what we know about the Mayas is based on archeological evidence that is still in the process of being studied by archeologists and anthropologists.

To begin with the geographical factor, The Mayan Lowlands where the Classic period developed are described as ecologically homogeneous, with climate, soil, and rainfall conducive to agriculture. Indigenous vegetation was edible and suitable for cultivation, and wild game was plentiful. Land topography and rivers provided for easy communication by foot or canoe, and surrounding mountains furnished a barrier against invaders. Sites were available for town or ceremonial edifices and soft stone to be worked without metal tools was abundant. Essentially, the environment provided for a simple and easy means of livelihood and lacked those environmental "challenges" that are alleged by some to stimulate human creative activity. On the other hand, the environment of early America was such that the English settlers were hard put to survive and would not have done so without help from the mother country. The economic development of the United States can be attributed largely to the presence of vast areas of land suited for various purposes and the ability of the people to exploit these natural resources. The disparate stimuli were available in much greater degree than they were for the Maya, and without this geographical largess it is reasonably certain that the United States would not have developed as it has. Also, the presence of oceans has had a significant impact on the American nation. So the geographical factor has played a significant role in terms of opportunity and stimuli.

Another factor to be considered is contacts with other societies. Earlier contentions that the Mayans developed in a virtual vacuum have been discounted and the contributions of the Olmecs have been acknowledged, if grudgingly, and early contacts had been made with Teotihuacan and other groups. The Mayans were active traders and, without indulging in speculation on possible influences from Egypt, the Orient, or outer space, they certainly were exposed to other peoples of various degrees of development. That they borrowed some of the elements that characterize their civilization is unquestionable even if there is disagreement on specifics. In the United States the case is more clear cut, for the immigrants brought with them the accomplishments of a highly developed and complex society, and they and their offspring continued this association while adapting European ideas and practices to fit their own particular needs. Most Europeans came to America in search of a higher standard of living and a more perfect society. The same motives may have prompted the people who settled in the Lowlands, but the cultural heritage they brought with them was considerably different, as were the contacts maintained with other groups. The nature of borrowed knowledge and skills is simply not comparable.

Related to the foregoing are tools, technology, science, and, essentially, those items that enable man to perform tasks more easily. The Mayans had no domesticated animals for hauling or transportation, and the wheel as a device was unknown to them. Scientific achievements in mathematics and astronomy did little to relieve the hardships of the people, and even the fundamentals of metallurgy were not mastered. The Americans benefited from thousands of years of scientific and technological advancement, and their nation was founded at the appropriate time to exploit the industrial age that was emerging in the West.

Ethnic factors are relevant in comparing the two societies, for basically the Mayans shared a similar language and similar physical characteristics as well as similar backgrounds. The United States was composed of immigrants from a variety of nations and their decendents, almost exclusively European in origin and predominantly white Anglo-Saxon Protestant of English stock. This diversity made for what an early writer called "a new man, the American," compelled to associate with peoples of different ethnic groups and being influenced by disparate heritages. The old term "melting pot" was to an extent applicable to America, and this mixture of ethnic backgrounds enriched this new nation and provided the stimulus that derives from contacts between societies and peoples.

Mayan society was highly structured, hierarchical in nature, with the priestly rulers a tiny minority and peasants constituting the vast majority, with no middle class and virtually no opportunity for upward mobility, with status being determined by birth. In the United States classes did exist but they were based on wealth and position, and while there was discrimination on ethnic and religious grounds, Caucasians did enjoy a greater opportunity to improve their lot than in any other nation. Ability was a major criterion for advancement and the presence of this incentive was an important factor in the growth of the United States.

Economically, the Mayan was a static but viable society. It never escaped its agricultural base, and the few artisans who practiced a craft were never employed in what could be considered even a primitive industry. Trade consisted of food and pottery and there were no resources to encourage other types of economic activity. The United States, of course, had not only the resources for a diversified economy but the "know how" imported from Europe and the ready contact for prosperous and stimulating commercial relations.

Politically, it seems that the Mayans were ruled by a priestly elite that gained its authority through religious sanction. Power was not highly centralized for the various settlements enjoyed considerable autonomy, and it appears that the rulers did organize and direct agricultural, building, and other activities. The United States was never a theocracy and political leaders were chosen to a greater or lesser degree by the people. The federalist system, intended to combine the virtues of centralization and decentralization of power, prevailed through numerous crises and seemed to provide a satisfactory form of government, or at least a government designed to offer the people freedom with restraints.

Militarily, the Mayans are referred to as a peace-loving people with no standing army, no protective walls, and no aggressive tendencies. Perhaps they were surrounded by satisfied neighbors who felt that the Mayans had nothing that they wanted, and, of course, the reverse could be true. Yet we are told of Mayan representations of soldiers returning from battle with prisoners, and it seems unlikely that they could have avoided serious quarrels with neighboring societies, quarrels that could have led to bloodshed, although the apparent peaceful nature of the Mesoamerican area probably enabled the Mayans to avoid diverting their time and resources to defense. The United States, on the other hand, has an almost continuous history of armed conflict. It was through warfare that the nation won and maintained its independence, displaced the native Indians, and rounded out its territory, to say nothing of enhancing trade and establishing itself as a leading power in world affairs. If, as has been said, war is a test of the nation's will, or as Adam Smith contended, man's noblest form of activity, then the United States has performed.

I hesistate to comment on cultural factors, although I shall submit to the temptation. Using the term "culture" to indicate intellectual and artistic achievements, we can say with assurance that here the Maya excelled and their works have warranted the society being labelled a "civilization." Their creativity in these fields is well known, and while some of it was borrowed the Mayans evidently improved considerably on what others had done. In contrast, the United States for many years was referred to condescendingly by Europeans as a cultural desert, arid in art and literature, merely producing bad modifications of European products. Perhaps, as some suggested, the Americans were too busy occupying and settling a continent while making money, devoting their energies to material rather than esthetic gratification. The leisure necessary for the creation of beauty was not available and the work ethic made functionalism an imperative. Understandably, the greatest contributions were in technology, and the occasional instances of intellectual and artistic creativity stand as exceptions to the rule.

One of the factors that I've ignored is the character of the people. A distinctive element of a successful society is a sharing of a common purpose, a mission if you will, a belief in fundamental values, in agreed upon ends and means, and an energy and vitality to spur the people on to attain specific goals. This combination produces a unity of effort that has been responsible for much human achievement. While I suspect this was true of the Mayans, I am convinced that it was for the United States.

In this brief time I've tried to compare some of the factors that were responsible for the development of two disparate societies. One, the Mayan, achieved eminence in its own world. The other, the United States, has achieved global eminence. But what are the criteria for eminence in each case? With the Maya it is intellectual and artistic excellence representing the highest flights of man's mind and spirit. With the United States it is economic and technical accomplishment, and tomorrow we will have a chance to discuss the implications for the present and the future.

WAR, DIPLOMACY, AND HISTORY

The Rhythm of History-Upbeat or Down?
II

Apropos of the title of this presentation, my musician wife tells me that the upbeat leads to the downbeat, and the latter is the stronger. No doubt the metaphor is intended to signify the reverse, for "down" usually means a decline and tonight we are to discuss "Causes of the decline of the Maya Culture, and analysis of present day parallels." Fortunately for our topic, there seems to be more information available on the Fall of the Mayan Civilization that there is on its rise, and material abounds on what is wrong with the nation and the world today. In keeping with the format used last night, I intend to deal with some of the reasons advanced to explain the fall of Mayan Civilization and see how they compare with what I understand of the situation in the United States. Since external relations are relevant in both cases my treatment may verge on the global. So, what components caused or accelerated the decline of the Maya from its Classic ascendancy and to what extent do we find them present today?

As you are aware, there is some dispute as to whether the so called Maya collapse took place at different times or concurrently in the Northern Lowlands and the Southern Lowlands, but I will continue to treat the Maya Civilization as a whole and concentrate on the Classic Period or what used to be referred to as the Old Empire.

It appears that the Classic Maya endured a period of crisis in the 6th century, possibly due to the decline of Teotihuacan power and the need to readjust trade. But the Maya overcame this crisis and a renewal or florescence occurred, again possibly due to the fall of Teotihuacan and the Maya being placed more on their own. A likely parallel with the United States would be the fading of European ascendancy and the emergence of America as the leading power, although interchange has, if anything, increased.

It seems that in the Late Classic period the class structure hardened, the elite consolidated, and a firmer division of labor was established with specialized bureaucrats and artisans. In the United States full-time officials have multiplied phenomenally as demands for public services have increased, and in both cases, that of the Maya and the United States, there is some question as to whether this element is a producer or a parasite on society.

We are told that rivalry among the various Maya regions stimulated activity during the late Classic times, although one might conjecture that it could have become self-defeating when it reached a point of hostility or antagonism. The

United States has had a similar experience, and the bloody Civil War is a monument to an excess of competition. Today, regionalism in America has been abetted by President Nixon's "New Federalism", the vagaries of daylight saving time, the gas shortage, and the appeals of California versus Florida. The question is directly related to the federalism controversy, namely, the degree to which authority should be centralized or localized. One could maintain that an effort to curtail the autonomy of Mayan regions brought resistance that contributed to the decline of the civilization. But I question whether the same would be true in the United States because of the rapidity of communications and a widespread feeling that Washington should assume more responsibility for the general welfare. As Alexander Hamilton said, "only a national government can govern in the interest of all the people."

The religious factor as a key to prestige and power is dealt with by Dr. Edmonson, but obviously it played a considerable authoritarian role in the Maya Society in contrast to its position in the United States, although the nation and its laws continue to function ostensibly in the Judeo-Christian tradition. Religion has played both a constructive and a destructive role in the past, and I doubt that it will have much effect on the immediate future. Yet religion does affect our beliefs, and what we believe determines what we do. Whether some amalgamation of the "higher religions," as Toynbee suggests, will or should happen is highly questionable.

Demographic factors have been given considerable attention by Mayanists and their findings have relevance. Evidently the earlier view that ceremonial centers were not towns has been discarded, and though urban population density was not so great as in other pre-Columbian civilizations a significant segment of the people did reside in these centers. It is possible that this drain on the food producing population placed strains on the economy and created dissension. There is evidence of malnutrition among the Mayans and the incidence of disease, with a resultant decline in births and an increase in early deaths. The aristocracy continued to multiply while the food producers decreased, and a larger percentage of females was born and survived. This imbalance in classes and in the proportion of sexes, and the functions they could serve, may have dislocated the economy to say nothing of its effect on the family and the military posture.

The earlier contention that soil exhaustion was a major factor in the Mayan collapse has been discarded, and replaced by the belief that food production was so close to meeting demand that no surplus was available to feed the populace in times of drought or other disaster. The marginal dimensions of wheat production in this country and the inordinate demands for this staple abroad and at home bear a striking resemblance. But better methods of control exist today and this nation, at least, seems unlikely to suffer too much.

Trade was a key factor in the rise of Maya society and the Mayans encountered more aggressive competitors to the west and south, competition often backed by force, with adverse effects on Mayan prosperity. Recent years have found the United States suffering from an unfavorable balance of trade and American products being priced out of the market. It has been said that Japan has accomplished by economic means what she failed to achieve previously by military aggression, and it has appeared that Japan and the Arab countries have been in the process of buying up the world. Whether the Mayan rate of exchange fluctuated the way the dollar has on the international scene is not known to me, but I suspect that a solution to the instability of the purchasing power of national currencies is imperative if a serious economic dislocation is to be avoided.

The military quotient in Mayan society is lacking, not necessarily because it did not exist but because of a paucity of information. Warfare was practiced, but how much and why eludes the researcher. The Toltec invasion came after the Classic period although it may have been occasioned by the noticeable weakening of the Maya state, and it is conceivable that prior to this time the Maya maintained a formidable or at least adequate defense posture. The evidence indicating a Classic Maya decline does not relate to military activity, and the most recent collective study of "The Maya Collapse" concludes by ruling "out a single 'internal' or 'external' phenomenon as the agent of the Classic Maya collapse."

Essentially, many authorities contend that the Classic collapse was due to the failure of the Maya managerial elite to cope with internal and external stresses that the society encountered. The internal strains could have been alleviated by better planning in the allocation of natural and human resources; by providing for social mobility to recruit administrators on the basis of merit rather than birth; by maintaining a balance between production, consumption, and trade; by establishing a military posture designed to provide for the safety and security of the people and protect the nation's interest in dealings with neighbors. Moreover, it is possible that the rulers, in attempting to institute reforms, began to exercise such control over people's lives that measures were resisted and the machinery of government broke down. In the United States laws have multipled to regulate virtually every aspect of human behavior on the grounds that they protect us from ourselves and each other, but the plethora of communication media, the openness of our society, and the responsibility of elected officials to the people should serve to prevent the government from taking action that will so alienate segments of the society that a collapse will occur. Also, the credentials of the decision maker must be appropriate to the needs of the time, and possibly the Mayan leadership was incapable of making the adjustment. In the U.S. we find the experts,--those who have and control scientific and technical knowledge,--exercising more influence in a hopefully beneficial manner.

The role of the elite, ruling minority is stressed by authorities in explaining both the rise and the decline of the Maya Civilization. The generative force provided by this group was manifest in creative and altruistic endeavor, and evidently deteriorated to self-aggrandizement and an egocentricity that resulted in governmental paralysis in attempting to cope with internal and external crises. In the United States today there seems to be a lack of confidence in the government. Not only is there a credibility gap but federal and local authorities seem incapable of anticipating or planning for emergencies or formulating policies when they do occur. In foreign affairs a degree of confidence has been established since the tragedy of Vietnam, which fostered violent dissention and contributed to the failure of President Johnson to achieve his "Great Society." The nature and extent of domestic reform often depends on which interest groups happen to dominate at a particular time, and legislation usually involves advantages for some to the detriment of others. In the field of foreign affairs the debate continues over the extent to which the United States should be involved, not only in regard to whatever we consider to be in the national interest, but to what degree humanitarian concerns should prevail. A year ago President Nixon said "The time has passed when America will make every other nation's conflict our own, or make every other nation's future our responsibility, or presume to tell the people of other nations how to manage their own affairs." The specifics of this so-called Nixon doctrine are still in dispute, although the principle seems to enjoy support.

Last night I mentioned that what people believe, consciously or unconsciously, determines what they do. Group activity is permeated by ideas that can be cohesive or divisive, and it is likely that the shared beliefs that contributed to the unity and growth of the Mayan civilization were challenged and contradicted to the point where the society was polarized and weakened. Was the cooperation that contributed to the rise of the Maya succeeded by a period of competition as the gulf between the poor and the rich widened? My study of history convinces me that certain beliefs can be constructive or destructive depending on the circumstances, most specifically in regard to the stage of development and the situation in which the group is functioning. While I have not seen material that would enable me to analyze the Mayans in this dimension, I do have some observations on certain "Western" beliefs or "hang ups," myths that seem to be more pronounced in the United States which contributed to our "rise" but may be obsolescent if not obsolete in regard to current tendencies and future survival.

1. Our concept of freedom, which may change as others have.

2. Our concept of the sanctity of the individual, an egocentric disregard of the admonition to "be our brother's keeper."

3. The associated economic absolutes of "rugged individualism", "free enterprise" and "private ownership."

4. Our emphasis on competition rather than cooperation.

5. Our belief in cut and dried solutions to problems --usually on our own terms.

6. The subordination of our values, in practice, to the dictates of a "standard of living concept" determined by technology and materialism, that compels people to buy things they don't need and can't afford, that substitutes obsolescence for quality and size for taste.

As Henry Kissinger noted some years ago, "it is hard for Americans to believe in tragedy," for what Henry James called "the bitch goddess success" has marked our progress.

We are told that this is a revolutionary era comparable to the great upheavals of the past, and unique at least in the sense that change has accelerated. The period may be referred to as one of rising expectations on the part of the vast majority of the world's population that has suffered from poverty, starvation, and exploitation. Yet the triple impact of technology, ideology, and new nations threatens to tear the world apart. Mankind has the means for controlling its destiny on this earth to a greater extent than ever before, and the reason we are holding this symposium in a building rather than a cave is because man has profited by his own experience and that of his predecessors. While the parallels are often inexact or uncertain, the Mayan experience may have some lessons for us all.

BOOK REVIEWS Chapter 24

I. Military

Miller, Nathan
Sea of Glory: The Continental Navy Fights for Independence, 1775-1783
New York: David McKay Co.
558 pp., $12.95, LC 72-92647
Publication Date: February 22, 1974

The subtitle of this book is misleading for it is not confined to an account of the Continental Navy which played a minor role in the immense maritime struggle that helped secure independence for the thirteen colonies. The author, described as a correspondent and a member of the investigative staff of the Senate Permanent Investigating Subcommittee, traces the evolution of colonial naval policy from the miniscule state navies and Washington's embryonic force to the gradual establishment by Congress of a truly Continental Navy. Spurred by the imperatives of denying supplies to the British Army and capturing them for the American forces, Congress first authorized the purchase of vessels and then their construction, formed committees that became the nucleus for an administrative organization, approved rules and regulations, and appointed officers. The final step in commerce raiding, which formed the substance of the American maritime contribution, was taken when Congress authorized the commissioning of privateers and the issuance of letters of marque with provision for the distribution of prize money and the creation of admiralty courts.

Set within the perspective of military and political developments on the domestic and international scene, this well-balanced narrative stresses the strategic and tactical operations of the major contestants. The British, while not fully exploiting their maritime superiority, maintained sufficient control of the sea to allow the Army a mobility that frustrated Washington, who desperately sought assistance from the French Navy to give him the opportunity to achieve a decisive military victory that finally materialized at Yorktown. Fleet actions and individual naval and privateer engagements are recounted in vivid detail with sufficient salt water flavor to satisfy the most ardent buff.

Although the author states that the book is based on primary as well as secondary sources, his few citations merely indicate the book or article that he relied on for his evidence or interpretation, and occasionally his paraphrasing deviates little or not at all from the text of the authorities to whom he gives general acknowledgment. Those familiar with published writings on the subject will find nothing new, and this work does not replace Charles O. Paullin's The Navy of the American Revolution and Gardner W. Allen's A Naval History of the American Revolution. But it does incorporate much recent scholarship and provides a well-written comprehensive account of combat maritime activities during the War of the Revolution that will appeal to the general reader if not the scholar.

History: Reviews of New Books, II (May/June 1974). Reprinted by permission.

"OLD BRUIN:" COMMODORE MATTHEW C. PERRY, 1794-1858. THE AMERICAN NAVAL OFFICER WHO HELPED FOUND LIBERIA, HUNTED PIRATES IN THE WEST INDIES, PRACTICED DIPLOMACY WITH THE SULTAN OF TURKEY AND THE KING OF THE TWO SICILIES; COMMANDED THE GULF SQUADRON IN THE MEXICAN WAR, PROMOTED THE STEAM NAVY AND THE SHELL GUN, AND CONDUCTED THE NAVAL EXPEDITION WHICH OPENED JAPAN. By Samuel Eliot Morison. (Boston: Atlantic-Little, Brown. 1967. Pp. xxii, 482. $12.50.)

This meticulous study of one of America's outstanding naval figures reveals an often slighted crucial segment of national development. Perry's career illustrates the role of the navy in protecting and promoting American interests abroad during the first half of the nineteenth century, and the comprehensive title enumerates the major accomplishments of this man whose fame has been overshadowed by the exploits of his older brother.

Setting the stage with a graphic portrayal of late eighteenth-century Rhode Island and the exciting life of busy Newport, the author sees Midshipman Perry entering the service at a time when "Madison shared Jefferson's irrational prejudice against the navy, as did the Western and Southern blocs which then controlled Congress." Unlike the dashing Oliver, Calbraith was "methodical, serious, conscientious, bent on becoming a good officer, getting on with his fellow reefers, winning the respect of the ratings and the esteem of his superiors." His service as a junior officer in the Atlantic during the War of 1812 was undistinguished, and the author shifts to the Battle of Lake Erie to defend Oliver's role against those who asserted that Elliot was the real hero. Following the war Calbraith served in the Mediterranean and then helped found Liberia by selecting a "healthy site" to promote a movement in which he had a deep interest. Subsequent duty in the Mediterranean provided an opportunity to gain diplomatic experience in dealing with the governments of Turkey and the Two Sicilies, in the latter case employing his squadron to make a "cumulative impression" which led to a treaty settling American claims and anticipated the method he was to follow in Japan. Digressing slightly, the author presents an account of the Somers mutiny and concurs with the decision to hang the three mutineers.

Perry's naval career reached its zenith during the Mexican War, first as vice-commodore and later as commander of naval forces in the Gulf of Mexico. A detailed account of blockade, amphibious, and river warfare provides the most recent scholarship on naval operations during the conflict and reveals exemplary interservice cooperation in establishing beachheads and furnishing support. But much of Perry's influence on the navy lay in his espousal of reforms that he vigorously promoted while at sea and during his intermittent tours ashore. He early embraced the introduction of steam propulsion; the author considers him the "father" of the steam navy. Shell guns, ironclads, and professional education were among other changes that he urged and partially succeeded in having adopted. But he opposed the abolition of flogging and doubted the effectiveness of what he called "moral suasion" to enforce discipline.

The expedition to Japan is treated fully. Perry's predecessor, Commodore Biddle, "was no diplomat," and his mistakes were heeded by his successor. By experience and temperament Perry was an ideal choice for the mission, although initially he resisted the assignment. When assured of the necessary authority and means for "securing a reasonable chance of success", the Commodore embarked on the task with his customary thoroughness and zeal. Perry's instructions, which he helped draft, granted him "large discretionary powers" and accorded him the rank of envoy extraordinary and minister plenipotentiary. The first visit to Japan was but a "preliminary demonstration," as the Commodore put it, intended to deliver a letter from the President to the Emperor, make known American demands, and allow the government time for reflection. Under no illusions regarding the magnitude and complexity of his task, Perry wrote that "a pursuance of the rules of ordinary diplomacy cannot have the least effect upon these sagacious and deceitful people." Returning with an augmented force, Perry's tactics were carefully designed to exploit the "forms" of Japanese intercourse. Being distantly formal, pompous or simple as seemed propitious, never obsequious, and ostentatiously displaying the military power at his disposal, Perry won major concessions from the Japanese government. Tense moments during the negotiations, when a break or even hostilities seemed likely, were forgotten when the Japanese Commissioners were entertained at a gala banquet livened by varieties of Western alcoholic beverages.

In his research for this work the author followed his customary method of visiting the scene of events, and material from Japanese and Mexican sources complements domestic primary documents and papers. The narrative is sprinkled with copious quotations from the writings of Perry and other contemporaries, and Morison's affection for the sea is obvious as he depicts life in the old navy in somewhat nostalgic prose. But the central figure emerges as the epitome of a breed of naval officer that regarded seamanship as merely a part of the job. Amateur scientist, educator, and accomplished diplomat, Perry came to view the Pacific as "America's sea of destiny" and exemplified the qualities necessary to make it so.

The American Historical Review, 73 (June 1968). Reprinted by permission. The paragraph on Japan was deleted in the published review to save space.

THE UNITED STATES NAVY IN THE PACIFIC, 1909-1922. By William Reynolds Braisted. Austin: The University of Texas Press, 1971. vii, 688 pp. Bibliography, Index. $15.00.

In this sequel to his earlier work, THE UNITED STATES NAVY IN THE PACIFIC, 1897-1909, Professor Braisted continues his study of naval policy and the use of this "first line of defense" as an instrument of American interests in the Far East. Bringing the story up through the Washington Conference on the Limitation of Armaments, 1921-1922, the book concludes on initial deliberations in the formulation of a "treaty navy."

The correlation of diplomatic and military policies so assiduously cultivated by Theodore Roosevelt was altered by his successor, whose "dollar diplomacy" in China helped push Russia and Japan together and brought an end to a rivalry that had contributed to American security in the western Pacific. The navy planners continued to envision as "most probable enemies" Germany in the Atlantic and Japan in the Pacific, and Taft's secretary of the navy, George von Lengerke Meyer, effected a reorganization of the department that weakened the bureau system and centralized control. A series of studies by the Naval War College in 1910-1911 revealed what the author considers "the basic problem that influenced American naval policy in the Pacific throughout the period of this study: the development of bases and other forms of support that would enable the United States to dispatch and maintain a fleet in the western Pacific sufficiently powerful to win naval dominance in those waters from Japan."(35) An initial overriding desire for a base in the Philippines was succeeded by enthusiasm for the development of Pearl Harbor, which the army and navy agreed was the key to control of the Pacific. The defense of Panama became a greater concern with completion of the canal scheduled for

1915, for "service men were nearly unanimous that the undefended canal would be a source of grave weakness rather than an element of strength."(43) Whether this new water route would permit the luxury of a one-ocean fleet that could move expeditiously from the Atlantic to the Pacific was an argument that rivaled the dispute over the most effective method of fighting Japan, whose ventures seemed likely to threaten American interests. An episode of American business penetration is revealed by a contract between China and the Bethlehem Steel Company that "committed the personnel and secrets of the United States Navy to the improvement of the Imperial Chinese Navy,"(77) with profit rather than strategic advantage as the motive. The shortcomings of American policy in China became apparent during the revolution, when efforts to pursue "concerted action" with other powers failed to prevent foreign exploitation of the strife-torn country.

During the Wilson administration the new secretary of the navy, Josephus Daniels, continued to exercise civilian control of the department, and he served as final arbiter of the perennial debates over the building program, war plans, and whether to divide the fleet. With the outbreak of war in 1914 the planners were faced with new considerations, for it appeared that the "international balances in the Pacific upon which the security of the United States had depended in large part" would be upset.(153) Thus the major impetus for the naval expansion program of 1916 came from apprehension over the consequences of the war in Europe, and "was primarily designed to prepare the nation for a later contest in which the United States might face a coalition attacking in both oceans."(201) Entry in the current struggle found the navy engaged in a war that "violated nearly all of the basic American naval assumptions."(289) But while adapting to the existing situation, the planners never lost sight of potential enemies, including Great Britain. Confrontation began at Paris in 1919 and reached its climax at Washington, when within the context of a settlement of Far Eastern questions the major naval powers established ratios of relative naval strength in capital ships and aircraft carriers. The treaties spawned by this conference provided the American authorities with a new set of assumptions, and debates resumed over war plans with inter-service and intra-service disagreements.

It is impossible to do justice to this comprehensive work in a short review. The list of topics covered alone would exhaust the word limitation, and the author has researched extensively in private and official papers, including Japanese sources, to provide the most authoritative account of the subject. British documents in the Public Record Office were not consulted, presumably becase the manuscript was completed before they were opened. Often quite detailed, this study places every event within the broad perspective of national strategy and the policies that the navy was expected to support and defend. This reader found little evidence of prejudice or bias, and although the author is not uncritical his treatment of the various controversies is remarkably even-handed.

Journal of Asian Studies, XXXI (November 1971). Reprinted by permission.

STEPHEN E. PELZ. Race to Pearl Harbor: The Failure of the Second London Naval Conference and the Onset of World War II. (Harvard Studies in American-East Asian Relations, 5.) Cambridge, Mass.: Harvard University Press. 1974. Pp. vii, 268. $17.50.

This book is essentially a study of naval rivalry between Japan, the United States, and Great Britain from the aftermath of the London Naval Conference of 1930 to the outbreak of war among the three nations. Japanese naval authorities were displeased with the established ratios and were successful in persuading the government to insist on more favorable terms at the parley scheduled for 1935. The United States was determined to maintain the existing equilibrium and reduce total tonnage, while Great Britain sought a compromise that would enable her to build more cruisers. The naval race reflected the international situation and the aspirations of the protagonists, with Japan bent on expanding her influence in the Pacific, the United States striving to maintain the status quo, and Great Britain faced with threats in Europe and the Far East. The second London Conference was followed by unbridled competition, with Great Britain financially unable to meet the Japanese challenge, to which the United States responded by a series of building programs.

So much for the familiar outline, but the author is not content with merely telling what happened and how, namely the intricate civil-military machinations in each nation and the labored negotiations between representatives. Carefully explained is the "why" of the naval limitation positions, most notably that of Japan, with details of strategy and the predominate role played by the navy in political and military policy. While the author's contention that the breakdown of disarmament led to subsequent developments and war may not be sustained (actually, he demonstrates that armaments were a symptom not a cause), his use of Japanese-language sources and British and American archival material provides new insights on the events that produced a world conflict.

American Historical Review, 80 (December 1975). Reprinted by permission.

BOOK REVIEWS

Bargaining for Supremacy: Anglo-American Naval Collaboration, 1937-1941. By James R. Leutze. (Chapel Hill: University of North Carolina Press, 1977. 328 pp. Appendix, notes, bibliography, and index. $17.95.)

The impetus for staff conversations between United States and British naval authorities, this study contends, was provided by President Franklin Roosevelt, who sought to gain British support for an embargo or quarantine in 1937 to halt Japanese aggression in the Far East. American and British naval units were to interdict Japanese trade routes, force a satisfactory termination of the Sino-Japanese conflict, and, presumably, ensure the preservation of the status quo in the Far East. Rebuffed by Prime Minister Neville Chamberlain, the President was not deterred from again taking the initiative as events in Europe seemed to reveal an accelerated and apparently coordinated effort by the Axis Powers to alter the existing territorial and political situation.

An initial reluctance of the British government to share naval secrets was overcome by the realization that America could be helpful in countering dangers to the Empire, although the discussions on technical and strategic matters proceeded slowly with a good deal of mutual suspicion. The correspondence between Roosevelt and Winston Churchill found the latter, on becoming prime minister, making frantic appeals for additional American support. Disagreements on strategy and theater priorities among the naval authorities of the two nations threatened military planning and efforts for contingency joint operations, while an exasperated Churchill exhorted his emissaries to avoid offending the hoped for ally. "The first thing is to get the United States into the war," he wrote the first sea lord. "We can then settle how to fight it afterwards" (p. 241). The detailed narrative concludes with the American-British-Canadian (ABC) conference in early 1941, which produced an agreement that conceded nearly all of the American demands and provided the basic strategy that was to prevail during the war. A brief epilogue covers meetings to December 1941.

The author's primary thesis is that during the course of these extended discussions the United States became the "superior" partner, succeeded in having its views adopted, and consciously strove to extend strategic planning control to wartime and even postwar naval dominance. Roosevelt's caution, ambivalence, and deception are described as he sought to avoid public or congressional reactions against his interventionist policies.

This study uses manuscript collections in the United States and England, both private papers and official documents, as well as printed primary and secondary sources.

The conversations are set within the context of developments on the international scene, although diplomatic negotiations between the democracies and the dictatorships are ignored, as is the tortuous course of United States-Japanese relations. Essentially, the author concentrates on his subject matter and provides an objective albeit not uncritical account of the steps by which Anglo-American naval collaboration was achieved.

Journal of American History, LXV (September 1978). Reprinted by permission.

The Navy League of the United States. By Armin Rappaport. (Detroit, Wayne State University Press, 1962. xi + 282 pp. $7.50)

During the 1920's and 1930's the Navy League was a favorite target of pacifist, isolationist, and disarmament groups. Accused of insidious lobbying activity designed to promote the interests of armaments manufacturers by creating a larger navy, the League found few vocal defenders outside its own ranks. Rappaport, provoked by the numerous but brief references to the organization by historians and other writers, embarked on this study in an effort to determine the extent and nature of the influence of the League on American naval policy.

This work traces the first fifty years of the League's history, from its founding in 1902 under the impetus of the nation's new role in world affairs to its position in the nuclear age of 1952. While considerable attention is devoted to the internal administrative problems of the organization, the author places his narrative in the context of America's naval and foreign policies. Thus the close correlation between League activities, the composition of the fleet, and national responsibilities is made clear at all times.

The Navy League, it appears, was formed by a group of dedicated citizens who were motivated solely by the desire to insure that the "first line of defense" would be adequate to meet the nation's needs. The task envisioned was that of providing information to popularize the navy and to persuade the public and its representatives that a larger fleet was necessary. News releases, a monthly publication, speeches, and personal contacts were the means employed to exert influence. On only two occasions, when the United States became involved in World Wars I and II, was the League satisfied with the naval program. Perhaps the most frustrating period in the League's history was the Republican era of 1921-1933, when public apathy, limitation of armaments and depression combined to reduce the navy far below its postwar opulence. Herbert Hoover proved to be the

League's most formidable antagonist, and Rappaport's account of the conflict is illuminating and objective.

The reader who expects sensational disclosures will be disappointed, for the author finds no evidence that the Navy League was a tool of industrialists. In fact, a deliberate effort was made to insure that the organization would not be controlled by any such vested interests. Furthermore, it was often difficult if not impossible to discover any clear connection between League activities and changes in the naval program. Success or failure usually coincided with the pressure of events over which the League had no control. Supplementation rather than implementation of new policies was generally the role played by the League, and it seldom strayed beyond the realm of seapower into the tempting areas of foreign and domestic policy.

Rappaport was granted unrestricted access to the League files, and they provide most of the material for this work. But he has also utilized government sources, private papers, contemporary writings and historical studies. Though displaying a general sympathy with his subject, the author's bias is reflected only in his obvious belief that a powerful fleet was necessity.

Pacific Historical Review, XXXII (February 1963). Reprinted by permission.

Strategy and Command: The First Two Years. By Louis Morton. United States Army in World War II, History of the War in the Pacific, Vol. X. (Washington, D.C., Office of the Chief of Military History, Department of the Army, 1962. xxii + 761 pp. $10.25)

World War II was not only the largest conflict in history but it was undoubtedly the best recorded. In the United States the respective services established historical divisions and arranged for professional historians, not military men, to present the story. The most ambitious project was established by the army, and the present volume is another in the series that will eventually run to approximately one hundred volumes. This book, however, can scarcely be classified as "army history." The naval dimensions of the war in the Pacific were in many respects more important than the land and air activities, and admirals and sea power occupy a considerable portion of the narrative.

The current volume begins with a brief but perceptive account of the geographical setting, the diplomatic background, and the development of military planning in the United States and Japan. The author then traces the steps which finally led the Japanese to choose war with the United States rather than accept what they thought would be an ignominious surrender. Though Morton believes that Japan would have been wiser to attack only British and Dutch territory, "the Japanese plan was not altogether as unrealistic as it has appeared to many" (p. 127).

The evolution of strategy for waging the war in the Pacific is the main theme of this book, and both allied and Japanese planning are included. Early agreement was reached between the British and American authorities on a "cardinal principle" of strategy, namely, "that only the minimum of force necessary for the safeguarding of vital interests in other theaters should be diverted from operations against Germany" (pp. 158-159). But this principle was interpreted differently by the British who insisted on an early defeat of Germany and the American authorities led by Admiral Ernest J. King who urged more attention to the Pacific. This dispute over the allocation of effort and resources is carefully described by the author. Moreover, this was a war of unified command and unified activity where only the proper coordination of land, sea, and air forces could defeat the enemy. Interservice rivalry added to the problems of coalition warfare, and "In the South Pacific the most serious disagreements between the Army and Navy commanders arose from differing views on the role of the air arm and the proper utilization of Army aircraft" (p. 352). Yet there were plenty of other areas of friction over the employment of forces and various jurisdictional matters, some due to Washington's failure to distinguish carefully between command authority.

The allied effort moved from defensive to defensive/offensive to offensive as the Japanese advance was halted and more resources became available. Planning was in a constant process of revision, and Morton weaves a fascinating tale as he presents the various plans, the arguments of their protagonists, and the factors which led to the final adoption of a plan or a compromise. The relationship between General Marshall and Admiral King is thoughtfully analyzed. Each of these men had strong convictions on certain issues, yet there was enough respect and possibly, affection, to avoid a break. Each seemed to sense the limit beyond which he could not go, either in making demands or resisting the demands of the other. Under their capable leadership, the war in the Pacific progressed to the point where, by the end of 1943, "There was no doubt about Japan's defeat--only when, how, and under whose command" (p. 605).

In addition to the text, which is thoroughly documented, the volume contains an Appendix in which are printed the texts of the more important directives and operational plans, both allied and Japanese. A superb bibliographical essay leads the reader through the intricacies of the organization and storage of official documents and records. Maps throughout the text are supplemented by others folded inside the back cover. This volume is a significant contribution to an understanding of the way in which war is waged at the highest military levels. The administration of combat forces reached its zenith in World War II, and for many its story is more exciting and rewarding than the conventional battle histories.

Pacific Historical Review, XXXIII (May 1964). Reprinted by permission.

D-Day: The Normandy Invasion in Retrospect. With a foreword by OMAR N. BRADLEY. (Eisenhower Foundation.) Lawrence: University Press of Kansas. 1971. Pp. xiii, 254. Cloth $7.50, paper $2.95.

This volume, with one exception, consists of papers read at the Eisenhower Library on the twenty-fifth anniversary of the Allied landing on the coast of France in June 1944. Several of the papers are followed by a commentary and all but one are accompanied by footnotes. Each of the authors was chosen for his expertise in the phase of the operation that he presented, and the appended bibliographies reflect their previous writings.

The stage is set by Forrest C. Pogue in "D-Day--1944," who places the event in the perspective of a combat historian-participant and then in the context of the world conflict and the politics of planning and executing the invasion. Don Whitehead provides "A Correspondent's View of D-Day," a highly personalized account of the landing at Omaha Beach with emphasis on the human element in the elaborate preparations and the chaos that prevailed during the assault. Bombing and strafing preliminaries and the controversy over targets and command are described in "Air Campaign Overlord: To D-Day," by Alfred Goldberg, who points out that the Allied air forces had performed their task so well that for them "D-Day was anticlimax." In a commentary Alfred Hurley faults Goldberg for exaggerating the role of air power and for not giving sufficient attention to the "turbulent milieu behind" the air effort. The limiting and often controlling factor of supply is stressed by Roland G. Ruppenthal in "Logistic Planning for Overlord in Retrospect," who finds tactics and even strategy determined by the imperatives of transportation and material, although in a commentary James A. Huston contends that logistic planners should anticipate the requirements of battlefield commanders and be prepared to satisfy their demands. The great debate over Allied military-political strategy in Europe is examined by Maurice Matloff in "Wilmot Revisited: Myth and Reality in Anglo-American Strategy for the Second Front," which concludes that "the final product was an amalgam of British caution and of American directness and perseverance." Shortcomings of the enemy defense are analyzed by

Friedrich Ruge in "German Naval Operations on D-Day," and George M. Elsey finds much to criticize on both sides in "Naval Aspects of Normandy in Retrospect," with gunfire support being overrated and ancillary vessels not given the credit they deserve. General Bernard L. Montgomery's recollections are questioned and his reputation is further tarnished by Martin Blumenson in "Some Reflections on the Immediate Post-Assault Strategy," with a display of historical investigation into meaning and substance. The final essay by Robin Higham deals with "Technology and D-Day," with an account of the development and utilization of many devices that contributed to the success of the Allied landing.

In many respects this volume represents a summary of the major studies that have appeared on this most ambitious amphibious operation in the annals of war. No single factor was responsible for victory but there were many without which the venture would have been doomed to failure. Most of the elements of human achievement or the lack thereof are depicted in these perceptive and authoritative papers.

American Historical Review, 79 (June 1974). Reprinted by permission.

Blair, Clay, Jr.
Silent Victory: The U.S. Submarine War Against Japan
New York: J. B. Lippincott Co.
1072 pp., $24.95, LC 74-2005
Publication Date: April 21, 1975

The title of this book conveys a double meaning: First, as a play on the customary designation of submarines and submariners as constituting the "silent service"; second, to signify that the contributions made by the undersea warriors to the defeat of Japan have never been adequately recognized by the public or other branches of the armed forces. The author, who has written about submarines in novels and nonfiction, has undertaken to correct the record in this massive, detailed study of submarine operations in the Pacific as they affected the course of the war against the Japanese Empire.

Beginning with a brief account of the development of these undersea vessels, Blair describes the design and building of prewar ships with scathing criticism of inefficient engines and defective torpedoes. When war came there was no established strategy, tactics were inadequate, many boats were not equipped for the task assigned, command relationships were strained, and in the early stages of the war submarines were as ineffectual as surface vessels in attempting to halt the Japanese advance. Commanding officers, trained in the peacetime lethargy, were often relieved for lack of aggressiveness, and coordination of effort was absent in the general confusion of trying to cope with the enemy and devise a policy. Gradually, experience, profiting by mistakes, and acquiring larger more modern boats combined with information furnished by the code breakers to enable the submarine force, Pacific, to emerge as a decisive factor in the eventual surrender of Japan.

As the author proceeds through the war year by year he places the operations of the submarines within the context of the major strategic and tactical campaigns in the Pacific. When the Americans moved from a defensive to an offensive strategy, the submarines became more integrated into overall operations. Throughout the conflict their primary function was to sink enemy naval and merchant vessels, although priorities varied according to the situation and the dictates of theater commanders. Often given assignments considered peripheral, such as transporting supplies and raiding groups or watching for downed aviators, the submarines served in many capacities to support the total effort. Essentially the submarine war against Japan, like the bombing of the Japanese homeland, was a war of attrition that complemented the more direct thrusts of the fast carrier task forces and the amphibious assaults on the Japanese-held islands that constituted the enemy's defense perimeter. The combined strategy destroyed Japan's capacity and will to resist.

This book covers the administrative, strategic, tactical, operational, and technological dimensions of the submarine war. Furthermore, it incorporates the human element and the drama, excitement, and horrors of combat. Unsparing in his criticism of every element of submarine activity, the author is also unsparing in his admiration and respect for those heroes of the deep. Although there are no footnote citations, an impressive annotated bibliography reveals that the author has consulted practically every available source, including patrol reports, official and unofficial correspondence, and interviews with numerous submariners. Only access to some of the code breaking material was denied. Maps of operational areas, photographs, and appendices containing statistics and lists of leading participants supplement the text.

This book will be of interest to former and current naval persons, military historians, and buffs, all of whom may read it for both pleasure and profit. It is unlikely that a better written, more comprehensive, and more authoritative book on the subject will ever appear.

<u>History: Reviews of New Books</u>, III (July 1975). Reprinted by permission.

THE QUIET WARRIOR: A BIOGRAPHY OF ADMIRAL RAYMOND A. SPRUANCE, by Thomas B. Buell (Boston, Little, Brown and Company, 1974). 486 pp., $15.00. Publication Date: July 30, 1974.

The aura surrounding military leaders often consists of a mixture of myth and fact. The elements of leadership and effectiveness in command are seldom capable of enumeration, less so of definition, and never subject to quantification. The contrasts in personality and demeanor between the top tactical naval commanders in the Pacific during World War II, Fleet Admiral William F. "Bull" Halsey and Admiral Spruance, were marked, yet their attributes were complementary rather than competitive, and each was effective in leading forces that brought destruction to the Imperial Japanese power. Admiral Spruance, the subject of this full length biography, apparently lacked many of the stereotypical characteristics deemed essential for successful leadership in war. Labeling the subject a quiet warrior conveys the impression that Spruance was unique within the framework of his contemporaries, and suggests that he possessed qualities uncommon in the military hierarchy. The author, a Naval Academy graduate and career officer, tries to portray the "whole man" within the context of an institution dedicated to the support of American policies during a half century of technological and strategic transition that culminated in the massive complexities of the second world war.

Spruance, the product of a midwestern upper middle class background, attended the Naval Academy because of financial necessity, and he "hated every minute" of the regimentation and the anti-intellectual curriculum that was designed to "condition" the midshipman to fit the mold. Plagued with seasickness throughout his career, Spruance had the usual duty assignments aboard various craft as he rose in rank and gained the training and experience to prepare those who survived the selection process for command at sea. The author recreates the atmosphere of the "old" and "transitional" Navy from the cruise of the Great White Fleet around the world in 1907-1909, through World War I, the disarmament negotiations and retrenchment of the 1920's and 1930's, and the controversies between those addicted to the combat efficiency of battleships, submarines, or aircraft carriers. Spruance's prewar assignments at the Naval War College--as a student and as a member of the staff--were significant in contributing to his understanding of international relations, his awareness of the multiple factors involved in modern warfare, and his perceptions of the reasoning process for solving tactical and strategic problems. The debate over whether decisions should be based on the enemy's intentions or his capability was lively, and with Japan designated as the most probably antagonist this experience at the Navy's institution of higher learning proved invaluable. As Admiral Spruance once remarked to this reviewer standing in the Mahan Library at the Naval War College, "This is where I got my education."

Spruance first visited Japan in 1908 on the Great White Fleet cruise, and while on duty in Washington he became acquainted with the Japanese naval attaches. When the war which he had foreseen finally came at Pearl Harbor, Spruance was appalled by the destruction and death but he never became vindictive toward the enemy, whom he respected as a foe, and he retained an affection for the Japanese people. Replacing the hospitalized Halsey in the fleet disposition for the defense of Midway Island, Spruance, although technically under the tactical command of Admiral Frank Jack Fletcher, was able to act independently and he was successful in thwarting the attempted invasion. The author defends Spruance's decision to refrain from pursuing the Japanese fleet, although he is critical of Spruance's action in this same regard at the Battle of the Philippine Sea. Subsequent Spruance-led invasions, including the final Okinawa operation, are described, and the interservice and intraservice squabbles over personalities and tactics are analyzed and judged. The Admiral's later career, including his presidency of the Naval War College and his ambassadorship to the Philippines, is presented in some detail.

For sources the author relies primarily on official published and unpublished materials, comtemporary and "after the fact" letters of Spruance and his colleagues, and interviews with former associates. Spruance emerges as a person dedicated to his profession, a moderately conscientious family man, and a cool, deliberate, essentially rational human being who went about his job in an efficient and unobtrusive manner. In a war that at the higher levels was administered rather than fought, whatever charisma he happened to possess was due to the impression he gave of being entirely in control of the situation, with no displays of temperament or emotion, and to his exuding that obscure quality "character." As a "black shoe" battleship officer he adapted to the carrier task force and amphibious strategies of the Pacific, and as a commander he selected the staff and delegated the authority necessary to organize and implement the operations required by a new kind of war. This sympathetic but not uncritical study will add considerably to an understanding of the man and the events in which he participated with such distinction, and undoubtedly will revive many altercations over the questions that plague the aftermath of battle.

This review was commissioned by the Washington Post Book World but was not published because of space limitations.

EDWIN BICKFORD HOOPER. Mobility, Support, Endurance: A Story of Naval Operational Logistics in the Vietnam War,

1967-1968. Washington: Naval History Division, Department of the Navy. 1972. Pp. xviii, 278. $4.25.

RICHARD G. HEWLETT and FRANCIS DUNCAN. Nuclear Navy, 1946-1962. Chicago: University of Chicago Press. 1974. Pp. xv, 477. $12.50.

The end of World War II found the United States Navy, which had established control of the seas to an extent never before approximated, faced with the task of defining its role as an instrument of national policy. It was a crucial time when the nation was assuming broader world-wide responsibilities, and advances in technology promised to render obsolescent the weapons that had produced victory. These books reveal two ways the navy responded to the challenge and the demands made on the service. Both are written by members of the government who had access to materials that will long be denied other historians.

Admiral Hooper presents a first-person narrative derived from his experience as commander of the Service Force of the U.S. Pacific Fleet, which furnished the supplies that made it possible to sustain military operations in Vietnam. Providing logistical support for the waging of limited war in distant parts of the world was a role few in the navy had visualized, but for which many were prepared by having mastered the enormous supply problems in the Pacific during the Second World War and the Korean War. This account of a less-publicized but no less vital dimension of the Vietnam involvement possesses the advantages and shortcomings of an eyewitness account by one who views the events with a detached perspective often lacking in autobiography.

The authors of Nuclear Navy, 1946-1962, both historians with the Atomic Energy Commission, have produced a detailed, heavily documented study of what amounted to one man's prevailing against the system. Although there had been an awareness at the top of the navy hierarchy of the implications of nuclear propulsion for warships, there was little awareness of how this should be accomplished. The selection of Hyman Rickover and the ways in which he overcame seemingly insuperable obstacles at virtually every stage constitute most of the story. Battling the navy, civilian firms, the Atomic Energy Commission, Congress, and almost everyone else involved, Rickover managed to supervise the development of practicable nuclear-propulsion systems, influence ship design, control the selection and training of crews, and intrude into command operations. Neither details nor personalities are lacking, with Rickover's single-minded dedication as a constant in the effort that saw thirty reactor-powered vessels at sea in 1962. The emphasis throughout is on technology, bureaucracy, and administration rather than on the strategic and tactical implications of nuclear-propelled warships.

BOOK REVIEWS

American Historical Review, LXXXI (June 1976). Reprinted by permission.

WEGENER, EDWARD. *The Soviet Naval Offensive: An Examination of the Strategic Role of Soviet Naval Forces in the East-West Conflict*. Translated by Henning Wegener. Annapolis: Naval Institute Press, 1975. vii, 135 pp.

This slim but substantive volume is a revision of a book published in Germany. Written by Rear Admiral Wegener, a retired officer of the Federal German Navy, it combines a virtual summary of the extensive writings on the Soviet Navy with an analysis of strategic and tactical implications for current and future international relationships.

The author begins with an exposition of the fundamentals of naval and maritime strategy, which he finds disparate but interrelated. Admittedly endorsing the sea power thesis of Alfred Thayer Mahan, he reduces the elements to three: "fleet, position, and sea-oriented mentality." Russian naval strategy, he believes, has evolved in the post-Stalin era from a defensive to an offensive role. While Russia's geographical position has imposed limitations on its ability to extend its radius of influence or control, militarily vast strides have been made in implementing the Soviet objective of world revolution and world dominance.

The first mission, Wegener contends, was to provide for territorial defense; next to establish potential or actual control of peripheral seas; currently the Soviets are striving to project their power onto the oceans or high seas. Essentially, it is a contest between the American and Russian navies, with the latter challenging the former's domination. The West, as exemplified by the United States and NATO, is finding itself in an increasingly deteriorating position. Technologically, or qualitatively, the Soviets have made impressive advances, and quantitatively they are outproducing the West. At present the decisive factor in control of the sea lies in the predominance of American aircraft carriers, although the author warns of a change in the situation due to Soviet construction of similar vessels.

Wegener presents scenarios of war from conventional through nuclear, limited and general, tactical and strategic, incorporating the Soviet "three wave" doctrine of successive stages of attack. Further, he expounds on the peacetime uses of naval force. The mere presence of warships has a psychological impact on nations, but in the final analysis the impression depends on the credibility of the war-making potential of the forces. In this respect the Soviets suffer from being incapable of supporting limited conflicts in many areas or waging a successful war in the Atlantic and the Pacific, although under certain conditions they could dominate much of the Indian Ocean. Wegener concludes that while the situation is precarious and actually dangerous, the outcome will depend on the will and determination of the West, primarily the United States, to meet the confrontation.

This study is an excellent introduction to the sea power competition that has reached dramatic proportions in recent years. It is well organized, simply and clearly written, and makes intelligible to the lay person and expert alike the basic factors involved in this dimension of the East-West struggle.

The Russian Review, XXXVI (January 1977). Reprinted by permission.

JAMES CABLE. Gunboat Diplomacy: Political Applications of Limited Naval Force. Pp. 251. New York: Praeger, 1971. $11.00.

The subtitle of this book is more descriptive than the title, a term that characterized what some have designated an age of imperialism, when the western powers imposed their will on weaker nations by sending a warship to intimidate a recalcitrant government or bombard a resistant people. Written while the author was on leave from the British Diplomatic Service as a research associate at the Institute for Strategic Studies, this work is an attempt "to assess the effectiveness of limited naval force in terms of its ability to achieve the results originally intended by the initiating government" (p. 13). In striving for a more precise definition and limited subject, the author produces the following: "Gunboat diplomacy is the use or threat of limited naval force, otherwise than as an act of war, in order to secure advantage, or to avert loss, either in the furtherance of an international dispute or else against foreign nationals within the territory or the jurisdiction of their own state" (p. 21). While cumbersome and conceivably less exact than the declared purpose, this elaboration is carefully explained and the reader is prepared for a further explication within the guidelines prescribed.

The author then plunges into an investigation of selected examples within the past fifty years to illustrate his categorization of the way limited naval force has been and can be applied to achieve certain objectives. Definitive force is exemplified by the Altmark and Pueblo incidents, although the former is "a classic case of gunboat diplomacy rather than an entirely typical one" (p. 31). The latter is a reversal of the axiomatic application of gunboat diplomacy, for the weaker nation prevailed. Corfu (1923) and Kuwait (1963) illustrate purposeful force and provide evidence for a quoted point, namely, "a resort to force is more likely to meet with acquiescence if it is immediate in its application, instantaneous in its effect and appropriate in its nature" (p. 48). Catalytic force is protrayed by the British involvement in the Baltic after World War I and the American intervention in Lebanon in 1958, while expressive force is symbolized by the Deutschland's appearance at Ceuta in 1936 and a few more recent instances.

But circumstances alter cases in gunboat diplomacy as in law, so the author assesses the impact of technological change, regional and international organizations, and superpower rivalry. Yet, "the sea still offers a neutral place d'armes open to all, where forces may be assembled, ready for intervention, but not yet committed" (p. 91). In the future, "the political applications of limited naval force will be less simple, less straightforward, probably less romantic than hitherto, but they may be even more effective" (p. 95). Naval capacities and doctrines are analyzed with the conclusion that "international capacity for the exercise of limited naval force thus resembles a pyramid, the number of potential assailants dwindling as we rise from one category to another, until the United States are left in solitary occupation of the summit" (p. 127). In this context the Soviet navy is given a chapter of its own, where the author visualizes its role being less aggressive than perceived by many authorities and offering a possible alternative to what could be more volatile confrontations. "Limited war, let alone limited force, finds no place in Soviet political or military doctrine" (p. 148).

In a final chapter entitled "Applications," the author postulates several possible situations, reiterates the impossibility of reducing the subject to simple generalizations, and concludes with a "more restricted thesis: the continuing utility of limited naval force" (p. 172). In some respects more philosophical and speculative than descriptive, this work at times confuses more than it illuminates, but it states the case and raises questions about many of the assumptions shared by decision-makers and strategists. Those searching for a new theory of sea power may well find the seeds in this juxtaposition of evidence and ideas. An appendix provides a chronology, and footnotes and a selective bibliography offer suggestions for further reading.

The Annals of the American Academy of Political and Social Science, 403 (September 1972). Reprinted by permission.

THE QUESTION OF NATIONAL DEFENSE: A CRITIQUE OF OUR MILITARY PREPARATIONS AND POLICIES, by Oskar Morgenstern. Vintage, (1961) $1.25.

WAR, DIPLOMACY, AND HISTORY

Of all the problems confronting man at the present time, the threat of war and thermonuclear annihilation is generally accepted as the most critical. Professor Morgenstern, an expert in "game theory" at the Massachusetts Institute of Technology, has written one of the most comprehensive and thought-provoking of a deluge of publications devoted to America's defense strategy and the way in which all-out war may be avoided.

THE STRUGGLE BETWEEN the Western World and the Communist bloc, coupled with the astounding technological advances in weapons systems, has created a situation in which "the problems raised are harder than the most difficult ever solved in science." A major obstacle to the solution of these problems, as Morgenstern sees it, is the complacency of the American people. Almost angrily, he decries the apathy that prevails in the face of the terrifying existent threat, not only to our institutions but to human life itself. Then, clearly and dispassionately, Morgenstern presents the alternatives and provides a blueprint for peace.

In short, the people must be made aware of the nature of the crisis and the sacrifices necessary to maintain the Western position, while at the same time efforts must be made to minimize the risk of war. Militarily, this involves the establishment of "invulnerable retaliatory forces" by both camps, so that each side is secure in the knowledge that a surprise attack will not be decisive. An essential element in creating this security is the immediate implementation of a vast and necessarily expensive civil defense program to insure that the population will survive a thermonuclear attack. Russia, the author shows, is far ahead of the United States in this respect, and her defense position is thereby strengthened. The retaliatory forces themselves will consist primarily of guided missiles, against which no defense exists, and the least vulnerable of launching platforms is the nuclear powered submarine. When each side possesses an adequate number of these vessels neither will be likely to risk an attack, knowing that sure, instant, and devastating retaliation would follow.

WITH THE CREATION of a thermonuclear stalemate, the prospect of "limited" war emerges. Here the nature and extent of the conflict must be determined by the aims or objectives, which must be defined and declared at the outset. In this way the chances of hostilities expanding will be minimized. Morgenstern cautions that "mathematical rigor in these areas is not to be expected," but the past furnishes examples where armed conflict has been confined to the achievement of limited ends and the high stakes provide an added inducement for success in the future.

In pungent, provocative chapters the author surveys the other facets of world competition and the steps which might reduce tensions. The nature of the challenge is exposed and proposed approaches are outlined on the role of research in strategy; economic rivalry; intelligence and secrecy; diplomacy amidst technological change; and the dilemma of arms controls. No review could do justice to the wealth of information and ideas presented in this impressive effort to help men control the forces they have unleashed, forces which the author fears may destroy the creator.

TOO OFTEN ONE HEARS that war now is so horrible that it is "unthinkable." Morgenstern believes, as do other writers such as Herman Kahn in his recent On Thermonuclear War, that unless men do think about it to the point of taking corrective steps, it will be too late. The eminent British scientist, civil servant, and novelist C. P. Snow has recently reminded us that "one of the overwhelming facts of our time is that the cardinal choices which lie before nations must be made by a handful of men acting in secret." By cardinal choices he means "those which determine in the crudest sense whether we live or die--as nations and individuals." Perhaps war has now become too serious a matter to be left to the generals or the politicians. When the experts predict casualties in terms of "mega-deaths," i.e., millions of dead, it is time to reappraise the social usefulness of this extreme form of human competition.

The University Daily Kansan, April 21, 1961. Reprinted by permission.

II. Diplomatic

PROLOGUE TO WAR: England and the United States, 1805-1812. By Bradford Perkins. Berkeley: University of California Press. 1961. $7.95.

In this volume Professor Perkins continues the work begun in his The First Rapprochement: England and the United States, 1795-1805. The current study has as its theme "the American search for national respectability and true independence from Europe, independence far transcending the recognition of an American state in 1783." Guiding the reader through the tortuous complexities of domestic and foreign affairs in both nations, the author presents his explanation of the events which led two reluctant nations into war.

In brief, Perkins concludes that the Republicans "took the nation into the War of 1812 as a consequence of specific

British actions, policies that threatened American interests and above all challenged the self-respect of the young nation." The British government underestimated the pride and determination of the Americans, and failed to understand the role of the irrational in human affairs. It also believed that Madison would behave as Jefferson had, and erred in allowing the past to determine its action.

England, engaged in a struggle for survival against the ruthless domination of Napoleon, was determined to take whatever steps were necessary to prevail. Her statesmen could not understand why the United States failed to accept the situation and accede to the British demands. Concessions on both sides were usually inadequate or ill-timed, either in light of partisan politics, public opinion, or military necessity. Leadership was inadequate when it might have proved decisive, and the nation drifted into war with a sigh of relief rather than a shout of exaltation.

The Orders in Council and impressment were the issues, both as they affected economic interests and national honor. Land hunger, Indian warfare, and other motives were, in Perkins' opinion, only peripheral. Impressively researched and carefully documented, this study provides stimulating insights into the diplomacy of the period.

<u>American Studies</u>, Volume III (Fall 1962). Reprinted by permission.

Grieb, Kenneth J. <u>The United States and Huerta</u>. Lincoln: The University of Nebraska Press, 1969. List of abbreviations, introduction, acknowledgments, note on the sources, index, maps and illustrations, xiv, 233 pp. $7.95.

Woodrow Wilson's policy toward the government of Victoriano Huerta in Mexico has been the subject of much criticism by historians. This book does not contest the conventional treatment of Wilson's first major effort at missionary diplomacy, but it does explore the episode in considerable detail and provides additional evidence for an excoriation of the president's behavior.

Beginning with an account of the circumstances under which Huerta came to power, the author reveals the involvement of U.S. Ambassador Henry Lane Wilson and the favorable reaction in Washington to the new government. The promise of stability appeared to determine the American attitude, although this stability was threatened by the prospect of a pro-Madero uprising and the uncertain position of Venustiano Carranza, governor of Coahuila. Ambassador Wilson recommended recognition of the new administration and Secretary of state Philander Knox indicated it would be extended provided outstanding issues between the two countries could be settled by formal agreement. Such was the situation when a new chief executive took office in Washington.

The president first applied pressure on the new government by denying recognition, and the author carefully recounts the steps by which Wilson escalated his coercive methods in an effort to remove Huerta. Detailed accounts of the Lind mission, the domestic upheaval in Mexico, the role of other nations, military incursions, and the Niagara Falls Conference reveal the complex maneuvers that contributed to Huerta's expulsion.

The author assesses Wilson as "an ardent moralist" who rejected compromise and was intolerant of opposition. Motivated by abstract ideas rather than the national interest, Wilson was inclined to impose his own beliefs on others, often to the detriment of the United States and the nations with which he was dealing. This reviewer does take exception to the seemingly over-simplistic view of Wilson's motives (which were multiple, as the author indicates in portions of the narrative) and his inflexibility, although the author mentions that the president in his subsequent diplomacy may have profited from this unpleasant involvement in Mexican affairs. In regard to nonrecognition, the author states: "By adopting this stance, Wilson reversed traditional American policy. Historically, the United States had always recognized de facto regimes, and such statesmen as John Quincy Adams and James Buchanan had affirmed this doctrine." Actually, Adams added a new criterion to American recognition policy, namely, that a government must observe accepted standards of international behavior. Recognition was denied the government of Buenos Aires until it cancelled letters of marque issued to privateers, and numerous other pre-Wilsonian examples exist. The "constitutional legitimacy" principle emerged when the Southern states seceded, and it was applied to the Maximilian regime when the United States continued to recognize the government of Benito Juarez.

But essentially this work is a well-balanced, generally objective explanation of this long and painful episode. The major figures, sharply drawn, emerge in full dimension as their characteristics and personalities are related to their actions under the circumstances. The author has utilized archival resources and personal papers in Mexico, Great Britain, and the United States to provide a valuable contribution to an understanding of these events.

Journal of Inter-American Studies and World Affairs, XIII (January 1971). Reprinted by permission.

Healy, David
Gunboat Diplomacy in the Wilson Era:
The U.S. Navy in Haiti, 1915-1916
Madison: The University of Wisconsin Press
268 pp., $15.00, LC 75-32074
Publication Date: May 14, 1976

As the subtitle indicates, this book deals with one example of President Wilson's missionary diplomacy in the Caribbean. The author, Professor of History at the University of Wisconsin-Milwaukee, established himself as a scholar of American ventures abroad by his previous U.S. Expansionism: The Imperialist Urge in the 1890s (1970); and The United States in Cuba, 1898-1902: Generals, Politicians, and the Search for Policy (1963). The current work continues the exploration of the correlation between diplomatic objectives and military means.

American interest in the fate of the impoverished black nation of Haiti increased in the early years of the 20th century as its strategic significance in relation to the Panama Canal and the threat of European imperialism became more apparent. Financial penetration by France and Germany was countered by American joint ownership in the National Bank of Haiti. But the monotonous regularity with which revolutionary movements overthrew the government provoked a feeling in Washington that the United States would have to take steps to prevent conditions that would invite European intervention. The outbreak of the first world war in August 1914 further alarmed Wilson and his advisors, and its adverse effects on Haitian trade aggravated the deteriorating Haitian economy.

In January 1915, when Rear Admiral William B. Caperton, commander of the Atlantic Fleet's Cruiser Squadron, arrived on the scene, a revolutionary army had established itself in part of the country. Initially striving to limit hostilities, Admiral Caperton was drawn into an escalation of involvement by successively landing forces to protect foreign lives and property, waging war and occupying territory to pacify the country, taking over customs and disbursing receipts, supervising the election of a new president, and negotiating and implementing a treaty with the United States that amounted to a virtual ultimatum and permitted American control of Haiti. Ably supported by his French speaking chief of staff, Captain Edward L. Beach, who handled much of the negotiation with the Haitian leaders, Admiral Caperton made numerous on-the-spot decisions, for he received little guidance from his superiors. Wilson was torn by diverse motivations and his concern over the constitutional power to intervene; his two secretaries of state were uninformed about conditions in Haiti and shared with the president an increasing concern with Europe; and Secretary of the Navy Josephus Daniels was indecisive. Finally, jurisdiction was turned over to the Marines, who, in the author's opinion, conducted affairs so abominably that the precarious structure established by the Navy commander soon collapsed.

The narrative carefully portrays the major protagonists--the Haitians, the Navy, and the Washington authorities. Further, the author has skillfully woven together the complex negotiations and the issues of security, economics, public opinion, domestic factors, and aspects of racism. The naval officers as diplomats, in the persons of Admiral Caperton and Captain Beach, emerge as the heroes of this incident, for they employed tact, persuasion, manipulation, intimidation, force, and perhaps bribes, to achieve a settlement satisfactory to most parties. Relying largely on materials in the Navy and State Department files, Haitian sources, newspapers, and periodicals, the author has produced a well-written scholarly multidimentional account that adds significantly to an understanding of this episode in gunboat diplomacy that will appeal to the historian, the diplomat, the military buff, and the general reader.

History: Reviews of New Books, IV (August 1976). Reprinted by permission.

THE UNITED STATES AND THE FAR EASTERN CRISIS OF 1933-1938: From the Manchurian Incident Through the Initial Stage of the Undeclared Sino-Japanese War. By Dorothy Borg. Cambridge, Massachusetts: Harvard University Press. 1964. $10.00

The extent to which the administration of Franklin Roosevelt was "isolationist" or "internationalist" prior to the war in Europe has been the subject of much controversy but disappointingly little scholarly research. In this substantial volume Miss Borg painstakingly reveals the policy followed by the United States toward the continuing Sino-Japanese struggle and offers answers to many questions.

Beginning with a brief account of the origins of the Hoover-Stimson nonrecognition doctrine and its acceptance by Roosevelt, Miss Borg leads the reader through the intricacies of Sino-Japanese relations, Britain's unsuccessful attempts to secure American cooperation in restraining Japan, and the vagaries of New Deal diplomacy. The complexities of internal affairs in China and the fluctuations of Japanese foreign policy are related in some detail with a commendable lack of bias. But the course followed by the United States, according to Miss Borg, was consistent if puzzling to many contemporaries. Both the President and Secretary of State Cordell Hull were determined to follow a neutral course for a variety of reasons. Until the resumption of the Sino-Japanese conflict in 1937 it was believed that a policy of conciliation toward Japan would lead to an amicable solution of her difficulties with China. Any attempts to apply concerted pressure would strengthen the position of the extremists and might escalate into war. Moreover, isolationist sentiment, representing a small but extremely vocal group, intimidated the administration out of all proportion to its real strength. Roosevelt and Hull were committed to the use of moral suasion and efforts to secure the support of world opinion to enforce certain principles of international law. The vaunted "Quarantine" speech represented the President's groping for a method to halt aggression which would be short of sanctions but stronger than mere moral condemnation, though he never could explain just what this entailed. The Brussels Conference revealed the bankruptcy of United States policy, for the American delegate, Norman Davis, was just as confused regarding his nation's intentions as were the delegates from other countries.

Miss Borg takes issue with the contention that the Roosevelt administration sought to aid China in her struggle with Japan but was prevented from doing so by the prevailing isolationist sentiment. Both the President and the Secretary of State followed a consistent policy of non-intervention and non-entanglement, and revealed no positive inclination to cooperate with the League or other nations, individually or collectively, to exert pressure on Japan. The United States would neither lead, nor follow, nor go along with others. Even the final awareness that Japan was bent on dominating China and the blatant attack on the gunboat PANAY brought no change in policy. Yet the reader detects a growing concern about the accelerating aggression in the world and a feeling that something should be done to halt it. Roosevelt's slow and almost imperceptible steps in this direction will presumably be the subject of another book.

American Studies, VI (Spring 1965). Reprinted by permission.

CHIN-TUNG LIANG. General Stilwell in China, 1942-1944: The Full Story. Pp. xviii, 321. Jamaica, N.Y.: St. John's University Press, 1972. $6.95.

This book is another contribution to the perennial controversy over the American role in China during World War II and, by implication, responsiblity for the ultimate Communist takeover. Given unprecendented access to the official archives of the Nationalist government, the author relies heavily on these materials as well as printed official and unofficial sources to produce a work originally published in Chinese in Taipei, where it was awarded the Sun Yat-sen medal.

When the United States formally entered the war, China had been fighting the Japanese invader since 1937, and Generalissimo Chiang Kai-shek believed that his government was entitled to an equal voice in the councils directing Allied activity. Quickly disabused of this belief by the Anglo-American agreement on a Europe first strategy, by the denial of membership in the Combined Chiefs of Staff, and subsequently by not being invited to participate in meetings of heads of state, the Generalissimo persisted in his efforts to support the common war effort. The appointment of General Stilwell and the promise of substantial military and material aid seemed to indicate full scale collaboration, but American and British obstructionism prevented an effective prosecution of the war against Japan, weakened the Nationalist government, and promoted the interests of the Chinese Communist regime. China was not only treated as a second class ally but, as a theater, was given a low priority in the scale of world conflict. Stilwell, in spite of his experience, did not understand the Chinese; as a strategist he was incompetent; and as Chiang's Chief of Staff he was insubordinate.

The United States simply did not understand that, "China was confronted by two different enemies: externally, the Japanese; internally, the Communists" (0. 230). The latter were supported by the "Davies-Service group," foreign service officers who produced voluminous reports critical of the Nationalist government and extolling the virtues of the "agrarian reformers." The Washington authorities, and especially General George C. Marshall, were influenced by the political assessments of these officials and the distorted versions of the military situation produced by Stilwell. Roosevelt, anxious to keep China in the war, made gestures to appease the Generalissimo by insisting that he not be treated as the head of a minor nation and by striving to induce Britain and Russia to include China as a partner in proclamations. But as American strategists lost interest in China as a major factor in the war against Japan and found the Soviet Union more useful, even the President ceased to uphold the Chinese cause.

Given the author's premises and point of view, it might be difficult to quarrel with him over the issues. One could argue, however, that just as he accuses the United States of a narrow view of the Chinese problem, so does he overlook the world problem that confronted the president. To allocate resources in the most effective way to prosecute this global struggle would have taxed the gods, and Churchill, Stalin, and Hitler were among the formidable antagonists who faced Roosevelt in military and diplomatic efforts. One might also fault the author on certain specifics, such as his table of reports and proposals filed by American authorities. In paraphrasing a report from Davies of July 24, 1943, and citing <u>Foreign Relations</u>, 1943 (China), he says:

"The feud between the Kuomintang and Communists has been long and deep-seated. If both are barred from external aid, the National Government will be overthrown" (p. 199). The document cited reads: "If Chiang and the Communists were to fight a civil war without external aid to either side there is little question that, unless it had by then been rendered impotent by the exhaustion of the prolonged war against Japan and by the centrifugal tendencies referred to above, the Central Government by sheer weight of arms would be able to crush the Communists" (p. 263). From a technical standpoint, there is considerable repetition, although in a foreword we are told that this is customary in Chinese writings, and numerous typographical errors mar the text and the footnotes.

This work presents a well known thesis, but the evidence from the Tachi Archives, often quoted at great length, provides a version of events somewhat different from the familiar accounts. While the book falls far short of its subtitle, it does add to our understanding of this complex episode.

The Annals of the American Academy of Political and Social Sciences, Volume 407 (May 1973). Reprinted by permission.

E. R. Stettinius, Jr., and James F. Byrnes. By Richard L. Walker and George Curry. The American Secretaries of State and Their Diplomacy, Volume XIV. (New York: Cooper Square, 1965. x + 423 pp. Notes, bibliographical essays, and index. $8.50.)

This volume, the fourth to be added to the original series, covers some of the most significant and controversial years in American foreign policy. In spite of obvious shortcomings in dealing with such a recent period, the authors approach their subjects with enthusiasm and deal with both the man and the issues. Hampered by not having access to the relevant Department of State materials and inhibited by a lack of space from providing a detailed account of complex diplomatic negotiations, these scholars have produced studies that are substantially consistent with the standards established by previous selections.

Stettinius, Walker observes, "hardly had time or opportunity to have a large influence on United States foreign policy." Appointed primarily for his administrative abilities and his invulnerability to charges of political partisanship, Stettinius was to concentrate on details and free President Franklin D. Roosevelt for the conduct of the major aspects of foreign relations. The author stresses the secretary's efforts to reorganize and "stream-line" the Department of State, but concludes that his greatest contribution was made at the United Nations conference in San

BOOK REVIEWS

Francisco where his patient and conciliatory tactics helped make the Charter a reality. Here all of Stettinius' diplomatic talents were employed in reconciling the differing viewpoints of members of his own delegation and representatives of other nations, and Walker is unrestrained in his admiration of the secretary's success. In dealing with the conference it is regrettable that the author did not avail himself of the Leo Pasvolsky papers in the Department of State, especially since he was denied access to the Stettinius files. It is also unfortunate that in his criticism of certain agreements made at Yalta he did not indicate their origins in earlier meetings of the Big Three.

James F. Byrnes as Secretary of State was scarcely a minor figure, and the part he played in policy formulation has not been so clear as his role in its execution. This reviewer, on first reading Byrnes' Speaking Frankly, was reminded of Mr. Dooley's observation that Theodore Roosevelt's Rough Riders should have been titled "Alone in Cubia." Subsequent works by Harry Truman and others have tended to redress the balance, but the break between the President and his former secretary of state has served to confuse the issue. Curry, who assisted Byrnes in preparing the latter's autobiographical All in One Lifetime, has attempted to refute many of the secretary's critics. Relying largely on Byrnes' published and unpublished writings, Curry provides a sympathetic and substantial account of the secretary's activities during this difficult period. His "patient but firm" attitude toward the Soviet Union is defended, his negotiating ability is extolled, and he is credited with having formulated and executed much of American policy in Europe. His early advocacy of more aid to Greece and Turkey and his awareness of Britain's precarious position may have furnished the seeds for the Truman Doctrine. Frustrated researchers might question the propriety or legality of citing official documents from the Byrnes manuscripts marked "Top Secret," although recent revelations by former presidential aides cast doubt on current security regulations.

The Journal of American History, LII (March 1966). Reprinted by permission.

Louis, William Roger. Imperialism at Bay: The United States and the Decolonization of the British Empire, 1951-1945. New York: Oxford University Press, 1978. 594 pp.

Perhaps the most enduring legacy bequeathed to posterity by the Second World War was the opportunity for nonwhite colonial peoples to secure their independence. In this impressively researched and solidly documented volume, Professor Louis provides a detailed account and substantive analysis of the thinking, planning, considerations, negotiations, and circumstances that preceded the dismemberment of the British Empire. As the title indicates, the focus is on U.S.-British relations and the future of British possessions and mandates, although related questions of holdings by other nations, both allies and enemies, are dealt with in the overall context.

Trouble over these issues began with the joint statement by President Franklin D. Roosevelt and Prime Minister Winston S. Churchill of 14 August 1941, the highly publicized Atlantic Charter, which affirmed "the right of all peoples to choose the form of government under which they will live," and expressed the "wish to see sovereign rights and self-government restored to those who have been forcibly deprived of them." The provisions of this Charter were included in the U.N. Declaration of 1 January 1942, signed by 26 nations, and on 23 February 1942 President Roosevelt stated that the principle of self-determination was applicable "to the whole world." Yet on 9 September 1941 Churchill told the House of Commons that the Atlantic Charter did not apply to "India, Burma, and other parts of the British Empire," and on 10 November 1942 he asserted, "We mean to hold our own. I have not become the King's First Minister in order to preside over the liquidation of the British Empire." These diametrically opposed positions taken by the leaders of the Western Allies did not disrupt the joint effort in prosecuting the war against the Axis Powers but they did provide a divisive issue in war aims and postwar settlements and created dissension in branches of the two governments. By untangling and explaining the diverse approaches taken by planners in the United States and Great Britain, the exchanges between representatives of both nations, and the eventual agreement, Louis makes his greatest contribution.

In Washington, the State Department under Secretary Cordell Hull and Under Secretary Sumner Welles worked to implement the ideas of Roosevelt in regard to trusteeship, i.e., the international supervision of colonies with accountability to the United Nations, self-government, and the objective of independence. The Joint Chiefs of Staff and the War and Navy Departments strove to carry out the President's concern for security in the Pacific, which required U.S. control of islands for bases and fortifications. Thus the State Department and the military were each pursuing ends that simply were not compatible.

In London a similar but not identical situation prevailed. The Foreign Office was more inclined to a compromise with the American position, while the Colonial Office was adamantly opposed to any tampering with the Empire or Commonwealth system. Australia and New Zealand were additional thorns in the side of the Colonial Office, for they endorsed the concepts of international supervision of colonies and accountability. Of great moment were the future of islands in the Southwest Pacific and the role the United States would play in providing security. One of the few issues on which all of the British authorities agreed, from Churchill on down, was that the American idea of "trusteeship" was merely a cover for American imperialism. The British statesmen were perfectly willing to allow the United States to take over Japanese islands, mandated or otherwise, but resented interference with portions of the Empire and Commonwealth that, among other things, would allow freer trade and the intrusion of American products. What struck the British as hypocrisy, or a double standard, was American insistence that no U.S. overseas possessions or any part of the Western Hemisphere could be included in the trusteeship system.

The intricate and tortuous course of deliberations among the departments and committees in both nations are analyzed at great length by Louis, and the factors tending toward compromise were revealed by the controversies that took place within each government. Roosevelt began to weaken somewhat before his death, especially on Indochina, but he held steadfast to his concept of trusteeship as a step toward the specified goal of independence. Harry Truman had no such commitment, and he accepted the advice of those who felt that cordial relations with England and France were more important than Roosevelt's belief that perpetuation of the colonial system would exacerbate international rivalry and provoke another war. The issue was resolved at San Francisco when pertinent provisions of the U.N. Charter were formulated and a face-saving formula was devised that completely satisfied few if any of the participants. Britain kept her colonies and mandates with stipulations for self-government and accountability, France retained her possessions, and what amounted to lip service was paid to "independence."

Louis does not indulge in moralizing, but he is not sparing in his judgments of the protagonists or the issues. On the basic conflict, he does fault the United States. "The Americans had raised expectations that they might unfurl an anti-imperial banner," he concludes, but "When it came to the test, the United States sided with the colonial powers." In Britain, the avowedly anti-imperialist Labour Party on gaining power found Prime Minister Clement Attlee and Foreign Secretary Ernest Bevin no more intent on breaking up the Empire and Commonwealth than were their Tory predecessors. Still, there was an acknowledgment in London as in Washington that conditions had changed, although few realized that the proliferation of sovereign states would occur as quickly and as drastically as it did.

This is a book not just to be read but to be chewed and digested. The writing style is clear and straightforward, although there are numerous quotations from speeches and writings of the various officials. Some readers may be distracted by the thorough detail in recounting the discussions in different echelons of the administrative hierarchy as the formulation of policy and the complexities of the decisionmaking process are revealed. The organization makes for some duplication, for Louis opens with a lengthy section on "Introductory and Parallel Themes," which provides something of an overview, then proceeds in a chronological manner through the deliberations in each country and between representatives. Also, except for Korea, little attention is given to the aspirations of the peoples whose fate was being determined with little or no consultation. These caveats, of course, are peripheral to the author's major theme, which illuminates the background of an upheaval that has significantly altered the world power structure. In sum, this work constitutes a landmark in the writing of diplomatic history.

Naval War College Review, XXXI (Winter 1979). Reprinted by permission.

Foreign Relations of the United States, 1946, Vol. VIII, The Far East. U.S. Department of State Publication 8554. (Washington, D.C., Government Printing Office, 1971. viii + 1137 pp. $5.75)

This volume appearing shortly before the President's order directing a reduction in the "time lag" between the events and publications in this series, is a veritable cornucopia of information on the situation in liberated and occupied areas of the Far East. We learn how our representatives perceived developments in these countries, what they reported and recommended to Washington, and the why of instructions that they in turn received. The chaotic domestic situations, the interplay among the victorious allies, and the role of the United States (varying from observer to arbiter), all are portrayed in their vivid complexity and leave the reader with the impression that American participants must have experienced at times a secret wish that Japanese control of these territories be restored.

Beginning with a brief section containing correspondence on United States interest in the independence of Burma, a more substantive and, in today's terms, relevant section follows dealing with "The Interest of the United States in Nationalist Opposition to Restoration of French Rule in Indochina." The wording of this cryptic title deserves analysis, for after a careful reading of 71 pages of documents this reviewer was convinced that Washington's interest in the situation was somewhat broader than indicated. Were the French negotiating with Ho Chi Minh? Would the Chinese troops move out? Were the Viet Minh actually communists and under the control of Moscow? Could the French troops subdue the Annamese? These and other questions were posed from Washington to emissaries in Hanoi, Saigon, Chungking, and Paris, with responses that left this reader with the impression that the negotiations revealed an incompatibility of objectives, that the Chungking government was somewhat reluctant to remove troops but did so, that Ho and his Provisional Government were nationalists first and communists second, that a French military effort might not succeed, and that American policy was somewhat ambivalent in pursuing the goal of an independent Vietnam without "international" communism. Americans in the field supplied Washington with clear, perceptive analyses of the situation based on interviews with the leading participants and other sources of varying degrees of reliability.

The major portion of this volume deals with the occupation and control of Japan, and the reader is privy to classified policy exchanges at the highest level. General Douglas MacArthur emerges as the most harassed of the protagonists, trying to rehabilitate Japan within the framework of the Allied Council in Tokyo and the Far Eastern Commission in Washington. Often at odds with both, notably in regard to the influence brought to bear on the formulation and adoption of a new constitution, MacArthur did point out the undesirability of designating the emperor as a war criminal. Some evidence is also included to support the contention that Hirohito was not enthusiastic about waging war against the United States and Great Britain.

For students of cold war origins, the most significant materials may be those pertaining to Korea. One sees the Soviet Union as determined to have a "friendly" government in a country whose location made it a strategic necessity to Russian security and interests in the Far East. This goal led the Soviets to oppose unification under an American sponsored government. The basic differences that led to a politically divided nation are graphically portrayed. Adding to the woes of the American authorities was the unpredictable Syngman Rhee, who is labelled a "nuisance in that he wants everything done his own impractical way and wants to head separate Govt [sic] of South Korea." (p. 786).

Developments in the Netherlands East Indies found the United States acting almost as an intermediary as nationalist elements strove for autonomy and the Dutch sought to retain the appearance if not much of the substance of empire. The implementation of Philippine independence necessitated lengthy negotiations over trade preferences, discrimination against foreigners, and the retention of military bases. In Siam [sic] the United States was involved with the British, exchange rates, claims, and the price of rice, and provided its good services to help resolve a boundary dispute with France.

These documents demonstrate the truism that American foreign policy is understandable only by an awareness of what is happening in other countries. The reader is fully aware of both dimensions, the domestic situation abroad and Washington's reaction. The editorial care expected in these volumes is evident throughout, including footnote identifications, cross references, and an elaborate index. A reduction in the time lag from 26 to 20 years is eagerly anticipated.

Pacific Historical Review, XLI (November 1972). Reprinted by permission.

Foreign Relations of the United States: Diplomatic Papers, 1946, Vol. X, The Far East: China. Department of State Publication 8562. (Washington, D.C., Government Printing Office, 1972. vi + 1427 pp. $6.95)

Foreign Relations of the United States: Diplomatic Papers, 1947, Vol. VI, The Far East. Department of State publication 8606. (Washington, D.C., Government Printing Office, 1972. ix + 1159 pp. $6)

Approximately half the volume on China embraces the mission of General George C. Marshall, and, in covering the period from August 1946 until the first part of 1947, represents a continuation of volume IX. Beginning with the pessimistic joint statement by Marshall and Ambassador John Leighton Stuart of August 10, 1946, it contains minutes of conversations, reports to Washington, memorandums, and assessments of the Chinese and international situations by various officials. Documents in the remainder of the volume relate to negotiations with the Nationalist government in regard to aid, the repatriation of Japanese, the American military presence, financial arrangements, consular posts, business opportunities, and similar details.

In shedding more light on the events that transpired in China during this troubled period, these documents should add fuel to the fires that have raged over the American role in the struggle. This material will not, however, in this reviewer's opinion, produce any significantly new interpretations or create any further alteration in the ranks of the various protagonists. Both Marshall and Stuart emerge as sincere, well-informed mediators, as advocates for neither party, and as desirous of promoting a peaceful, prosperous and independent nation that would take its place in world affairs. The specter of Russian domination emerges as a major factor in American concern, but the mediators seemed convinced that the Chinese communists were nationalists first. The numerous conversations with Chou En-lai, reported in detail, were conducted with a surprising degree of candor and frankness, and only deteriorated when Chou openly accused Marshall of supporting the Kuomintang cause. The general's relations with Chiang Kai-shek seemed more formal, although after one exchange Marshall could state that "we agreed to disagree" (p. 57). Subjected repeatedly by each side to assertions that the other could not be trusted and was only maneuvering to establish its own ascendancy, General Marshall pursued his task with patience and determination until convinced that it was hopeless.

Brief portions of volume VI, 1947, are devoted to relations with Burma, the Netherlands East Indies, the Philippines, and Siam. A substantive section on French Indochina contains numerous reports from the consuls at Hanoi and Saigon concerning the nature of the struggle and analyzing the issues. Ho Chi Minh is portrayed as an intense nationalist, not controlled by the Soviets, oriented toward the West, but willing to accept aid from any source to achieve his objective. The French, not willing to grant full independence even within the French Union, selected Bao Dai to head a more amenable government. Material on the occupation of Japan reveals wrangling among the erstwhile allies over methods for restoring the disrupted economy, arranging for reparations, and preparing for a peace conference. Of considerable interest are documents relating to the failure of the Joint Commission in Korea to agree on the procedure for a nation-wide election and the American decision to place the matter before the General Assembly, and a top secret memorandum from the Secretary of Defense stating, "The Joint Chiefs of Staff consider that, from the standpoint of military security, the United States has little strategic interest in maintaining the present troops and bases in Korea. . ." (p. 817). Although the substance of this recommendation has been known, it is possible that some day the Foreign Relations series will achieve the notoriety accorded the Pentagon Papers.

Pacific Historical Review, XLII (February 1973). Reprinted by permission.

Foreign Relations of the United States, 1947, Volume VII: The Far East: China. Department of State Publication 8613. (Washington, D.C., Government Printing Office, 1972. vi + 1477 pp. $6.75)

Foreign Relations of the United States, 1948, Volume VII: The Far East: China. Department of State Publication 8678. (Washington, D.C., Government Printing Office, 1973. v + 887 pp. $6.50)

These volumes are a valuable supplement to the so-called "White Paper," United States Relations with China, published by the Department of State in 1949. The Marshall mission had terminated without ending the civil strife, and the general, as Secretary of State, was able to bring his experience to bear in attempting to clarify the role that the United States should play in furthering the development of a stable, prosperous, and democratic China that would be a responsible force in world affairs.

The documents--consisting primarily of official dispatches, department memoranda, and records of conversations --reveal an almost monotonous account of the deterioration of the National Government's position and the search for methods to salvage the situation. Reports of corruption and inefficiency, skyrocketing inflation, and Communist military success fill the numerous embassy and counsellor communiques and provide an illuminating picture of the factors that contributed to the expulsion of the Nationalists. Generalissimo Chiang Kai-shek is portrayed as a well meaning, dedicated but stubborn leader who could not be convinced, as Marshall put it, "that China could only be saved by drastic political and military reforms" (1947, p. 796). In response to repeated and increasingly frantic requests from the Chinese government and Ambassador John Leighton Stuart for increased American financial and military aid, the Secretary insisted that the United States would not become involved in the civil war even to the point of providing formal advice or its good offices to help resolve the conflict. While continuing to support the Nationalist Government (and this reviewer found no evidence in these materials of Communist support on the part of any American official), Washington refused to be drawn further into what it considered a domestic struggle.

Expectations that the Wedemeyer mission would be the prelude to massive aid were dashed when Marshall advised that drastic reforms should be effected prior to any escalation of American assistance, and when Nanking's efforts to use the specter of the Soviet threat were frustrated by Marshall's refusal to accept the Far Eastern crisis as analogous to the crisis in Europe. Yet Ambassador Stuart could report in December 1948 that Chiang Kai-shek "has been counting on immediate American military aid and the imminence of the Third World War when China would join with her anti-Soviet allies" (1948, p. 626).

There is, unfortunately, little information in these papers on what was going on in areas controlled by the Communists. Evidence of direct Soviet military aid was sought but not found, and second-hand reports seemed to indicate that the Communists were striving to win the support of the populace by conciliatory measures. The future of American diplomatic representatives was revealed when the

BOOK REVIEWS

Communists captured Mukden, the first city taken that contained a consulate. Initially the Communists seemed willing to tolerate the consular activity but their attitude changed and they instituted repressive measures to curtail normal activities. In the meantime, the State Department began to consider the prospects of a government succeeding that of the Nationalists, perhaps a coalition of factions or one representing only the Communists, and the circumstances under which formal recognition should be extended.

These documents reveal a deep sympathy for the Chinese people and nation on the part of American officials and contain perceptive analyses of the conditions prevailing in China under the Nationalist Government. Also included in the 1947 volume is material on the Formosa (Taiwan) reoccupation and maladministration, and on difficulties with the Soviet Union over rights in the port of Dairen. The usual table of contents, detailed index, and footnotes with cross references and full identification of individuals continue to attest to the high editorial quality of this series.

Pacific Historical Review, XLIII (May 1974). Reprinted by permission.

CONTAINMENT AND REVOLUTION, edited by David Horowitz (Boston: Beacon Press, 1967)

This is a revisionist work on the origins and nature of the Cold War, with footnoted studies ranging from American intervention in Russia during and after the first world war to the current conflict in Vietnam. The general theme is stated by Bertrand Russell in a preface: "There is an essential unity in the cold war, economic and foreign policies of the United States. This is created by the constant search for raw materials and markets, the imposition of poverty upon a large proportion of the world's population and the use of US military power in dozens of countries to protect the interests of American capitalism and destroy those who dare to resist." The editor, in his Introduction, concludes: "Even on the evidence of the early cold war period, therefore, it is clear that the global scale of the conflict was the result of a real global phenomenon: the spread of revolution in the contemporary era of world social development, and the decision of the United States to assume its role, as the newly dominant capitalist world power, of guardian of the global status quo." Isaac Deutscher, writing on "Myths of the Cold War," finds that "for nearly two decades western policy has moved in a maze of misconceptions and miscalculations, and amid the wreckage of its own illusions, in order to run now into a blind wall." The world, he says, has come "very close, dangerously close, to a division between revolutionary and counter-revolutionary nations." William Appleman Williams, dipping into the past in his essay "American Intervention in Russia: 1917-20," claims "The increasingly antagonistic policy of the United States towards the Soviet Union during the last months of World War II, and on into the years of the cold war, was not the result of a fundamental change in the outlook of American policy-makers. American leaders had never either in the Mid-1930s or between 1941 and 1944, abandoned or reversed the basic opposition displayed by the United States from the outset of the Bolshevik Revolution." In an analysis of "The World War and the Cold War," John Bagguley asserts that "the discord and hostility arising after Yalta were less the signal of a western firmness in the face of Soviet aggression, than an indication of the acrimony naturally occurring when two of those who had agreed to divide the continent of Europe--the United States and Britain--attempted to deprive the third party of its share." Senator Robert Taft emerges as a perceptive and far-sighted statesmen in "A Conservative Critique of Containment: Senator Taft on the Early Cold War Program," by Henry W. Berger. In a study of "Counter-Insurgency: Myth and Reality in Greece," Todd Gitlin concludes that "British and then American policy were, under the surface, as crude as the strategy that governed them: not to contain foreign aggression but domestic revolution; not to bring democracy but to maintain its absence; not to avoid violence but to thwart radical change by violence if necessary; not to bring freedom, but bases."

Shifting to the Far East, John Gittings explains "The Origins of China's Foreign Policy" in terms of her "entire experience of imperialist and semi-colonial aggression," although "the modality of this position could still have been affected by different policies, especially by the United States, during the civil war and since 1949-50." The final article by Richard Morrock, "Revolution and Intervention in Vietnam," finds Vietnam "proof of the fact that whenever a nation tries to put an end to the capitalist system, or even whenever a dependent nation seeks the abolition of its inferior status relative to some industrialized power, these efforts will be resisted by force and violence."

This year has seen the publication of a number of books contesting the responsibility of Communist nations for the Cold War and criticizing American policies of the past twenty five years. While this work is more extreme than are those by Louis Halle, George Kennan, and Walter LaFeber, for example, it deserves the attention of every serious student of world affairs.

BOOK REVIEWS

Written and distributed at the Naval War College, 1967.

Slater, Jerome. Intervention and Negotiation, The United States and the Dominican Republic. New York, Evanston, and London: Harper & Row, Publishers, 1970. Foreword by Hans J. Morgenthau, preface, notes, bibliography, index, illustrations. xviii, 254 pp. $7.95.

When United States troops landed in the Dominican Republic in April 1965 some observers foresaw a "Johnson Corollary" to the Monroe Doctrine to the effect that intervention in the domestic affairs of Caribbean nations was justified in order to prevent the spread of Communism. Critics of what many considered a precipitate and unwise action were vociferous in their condemnation of the affair, and piecemeal defenses of the administration policy failed to quiet the uproar. Now, with the perspective of some five years, the author of this work has set out to analyze "the full range of U.S. policy in the Dominican revolution from the military intervention of April, 1965, to the withdrawal of United States troops in September, 1966."

Events in Cuba led Washington to adopt a new policy toward Latin American dictatorships and exert pressure for more liberal governments and the institution of economic and social reforms, and OAS support was secured for sanctions against Trujillo in the Dominican Republic. These efforts continued after the dictator's assassination as the Kennedy administration strove to insure a democratic regime, and the election of Juan Bosch was widely heralded as ushering in a new era in Dominican affairs with the promise of significant reforms, although the United States Ambassador, John Bartlow Martin, was less optimistic about the new president and his Partido Revolucionario Dominicano (PRD). Finally, as even the State Department became disillusioned over the new government, a military group led by Colonel Elias Wessin y Wessin took control. The author contends that while Bosch was not the most astute politician, "the crucial reason for Bosch's downfall was that he meant what he said about ruling by democratic methods, respecting the civil liberties of leftist opponents, and effecting major political, economic, and social changes."

During the next eighteen months Donald Reid Cabral emerged as leader of the junta, but he failed to secure popular support and even antagonized the military. The revolution began in April 1965 as a coup, with the original participants being "a rather mixed bag" of liberals, reactionaries, and less reputable opportunists. Yet the uprising gained popular support, the PRD began to dominate, and it became clear that success would mean a return of Bosch to the presidency. At this point, and apparently with the urging of U.S. Embassy officials, the military under the leadership of Wessin y Wessin decided to oppose the rebellion. While United States officials distrusted Bosch and the PRD, "by far the more important factor in the decision to intervene was the embassy's specific assessment, reached almost at the outset, that there was a significant degree of Communist participation in the revolution." At this point the author begins a day-by-day and almost hour-by-hour account of the events that followed.

As the fighting continued and it appeared that the revolutionists were on the verge of victory, Ambassador W. Tapley Bennet on April 28, at the request of one member of the governing triumvirate, advised Washington to provide United States troops, and the first contingent arrived at San Isidro that night. "There is not the slightest doubt," says the author, "that the primary, indeed the overwhelming factor in the U.S. decision to intervene was the belief in both the embassy and the State Department that the apparently imminent contitutionalist victory would pose an unacceptable risk of a Communist takeover." Washington, however, in attempting to justify the intervention, exaggerated the number of Communists or Castroites in the revolutionary group and their degree of influence, thereby casting further doubts on the validity of the operation. Yet the author does not question United States intentions so much as he does the intervention itself, for he rejects the contention that Washington was motivated by a desire to prevent reform by supporting a reactionary military oligarchy that would provide stability. Although there is no clear evidence that United States troops participated in the fighting, they did prevent the rebel forces from uniting and allowed Wessin to destroy the weakened segments. The Washington authorities began a series of moves designed to restore a damaged reputation, bring respectability to the operation, and prepare for a restoration of constitutional government. The Organization of American States sought through the Special Committee of the Tenth Meeting of Consultation to arrange for a political settlement, but this committee "was almost a total disaster," and "the real power to arrange a settlement continued to remain in the hands of the United States." After a succession of Washington emissaries had failed to achieve a solution, Ellsworth Bunker arrived on the scene as chairman of an OAS ad hoc committee with wide authority. Dominating the negotiations, Bunker finally brought about agreement among the various factions on a Provisional Government under Hector Garcia-Godoy pending the outcome of elections. This interim government survived a number of crises as Garcia-Godoy and Bunker worked closely together to establish a foundation for free elections and acceptance of the outcome by all groups. The United States was committed to scrupulous neutrality and went to great lengths to demonstrate its impartiality, and the author maintains that "the issue of fraud or deliberately rigged elections can be dismissed as unfounded." The new government of Joaquin

Balaguer instituted a number of programs and the gross national product rose seven percent in 1969, but at the time of writing the Dominican Republic was "again on the edge of a new explosion."

The author takes great pains to explain the reasons for United States policies, i.e., first to understand, then to judge, and his judgments are very critical. Substantial errors were made in the pre-intervention period by not supporting particular groups at crucial times; the military intervention was a mistake because of the "predictably enourmous political and moral costs," and "the venture would not have been justified even if the revolution had been "unmistakably Communist;" domestic considerations and worldwide responsibilities played an unwarranted role in the decision to intervene; and serious errors were made in the post-intervention period when opportunities were lost to effect the "really sweeping military reform" essential for political and social change. Rejected are parallels with the Vietnam war and the Soviet invasion of Czechoslovakia, as are charges that the Dominican affair reflects an antiliberal or counterrevolutionary policy on the part of the United States.

There are perils involved in the writing of what some call "instant history," accounts produced so close to the events that relevant documents are not available. In this book the author has supplemented published materials, official and unofficial, by interviews with a number of participants, some of whom he is not allowed to identify. When taking issue with existing works the author is careful to indicate the other points of view, and he obviously strives to be fair and even-handed in his treatment of other interpretations as he does in dealing with the issues. Still his own position is clear, and he does not hesitate to draw his own conclusions. Whether, as contended, "Along with the war in Vietnam, the U.S. intervention in the Dominican revolution of 1965 has come to represent in the United States and all over the world the bankruptcy of recent American foreign policy" is another question. How many examples does one need for a generalization of this sort?

Journal of Inter-American Studies and World Affairs, XIII (July-October 1971). Reprinted by permission.

From Colony to Empire: Essays in the History of American Foreign Relations. Edited by William Appleman Williams. New York, N.Y.: John Wiley & Sons, Inc., 1972. Pp. x, 506. Clothbound. $10.95.

Eight historians here present what is more an analysis and interpretation of American foreign policy than a straightforward narrative factual account. The imperialist urge is emphasized, from the "dream" of Benjamin Franklin and James Madison to its culmination in Lyndon Johnson and Richard Nixon. Leading Americans of virtually every generation sought to extend the nation's boundaries, promote commerce and investment, control trade routes, and influence if not dominate other countries in order to enhance economic opportunities and pursue what were conceived of as the national interest. The growth of the American Empire was deliberate, not inadvertent or fortuitous, and "greatness" was sought, not thrust on the United States. The expansionist tendency is stressed throughout, and relations with other countries not bearing on this topic or what might be termed predatory motivations are slighted or ignored.

Essentially, these writers contend, the United States has been an aggressor--territorially, ideologically, and economically. Highly critical, this work can be regarded as a supplement to more conventional accounts, and the authors have researched their respective areas with considerable diligence. Representing what some call the "new left" point of view, these essays provide a version of American aggrandizement and exploitation that is provocative and often stimulating.

The Social Studies, LXIV (November 1973). Reprinted by permission.

COMPETITIVE INTERFERENCE AND TWENTIETH CENTURY DIPLOMACY. By Richard W. Cottam. (Pittsburgh: University of Pittsburgh Press. 1967. Pp. 243. $5.95.)

The marriage of history and political theory has been long delayed, and exponents of the separate disciplines have had their problems with methodology and terminology. In this work the author has made another of the valiant attempts to correlate experience and conjecture in order to understand the past and work more effectively for control of the future.

Confining his treatment to the shadowy area of intervening in the affairs of other nations without appearing to do so, or at least not being obnoxious about it, Professor Cottam deals with the amount of or "levels" of interference that a nation will tolerate, discusses "leverage" as a manifestation of power, censures the "ad hoc" American approach to foreign policy and argues that a long-range strategic design could be followed in spite of our "democratic society," postulates "an ideal type model for foreign policy planning," explores United States-Iranian relations as a case study, and concludes with a critique of "The Institutional Base for American Diplomacy."

In a lengthy introduction Cottam reveals many of his premises, conclusions, and what some would regard as his prejudices. The "intuitive," "ad hoc," "crisis interference" policy pursued by the United States is deplored. Conventional diplomacy is no longer adequate, and the traditional final arbiter in disputes between nations, the "ultimate recourse," has been replaced by "political warfare, economic warfare, and psychological warfare." Recognizing what some may consider obvious, the author contends that "a government seeking to influence the policy of another government should, at this point, have expanded its scope of activities to attempt to influence decision-making at levels other than the top governmental." Institutionally alone, the United States is not organized to cope with the situation, but steps can be taken to remedy this and other shortcomings.

The methods and degree of intervention in the affairs of other nations are governed by numerous factors, primarily the outmoded concept of the sovereign nation-state. Yet the amount of interference that a nation will tolerate varies depending on circumstances, and the author enumerates "ten types of interference that are commonly resorted to," ranging from diplomatic procedures to the use of force. He then considers the conditions under which a nation will accept what sort of interference and how a predictable reaction can be determined. In assessing the "leverage" that can be brought to bear to influence the policy of another nation, the author takes issue with Hans Morgenthau and Thomas Schelling's espousal of game theory. "Variables," especially of the "situational" type, are imperative considerations, and these, too, are categorized. Tactical and strategic plans must be considered in the context of long-range objectives with reference to multidimensional models constructed for illumination but not deification. Since covert and overt intervention are going to play a major role in foreign relations, the Central Intelligence Agency should be more involved in the formulation and execution of policy.

One might suspect that the marriage attempted by the author has proved to be morganatic, with history being relegated to the lower station. Post-World War II diplomacy is treated, not that of the twentieth century, and much of the evidence is drawn from events in the Middle East consonant with the author's experience and expertise in that area. Citations are confined largely to the New York Times and various secondary accounts. Still, while fault can be found with certain aspects of this work, it deals ambitiously with one of the more pressing problems of our time and is stimulating and original in many of its precepts.

American Historical Review, LXIII (April 1968). Reprinted by permission.